Understanding and Managing Parei Alienation

In *Understanding and Managing Parental Alienation: A Guide to Assessment and Intervention*, Janet Haines, Mandy Matthewson and Marcus Turnbull offer a comprehensive analysis of contemporary understanding of parental alienation. Grounded in recent scientific advances, this is the first book of its kind providing resources on how to identify parental alienation and a guide to evidence-based intervention.

Parental alienation is a process in which one parent manipulates their child to negatively perceive and reject the other parent. Recognising this phenomenon and knowing when to intervene is often the biggest challenge faced by practitioners and this book provides a guide to this process. Divided into six parts, it examines what parental alienation is and how it is caused, how it affects each family member as a mental health concern and form of violence, and how to assess, identify and intervene successfully from a legal and therapy standpoint. Taking on a gender-neutral approach, the book is filled with contemporary case examples from male and female perspectives, cutting-edge research, practitioner–client dialogues, and practitioners' reflections to show the difficult realities of parental alienation.

Practical and accessible, this is an essential resource for mental health professionals working with families experiencing parental alienation, as well as postgraduate students of clinical psychology, counselling, family therapy, social work, and child and family psychology. This book will also be of immense interest to family lawyers and mediators due to its multidisciplinary approach.

Janet Haines is a psychologist with over 20 years' experience in private clinical practice. She has extensive experience in matters involving psychology and family law, including acting as a single expert for the Family Law Court of Australia and Federal Circuit Court.

Mandy Matthewson is a senior lecturer in psychology at the University of Tasmania (UTAS) and a clinical psychologist in private practice. She is the lead researcher in the Family and Interpersonal Relationships Research Lab at UTAS and Chair of the Parental Alienation Study Group's Research Committee.

Marcus Turnbull is a senior partner specialising in family law, including child support and de facto relationship matters. Marcus is a child representative in the child protection jurisdiction and an independent children's lawyer in the Family Court and Federal Circuit Court of Australia. Currently, Marcus is the Tasmanian representative of the Family Law Section of the Law Council of Australia, the Chair of the Family Law Practitioners' Association of Tasmania, and member of the executive of Australian Institute of Family Lawyers and Mediators.

"Matthewson, Haines and Turnbull have authored a deeply researched and compassionately written work on a pernicious form of family violence Parental Alienation. Calling on their decades of experience in clinical psychology and family law, these experts give us a comprehensive look at how Parental Alienation begins, develops and resists attempts at intervention. Using the literature of family and clinical psychology, the authors provide a methodology for assessment and intervention. Drawing on their experience in forensic psychology and law, the authors provide immediately practical guidance to help legal professionals craft lasting remedies."

Demosthenes Lorandos, PhD, J.D, Licensed Psychologist
and Attorney at Law, PsychLaw, USA

Understanding and Managing Parental Alienation

A Guide to Assessment and Intervention

Janet Haines, Mandy Matthewson and Marcus Turnbull

Routledge
Taylor & Francis Group

LONDON AND NEW YORK

First published 2020
by Routledge
2 Park Square, Milton Park, Abingdon, Oxon OX14 4RN

and by Routledge
52 Vanderbilt Avenue, New York, NY 10017

Routledge is an imprint of the Taylor & Francis Group, an informa business

© 2020 Janet Haines, Mandy Matthewson and Marcus Turnbull

British Library Cataloguing-in-Publication Data
A catalogue record for this book is available from the British Library

Library of Congress Cataloging-in-Publication Data
A catalog record has been requested for this book

ISBN: 978-0-367-31290-9 (hbk)
ISBN: 978-0-367-31294-7 (pbk)
ISBN: 978-0-429-31611-1 (ebk)

Typeset in Times New Roman
by Newgen Publishing UK

I am grateful for the opportunities I have had to undertake such challenging work and for my husband, Dr Chris Williams, who has never doubted I could rise to that challenge.

Janet

To my mum and dad who gave me the secure base all children should have.

Mandy

To Lisa, Maya and Juliette, the three women in my life keeping my boat steady.

Marcus

Contents

List of tables

Preface

Nothing really can prepare you for your first encounter with an alienated family. The behaviours of the alienating parent can be outrageous, the plight of the targeted parent can be devastating, and the reality of the alienated child's predicament can be heartbreaking. You think you can understand their world view and you believe that logic and rationality, as you see it, will prevail. However, you are then overwhelmed by the complexity of the family members' situations. Despite this, you feel compelled to help.

In writing this book, we have reflected on our professional experiences and the influences that brought us to the decision to devote the time and attention needed to organise our thoughts about parental alienation and prepare this book. Each of us had a different pathway to developing an interest in parental alienation that resulted in cohesive viewpoints from our different perspectives.

When considering the evolution of our interest in parental alienation, it began from a different viewpoint for each of us. Marcus, as a senior partner in his law firm and an experienced family law practitioner, dealt with the challenges of working with cases involving parental alienation. Both as a lawyer for people trying to resolve parenting disputes to his work as an independent children's lawyer, Marcus was faced with having to understand complicated psychological presentations of the people involved in parenting disputes who were influenced by parental alienation.

In her role as a court-appointed single expert, Janet kept encountering the complex behaviours that constitute parental alienation. The tasks of making sense of the counter-intuitive presentations and wading through allegations of family violence and abuse with no supporting evidence was challenging. In her role as an academic, Janet found herself having to teach postgraduate clinical psychology students about these complicated presentations, knowing that, without ever having met an alienated family, the students would struggle to conceptualise the complexities of the family dynamics and the individual contributors to these dynamics.

Janet's understanding of the complexities of the presentations of alienated families did not assist her to know how to address these problems. She turned to Mandy, an academic and practising clinical psychologist with an interest in family dynamics and family therapy. Mandy took on the challenge.

However, when Mandy met her first alienated family, she had no idea what to do. The family was court-ordered to see her for family therapy in the hope that such therapy would reunify the children with the parent they had rejected. Mandy was able to help this family as she stumbled into the frightening world of parental alienation and the endlessly intriguing world of parental alienation research.

So, from our various perspectives, many discussions ensued that resulted, eventually, in the writing of this book. We wanted to be able to describe parental alienation, provide some guidance on how to identify it, and to offer suggestions on how to resolve it. We wanted to write a book that would be an invaluable resource for legal and mental health practitioners. If the reader is a member of an alienated family, we hope the book provides information that helps in some way.

Part One

The nature of parental alienation

Chapter One

What is parental alienation?

Introduction

Parental alienation is the term used to describe the process where a child's relationship with one parent (the targeted parent) is negatively influenced by the actions of the other parent (the alienating parent). It represents a noteworthy deviation from what is expected in a parent–child relationship and is of clinical and legal significance (1). *Definition*

Parental alienation differs from what is typically understood to be parental estrangement (2). In the case of alienation, the child's rejection of the parent occurs in the absence of a reasonable justification for the rejection. In the case of estrangement, there is usually a sound rationale for the child's rejection of the parent. It has been proposed that parental alienation and estrangement may be differentiated using appropriate assessment techniques (3).

Despite views being held to the contrary, alienating parents can be either mothers or fathers (1), although there is some suggestion that the alienation strategies used by mothers and fathers may differ (4). It is interesting to note that research results indicate that alienating behaviours *PA basics* by mothers are considered to be more acceptable than are the same behaviours demonstrated by fathers (5).

Parental alienation as a psychological and legal entity has been the focus of debate. This debate has centred on the legitimacy of the phenomenon, the nature of its presentations, and the mechanisms that underlie it. Despite these controversies in the literature, we believe that most practitioners who work with family law cases or parenting disputes have been confronted with evidence of the existence of parental alienation.

We will examine aspects of parental alienation, how it influences family relationships and how we can identify its existence in individual cases. Further, we will be moving towards suggestions for resolution of the relationship/family dynamic problems that underlie parental alienation.

Parental alienation

Parents' behaviour affects children's wellbeing

After separation and divorce, most parents can work in a reasonably collaborative manner to allow for co-parenting of their children. They are able to achieve this by distinguishing between their role as a partner or former partner in a relationship and their role as a parent (6).

Parents who do not have a functional relationship, whether they remain within the relationship or whether the relationship has ended, may behave in ways that negatively impact on their child's psychological adjustment. Certainly, in the context of parenting disputes, children can be used in ways that meet the needs of unhappy parents.

In parenting disputes, attachment theory is often used to present an argument for why a child should remain with one parent and have limited time with the other parent (7–8). This is clearly a distortion of attachment theory and the nature of attachment. Our bottom line, a view that is held by others, is that children can be strongly attached to both parents and that both parents have significant and important roles to play in raising their child (7). Also, whenever possible and if the circumstances allow it, it is preferable for a child to spend significant overnight time with both parents (9–10).

Children's rejection of a parent

If regular contact takes place, most children are attached to both their parents. So, it is a conundrum why children who once were strongly attached to a parent can then reject that parent without there being an identifiable event or events that would trigger such a response in the child.

It has been suggested that there are numerous reasons for the breakdown of a parent–child relationship following divorce or family separation (11). For example, a child's rejection of a parent may reflect a normal developmental separation difficulty that is a function of the child's age. It is a normal enough phenomenon for a child to shift their preference for one parent or the other over the course of their early life.

It may also be the case that children will express a preference for one parent over the other in certain circumstances. Consider the following comment.

Box 1.1 Psychologist: Young children who are attached to both their parents will benefit from the presence, interaction with and caregiving of their mothers and their fathers. However, when small children are distressed, they tend to want to be comforted by their primary caregiver. In our society, the primary caregiver is most often, although not always, the mother. This is not to say that a child cannot be comforted by the other parent. It just means that, if faced with a choice, a young child will reach for their primary caregiver if they are upset. Unfortunately, parents in dispute tend to use this normal developmental preference to support their legal position in a parenting dispute.

Alternatively, the rejected parent may have inadequate skills to care for the child and the child's rejection may be an expression of dissatisfaction with that parent's capacity to demonstrate adequate parenting skills. The child will express a preference for the parent with the better parenting skills because it is more comfortable for the child to be in the environment offered by that parent.

Box 1.2 Psychologist: Young children feel most secure when they are offered good quality care. Not all parents are created equal when it comes to their parenting skills. Quite separate from the depth of feeling a parent may have for their child, some parents are less able to identify their child's needs and respond in a manner that will meet those needs than other parents. Some parents are not particularly skilled at carrying out care tasks. They can be too nervous, too self-absorbed, or too impractical. Children can be more settled when they are being looked after by the most skilled parent. A child turning to one parent with superior caring skills can be misinterpreted as a rejection of the other parent.

What PA is not

Further, rejection of a parent may reflect oppositional behaviour that may have pre-existed or exists separately from the parenting dispute problems. Some children struggle to do what is asked of them or expected of them. These children may reject a parent because the parent expects the child to spend time with them or because one parent has more rigid rules than the other parent.

> **Box 1.3 Psychologist:** Some children will tend to dig in their heels and refuse to follow the rules or will act in an oppositional way when they have little choice but to comply. For example, I recall working with a parent whose child would deliberately shuffle her feet across the floor and take up to half an hour to walk to the bathroom when asked to brush her teeth at bedtime. A child like this would not find it particularly comfortable to spend time with a parent who made lots of demands on them to comply with the parent's wishes. They may opt to be with the parent who does not seem to care if teeth are brushed at bedtime.

The child's rejection of the parent may also reflect the child's response to the high level of conflict between the parents that exists with some divorced parents. Children may find it stressful to spend time with the parent who demonstrates little ability to control their negative feelings about the other parent. Also, children may opt to spend time with the parent they perceive to be the one more negatively affected by the parental conflict. They form a view, rightly or wrongly, that one parent is better able to look after themselves and the other parent is needier of the child's time and attention.

> **Box 1.4 Psychologist:** Children who are exposed to parental conflict tend to fall into three categories. There are the children who cope well enough, understanding their parents are not on friendly terms. There are children who reject the parent who complains about the other parent. These children do not like being in a situation where they have to choose whose side they will take. There are children who have chosen a side and it is usually the side of the parent they feel is being persecuted by their other parent. The children act as supporters of the 'attacked' parent.

Also, the child's rejection of a parent may be a function of experienced abuse or some other problem being experienced by the child. A child may be genuinely concerned for their own well-being or the wellbeing of siblings and refuse to spend time with a parent for that reason.

> **Box 1.5 Psychologist:** Although it is recognised that most maltreated children still love their parents, there are some children who are frightened of their parents or cannot cope with their parent's behaviour. These children are reacting to the parenting failures being demonstrated by the problematic parent. With no other way of coping with the unsatisfactory situation, these children may opt to avoid spending time with the parent with the troubling behaviour.

Of course, it is also the case that a child's rejection of a parent is a function of a campaign of alienation carried out by one parent. This campaign of alienation is a reflection of a complicated reaction to the targeted parent and the end of the parents' romantic relationship. This alienation process tends to reflect problematic parental attitudes and beliefs and not choices made by the child, although it can seem that way to the parents involved and others. It is our view that parental alienation is something that is done to a child and not a manifestation of a problem within the child.

Parental alienation and the alienated family

The focus of this book will be on parental alienation and the alienated family. Although it has been argued that parental alienation is a normative outcome following separation and divorce (6), it has been considered that parental alienation reflects a deviation from normal family behaviour or interactions (1), thus making parental alienation a phenomenon that is worthy of clinical, legal and research attention.

It has been suggested that when you consider the large number of separated or dysfunctional families, parental alienation occurs infrequently (12). Indeed, most cases of the rejection of one parent and an alignment with the other are not extreme manifestations of these reactions. In this way, the majority of cases relating to problematic parent–child relationships do not reflect a process of parental alienation and are likely to resolve with the passage of time or a change in circumstance. It has been suggested that these less extreme forms of rejection or alignment are multi-determined and reflect problems with the parents and the child (12).

What is parental alienation?

The term 'parental alienation' is used to describe a process involving one parent teaching or influencing a child to disregard the child's other parent, to experience fear when they are around that parent, and to avoid having any contact with them (13). The genesis of the alienation process seems to be the poor functioning of the parent whose actions trigger the alienation process and reflects the negative feelings this parent has for the other parent (11,14).

Parental alienation is not a single strategy but a complex cluster of strategies that share a similar goal. One study recorded 66 types of parental alienation strategies, with 11 reported by at least 20 percent of the sample of 907 participants (15). Although alienating behaviours can be experienced within many families, this study demonstrated that those people who had been alienated from a parent reported more alienating behaviour types by their parent than did those not alienated from a parent (1).

It has been suggested that parental alienation is best understood in the context of family violence. In this way, it is considered to be an abusive process that negatively affects psychological wellbeing, relationships and functioning in a range of life domains. Certainly, parental alienation often occurs in conjunction with high levels of conflict between the parents (16–17). This conflict can occur before the parental relationship ends, during the process of separation or after separation (18).

The consequences of parental alienation

The result of parental alienation is the breakdown of the relationship a child has with a parent or damage to that relationship. Targeted parents have reported that the effect on their relationship with their child can be severe (15). The effects of parental alienation on the parent–child relationship can be felt for years or, indeed, a lifetime (19).

Box 1.6 **Psychologist:** I have evaluated parenting dispute cases where there has been a complete termination of the parent–child relationship. There have been cases where, prior to the cessation of the parents' relationship, the children of the family spent considerable, good quality time with the targeted parent engaging in rewarding activities. The bond between these children and their targeted parent would have been described as strong. Nevertheless, the children end up refusing to have any contact with the targeted parent and they seem to have little feeling for the plight of the targeted parent and the targeted parent's grief at the loss of their relationship with their children.

Is there something broken in the parent–child relationship?

It is interesting that the breakdown of the relationship between the child and the parent can occur even if the relationship was once a very positive one for the child (19). So, a close and loving relationship with a parent will not protect a child from the influence of a process of parental alienation. It is confusing for the targeted parent who experiences the withdrawal of their loved and loving child from them.

Also of interest is the fact that, in some cases, the damage to the relationship can quickly resolve if the circumstances change. Appropriately targeted intervention can result in the problem situation being rectified, although it is acknowledged that this is not always easy to achieve, especially when the alienation campaign is still in effect. Further, a child's rejection of the targeted parent can abruptly cease when, during the course of a legal hearing, the alienating parent recognises the damage they are doing and, in effect, then gives the child permission to once again love the targeted parent.

When does parental alienation occur?

Although most often parental alienation occurs in separated families (1), it may be evident within intact families where the dynamics within the family are unhealthy and parental conflict exists (20–22). When enquiring about childhood experiences of parental alienation, young adults are able to identify the types of behaviours they experienced during childhood that are understood to be indicators of parental alienation. It is from this type of research that it was identified that parental alienation strategies can be used within intact, albeit dysfunctional, families (20). The feature that seems to link the separated and intact families in which parental alienation occurs is the poor quality of the parental relationship. Indeed, it has been reported that parental conflict is a better predictor of the development of parental alienation than is marital status (22).

However, it is worthy of note that there is research that has indicated that the alienation experiences in divorced and intact families differ in terms of their degree or severity (1). It has been reported that there is a higher degree of alienating behaviour by parents who are separated or divorced compared with parents who remain in a relationship, at least as reported by university aged young adults providing information about their childhood experiences.

How often does parental alienation occur?

It has been estimated that about two-thirds of divorced parents will be able to develop healthy co-parenting relationships, even if there are some initial difficulties in establishing a workable arrangement. Of the other one-third of cases, some parents will still be able to establish a good working relationship if they are provided with the right type of assistance. However, within this one-third of cases, there will be parents who are unable to jointly raise their children and a process of parental alienation will influence this inability to work together (6).

Others have suggested that the experience of parental alienation is more widespread than this. Certainly, the pervasiveness of the problem is evident when consideration is given to the international scope of published material about the phenomenon (19). It is recognised as a problem even in jurisdictions where there is no legal definition for the process (23).

It has been reported that about 80 percent of adult children of divorced parents are able to identify the experience of at least one parental alienation tactic during their childhoods. A smaller number of people surveyed, 20 percent, reported that one parent actively tried to turn them against the other parent (24).

Although it has been suggested from other research that about 1 percent of the population in the US are the victims of parental alienation (19), it is apparent that parental alienation is more likely to be observed in certain samples. For example, it has been reported that about 6 percent of children involved in a parenting dispute or referred for counselling expressed extremely rejecting views related to one parent (25).

So, it is evident that there is too little information available to give an accurate picture of the pervasiveness of the problem. Of course, it is the case that the process is more likely to be evident when working with parenting disputes, although it seems that this is not the only time you are likely to come across this phenomenon.

Concluding comments

So, parental alienation is a negative process that occurs within families. It has been associated with a range of detrimental experiences during childhood. For example, parental alienation strategies have been reported to occur in conjunction with low levels of parental caring and higher levels of parental maltreatment of children (20). In addition, the experience of parental alienation during childhood has been associated with poor outcomes for the children involved. These include problems associated with depressive symptoms, adult relationships, alcohol misuse, and difficulties determining self-direction and engaging in cooperative exchanges with others (20). Certainly, it seems that the experience of parental alienation during childhood can have effects throughout the person's life.

Before moving on, it is important to consider one other matter. Currently, there is no way of definitively determining if parental alienation is occurring. There is no number of alienation strategies that have to be present, no cut-off score on an assessment instrument, and no means of determining severity of experience that is universally accepted. As a result, it is necessary to express caution about the interpretation of some of the research investigating parental alienation.

In reality, we believe that some parents, some of the time, will behave in ways that are not exemplary because they are hurt, bitter and unhappy. Many parents will see the errors of their ways and recognise the potential damage they are doing to their children and change their behaviour as a result. We do not consider this to be the same thing as the persistent and driven campaign of distancing a child from a parent that we see as characteristic of parental alienation.

References

1.   Hands, A.J., & Warshak, R.A. (2011). Parental alienation among college students. *The American Journal of Family Therapy, 39,* 431–443. doi:10.1080/01926187.2011.575336

2. Bernet, W., Ongider-Gregory, N., Reay, K., & Rohner, R.P. (2016). An objective measure of splitting in parental alienation: The Parental Acceptance-Rejection Questionnaire. *Journal of the American Academy of Child and Adolescent Psychiatry, 55*, S201. doi:10.1016/j.jaac.2016.09.313

3. Lee, S.M., & Olesen, N.W. (2001). Assessing for alienation in child custody and access evaluations. *Family Court Review, 39*, 282–298. doi:10.1111/j.174–617.2001.tb00611.x

4. Lopez, T.J., Iglesias, V.E.N., & Garcia, P.F. (2014). Parental alienation gradient: Strategies for a syndrome. *The American Journal of Family Therapy, 42*, 217. doi:10.1080/01926187.2013.820116

5. Harman, J.J., Biringen, Z., Ratajack, E.M., Outland, P.L., & Kraus, A. (2016). Parents behaving badly: Gender biases in the perception of parental alienating behaviours. *Journal of Family Psychology, 30*, 866. doi:10.1037/fam0000232

6. Campbell, T.W. (2005). Why doesn't parental alienation occur more frequently? The significance of role discrimination. *The American Journal of Family Therapy, 33*, 365–377. doi:10.1080/01926180500274567

7. Lowenstein, L.F. (2010). Attachment theory and parental alienation. *Journal of Divorce and Remarriage, 51*, 157–168. doi:10.1080/10502551003597808

8. Whiteside, M.F. (1998). Custody for children age 5 and younger. *Family and Conciliation Courts Review, 36*, 479–502. doi:10.1111/j.174–1617.1998.tb01092.x

9. Bernet, W. (2016). Children of divorce: Breaking news for clinicians and forensic practitioners. *Journal of the American Academy of Child and Adolescent Psychiatry, 55*, S27. doi:10.1016/j.jaac.2016.07.538

10. Nielsen, L. (2014). Shared physical custody: Summary of 40 studies on outcomes for children. *Journal of Divorce and Remarriage, 55*, 613–635. doi:10.1080/10502556.2014.965578

11. Lund, M. (1995). A therapist's view of parental alienation syndrome. *Family and Conciliation Courts Review, 33*, 308–316. doi:10.1111/j.174–1617.1995.tb00373.x

12. Johnston, J.R. (2003). Parental alignments and rejection: An empirical study of alienation in children of divorce. *Journal of American Academy of Psychiatry and Law, 31*, 158–170.

13. Darnall, D. (2011). The psychosocial treatment of parental alienation. *Child and Adolescent Psychiatric Clinics of North America, 20*, 479–494. doi:10.1016/j.chc.2011.03.006

14. Dunne, J., & Hendrick, M. (1994). The parental alienation syndrome: An analysis of sixteen selected cases. *Journal of Divorce and Remarriage, 21*, 21. doi:10.1300/j087v21n03_02

15. Baker, A.J.L., & Darnall, D. (2006). Behaviors and strategies employed in parental alienation: A survey of parental experiences. *Journal of Divorce and Remarriage, 45*, 97–12. doi:10.1300/J087v45n01_06

16. Godbout, E., & Parent, C. (2012). The life paths and lived experiences of adults who have experienced parental alienation: A retrospective study. *Journal of Divorce and Remarriage, 53*, 34. doi:10.1080/10502556.2012.635967

17. Mone, J.G., MacPhee, D., & Anderson, S.K. (2011). Family members' narratives of divorce and interparental conflict: Implications for parental alienation. *Journal of Divorce and Remarriage, 52*, 642. doi:10.1080/10502556.2011.619940

18. Lowenstein, L.F. (2013). Is the concept of parental alienation a meaningful one? *Journal of Divorce and Remarriage, 54*, 65B. doi:10.1080/10502556.2013.810980

19. Bernet, W., von Boch-Galhau, W., Baker, A.J.L., & Morrison, S.L. (2010). Parental alienation, DSM-V, and ICD-11. *The American Journal of Family Therapy, 38*, 76–187. doi:10.1080/01926180903586583

20. Baker, A.J.L., & Verrocchio, M.C. (2013). Italian college student-reported childhood exposure to parental alienation: Correlates with well-being. *Journal of Divorce and Remarriage, 54*, 609–628. doi:10.1080/10502556.2013.837714

21. Cartwright, G.F. (1993). Expanding the parameters of parental alienation syndrome. *The American Journal of Family Therapy, 21*, 205–215. doi:10.1080/01926189308250919

22. Mone, J.G., & Biringen, Z. (2006). Perceived parent–child alienation: Empirical assessment of parent–child relationships within divorced and intact families. *Journal of Divorce and Remarriage, 45*, 131–156. doi:10.1300/j087v45n03_07

23. Gith, E. (2013). The attitude of the Shari'a Courts to parental alienation syndrome: Understanding the dynamics of the syndrome in Arab society. *Journal of Divorce and Remarriage, 54,* 537–547. doi:10.1080/10502556.2013.828982

24. Baker, A.J.L., & Chambers, J. (2011). Adult recall of childhood exposure to parental conflict: Unpacking the Black Box of parental alienation. *Journal of Divorce and Remarriage, 52,* 55–76. doi:10.1080/10502556.2011.534396

25. Johnston, J.R., Walters, M.G., & Olesen, N.W. (2008). Is it alienating parenting, role reversal or child abuse? A study of children's rejection of a parent in child custody disputes. *Journal of Emotional Abuse, 5,* 191–218. doi:10.1300/j135v05n04_02

Chapter Two

The great syndrome debate

Introduction

Before moving on to examine parental alienation more fully, it is important to address the fact that there has been considerable debate about the validity of the concept. This seems to be based on the rejection of the notion of the characteristics of parental alienation representing a syndrome, although some refute the existence of a parental alienation process in any form.

The debated idea of a parental alienation syndrome was proposed by Gardner (1), who identified a range of features that supposedly were characteristic of this syndrome. This push for the phenomenon of parental alienation to be viewed as a syndrome was rejected by some who considered that there were insufficient grounds for making such a claim (2).

Unfortunately, the result of the debate was not clarification of whether parental alienation occurred and could be identified. It seemed to lead to confusion about parental alienation versus a parental alienation syndrome, with supporters and rejecters retreating to their own corners and maintaining their views. In the literature, there was opinion offered but not very much actual research that would help clarify the situation. In effect, rather than the debate advancing science, as it often does, it created an adversarial reaction where the position held was strongly defended.

Gardner's parental alienation syndrome

The parental alienation syndrome that Gardner proposed was identified by eight characteristics (3). These characteristics were reportedly evident in the alienated child. They included:

1.   *A campaign of hatred and denigration of the parent who is the target of the alienation process.*

> **Box 2.1 Interviewer:** Tell me about your mother.
> **Alienated child:** My mother is hopeless. She can't do anything right. She doesn't know how to be a proper mother. Dad knows. He knows how bad she is as a mother. We don't need her. She's stupid and we hate her.

2.   *The rationalisations provided by the child for the deprecation and hatred are inadequate and frivolous or absurd.*

> **Box 2.2 Interviewer:** Why do you think Mum is hopeless?
> **Alienated child:** She just is. When she left Dad, she had her hair cut and she dyed it a different colour. That's how stupid she is.
> **Interviewer:** Lots of people have their hair cut and dyed but that doesn't make them hopeless. Why do you think that makes your Mum hopeless?
> **Alienated child:** Dad said she spends all the money he has to give her on things like having her hair cut. That makes her stupid. Anyway, it's Dad's money, not her money.

3.   *Absence of the usual or expected ambivalence about the targeted parent.*

> **Box 2.3 Interviewer:** You have told me lots of things that annoy you about Mum. What about the things that you like about her? What are some nice things about Mum?
> **Alienated child:** There is nothing nice about my mother. Nothing at all. I can't think of one single thing. Not like Dad. Everything about Dad is nice. There is nothing bad about Dad. Everything is bad about my mother.

4.   *Insistence that the negative views about the targeted parent are their own and their decision to reject that parent is their own.* This is entitled the independent-thinker phenomenon.

> **Box 2.4 Interviewer:** You told me lots of reasons why you don't want to spend any time with Mum, but a lot of these things happened when you were a baby. Did someone remind you about these things that happened when you were a baby?
> **Alienated child:** No, no-one. I just remembered them myself. I just know I don't want to see Mum. It's my idea, not Dad's. I made up my own mind.

5.   *Unquestioning support of the alienating parent in the conflict between the parents.*

> **Box 2.5 Interviewer:** Your Dad and Mum are finding it hard to be friends.
> **Alienated child:** Well, that's my mother's fault. Dad always does the right thing but then she picks a fight. Like, she keeps taking Dad back to court about me when she could just leave us alone. That makes it her fault. Dad would be happier if she would just go away.

6.   *Absence of guilty feelings about the way the targeted parent is treated.*

> **Box 2.6 Interviewer:** Mum was a bit sad she didn't hear from you on Mother's Day.
> **Alienated child:** Too bad for her. If she was a better mother, I might have called her. But she doesn't deserve to have a call from me.

7. *The adoption of experiences of the alienating parent or phrases they use in relation to the targeted parent.*

Box 2.7 Interviewer: You seem angry with Mum.

Alienated child: Of course I'm angry with her. I remember when she threw Dad out of the house and wouldn't let him come back, even to see me. He had to go and stay with his friend, Jack.

Interviewer: But both Mum and Dad told me that happened before you were born. So, who told you that happened?

Alienated child: No-one … no-one told me. I just knew. I remember it happening. She was really mad for no reason and threw Dad out of his own house. She put all his clothes in the garage, and he had to go and stay with Jack.

---

8. *The denigration can extend beyond the targeted parent to the targeted parent's extended family.*

Box 2.8 Interviewer: As things are at the moment, you don't get to see Grandma and Grandpa or Uncle Stephen. Do you miss them?

Alienated child: No, I don't miss them. I hate them. They're stupid, too. I have my other grandparents, so I don't need those ones. They just take her side … that's how stupid they are.

Gardner (4) proposed parental alienation syndrome as a disorder of childhood. He understood it to be evidenced in a "campaign of acrimony against a parent". It seems that this notion of a 'parental alienation syndrome' was conceptualised as occurring as a consequence of high conflict divorce (5).

There has been support for Gardner's parental alienation syndrome. In general, research has demonstrated that professionals who conduct parenting dispute evaluations are familiar with the notion of a parental alienation syndrome and address its presence as an important consideration in the evaluation process (6). This is despite there being some more contentious issues, such as whether or not it should be classified as a mental disorder.

Interestingly, this research has also shown that the parenting dispute evaluators who reported greater familiarity with parental alienation syndrome were the ones who had experienced greater need to consider it in the cases with which they dealt and more cases where parental alienation syndrome was assessed to have occurred (6). This suggests that the more a professional is exposed to cases involving parental alienation, the more likely they are to consider it to be a real phenomenon.

Of course, the validity of Gardner's proposal would require that the indicators can be consistently identified in suggested cases of parental alienation syndrome. One study of targeted parents found there was general support for Gardner's indicators of his parental alienation syndrome as demonstrated by the children from whom they were alienated (3). Further, the criteria outlined by Gardner for parental alienation syndrome were supported by a group of therapists who already were familiar with the concept of parental alienation (7).

Criticisms of parental alienation syndrome

Of course, support for Gardner's parental alienation syndrome is not universal. Some authors have suggested there is limited support for some aspects of Gardner's views and lack of support for other aspects (8). Other people working with families or in matters related to parenting disputes strongly oppose the notion of a syndrome and state their opposition using the strongest of terms (9). Although Gardner (10) rejected the criticisms directed at his proposal and considered denial of the existence of a parental alienation syndrome was damaging to families, some authors strenuously refute his arguments.

Some have suggested that Gardner failed to provide the evidence needed to support the proposition of a syndrome (2). In general, the criticisms of Gardner's conceptualisation of parental alienation relate to the following.

Inadequate evidence base

Critics of a parental alienation syndrome have highlighted an absence of an adequate evidence base for the proposition (11) founded on rigorous scientific study (12). With the burden of proof falling on the proposer of any new syndrome, it is argued that Gardner fell short of doing so because his ideas are inconsistent with any minimal scientific standard of proof (2).

Although this may have been true at the time the syndrome was proposed, there is an increasing body of knowledge based on research efforts in a process of building an evidence base that was recognised as necessary soon after the introduction of the notion of parental alienation syndrome (13). However, the extent to which this subsequent research supports the existence of a syndrome rather than merely supporting parental alienation as a concept separate from the proposed syndrome should be discussed.

Inadequate theoretical foundation

The critics of Gardner's parental alienation syndrome point to inadequate theoretical foundations that fail to take into account the complexity of factors that may contribute to parental alienation, such as dysfunctional families and problems of attachment (14). The difficulties with this lack of theoretical base are highlighted when consideration is given to the fact that legal decision-making is relying on unsubstantiated propositions (15).

This is probably a fair criticism when directed at the notion of a parental alienation syndrome. However, the concept of parental alienation separate from the proposition of a syndrome does not deserve the same criticism. How parental alienation presents, who experiences it, and the factors that affect both the people who experience parental alienation and contribute to its onset and maintenance need to be identified before theoretical formulations can be developed. The complexity of parental alienation suggests multiple underpinnings that need to be integrated into a cohesive account of why parental alienation occurs.

Misinterpretation of a child's normal reactions

It has been suggested by the critics of parental alienation syndrome that Gardner has misinterpreted a child's normal reaction to divorce that is determined by developmental status as something more psychopathological.

This is not a particularly helpful argument about the validity of the proposed parental alienation syndrome. In coming chapters, the way in which an alienated child presents will be covered.

It should be apparent from this coverage that an alienated child's response to the targeted parent is not a normal reaction to divorce, irrespective of developmental status. However, this presentation, in itself, will not determine whether those characteristics of the child can be understood as a syndrome.

Validity of child sexual abuse allegations

Critics of a parental alienation syndrome hold the view that, generally, child sexual abuse allegations have validity and that a parent's protective efforts are misinterpreted as a parental alienation process.

In practice, many child sex abuse allegations have validity. It does not follow that all allegations have the same validity. The high rates of false allegations of sexual abuse in parenting disputes are well reported (16), including in cases where parental alienation is suspected (17). To hold the view that a parental alienation syndrome cannot exist because all cases of alleged child sexual abuse have validity is erroneous and does not reflect the tactics used by parents in the adversarial system that is family law.

Over-estimation of threat to child of parental alienation

According to the critics of parental alienation syndrome, the proposed potential damage to the child of this parental alienation process is over-estimated. In reality, the increasing body of knowledge derived from current research has supported the view that the damage to alienated children is considerable and can be long-lasting (18). The effects on children exposed to parental alienation will be covered in coming chapters.

Errors in suggesting the primary cause is the alienating parent

It has been suggested that the view of parental alienation syndrome as a manifestation in the alienating child of the effects of the negative views of the alienating parent is overly simplistic and incorrect (19). Therefore, these critics have suggested that the fundamental underpinnings of Gardner's view about parental alienation syndrome are flawed, causing them to reject both the notion of the parental alienation syndrome and the remedies that have been suggested by Gardner. These alternative views that focus on the contribution to parental alienation of the alienated child and the targeted parent will be considered in later chapters.

Inappropriate remedies

Gardner advocated the removal of the child from the care of the alienating parent and placement of that child with the targeted parent as a way to manage parental alienation and, in effect, as a treatment of the symptoms of parental alienation syndrome. Critics of his proposals consider the suggested remedies to be unwarranted.

In family law in Australia, a concern seems to relate to Gardner's suggestions regarding the resolution of the problem. He suggested that the approach to resolution should be dependent on the severity of the alienation process. It was suggested that the alienated child should be removed from the alienating parent (who they love, who they are dependent on, and with whom they have the strongest alliance) and placed with the targeted parent (who they have come to hate and fear, and with whom they do not wish to spend time) when the alienation is severe. It has been reported that mental health experts giving evidence in the Family Court of Australia expressed concern about the impact on the alienated child of placing the child with a parent they had learned to fear or hate without there being some effort to resolve the relationship difficulties. Unfortunately, this concern may have created a tendency to believe that nothing can be done to rectify the situation if parental alienation has occurred, although this is not so.

Despite this claim that a transfer of the living circumstances of the alienated child from the alienating parent to the targeted parent is problematic, recent research has supported this intervention as contributing to a better outcome in cases where the behaviour of the alienating parent is intractable (20). Therapy options for the management of parental alienation will be discussed in coming chapters.

The debate relating to whether or not Gardner's parental alienation syndrome has validity is made more complex by the distinction that can be made between parental alienation syndrome and parental alienation in the absence of the notion of a syndrome. This issue needs to be considered.

Parental alienation without the syndrome

Despite these debates related to the validity of Gardner's parental alienation syndrome, there does appear to be considerable consensus among mental health professionals who conduct parenting dispute evaluations or work with separated families that parental alienation exists (7), separate from any consideration of a syndrome. This is certainly our experience. It seems to be the case that even those people who have indicated that the idea of parental alienation is too simplistic an account of why a child will reject a parent (21) have identified that parental alienation is a significant contributor to this rejection process, along with factors related to the targeted parent and the 'parentification' of the child by the alienating parent (22). So, despite the specific rejection by some of the notion of a parental alienation syndrome (23), there is a more general acceptance of the notion of parental alienation and no substantive evidence that parental alienation lacks scientific basis (24).

However, this more general consensus does not necessarily eliminate controversy about the merit of parental alienation (25–26) or create uniformity in an approach to parental alienation. Indeed, ten false beliefs about parental alienation have been identified, with these beliefs potentially compromising parenting dispute evaluations (11). These false beliefs include the following:

1. *Children never unreasonably reject the parent with whom they spend the most time.*

This belief assumes that there are justifiable reasons for a child to reject a parent where there is a history of that parent being the primary carer of the child. That is, holding this belief points to the underlying view that the targeted parent must have done something to trigger this rejection and, therefore, the targeted parent is responsible for this process.

There is not strong evidence that this is the cause of parental alienation. Even those who believe targeted parents contribute to the development of alienation will say that this is one aspect of a complex pattern of influences, including the child being influenced by the alienating parent to hold unreasonable views about the targeted parent (21).

The very nature of parental alienation is based on the fact that children do reject a parent with whom they had spent most of their time. It is the unreasonableness of this rejection that makes parental alienation problematic. The alienated children's explanations for the rejection of the targeted parent highlight the fundamental unreasonableness or irrationality of the rejection.

2. *Children never unreasonably reject their mothers.*

This belief seems to be based on the erroneous view that a child's strongest attachment relationship is always with their mother and that the child will not act in a way that threatens this attachment relationship (11).

Firstly, this belief seems to be based on an outdated and incorrect view of attachment. Rather than a single, important attachment figure, a child will have a hierarchy of attachments, and the placement on that hierarchy may alter as a function of the child's current needs (27). The existence of this attachment hierarchy means that although one parent may currently hold the place associated with the strongest attachment, the child still may be strongly attached to the other parent.

Secondly, it may be the case that a child is most strongly attached to their mother, but this will not prevent the development of parental alienation with the rejection of the mother. Parental alienation is problematic because a child will reject a relationship with a person with whom they were previously strongly attached, even if that parent is their mother.

Therefore, the child is not protected from parental alienation because they have a strong attachment relationship with their mother. The fundamental unreasonableness of the rejection will apply, even if the parent being rejected is the mother.

It is interesting that people continue to view mothers as the alienating parents and fathers as the targeted parents in all cases, despite evidence that both mothers and fathers can be alienating parents and targeted parents (28). Some authors in this area push so strongly to reject parental alienation that they label it 'an affront to mothers' (9) but, apparently, not to fathers.

3. Each parent contributes equally to a child's alienation.

Some researchers hold the view that the person solely responsible for the development of parental alienation is the alienating parent (29). Others say that the targeted parent contributes to this development (21). It also has been questioned whether the problematic presentation of targeted parents is a reflection of the alienating parent's behaviour and the alienated child's rejection rather than a contributor to the onset of parental alienation. However, it would be difficult to argue that the single greatest contributor is other than the alienating parent's actions.

4. Alienation is a child's transient, short-lived response to the parents' separation.

There is growing evidence that it is simply not true that the rejection of the targeted parent by an alienated child is a transient response to the parents' separation. For some people alienated from a parent during childhood, the effects will be lifelong. This is not only in terms of the damage to their relationship with the targeted parent that may not recover (18). The negative effects may persist in terms of the individual's social and psychological functioning. Further, there is evidence of intergenerational transmission of alienation, with alienated children becoming alienating parents or targeted parents. These issues will be discussed more fully in coming chapters.

5. Rejecting a parent is a short-term healthy coping mechanism.

As previously stated, the effects of parental alienation often are not short-term. The damage to the parent–child relationship can be lifelong and the social and psychological consequences of parental alienation can extend into adult life. Also, the effects can be intergenerational.

It is difficult to discern how the rejection that results in damage to a previously loving and close relationship can be considered to be a healthy coping mechanism. This is especially the case as the effects of the choice to reject a parent can be difficult for the alienating child (18). This is the reason why the child adjusts to the demand of having to choose sides and reject a loved parent by using a range of strategies that are psychologically unhealthy. These will be discussed later in other chapters.

This belief that rejecting a parent is a short-term healthy coping mechanism is a misinterpretation of the alienation of the parent and the rejection by the alienated child as being the same as a child expressing upset and resentment by briefly withdrawing. The differences between an alienated child and a child briefly estranged from a parent can be discerned (21,30). This low-level estrangement can be managed easily, in contrast to parental alienation that cannot be as easily rectified.

6.   Young children living with an alienating parent need no intervention.

Given what will be covered in coming chapters about the way in which an alienated child's rejecting behaviour manifests, and the short- and long-term effects of being involved in the process of parental alienation, it is difficult to sustain an argument that no intervention is needed for a child living with an alienating parent. Take, for example, the unhealthy alliance that develops between the alienating parent and the alienated child (31). This colours the way a child sees the world and causes the child to act in ways that, in any other circumstance, would be considered to be problematic for the child.

The apparent distortions in a child's thinking that develop as a consequence of exposure to an alienating parent's alienation tactics are problematic and detrimental to the child (31). If these distortions are generalised to other areas of the child's life or manifested in other ways, this type of distorted thinking would be considered to be problematic for the child.

Also, there are a number of unhealthy alienating parent-alienated child relationship features that would be considered to be problematic if they occurred in any other context. To dismiss the importance of these issues because they occur in a close relationship between the alienating parent and the alienated child is short-sighted, unwarranted and wrong.

7.   Alienated adolescents' stated preferences should dominate parenting decisions.

In Australia, there is provision in family law for the views expressed by the child about parenting dispute matters to be taken into consideration. However, the weight the court gives to these expressed views is determined by a range of factors, such as, the maturity of the child and the extent to which the child can understand the consequences of the decisions they make in relation to where they wish to live.

In the case where a child's views are being influenced by a process of emotional manipulation that is evident in cases of parental alienation, the court would identify such a factor as being an indicator that considerably less weight be given to the child's expressed views about living/parenting arrangements. The way in which parental alienation manifests in a child's behaviour highlights the fact that the views being expressed by the child that they wish only to have contact with the alienating parent should sound alarm bells for therapists, parenting dispute evaluators and the court. For example, such manifestations of parental alienation would include the irrationality of the child's thinking or the lack of ambivalent feelings about their parents (31).

8.   Children who appear to function well outside the family need no intervention.

One of the characteristics of an alienated child's presentation is that they may behave well in circumstances other than those relating to the targeted parent (31). This is not a sign of good adjustment when good behaviour outside the family sharply contrasts with the dysfunctional behaviour that occurs within the family.

Interestingly, in other cases, this belief that children need no intervention if they function well outside the family would not be endorsed. For example, a child may be reasonably well behaved at school but their behaviour at home may be uncontrolled. This is a common enough scenario. To say that no intervention was needed in this case because the child appears to function well outside of the family is wrong.

Another example would be the case of a child incest victim who managed to behave well at school, even to the point of being highly achieving. The child is functioning seemingly well outside of the family but is suffering abuse at home. No-one would say that intervention was not needed in this case. Given that a child's home should be the place where they feel most secure, where they are offered the greatest stability, and where they are given the greatest encouragement, the fact that problems exist within the family should not be ignored.

9. *Severely alienated children are best treated with traditional therapy techniques while living primarily with their favoured parent.*

There is no evidence that traditional therapy techniques are effective in rectifying parental alienation (20). Also, they are not effective while the child remains living with the alienating parent if the alienating parent's behaviour remains unchecked. Certainly, the efficacy of any therapeutic intervention is going to be reduced in those circumstances. Traditional, one-on-one therapies do not address the problems that exist with the dynamics in the child's family.

10. *Separating children from an alienating parent is traumatic.*

There is no evidence that separating children from an alienating parent is traumatic. Even if it may be stressful for the child as the transition takes place, it is our experience that children generally settle into their new circumstances after they are removed from the alienating parent's negative influence. It is worth remembering that the child used to have a loving relationship with the parent with whom they are being placed.

It should be noted that the goal of intervention is not separation of the child from the alienating parent in all cases. This only occurs in cases where the alienation process is the most severe. It occurs in situations where the alienating parent will not or cannot moderate their behaviour in the best interests of their child.

Again, if this was occurring in a different context, this issue would not need to be discussed. For example, maltreated children love their parents and their preference is usually to remain with their parent. However, no-one would advocate allowing a child to be abused because the child would find it difficult to be removed from the abusive parent's care. Efforts would be made to ease the transition, but it would still be considered necessary to make other care arrangements if the abusive parent's behaviour was not amenable to change. The transient stress the child may experience would be considered of secondary importance to the need to protect the child from harm. It is argued that parental alienation causes a child harm.

Concluding comments

This book adopts the view that parental alienation exists and is of significant clinical importance to warrant concern and intervention. We have adopted the view that insufficient support exists for

Gardner's notion of a parental alienation syndrome and that, although the proposition may be revisited in the future, the current research base supports the notion of parental alienation without reference to a syndrome. We and others hold the view that it is important to continue to examine the concept of parental alienation and to learn more about its onset, the factors that maintain it, how it presents and how it affects those involved (32).

As we work our way through this topic of parental alienation, you will see that these features can be applied to the notion of parental alienation in the absence of the need to consider it in terms of a syndrome. In examining the broader understanding of parental alienation, let us start by identifying the processes that underlie it.

References

1. Gardner, R.A. (1992). *The parental alienation syndrome. A guide for mental health and legal professionals.* Cresskill, NJ: Creative Therapeutics.
2. Emery, R.E. (2005). Proponents bear the burden of proof. *Family Court Review, 43,* 8–13. doi:10.1111/j.1744-1617.2005.00002.x
3. Baker, A.J.L., & Darnall, D. (2007). A construct study of the eight symptoms of severe parental alienation syndrome: A survey of parental experiences. *Journal of Divorce and Remarriage, 47,* 55–75. doi:10.1300/j087v47n01_04
4. Gardner, R.A. (2004). Commentary on Kelly and Johnston's "The Alienated Child: A reformulation of parental alienation syndrome". *Family Court Review, 42,* 611–621. doi:10.1177/1531244504268711
5. Rand, D.C. (1997). The spectrum of parental alienation syndrome (Part I). *American Journal of Forensic Psychology, 15,* 23–51.
6. Baker, A.J.L. (2007). Knowledge and attitudes about the parental alienation syndrome: A survey of custody evaluators. *The American Journal of Family Therapy, 35,* 1–19. doi:10.1080/01926180600698368
7. Rueda, C. (2004). An inter-rater reliability study of parental alienation syndrome. *The American Journal of Family Therapy, 32,* 391–403. doi:10.1080/01926180490499864
8. Spruijt, E., Eikelenboom, B., Harmeling, J., Stokkers, R., & Kormos, H. (2005). Parental alienation syndrome (PAS) in the Netherlands. *The American Journal of Family Therapy, 33,* 303–317. doi:10.1080/01926180590962110
9. Clemente, M., & Padilla-Racero, D. (2016). When courts accept what science rejects: Custody issues concerning the alleged "parental alienation syndrome". *Journal of Child Custody, 13,* 126–133. doi:10.1080/15379418.2016.1219245
10. Gardner, R.A. (2002). Denial of the parental alienation syndrome also harms women. *The American Journal of Family Therapy, 30,* 191–202. doi:10.1080/019261802753577520
11. Warshak, R.A. (2015). Ten parental alienation fallacies that compromise decisions in court and in therapy. *Professional Psychology: Research and Practice, 46,* 235–249. doi:10.1037/pro0000031
12. Houchin, T.M., Ranseen, J., Hash, P.A.K. et al. (2012). The parental alienation debate belongs in the courtroom, not in DSM-5. *Journal of the American Academy of Psychiatry and the Law, 40,* 127–131.
13. Cartwright, G.F. (1993). Expanding the parameters of parental alienation syndrome. *The American Journal of Family Therapy, 21,* 205–215. doi:10.1080/01926180500274567
14. Waldron, K.H., & Joanis, D.E. (1996). Understanding and collaboratively treating parental alienation syndrome. *American Journal of Family Law, 10,* 121–133.
15. Zirogiannis, L. (2001). Evidentiary issues with parental alienation syndrome. *Family Court Review, 39,* 334–343. doi:10.1111/j.174–1617.2001.tb00614.x
16. Trocme, N., & Bala, N. (2005). False allegations of abuse and neglect when parents separate. *Child Abuse and Neglect, 29,* 1333–1345. doi:10.1016/j.chiabu.2004.06.016

17. Lowenstein, L.F. (2012). Child contact disputes between parents and allegations of sex abuse: What does the research say? *Journal of Divorce and Remarriage, 53,* 194–203. doi:10.1080/10502556.2012.663267

18. Baker, A.J.L. (2005). The long-term effects of parental alienation on adult children: A qualitative research study. *The American Journal of Family Therapy, 33,* 289–302. doi:10.1080/01926180590962129

19. Johnston, J.R., & Kelly, J.B. (2004). Rejoinder to Gardner's "Commentary on Kelly and Johnston's 'The Alienated Child: A reformulation of parental alienation syndrome'". *Family Court Review, 42,* 622–628. doi:10.1177/1531244504268658

20. Templer, K., Matthewson, M., Haines, J., & Cox, R. (2017). Recommendations for best practice response to parental alienation: Findings from a systematic review. *Journal of Family Therapy, 39,* 103–122. doi:10.1111/1467–6427.12137

21. Kelly, J.B., & Johnston, J.R. (2001). The alienated child: A reformulation of parental alienation syndrome. *Family Court Review, 39,* 249–266. doi:10.1111/j.174–1617.2001.tb00609.x

22. Johnston, J.R., Walters, M.G., & Olesen, N.W. (2008). Is it alienating parenting, role reversal or child abuse? A study of children's rejection of a parent in child custody disputes. *Journal of Emotional Abuse, 5,* 191–218. doi:10.1300/j135v05n04_02

23. Bow, J.N., Gould, J.W., & Flens, J.R. (2009). Examining parental alienation in child custody cases: A survey of mental health and legal professionals. *The American Journal of Family Therapy, 37,* 127–147. doi:10.1080/01926180801960658

24. Erard, R.E. (2016). Maybe the sky isn't falling after all: Comment on Kleinman and Kaplan (2016). *Journal of Child Custody, 13,* 88–96. doi:10.1080/15379418.2016.1130597

25. O'Donohue, W., Benuto, L.T., & Bennett, N. (2016). Examining the validity of parental alienation syndrome. *Journal of Child Custody, 13,* 113–125. doi:10.1080/15379418.2016.1217758

26. Pepiton, M.B., Alvis, L.J., Allen, K., & Logid, G. (2012). Is parental alienation a valid concept? Not according to scientific evidence. A review of parental alienation, DSM-5 and ICD-11 by William Bernet. *Journal of Child Sexual Abuse, 21,* 244–253. doi:10.1080/10538712.2011.628272

27. Bretherton, I. (2010). Fathers in attachment theory and research: A review. *Early Child Development and Care, 180,* 9–23. doi:10.1080/03004430903414661

28. Hands, A.J., & Warshak, R.A. (2011). Parental alienation among college students. *The American Journal of Family Therapy, 39,* 431–443. doi:10.1080/01926187.2011.575336

29. McIntosh, J.E. (2011). Guest editor's introduction to special issue on attachment theory, separation, and divorce: Forging coherent understandings for family law. *Family Court Review, 49,* 418–425. doi:10.1111/j.1744-1617.2011.01382.x

30. Lee, S.M., & Olesen, N.W. (2001). Assessing for alienation in child custody and access evaluations. *Family Court Review, 39,* 282–298. doi:10.1111/j.174–617.2001.tb00611.x

31. Ellis, E. (2008). A stepwise approach to evaluating children for parental alienation syndrome. *Journal of Child Custody, 4,* 55–78. doi:10.1300/j190v04n01_03

32. Shaw, M. (2016). Commentary for "Examining the use of 'parental alienation syndrome'". *Journal of Child Custody, 13,* 144–146. doi:10.1080/15379418.2016.1219244

Chapter Three

Processes underlying parental alienation

Introduction

Parental alienation does not occur in a vacuum. Undoubtedly, there are factors that encourage the onset of parental alienation and maintain it as a strategy that is adopted to meet the various needs of the alienating parent. Although the issue has received relatively limited research attention, it is likely that there are influences on the occurrence of parental alienation that exist before its onset, that occur during separation, and that develop after separation. For the most part, these reflect factors associated with the relationship between the parents or individual contributors from each parent. Many of these factors will be discussed in coming chapters. There is little to suggest that there are child-related or child-initiated characteristics that trigger parental alienation.

It can be argued that parental alienation is a normative response to divorce, given that it is an outcome that occurs following a proportion of separations and divorce. Although most separated parents can develop an effective co-parenting relationship, some cannot do so. To understand why this is the case, the processes that may underlie parental alienation should be considered. The processes that are of most interest here are those that link the tactics used by the alienating parent with the effect on the child resulting in the child rejecting a previously loved parent.

Psychologically abusive group processes

Interestingly, it has been suggested that the processes associated with parental alienation are similar to those evident in cultic groups (1). When dealing with the child, the alienating parent insists upon complete allegiance, even while claiming that they support the child's relationship with the targeted parent. The alienating parent disregards the costs associated with this allegiance because their action is motivated by the goal of having their own needs met.

It is understood that the influence on members of cults is characterised by such factors as compliance, exploitation, mind control and anxious dependency. Individuals are taught what to think and how to behave and they tend to feel intense anxiety at the thought of withdrawal of support from the influential person or cult leader (2). The similarities between these processes and those associated with parental alienation are evident. Parental alienation can be understood as a process of influencing a child to hold a certain point of view that suits the alienating parent. This is achieved through a variety of means that have similar characteristics to these cultic group processes.

Certainly, some authors have described a process of brainwashing of the alienated child by the alienating parent (3–4). This process of brainwashing is characterised by the alienating parent intentionally acting in specific ways, or making particular comments, for the purpose of turning the child against the targeted parent. These behaviours include, for example, labelling the targeted parent in a negative way, such as 'unfit parent' or 'adulterer'; alleging the targeted parent demonstrates mental health problems, such as substance use problems or anger management problems; accusing the targeted parent of abandoning the family, either in a direct manner, such as leaving the family to pursue a relationship with another person, or in an indirect manner, such as failing to make child support payments.

It has been suggested that the above information is repeatedly presented to a child until the child assimilates the information. At this point, the child starts to make statements reflecting this assimilated information. The alienating parent then claims that the child is expressing personal or independent views. Later, it will be discussed how easy it is to create false memories in children. Suffice to say here that this process can occur without obvious behaviours by the alienating parent that directly instruct the child to believe certain things to be true even though they have not experienced them.

If the processes underlying parental alienation are similar to those that encourage engagement of cultic group members, the same influences evident in cultic groups should be able to be applied in the case of parental alienation. The parental alienation strategies considered below will be discussed in more detail in coming chapters.

Isolation

Cultic groups attempt to ensure engagement by members by isolating them from the people with whom they have significant relationships and from the environments that are familiar to them. This is achieved by isolating group members from the people who form their support network, including family members and friends. They are separated from activities that tend to define a person's life, such as work, study and familiar and enjoyable activities. They are kept from these things and placed in an isolated environment where the likelihood of inadvertent contact with people known to them is reduced.

When considering parental alienation, alienating parents act to separate the child from both the targeted parent and, often, the extended family members of the targeted parent (6). The consequence of this is that the alienated child is not exposed to views that are different from the ones being presented to the child by the alienating parent. This goal of eradicating the targeted parent from the life of the alienated child is facilitated by the information gatekeeping conducted by the alienating parent (7). Information that is contrary to the view being espoused by the alienating parent is not shared with the child, but they are exposed to information that supports the alienating parent's point of view. To encourage the rejection of the targeted parent, the alienating parent denigrates the targeted parent and vilifies them, making them seem dangerous or uncaring to the alienated child (7–10). The combination of these strategies results in the isolation of the alienated child from the targeted parent.

Control and manipulation of behaviour

To ensure commitment to the group, cultic group leaders aim to control group members. It is necessary that the behaviour of group members does not deviate from the goals of the group. Manipulation is used as a strategy to achieve this aim. By manipulating the information to which the group members have access and using language that fosters belief in the misinformation, group members are more likely to adopt the doctrine of the group and not act to defy the demands of the group leaders.

Alienating parents talk about the targeted parent in denigrating ways, influencing how the alienated child comes to view that parent. They also use vilification to make the targeted parent seem more threatening to the child than is actually the case (8–9). In addition, alienating parents disclose inappropriate information to the child while withholding information that does not support the case being presented to the child by the alienating parent (8–9). Deliberate actions are taken to damage the loving connection between the child and the targeted parent to advance the goal of alienation, such as telling the child the targeted parent does not love them (8–9). This may involve a variety of emotionally manipulative means (7–9). In the end, these actions enhance the chances of the child expressing their loyalty to the alienating parent, that is the parent who seems to be telling them the truth and who has protected them from the targeted parent who has been presented to them as untrustworthy and potentially dangerous.

Control over personal life

It is necessary for group members to sublimate their own views and needs to those of the cultic group. To achieve this, group leaders take over control of the lives of group members by taking away their need to make decisions. To facilitate this process, group leaders take control of group members' finances, how they use their time, with whom they can develop affectionate relationships, and their mental and physical health. By keeping group members' behaviour under scrutiny, any deviation from group goals can be identified and suppressed.

Alienating parents exert similar control over their children. They interfere with the time the child spends with the targeted parent in an effort to exert control over the activities in which the child engages with the targeted parent and how their time is used (7,10). Alienating parents can encourage defiant behaviour by the child while they are with the targeted parent in an effort to influence the targeted parent–child relationship even when they do not have direct influence on the child's behaviour (4). They attempt to control the child by interrogating them on their return from spending time with the targeted parent (10). Alienating parents aim to damage the loving connection the child has with the targeted parent (8–9), often by emotionally manipulative means (7).

Emotional abuse

To ensure group member compliance and to create a situation where group members are subservient to cultic group needs, emotionally abusive strategies are used. This involves creating a situation where group-focused activities and views are strongly rewarded, whereas deviant attitudes or behaviours are strongly punished using threats, humiliation and rejection. However, group members are provided with a means of redeeming themselves by confessing to wrongdoing for which they are offered forgiveness and welcomed back into the loving fold.

Alienating parents force the loyalty of the alienated child by use of specific alienation strategies. They encourage an unhealthy alliance between the alienating parent and the child (7) by rewarding the child for actions that reject the targeted parent and support the alienating parent. This process can also be achieved through the use of emotional manipulation (8–9). This can occur in a number of ways. For example, the alienating parent may manipulate the child by disclosing inappropriate information about the targeted parent (8–9) that results in the child developing negative views of the targeted parent that would otherwise not develop. Alternatively, the alienating parent may threaten to withdraw love and affection if the child does not demonstrate loyalty to the alienating parent and rejection of the targeted parent (8–9). When the child who is threatened in this way demonstrates the desired commitment to the alienating parent, that parent then rewards the child with loving and affectionate interaction.

Indoctrination in an absolute belief system

For an individual to demonstrate complete engagement with a cultic group, it is necessary for there to be processes in operation that encourage group members to reject their previously held ideas in favour of the views being offered by the group. This is achieved by discrediting these previously held views and any critical thinking that might cause an individual to discount the alternative view being offered. In place of these previously held views, an alternative viewpoint is encouraged and rewarded, with this alternative viewpoint being presented as being above question, above the needs of the individual and above the law.

The alienated child is encouraged to favour the views of the alienating parent. This is done in a variety of ways. The alienating parent damages the child's loving connection with the targeted parent by attacking the fundamentals of an attachment relationship, that is warmth, intimacy and continuity (11–12). This is achieved by the child being exposed to denigrating comments about the targeted parent and views about the targeted parent that are vilifying. The child is exposed to information about the targeted parent that would change the child's view and alter the warmth and intimacy in the relationship, while contradictory information is withheld. By encouraging defiant behaviour on the part of the child and then interpreting the targeted parent's reaction to that defiance in a negative way, the child's growing negative view of the targeted parent is encouraged. While this is occurring, the child is encouraged to form an unhealthy alliance with the alienating parent with the child being expected to engage in actions that are detrimental to the targeted parent. This damages the relationship further between the child and the targeted parent, increasing the likelihood that the child will demonstrate greater loyalty to the alienating parent.

Imposition of a single and extraordinary authority

If a person's previous belief system is going to be successfully replaced with an alternative belief system, there must be a reason for doing so that seems compelling for that individual. In cultic groups, typically, the leader is presented to the individual as someone who has special qualities. These qualities are presented as so special that they provide the leader with extraordinary authority that should not and cannot be challenged. This allows the group leader to ask of the group members things that might be rejected if they came from a person with lesser perceived authority.

In the case of parental alienation, the alienating parent presents him or herself as the devoted and consistently stable parent, while undermining the relationship between the child and the targeted parent. The child comes to believe the alienating parent is the truthful parent and the targeted parent is viewed as having attributes that are negative, dangerous and unloving. As the child is kept from spending time with the targeted parent, the relationship between the child and that parent weakens. The child is encouraged to believe that it is their independent wish to distance themselves from the targeted parent. The alienating parent may use 'experts', such as psychologists, to support the view that the child should not spend time with the targeted parent, further strengthening the view held by the alienated child that the targeted parent is unloving and the alienating parent is the one who is most devoted.

Overall, there are considerable overlapping points in cultic group processes and those of parental alienation. With regard to cultic groups, the goal is devotion to the group leader, loyalty to the group and dedication to the group ideals. In the case of parental alienation, the goals are devotion to the alienating parent, loyalty to the alienating parent's position and dedication to the alienating parent's point of view. Examination of these processes provides some understanding of how something seemingly inconceivable could occur, such as a child, without apparent justification, rejecting a parent with whom they previously had a loving relationship. It is also worth considering if there are other processes occurring in the alienating parent–child relationship that facilitate the alienation of a child from a loving parent.

Parent–child relationship patterns

Attention has been paid to the dysfunctional nature of the relationship or interaction between the alienating parent and the alienated child that may contribute to the development of parental alienation or its maintenance. It has been suggested that parental conflict causes a change from a parent–parent alliance to an unhealthy parent–child alliance (13). Parents who avoid this shift are those who can differentiate between their role as a partner in an adult relationship and the role of parent (14). Failure to make this distinction can create a situation where the nature or function of the parent–child relationship is negatively altered. Consider the following relationship patterns that have been described as forms of role corruption in the relationship between parents and children (13). These problems have been reported to occur often in the context of parental alienation.

Adultification

> **Box 3.1 Example:** Robert is the father of three boys aged 13, 11 and 8 years. An acrimonious separation from the children's mother resulted in the boys living with their father, with the boys irrationally rejecting their mother. The mother had been the caring and consistent parent prior to separation and, the evidence would suggest, Robert had been emotionally and physically abusive towards the children. The middle child found himself in the role of his father's confidant. Matters related to the parenting dispute that was before the Family Court were discussed with this child, with him being encouraged to form an alliance with his father to ensure that the dispute was resolved in his father's favour. Long hours were spent at night working out strategies to 'win'.

Adultification is a process that distorts the parent–child relationship. The child is placed in the role of friend or pseudo-partner. The parent turns to the child and discloses information about themselves to the child they see as a confidant. The parent considers the child to be an ally.

The interaction patterns in a parent–child relationship characterised by the adultification of the child are closer in nature to a partner–partner relationship than a parent–child relationship. The child is prematurely provided with information from the alienating parent that is adult in content and, thus, age-inappropriate (15).

A child will slip into this role because it brings with it a parent's attention. The child's pleasure at the attention and, indeed, desire to please the parent is mistaken by the parent as a sign that the child is mature and able to deal with the information being disclosed. In the case of parental alienation, this process increases the chances that the child will side with the alienating parent. There is a desire to maintain the special status of the parent–child relationship, so the child will agree with statements made by the alienating parent, sympathise with that parent and side against the targeted parent.

Promoting a child to the role of friend or ally means that the child will be exposed to information or situations that are beyond their emotional developmental capacity to handle. Therefore, this adultification comes at a cost to the child. It is associated with the child experiencing depression and anxiety, interferes with the child's relationships with others, and fosters sub-optimal academic and work-related performances (13).

Let us examine how this process of adultification can be identified from an interview with the alienating parent. Consider the following example.

Box 3.2 Interviewer: Tell me about your relationship with your daughter.

Alienating parent: Our relationship is great. We are so close. She's my best friend. We aren't really like mother and daughter. We like the same things and we really understand each other. We like to hang out together. We talk about things and she is such a good listener. She's so grown up.

Note here how the comments made by the mother indicate relationship equivalence. The mother and the daughter are on an equal footing in the relationship. The role of parent has been abandoned in favour of a friendship. Such a shift places pressure on the child to act as an ally to the alienating parent. Consider another example.

Box 3.3 Interviewer: Tell me about your relationship with your daughter.

Alienating parent: We share everything. I don't keep anything from her. She's an intelligent girl and I know she copes better if she knows what's going on. She has a right to know. In any case, she knows what her father is like. She remembers everything that happened. We discuss it all the time. It makes us both feel better. She knows what he's done to me.

Here the alienating mother is treating the child as a confidant. A child in this situation is likely to be overburdened by adult information. Bearing in mind that the information being provided by the alienating parent is offered from one frame of reference only, it is likely to have a significant and negative influence on the way the child views the other parent. Additionally, the information given to the child is repeated to reinforce the narrative.

Parentification

The term 'parentification' emerged out of family systems theory. It is a term used to describe a parent–child role change characterised by the parent encouraging the child to act in ways that fulfil the parent's need to be cared for or looked after. It denotes a pattern of pathological dependency needs in the parent.

In general, mothers are more likely to 'parentify' their children than are fathers, although fathers can do it as well. These mothers may have problems with their own family of origin and may have missed out on the type of parenting they needed to function more independently as adults (16). Also, these alienating mothers may be overwhelmed by the demands of single parenting after the breakdown of the parental relationship and they increasingly rely on the child to ease their burden and meet their need to be looked after (17).

It is unhealthy for a child to be thrust into the role of parent to their parent. Whether there is a process of passive acceptance of the shift from the child fulfilling a child's role to fulfilling a parenting role or whether the alienating parent actively enlists the child for this role, parentification is a destructive process. A child's developmental needs are not met in such a situation, their peer relationships are affected, and their ability to function in a normal parent–child relationship with their other parent is compromised.

The longer-term consequences for children who have been thrust into a parenting role are negative. Children placed into that position of having to parent their parent are at increased risk of depression, suicidal ideation, negative emotional states related to shame, guilt and worry, isolation from peers, and a range of internalising problems, such as psychosomatic symptoms (18).

Here are presented some examples of how this process might be identified in interview. Consider this example.

Box 3.4 Interviewer: Tell me about your relationship with your daughter.

Alienating parent: She is really good. She knows when I'm sad, so she gives me a cuddle. She understands why I'm upset. I don't have to explain it to her. She makes me feel better. I know I can turn to her. I don't know what I'd do without her. I tell her what I'm worried about and she seems to be able to come up with the best solution.

In this case, the alienating mother is turning to the child seeking to have her emotional needs met. The responsibility for the emotional wellbeing of a parent is a considerable burden for a child. It does create in the child a desire not to act in a way that will further jeopardise the parent's adjustment. The alienated child becomes more strongly aligned with the alienating parent and more rejecting of the targeted parent. The child comes to see the targeted parent as contributing to the problem by causing the emotional disturbance in the alienating parent in the first place. Consider a different example.

Box 3.5 Interviewer: Tell me about Jack. What is he like?

Alienating parent: He is my rock. I can rely on him completely. Since his father ran off, he has been the man of the house. He does a better job than his father. He is so reliable, and I know I can trust him to look after us. He looks after his younger sister. It is funny, really. He tells her to eat her vegetables and reminds her when it's bedtime. He makes my job easy.

In this case, the alienating mother is turning to the child for instrumental or physical support. The role typically fulfilled by the father in the home is now being filled by the alienated child. The failure of the alienating parent to cope with the day-to-day demands within the family home is likely to foster a belief in the alienated child that the alienating parent is overburdened, that the parent's capacity to cope has been damaged by the targeted parent, as claimed or implied by the alienating parent, and that the alienating parent needs the child more than does the targeted parent.

Infantilisation

Infantilisation is the term used to describe a situation where a parent will treat a child as if the child is much younger than their chronological age. The process is associated with the alienating parent's need to be needed and loved. The child is held back in relation to their emotional and social development. Attempts by the alienated child to demonstrate even normal independence is likely to elicit an escalation in the alienating parent's efforts to ensure the child's dependence.

A child in this situation becomes aware of the futility of trying to demonstrate independence. In a process of 'learned helplessness', the child begins to understand that there is nothing they can do to rectify the situation, so they give up trying and slip into the role of a child much younger than their chronological age. If the child is unable to accept the situation, they are likely to feel angry and resentful much of the time.

Let us examine an interview presentation of an alienating mother who is treating her nine-year-old daughter child in this manner. Consider this example.

Box 3.6 Interviewer: What are your objections to your daughter spending time with her father?

Alienating parent: It isn't appropriate for her to be there. Her father expects her to fend for herself. It would be better for him to wait until she is 18. Then she can decide for herself if she wants to see her father and she will be able to protect herself from everything that goes on in that house.

Interviewer: What sort of things are you worried about?

Alienating parent: Well, he makes her spend time with his new so-called girlfriend or partner or whatever she calls herself. He expects her to help clean up the kitchen after dinner. He lets her stay up later than I let her. He only has one bathroom at his place, so she has to share with him and his partner. It is just inviting trouble. If she needs my help, he won't let her call me.

Interviewer: What sort of help do you think she might need?

Alienating parent: Well, if she can't sleep. If she has trouble sleeping, I usually sit with her and rub her back. He won't do that for her, and I am too far away. He won't let me go there and settle her to sleep.

The alienating mother presents the case, both to the interviewer and, presumably, to the alienated child, that the child is at risk of harm in the targeted parent's care and is in need of protection. The alienating mother's needs are met by maintaining the role of the parent who is most able to offer support to the child who is considered to be unable to negotiate the normal challenges of life. Consider another example.

Box 3.7 Interviewer: You've been expressing concern about your daughter spending overnight time with her father.

Alienating parent: Yes, she's too young to be away from me. She's not ready to be away from me overnight. For a while during the day is ok, if she wants, but not overnight.

Interviewer: What are your concerns about her spending overnights with her father?

Alienating parent: She's too young to be away from me.

Interviewer: But your daughter told me she spends overnights away from you with your mother and your sister. She told me how much fun she has when she gets to stay with them.

Alienating parent: That's different. I know I can go to their homes if my daughter needs me. They won't prevent me from going there to comfort her.

Interviewer: Has that need ever arisen?

> **Alienating parent:** No, but then my mother and my sister know my daughter very well and know what she needs.
> **Interviewer:** And her father doesn't?
> **Alienating parent:** No, not as far as I'm concerned. He doesn't do a good enough job.
> **Interviewer:** Your daughter also told me she spends overnights at her friends' homes on a reasonably regular basis.
> **Alienating parent:** Well, that's a normal part of childhood.
> **Interviewer:** I agree. And she seems to cope well with those overnight stays.
> **Alienating parent:** Well, again, it's different. Little girls spend time with their friends. It's not the same thing as spending overnights with her father. He expects things of her, like feeding their dog. It's too much.

Despite there being reasonable indications that the child can cope well with being separated from her mother, this mother still refuses to acknowledge that her child is old enough to cope with overnights with her father. Her reasons relate to the child's developmental stage. She discounts the father's capacity to care for their child in an adequate manner, suggesting that the child is too young to be able to cope with the demands the father places on the child, even though those demands are not particularly burdensome and are age-appropriate.

Concluding comments

There is information available about ways in which people can be encouraged to hold views that seem to be contrary to one's experience and previously held world view. These same processes can be applied to the case of parental alienation. In addition, it seems that parental alienation can have a profound effect on the nature of the child's relationships with other people in their lives, including the alienating parent. In each of these cases outlined above, it is the alienating parent's needs that are being met and not the child's needs. As a result, we must consider how the effect of this process on the child can be understood.

References

1. Baker, A.J.L. (2005). The cult of parenthood: A qualitative study of parental alienation. *Cultic Studies Review, 5,* 1–29. doi:10.1080/019261805 90962129
2. Chambers, W.V., Langone, M.D., Dole, A.A., & Grice, J.W. (1994). The Group Psychological Abuse Scale: A measure of the varieties of cultic abuse. *Cultic Studies Journal, 11,* 88–117.
3. Baker, A.J.L. (2007). *Adult children of parental alienation syndrome: Breaking the ties that bind.* New York: W.W. Norton.
4. Turkat, I.D. (1994). Child visitation interference in divorce. *Clinical Psychology Review, 14,* 737–742. doi:10.1016/0272-7358(94)90039-6
5. Rodriguez Carballeira, A., Saldana, O., Almendros, C., Martin-Pena, J., Escartin, J., & Porrua-Garcia, C. (2015). Group psychological abuse: Taxonomy and severity of its components. *The European Journal of Psychology Applied to Legal Context, 7,* 31–39. doi:10.1016/j.ejpal.2014.11.001
6. Golly, C.H. (2016). Pruning the family tree: The plight of grandparents who are alienated from their grandchildren. *The International Journal of Aging and Society, 7,* 21–31. doi:10.18848/2160-1909/CGP/v07i02/21–31

7. Baker, A.J.L., & Darnall, D. (2006). Behaviors and strategies employed in parental alienation: A survey of parental experiences. *Journal of Divorce and Remarriage, 45,* 97–12. doi:10.1300/J087v45n01_06
8. Baker, A.J.L. (2005). The long-term effects of parental alienation on adult children: A qualitative research study. *The American Journal of Family Therapy, 33,* 289–302. doi:10.1080/01926180590962129
9. Baker, A.J.L. (2005). Parental alienation strategies: A qualitative study of adults who experienced parental alienation as a child. *American Journal of Forensic Psychology, 23,* 1–23.
10. Vassiliou, D., & Cartwright, G.F. (2001). The lost parents' perspective on parental alienation syndrome. *The American Journal of Family Therapy, 29,* 181–191. doi:10.1080/019261801750424307
11. Bowlby, J. (1963). *Attachment and loss: Attachment* (Vol. 1). London: Hogarth.
12. Bowlby, J. (1988). *A secure base. Clinical applications of attachment theory.* London: Routledge.
13. Garber, B.D. (2011). Parental alienation and the dynamics of the enmeshed parent–child dyad: Adultification, parentification, and infantilization. *Family Court Review, 49,* 322–335. doi:10.1111/j.1744-1617.2011.01374.x
14. Campbell, T.W. (2005). Why doesn't parental alienation occur more frequently? The significance of role discrimination. *The American Journal of Family Therapy, 33,* 365–377. doi:10.1016/j.jaac.2016.09.313
15. Burton, L. (2007). Childhood adultification in economically disadvantaged families: A conceptual model. *Family Relations, 56,* 329–345. doi:10.1111/j.1741-3729.2007.00463.x
16. Wells, M., Glickauf-Hughes, C., & Jones, R. (1999). Codependency: A grass roots construct's relationship to shame-proneness, low self-esteem, and childhood parentification. *American Journal of Family Therapy, 27,* 63–71. doi:10.1080/019261899262104
17. Boyd-Franklin, N. (1989). *Black families in therapy: A multisystems approach.* New York: Guilford Press.
18. Jurkovic, G. (1997). *Lost childhoods: The plight of the parentified child.* New York: Brunner/Mazel.

Chapter Four

Parental alienation as a mental disorder

Introduction

Some authors have stressed the need for parental alienation to be recognised in psychiatric classification systems (1) and there has been a move toward labelling parental alienation as a mental condition (2). This view of a Parental Alienation Disorder is held because parental alienation does not reflect a transient disruption to a child's relationship with the targeted parent but an enduring pattern of altered belief that may influence a child's relationship with that parent in the long term (1).

In the proposed classification of Parental Alienation Disorder, the diagnostic label would be applied to the child who experiences the consequences of the alienation process rather than the perpetrator of the alienation whose distorted thinking about the matter resulted in the alienation of the child from the targeted parent. In this way, the proposed Parental Alienation Disorder is considered to be a condition, the symptoms of which manifest in the child (1).

Parental alienation as a psychiatric disorder

There are a variety of reasons put forward for labelling parental alienation as a disorder. These reasons relate to the way in which the symptoms manifest and the advantages to be gained from formal recognition of parental alienation that would follow on from the classification of the symptoms of parental alienation. These reasons are as follows.

Parental alienation disorder is clearly a prototypical example of what has been termed a relational disorder. In this way, its characteristics do not exist outside of the experience of relationships (2).

The identification of the problem of parental alienation existing in the context of relational disorders indicates that the proposed condition is associated with significant psychological maladjustment. Also, it is the case that a framework exists for the understanding of parental alienation as a disorder. The consideration of parental alienation as a relational disorder will be considered later in this chapter.

Parental alienation is almost universally recognised and accepted. It is argued that the notion of parental alienation is recognised by people who work with children and families (2), particularly in relation to parenting disputes. This is despite the fact that there is less agreement with regard to the presence of a parental alienation syndrome.

Although there is still considerable debate about parental alienation, it is becoming increasingly difficult to sustain an argument that the phenomenon of parental alienation does not exist. Although more fully discussed in Chapter Two, the acceptance of parental alienation by mental health professionals and the legal system means that it must be dealt with as an existing phenomenon. As argued in Chapter Two, it is not really necessary for universal acceptance of a condition for that condition to be recognised in classificatory systems. For example, debate still exists in relation to Dissociative Identity Disorder despite it being recognised as a diagnosable condition for some time (3–4).

Parental alienation is a valid and reliable construct. In this way, the characteristics of parental alienation are known and can be measured against other, similar presentations. Further, these characteristics are stable over time (2).

The understanding of the ways in which parental alienation manifests and the strategies used by alienating parents are becoming increasingly well known. These will be discussed in upcoming chapters. Without necessarily rejecting the propositions of Gardner (5) with regard to the ways in which an alienated child presents, there has been an increasing understanding of the complexity of the strategies used to facilitate the process of parental alienation (6–7), the ways in which these strategies affect the alienated child and how that child's attitudes and behaviour are altered as a function of this process. Despite this complexity, there are limited ways in which the alienation process or the effects of the alienation process present. Further, there is growing indication that parental alienation can be differentiated from other forms of a child's rejection of a parent, for example as a consequence of maltreatment (8). This growing body of knowledge about parental alienation indicates its validity.

The severity of parental alienation may alter over the course of the alienation process and a child's attitude and behaviour towards the targeted parent can be increasingly more rejecting as the alienation campaign affects the child's views. However, there is no indication that the fundamental nature of parental alienation alters over time if measured at different time points once the rejection of the targeted parent has been established. Although this rejection may be resolved, either through therapy, a change of attitude of the alienating parent, or a significant life experience, while the child is affected the alienation is measurable across this time. This indicates that the concept of parental alienation is a reliable one.

By adopting diagnostic criteria for parental alienation disorder, the likelihood of systematic research will be increased (2). It is likely that both the quantity of research would increase and the quality of the research would improve. There would be greater consistency across studies so that useful comparisons could be made between the results of one study and the results of another. Certainly, agreement between researchers on the focus of studies allows for the formulation of a body of knowledge about parental alienation that provides an accurate reflection of the current state of understanding of parental alienation.

Further, the use of diagnostic criteria to identify group membership would allow for the research focus to be on people who had experienced the impact of parental alienation rather than people who may have experienced one or two parental alienation tactics by a parent. This would allow for the results of any research to be properly interpreted. That is, the results would be relevant to actual cases of parental alienation rather than being diluted by inclusion of participants who had been exposed to the effect of divorce but were not experiencing parental alienation.

By adopting agreed upon diagnostic criteria, the misuse of the construct will decrease (2). There are numerous ways in which the construct of parental alienation is misused. For example, some have argued that labelling the phenomenon parental alienation is a feminist issue that is an attack on mothers (9). Of course, this fails to take into account the fact that alienating parents may be mothers or fathers (10). An adequate description of parental alienation that would occur with the recognition of it as a disorder would prevent these types of accusations from being made.

The concept of parental alienation can be misused in the legal system. In these cases, parents may claim that the other parent is alienating them from children who do not want to see them for legitimate reasons. Rather than acknowledging their contribution to the rejection by the child, these parents tend to divert blame to the other parent without justification or evidence of the accepted indicators that parental alienation has occurred. Proper description of the indicators of parental alienation would make it more difficult for people to claim the other parent aims to alienate them from their child when that is not the case.

Proper description of the indicators of parental alienation that increases understanding by professionals involved in these cases would reduce the chances that these professionals would be co-opted by alienating parents into supporting their goal of restricting the input of the other parent into the child's life. Professionals tend to leave themselves vulnerable to this process of tri-angulation because of too little knowledge about parental alienation.

By adopting diagnostic criteria, there will be improvement in treatment options for children with the disorder (2). The clarification of the indicators of parental alienation associated with diagnostic criteria would allow for the development of an evidence base for the efficacy of therapeutic interventions to treat the condition. Such an evidence base is fundamental to appropriate selection of treatment choices for this problem. Intervention for parental alienation will be covered later in this book.

Criticisms of the notion of a disorder

Criticisms of the suggestion that parental alienation should be classified as a mental disorder have been noted, highlighting the controversy that has dogged the concept of parental alienation since its introduction (11). For example, some people do not feel confident enough that proper distinctions can be made between alienated/estranged children and abused/traumatised children (12). It is recognised that children who are expressing genuine anger and distress as a result of being exposed to abuse and violence should be managed differently from those who have been deliberately alienated from a parent. So, it is important to be able to distinguish these two groups of children. Others have suggested that it is possible to distinguish alienated from abused or otherwise estranged children by following robust evaluation procedures (13).

Despite the fact that most practitioners agree that parental alienation exists, particularly in divorced populations, there is little consensus on whether parental alienation should be classified as a mental disorder, or how such a mental disorder may present. Although some support the notion of parental alienation being classified as a mental disorder, others disagree. The supporters of the classification of parental alienation as a mental disorder consider that those who reject the notion are doing so on the basis of misunderstandings about the condition (15).

The arguments for rejecting the notion of parental alienation as a mental disorder need to be considered.

I. Insufficient evidence base for parental alienation.

Firstly, it has been claimed that the evidence base for parental alienation is not robust enough. It has been argued that there has been insufficient research conducted examining the concept. Without this evidence base, the validity of any diagnostic criteria would be limited.

The proponents of the classification of parental alienation as a mental disorder disagree with this notion. It is claimed that there is an increasing body of knowledge about parental alienation that is based on the increasing research interest it has attracted. Certainly, the initial focus in the literature based on anecdotal accounts of parental alienation has given way to more methodologically sound research being conducted. As a result, there is a growing knowledge base that is beginning to clarify issues about parental alienation.

However, there are obvious limitations to obtaining good research results. For example, with few alienating parents identifying themselves in this way, it is unlikely that they would volunteer to participate in research that is designed to identify their problematic behaviour. In fact, one of the arguments for classifying parental alienation as a mental disorder is to encourage more and more methodologically robust research. If such a classification can only be accepted after research results are obtained (the rejecters' position) and research results are more likely to be obtained after classification has occurred (the proponents' position), then a stalemate exists.

2. The label of a mental illness has detrimental effects on the recipient of the diagnosis.

Those who reject the notion of parental alienation as a mental disorder argue that being labelled with a 'disorder' would have negative consequences for the recipient of that label. This is particularly problematic given that the label would be applied to children who would potentially then bear the burden of that diagnosis into the future.

The issue of the stigmatising nature of a psychiatric diagnosis has been an important one (15). Concern has been raised that labelling an individual with a mental condition causes them to be treated differently and in a way that may limit their achievements and functioning.

However, having a classified mental illness may be considered to be advantageous in some cases. It certainly identifies an individual as a person in need of assistance. This can tend to become forgotten when dealing with cases of parental alienation. Further, the identification of a person having a certain mental disorder directs therapeutic intervention.

3. Those seeking to classify parental alienation as a mental disorder are driven by needs other than those associated with the greater good.

It has been suggested that the supporters of the notion of parental alienation being classified as a mental disorder are motivated by the need to do what suits them the best or for purposes that may not be in everyone's best interests. However, an argument that questions the motivations of those promoting the action can be applied in any circumstance. Also, it could also be argued that the motivations of those acting to prevent the classification of parental alienation as a mental disorder should be questioned. It seems to fail to advance the debate to any useful degree.

4. The rejection of Gardner's parental alienation syndrome.

Finally, and probably most significantly, it has been suggested that the reason people are reluctant to accept parental alienation as a mental disorder is because of negative views held about Gardner, his conceptualisation of parental alienation, and his decision to self-publish his ideas. His push for the acceptance of a syndrome seemed premature and, for many, ill-considered.

However, it seems unwarranted to reject the notion of parental alienation and the proposition of it being classified as a mental disorder on the basis of dissatisfaction with the earliest conceptualisation of the phenomenon. The development of most ideas has a starting point that marks the beginning of the formulation of the finished project. There is no reason to suppose that the understanding of parental alienation would be any different in this regard.

In any case, the notion of a parental alienation disorder is still too under-developed at this point to be able to be considered as a valid and reliable formulation. There are still issues that need to be addressed, such as whether parental alienation is better considered to be a manifestation of an already existing disorder or whether it is best to apply the diagnosis to the children affected by parental alienation rather than the alienating parent. When these and other issues are considered, decisions could then be made about whether or not this clearly complex phenomenon is best understood as a disorder in its own right.

Other psychological conceptualisations

Rather than the proposed Parental Alienation Disorder, it is worth considering whether or not parental alienation can be subsumed under existing conditions or those more broadly proposed. There is a feature of parental alienation that needs to be taken into account when considering the classification of the entity as a disorder. That is, parental alienation does not exist for one individual in isolation of other individuals. In this way, any case of parental alienation involves, at least, an alienating parent, an alienated child and a targeted parent. The most problematic and dysfunctional relationship in this triad is the one that exists between the alienating parent and the alienated child although, by saying this, the intention is not to diminish the impact of parental alienation on the targeted parent.

In an attempt to understand this dysfunctional relationship between the alienating parent and the alienated child, the previous notion of *folie a deux* should be considered. Although no longer listed in the *Diagnostic and Statistical Manual* (DSM) (16) as a mental disorder, *folie a deux* was used to describe a shared psychotic illness where the delusional belief system of one individual was adopted by another individual, typically occurring in two people who shared a close relationship. When considering parental alienation and the relationship between the alienating parent and the alienated child, there appears to be a shared belief system. Certainly, it is case that this parent and child form an alliance with a common goal of rejecting the targeted parent.

However, it needs to be questioned whether or not this shared belief system is the same as that experienced in cases of *folie a deux*. In particular, consideration needs to be given to whether or not the alienating parent is holding beliefs that are delusion-like in character or whether they are knowingly generating that type of belief in the alienated child. If it is the latter, the nature of the shared views would be different from those characterised in the notion of *folie a deux*. It might be worth considering this in the context of two cases.

Box 4.1 Case One: Jennifer, the mother of two teenaged boys, has been divorced for ten years. When talking to her, she refuses to use the children's father's name. She refers to James, the father, as a 'psychopath', although the 'evidence' she presents for her viewpoint is irrelevant and unconvincing. Jennifer considers it to be her mission in life to warn anyone who is associated with James of his shortcomings. She has approached people she has never met but who she has learned have friendships or relationships with James and vilified him. She is astonished that the reception she receives from these people is not always welcoming. Over the course of this ten-year period, Jennifer has repeatedly interfered with the relationships between James and the boys although she denies ever doing so. The younger of the two boys, aged 13, rejects his father and holds the view that James is a dangerous man who ruins people's lives. The older boy, at 15 years of age, is more ambivalent about his father and he is able to identify that his father is not the person his mother describes. Although also choosing to reject his father, his feelings are not quite as rigid as those of his younger brother. Repeated attempts have been made in therapy to moderate Jennifer's thinking about James. She continues to strongly endorse the view that

James has no redeeming characteristics and he is a threat to her children. She does not understand why James continues to pursue time with his sons. Despite there being no collateral information to support the notion that James is a psychopath, efforts to challenge Jennifer's thinking leave her confused. She struggles to understand how others cannot see her point of view.

Box 4.2 **Case Two:** Therese is the mother of two children, a son aged seventeen years and a daughter aged six years. The children have different fathers. Therese's son does not have contact with his father. Tim is the father of the six-year-old daughter. Therese has repeatedly claimed that her daughter is frightened of her father and does not wish to spend time with him. She claims that the child's fear is genuine although she cannot say what is causing the fear. The daughter has been observed by her teachers at school hiding behind her mother's car when Tim has arrived to collect her to spend time with her. Therese is insistent that she has never done or said anything to influence how the child feels about her father. She acknowledges that Tim and their daughter used to have a loving relationship. However, she said that changed after Tim ended their relationship and became involved with another partner. Therese was furious about Tim's new relationship. Over the past year, Therese made a series of serious allegations of wrongdoing by Tim, all of which proved to be false. She now claims only that she does not know why her daughter is rejecting Tim. Nevertheless, Therese claims that the child is not safe in Tim's care. Despite her young age, when she is interviewed, it is apparent that this six-year-old child knows more than she should about the parenting dispute in which her parents have been involved. She reports that she has been shown documents by her mother that make it clear that Tim is hurting her mother and not telling the truth. The child claims that she does not want to spend time with her father and that she only loves her mother.

Although both cases are clearly more complex than presented here, there is a fundamental difference with implications for the notion of a shared belief system. Case One involves an alienating parent who has deeply entrenched beliefs about her former partner and the father of her children that could not be shifted easily. She was rejecting of the notion that she might be mistaken and used arguments to support her view that could not be sustained and would not be considered to be 'evidence' in the usual sense.

In Case Two, the alienating parent deliberately acted in a way to undermine the relationship between the targeted parent and their daughter. She knowingly made false accusations about the targeted parent's behaviour and continued to do so even after these allegations were demonstrated to be false. Disregarding the impact on her daughter's wellbeing, this alienating parent fostered a fear response in the child by providing her with information that her father represented a threat to her.

There seems to be a fundamental difference between the belief systems of these two alienating parents. The parent described in Case One appeared not to understand that her views about the targeted parent were not shared by others or would not be shared by others because they lacked foundation. Attempts to challenge her thinking and moderate it resulted in feelings of confusion for her. She could not understand that others might view her beliefs about the targeted parent as faulty and problematic. Her beliefs about the targeted parent have been shared with the children and the youngest child, in particular, endorsed these views as strongly as did his mother.

In contrast, the Case Two alienating parent has been expressing her animosity and need for revenge in specific actions that can be interpreted as intentional, with the alienating parent being aware of the purpose of her actions. It would be difficult to reach a conclusion that her thoughts about the targeted parent were delusional in their character although they clearly are cognitively distorted.

It is not possible to consider all cases of parental alienation in the context of a shared delusional belief system. Although alienated children come to hold the views instilled in them by the alienating parent, there is variation in the extent to which alienating parents are aware of the purpose of their actions and understand their deliberate nature, even if they deny this to be so. As a result, the concept of a shared delusional system is inadequate to account for all cases of parental alienation.

As an alternative conceptualisation of parental alienation, it has been suggested that it is best described as a relational disorder (8). In the DSM-5 (16), under the section considering conditions that may be the focus of clinical attention, relational disorders are presented. These include problems that relate to family upbringing. Of relevance to the notion of parental alienation, mention is made of children affected by parental relationship distress. Clarifying this, relationship distress is characterised as occurring in situations such as high levels of conflict and in cases where one parent disparages the other or parents disparage each other.

It does seem that parental alienation could be considered to fall into this category. However, with only the basic notion of the events that might cause a child to be affected by parental relationship distress, it is difficult to ascertain the extent to which parental alienation fits. Also, it seems that the suggestion is broad enough to reflect a wide range of events that could affect a child, with parental alienation being one of potentially many outcomes for the child.

Parental alienation may also be incorporated in the classification of problems associated with child maltreatment and neglect (16). In particular, it could be argued that parental alienation should be identified as a disorder associated with child psychological abuse. The notion of parental alienation as a form of child abuse will be discussed more fully in the next chapter.

Who should be diagnosed?

It is interesting that the proposition is that the mental disorder label be applied to the alienated child. There is little evidence to suggest that parental alienation reflects a dysfunction in the targeted parent to any significant degree or that there is a fundamental flaw in the targeted parent–child relationship that would trigger this process (17). The alienated child, in effect, is the victim of the process. It is acknowledged that some authors have suggested that there are characteristics in the targeted parent that may contribute to parental alienation (18); however, it is not known if these characteristics are associated with the onset of parental alienation or occur as a consequence of parental alienation. The research that is available would suggest that parental alienation is a reflection of psychopathology in the alienating parent (17).

It is worth considering whether the focus of the formulation of a mental condition should be on the alienating parent rather than the alienated child. Undoubtedly, there are negative psychological consequences of parental alienation for the alienated child and the targeted parent that will be discussed in upcoming chapters. However, the outcome of exposure may be differentiated from the features of the individual whose beliefs and actions are the cause of the problem.

Concluding comments

Proposals have been made to consider parental alienation as a mental condition with clearly identified diagnostic criteria. Others have objected to these propositions, highlighting a range of problems that bring into question the validity of such a proposed condition. It is unlikely that parental alienation will be considered in classification systems until the disagreements about the existence and nature of parental alienation are resolved. This will occur when more research is conducted.

However, parental alienation exists whether or not it is classified as a diagnosable mental condition. It is a complex phenomenon that has a negative influence on the alienated child, the targeted parent, and even the alienating parent. The clarification of whether parental alienation might fit with the understanding of family violence because of potentially abusive characteristics is one of those complexities that needs to be addressed.

References

1. Bernet, W., von Boch-Galhau, W., Baker, A.J.L., & Morrison, S.L. (2010). Parental alienation, DSM-V, and ICD-11. *The American Journal of Family Therapy, 38,* 76–187. doi:10.1080/01926180903586583
2. Bernet, W. (2008). Parental alienation disorder and DSM-V. *The American Journal of Family Therapy, 36,* 349–336. doi:10.1080/01926180802405513
3. Boysen, G.A. (2011). The scientific status of childhood Dissociative Identity Disorder: A review of published research. *Psychotherapy and Psychosomatics, 80,* 329–334. doi:10.1159/000323403
4. Kihlstrom, J.F. (2005). Dissociative disorders. *Annual Review of Clinical Psychology, 1,* 227–253. doi:10.1146/annurev.clinpsy.1.102803.143925
5. Gardner, R.A. (1992). *The parental alienation syndrome. A guide for mental health and legal professionals.* Cresskill, NJ: Creative Therapeutics.
6. Baker, A.J.L., & Darnall, D. (2006). Behaviors and strategies employed in parental alienation: A survey of parental experiences. *Journal of Divorce and Remarriage, 45,* 97–112. doi:10.1300/J087v45n01_06
7. Baker, A.J.L., & Eichler, A. (2016). The linkage between parental alienation behaviors and child alienation. *Journal of Divorce and Remarriage, 57,* 475–484. doi:10.1080/10502556.2016.1220285
8. Bernet, W., Wamboldt, M.Z., & Narrow, W.E. (2016). Child affected by parental relationship distress. *Journal of the American Academy of Child and Adolescent Psychiatry, 55,* 571–579. doi:10.1016/j.jaac.2016.04.018
9. Clemente, M., & Padilla-Racero, D. (2016). When courts accept what science rejects: Custody issues concerning the alleged "parental alienation syndrome". *Journal of Child Custody, 13,* 126–133. doi:10.1080/15379418.2016.1219245
10. Hands, A.J., & Warshak, R.A. (2011). Parental alienation among college students. *The American Journal of Family Therapy, 39,* 431–443. doi:10.1080/01926187.2011.575336
11. Houchin, T.M., Ranseen, J., Hash, P.A.K. et al. (2012). The parental alienation debate belongs in the courtroom, not in DSM-5. *Journal of the American Academy of Psychiatry and the Law, 40,* 127–131.
12. Walker, L.E., & Shapiro, D.L. (2010). Parental alienation disorder: Why label children with a mental diagnosis? *Journal of Child Custody, 7,* 266–286. doi:10.1080/15379418.2010.521041
13. Lee, S.M., & Olesen, N.W. (2005). Assessing for alienation in child custody and access evaluations. *Family Court Review, 39,* 282–298. doi:10.1111/j.174–1617.2001.tb00611.x
14. Bernet, W., & Baker, A.J.L. (2013). Parental alienation, DSM-5, and ICD-11: Response to critics. *The Journal of the American Academy of Psychiatry and the Law, 41,* 98–104. doi:10.1080/01926180903586583

15. Patten, S.B., Williams, J.V.A., Lavorato, D.H., Bulloch, A., Charbonneau, M., et al. (2016). Perceived stigma among recipients of mental health care in the general/Canadian population. *Canadian Journal of Psychiatry, 61,* 480–488. doi:10.1177/0706743716639928

16. American Psychiatric Association. (2013). *Diagnostic and statistical manual of mental disorders* (5th edn.). Arlington, VA: American Psychiatric Publishing.

17. Dunne, J., & Hendrick, M. (1994). The parental alienation syndrome: An analysis of sixteen selected cases. *Journal of Divorce and Remarriage, 21,* 21–38. doi:10.1300/j087v21n03_02

18. Friedlander, S., & Walters, M.G. (2010). When a child rejects a parent: Tailoring the intervention to fit the problem. *Family Court Review, 48,* 98–111. doi:10.1111/j.1744-1617.2009.01291.x

Chapter Five

Parental alienation as a form of family violence

Introduction

A recent shift in the literature has seen parental alienation being conceptualised as family violence rather than psychopathology (1). Alienating behaviours can be viewed as acts of aggression with the main aim of altering or terminating the relationship between the child and the targeted parent. By conceptualising parental alienation in this way, the focus of attention shifts from the aberrant behaviour of the child to the problematic behaviour of the alienating parent.

Just as there is yet to be consensus in the literature on what constitutes parental alienation, there is a lack of consensus on the definition of family violence. The term *family violence* can be defined as any act of violence perpetrated by one member of a family against any other family members (2). To this end, family violence includes harm perpetrated against children and adults within the family.

Family violence encompasses intimate relationship violence and child maltreatment. Intimate relationship violence includes violence perpetrated against cohabitating or non-cohabiting partners as well as ex-partners. Child maltreatment includes abuse and neglect of children (2). Family violence includes harmful acts such as physical and sexual violence, threats and intimidation (psychological abuse), neglect and endangerment (3) and financial abuse (4).

Theories of family violence: A brief overview

There are numerous theories of family violence. Consideration here will be given to some of the prevailing theories.

Feminist theory

Feminist theorists maintain that family violence is the consequence of male domination over women in society. Feminist theorists believe family violence is grounded in the patriarchal structure of society in which men use violence to maintain power and control over women. According to this view, family violence occurs because of male privilege and men's need to maintain this (3). Men's violent behaviour is understood to be the result of socialisation.

Let us consider the following case of parental alienation.

Box 5.1 **Judy and Laura's story:** When Judy met Paul, she was impressed by his confidence and self-assurance. Judy felt safe when she was with Paul and he made every effort to make her feel special. Judy and Paul married soon after they met. Paul promised to always look after Judy. Judy thought Paul was the love of her life and she thought he felt the same way about her. Early in their marriage, Judy realised that when Paul said he would always look after her that meant everything had to be his way. He insisted on a shared bank account and quickly took control of their finances. Paul wanted to know where Judy was and what she was doing throughout the day. By the time Judy was ready to leave Paul, five years later, Paul had to know of her whereabouts at all times. If he did not know where she was, Judy would be accused of having an affair. Judy was not having an affair. Judy no longer had access to their shared bank account and relied on the small cash allowance Paul gave her. When Judy behaved in ways with which Paul disagreed, Paul would shout at her and, on occasions, he slapped her and threw small household objects at her. Judy was not allowed to have an opinion that was different to Paul's. By the time Judy was ready to leave Paul, she and Paul had a four-year-old daughter, Laura. Laura was the apple of Paul's eye, but that did not stop him from exposing Laura to the way he treated Judy. When Judy left Paul, she took Laura with her. But she knew Laura loved her father, so she agreed to a shared care arrangement with Paul. After 12 months of sharing the care of Laura, Judy re-partnered. At this time, Paul decided that Laura was better off in his care because he did not trust Judy's judgement. He refused to return Laura to Judy's care and he alleged that Judy was an unfit parent. He accused Judy of having an alcohol addiction and neglecting Laura. He also accused Judy of physically abusing Laura. None of these allegations were substantiated, but Laura emphatically maintained she wanted to live with her father and she claimed her mother was an unfit parent. Consequently, the court decided that Laura should live with Paul. Paul thwarted all of Judy's attempts to have a relationship with Laura. Judy did not see Laura again until Laura was 22 years old. Paul had died and Laura was able to reach out to her mother. While living with her father, Laura's life was tightly controlled by Paul. Paul made all of her decisions, including who she could befriend, the subjects she took in school and her career path. Paul maintained control over Laura by a schedule of punishment and reward. If Laura stepped out of line, her father would shout at her. On occasions, he slapped her and threw small household objects at her. He controlled her finances and monitored her electronic devices. He even tracked her movements with a GPS tracker on Laura's watch. For years Laura believed her mother had chosen alcohol over her. She believed all the negative things her father said about her mother. By the time mother and daughter reconnected, they both experienced anxiety, episodes of depression and did not trust others easily.

Feminist theory can be used to explain the behaviours displayed by Paul in the case example. Feminist theorists may argue that Paul used violence to ensure his dominant male role in the family. Paul's behaviour resulted from a socialisation process that favours male dominance in society. He ensured power and control over Judy during their relationship through psychological, physical and financial abuse and maintained it post-separation by denying Judy her role of mother to Laura. Paul reinforced his male dominance by perpetrating family violence against Laura.

Although this is the predominant theory in family violence research and practice, feminist theory of family violence has been widely criticised because it fails to acknowledge female perpetrators of family violence. Let us consider the case of Peter and William.

Box 5.2 **Peter and William's story:** When Peter met Samantha, he was impressed by her confidence and self-assurance. Peter felt like he could achieve anything with Samantha by his side and she made every effort to make Peter feel special. Peter and Samantha married soon after they met. Samantha promised to always look after Peter. Peter thought Samantha was the love of his life and he thought she felt the same way about him. Early in their marriage Peter realised that when Samantha said she would always look after him that meant everything had to be her way. She insisted on a shared bank account and quickly took control of their finances. Samantha wanted to know where Peter was and what he was doing throughout the day. By the time Peter was ready to leave Samantha, five years later, Samantha had to know of his whereabouts at all times. If she did not know where he was, Peter would be accused of having an affair. Peter was not having an affair. Peter no longer had access to their shared bank account and relied on the small cash allowance Samantha gave him. When Peter behaved in ways with which Samantha disagreed, Samantha would shout at him and, on occasions, she slapped him and threw small household objects at him. Peter was not allowed to have an opinion that was different to Samantha's. By the time Peter was ready to leave Samantha, he and Samantha had a four-year-old son, William. William was the apple of Samantha's eye, but that did not stop her from exposing William to the way she treated Peter. When Peter left Samantha, he agreed to a shared care arrangement of William because he knew William loved his mother and his father. After 12 months of sharing the care of William, Peter re-partnered. At this time, Samantha decided that William was better off in her care because she did not trust Peter's judgement. She refused to return William to Peter's care and she alleged that Peter was an unfit parent. She accused Peter of having an alcohol addiction and neglecting William. She also accused Peter of physically abusing William. None of these allegations were substantiated, but William emphatically maintained he wanted to live with his mother and he claimed his father was an unfit and abusive parent. Consequently, the court decided that William should live with Samantha. Samantha thwarted all of Peter's attempts to have a relationship with William. Peter did not see William again until William was 22 years old. Samantha had thrown William out of her house following a disagreement and being rejected by his mother allowed him to reach out to his father. While living with his mother, William's life was tightly controlled by Samantha. Samantha made all of William's decisions including who he could befriend, the subjects he took in school and his career path. Samantha maintained control over William by a schedule of punishment and reward. If William stepped out of line, Samantha would shout at him. On occasions, she slapped him and threw small household objects at him. She controlled his finances and monitored his electronic devices. She even tracked his movements with a GPS tracker on William's watch. For years William believed his father had chosen alcohol over him. He believed all the negative things his mother said about his father. By the time father and son reconnected, they both experienced anxiety, episodes of depression and did not trust others easily.

If Peter and William's experience is viewed through a feminist lens, the acts of violence perpetrated by Samantha against Peter and William could easily be overlooked. Indeed, parental alienation challenges prevailing views of family violence because early parental alienation literature indicated that alienating parents (the perpetrator of abusive behaviours) were more likely to be mothers than fathers (5–8).

When an alienating mother uses vilification as an alienating tactic, alienating behaviours can be misconstrued as mothers acting to protect their children from neglectful and abusive men. Vilification and false allegations of abuse as an alienating tactic will be discussed in detail in Chapter Eleven. If family violence is viewed as acts of coercion and control regardless of the gender of the perpetrator, alienating behaviours clearly are acts of violence. Indeed, current research has shown that both mothers and fathers engage in alienating tactics (9–11). Fathers are more likely to encourage the alienated child to be defiant, whereas mothers tend to denigrate the targeted parent in front of others more often than do fathers (7,9,11).

Family systems theory

This theory views family violence as being grounded in the internal structure of a family system. According to family systems theorists, family violence can occur as a result of misunderstandings, unmet expectations and financial stress (3). When these factors are coupled with an individual family member's aggressive traits, jealousy and mistrust, family violence can occur. As can be seen in the cases of Judy and Peter, family violence escalated as both Paul and Samantha raised their expectations of their respective partner's behaviour. Eventually, Judy and Peter could not meet these expectations and experienced harmful sanctions for not maintaining the family system Paul and Samantha expected. When the family system dissolved, Paul and Samantha continued to maintain control over the changing family system by ongoing acts of aggression.

Attachment theory

Attachment theorists posit that, during childhood, perpetrators of family violence develop maladaptive internal working models of relationships when their own caregivers are undependable and insensitive to their needs or are absent. Under these conditions, children can have difficulty learning how to regulate their emotions, experience fear, anxiety and anger and, subsequently, have difficulty in forming secure adult relationships. Instead, they use dysfunctional emotion regulation strategies in close relationships (12). Therefore, children who are exposed to family violence are more likely than other children to display insecure attachment styles and perpetrate family violence.

Let us hear Samantha's story.

Box 5.3 Samantha's story: Samantha was raised by her mother and grandmother. Samantha did not know her father. Her mother and grandmother told her that her father was an abusive alcoholic and left when Samantha was two years old. Samantha heard only negative stories about her father and never had the opportunity to have experiences that may have contradicted the narrative of him her mother and grandmother recounted on numerous occasions. Samantha came to believe that men cannot be trusted and must be monitored closely and controlled in order to avoid being hurt by them. Samantha's mother's behaviour could be volatile at times. She was prone to fits of rage, sometimes without any apparent rhyme or reason. Samantha spent her childhood walking on eggshells to try and avoid upsetting her mother. This experience reinforced Samantha's internal working model that others cannot be trusted and it perpetuated her need to take control of situations in order to feel safe. When Samantha met Peter, she was relieved to meet a man she thought she could trust. However, the inevitable stresses of life triggered her need to take control and coerce Peter to meet her ever-increasing expectations.

Social learning theory

Social learning theorists consider family violence as a learned behaviour. Violence is learned through modelling, and classical and operant conditioning (13). According to social learning theorists, individuals learn that violence is effective in resolving conflicts and maintaining control. If you consider the case of Samantha, it could be argued that she learned her behaviours, including her patterns of abusive behaviours, from her mother.

Social learning theory and attachment theory support the intergenerational nature of trauma and family violence. Research shows that parental alienation is an intergenerational problem with alienated children growing up to either perpetrate parental alienation themselves or become a targeted parent (14–16).

Psychopathology

A wealth of research shows that perpetrators of family violence tend to display pathological personality traits. Antisocial, borderline, narcissistic and dependent personality disorders are prevalent in the population of family violence offenders (17). According to psychopathological perspectives, family violence is the result of individual's psychopathologies, such as mental illness, personality disorders, and substance abuse. Certain psychopathologies may predispose individuals to act violently or certain psychopathologies reduce an individual's coping resources rendering them open to respond to stressors in a dysfunctional manner.

The literature pertaining to parental alienation suggests that alienating parents exhibit narcissistic personality traits, a paranoid orientation to interactions with others, severe cognitive distortions, and a tendency to externalise unwanted emotions and responsibilities (7-8,18-22). All of these characteristics are similar to those seen in populations of family violence perpetrators. If we reconsider the case of Samantha and Paul, it would not be surprising to discover that they both demonstrated traits associated with personality disturbance.

A limitation of this approach to understanding family violence is it fails to consider the role of the external environment. Indeed, all theories of family violence have their limitations, however, they all identify coercion and control as central elements in family violence. As we have already seen in previous chapters, coercion and control are central to parental alienation (1). Some jurisdictions, including Brazil and Mexico, consider parental alienation to be sufficiently harmful to children that it is considered a criminal offence. To this end, it would be important to consider how Australian law defines family violence and whether parental alienation and alienating behaviours fall within it.

What does the law say about family violence?

The Family Law Court of Australia recognises the association between family violence and family breakdown and the serious impact family violence has on adults and children. In 2011, the legal definition of family violence in the *Family Law Act 1975* (23) was updated to include coercion and control and the serious psychological damage exposure to family violence has on children. The definition of family violence provided by the *Family Law Act 1975* (23) is seen below.

> **Family Law Act 1975 – Section 4AB Definition of family violence etc.**
> (1) Family violence means violent, threatening or other behaviour by a person that coerces or controls a family member or causes the family member to be fearful.

(2) Examples of behaviour that may constitute family violence include (but are not limited to):

(a) an assault;

(b) a sexual assault or other sexually abusive behaviour;

(c) stalking;

(d) repeated derogatory taunts;

(e) intentionally damaging or destroying property;

(f) intentionally causing death or injury to an animal; or

(g) unreasonably denying the family member financial autonomy;

(h) unreasonably withholding financial support needed;

(i) preventing the family member from making or keeping connections with his or her family, friends or culture; or

(j) unlawfully depriving the family member of his or her liberty.

(3) A child is exposed to family violence if the child sees or hears family violence or otherwise experiences the effects of family violence.

(4) Examples of situations that may constitute a child being exposed to family violence include (but are not limited to) the child:

(a) overhearing threats of death or personal injury by a member of the child's family towards another member of the child's family;

(b) seeing or hearing an assault of a member of the child's family by another member of the child's family;

(c) comforting or providing assistance to a member of the child's family who has been assaulted by another member of the child's family;

(d) cleaning up a site after a member of the child's family has intentionally damaged property of another member of the child's family;

(e) being present when police or ambulance officers attend an incident involving the assault of a member of the child's family by another member of the child's family.

Is parental alienation family violence against children?

It needs to be considered whether parental alienation is a manifestation of violence against children. To address this, it is necessary to consider each component of the above definition as it applies to parental alienation research. As previously seen, central to parental alienation is coercion and control. Alienating parents control their children by denying them a relationship with their other parent. Alienating parents use coercion and control in ways consistent with the behaviour of cult leaders (14-16,18,24).

Additionally, alienating parents deliberately engage in violent behaviours in front of the children as a means of exerting control through fear. Alienating parents will set up incidents where they become aggressive towards the targeted parent in the presence of the child to (a) reinforce the notion that the targeted parent is dangerous and, therefore, such displays of aggression are needed as a preventative measure and (b) show the child how aggressive the alienating parent can be in order to maintain behavioural control of them (24). When staging a violent scene, alienating parents will have no qualms in ensuring the child sees emergency services attend the incident.

There have been reports of children experiencing acts of violence listed in the *Family Law Act, 1975* (23). Table 5.1 is a summary of examples from the literature of violent acts perpetrated by alienating parents against their children.

Table 5.1 Violent acts by alienating parents against their children.

Violence acts as per Family Law Act 1975	Examples from the literature	Example citations
Assault	Physical assaults perpetrated by alienating parent before and after alienation.	8,18–19,23–24
	Physical assault and threatened physical assault in response to lack of compliance with the alienating parent's wishes.	
Sexually abusive behaviour	Sexual abuse perpetrated by the alienating parent with alienation used as a means of concealing and maintaining the abuse.	23
	Sexual abuse perpetrated by others as a consequence of the alienating parent's neglect of the child.	
	Subjecting children to unnecessary physical examinations when false allegations of sexual abuse are made.	
Stalking	Alienating parents will use children to stalk and 'spy-on' the targeted parent for them.	19,23,25–28
Repeated derogatory taunts	Repeated denigration, belittling, mocking before and after alienation.	14–15,18,23–28
Damaging property	No known references in the literature.	
Death or injury to an animal	No known references in the literature.	
Denying financial autonomy	Alienating parent taking control of the child's bank account even when the child reaches adulthood.	29
Withholding financial support	Leaving the child without necessary financial support if the child reunites with the targeted parent.	29–30
Preventing the family member from making or keeping connections with his or her family, friends or culture	Preventing the child from having contact with the targeted parent and any family members connected to the targeted parent, such as grandparents, uncles, aunties, half-siblings.	14–15,18,23–28
	Ensuring relationships with peers cease by changing schools.	
Unlawfully depriving the family member of his or her liberty	Child abduction as the ultimate alienation tactic.	23,31
	Child abduction keeps the child away from everything that is familiar to them.	
	In extreme cases, children are kept hidden from society.	

Alienating parents will use emotional manipulation, verbal abuse, physical violence and financial abuse to maintain control over their children. Children soon learn that the mere mention of the targeted parent results in violent sanctions. Moreover, the repeated pairing of acts of violence with the targeted parent means the child begins to associate their once much-loved parent with themes of aggression even when the targeted parent displays no aggressive behaviour themselves.

It can be difficult for therapists and the judiciary to understand why children would consider the abusive parent to be their preferred option when the simplest solution to their suffering would be to express a desire to live with the targeted parent. The alienating parent–child alliance can be viewed similarly to the Stockholm Syndrome. The Stockholm Syndrome refers to a process of trauma bonding where an emotional attachment is formed, bonding the victim of abuse to the abuser (33). Although receiving little research attention, cases of this type of bonding in victims of child abuse and interpersonal violence have been noted.

Table 5.2 Family violence acts perpetrated by alienating parents against targeted parents.

Violence acts as per Family Law Act 1975	Examples from the literature	Example citations
Assault	Physical assault and threatened physical assault before and after separation.	33
Sexually abusive behaviour	No known reference.	
Stalking	Monitoring movements. Monitoring movements on social media. Following the targeted parent. Using the child to spy on the targeted parent and report back to the alienating parent.	33
Repeated derogatory taunts	Repeated denigration, belittling, mocking, verbal abuse.	9,24,31,33–35
Damaging property	Property damage post separation.	24
Death or injury to an animal	No known reference.	
Denying financial autonomy	Repeated costly legal involvement results in significant financial burden to the targeted parent. Alienation used to obtain maximum child support also resulting in financial burden to the targeted parent.	33–34
Withholding financial support	Controlling targeted parent's finances pre-separation.	33
Preventing the family member from making or keeping connections with his or her family, friends or culture	This is the corner-stone of alienating behaviours.	9,24,31,33–35
Unlawfully depriving the family member of his or her liberty	No known references to this in the literature.	

Parental alienation also is seen as a continuation of pre-separation family violence where the perpetrator uses the children to continue to control their ex-partner (34). In doing so, the children suffer in a collateral way as a result of the violence playing out in the relationship.

Is parental alienation family violence against targeted parents?

Many targeted parents report instances of family violence pre-separation (34). Table 5.2 offers a summary of examples from the literature of family violence perpetrated by alienating parents against targeted parents.

Tables 5.1 and 5.2 show that alienating behaviours described in the literature are consistent with acts of family violence as defined by the *Family Law Act, 1975* (23). Targeted parents and children are exposed to acts of violence before and after family separation. In instances of parental alienation, the abuse is triggered by family separation and exacerbated post family separation. Perpetrators continue to abuse their ex-partners in order to maintain power and control over them (37).

A common alienating tactic used by alienating parents is to make false allegations of abuse against the targeted parent (38). This tactic is not only employed by alienating parents to alienate their child from the targeted parent, it also achieves the aim of psychological abuse, such as control, isolation, and intimidation of the targeted parent and child.

Concluding comments

There are strong arguments for the consideration of parental alienation as family violence. Exposure to alienating behaviours negatively impacts the psychological wellbeing of alienated children (18,25) and targeted parents (9). Parental alienation affects the alienated child and targeted parent. Understanding parental alienation as a form of family violence shifts the focus of the problem from a psychological disorder diagnosed in the child to a wider problem that affects the entire family system for generations. Considering parental alienation as a form of family violence has important legal and clinical practice implications, because leaving a child in the care of the alienating parent is tantamount to leaving them in the care of an abusive parent.

References

1. Harman, J.J., Kruk, E., & Hines, D.A. (2018). Parental alienating behaviors: An unacknowledged form of family violence. *Psychological Bulletin, 144,* 1275–1299. doi:10.1037/bul0000175
2. Chalk, R., & King, P. (1998). Assessing family violence interventions. *American Journal of Preventive Medicine, 14,* 289–292.
3. Lawson, D.M. (2013). *Family violence: Explanations and evidence-based clinical practice.* Alexandria, VA: American Counseling Association.
4. Adams, A.E., Sullivan, C.M., Bybee, D., & Greeson, M.R. (2008). Development of the Scale of Economic Abuse. *Violence Against Women, 14,* 563–588. doi:10.1177/1077801208315529
5. Bow, J.N., Gould, J.W., & Flens, J.R. (2009). Examining parental alienation in child custody cases: A survey of mental health and legal professionals. *The American Journal of Family Therapy, 37,* 127–145. doi:10.1080/01926180801960658
6. Johnston, J.R. (2003). Parental alignments and rejection: An empirical study of alienation in children of divorce. *Journal of American Academy of Psychiatry and Law, 31,* 158–170.
7. Rand, D.C. (1997). The spectrum of parental alienation syndrome (part I). *American Journal of Forensic Psychology, 15(3),* 23–51.
8. Rand, D.C. (1997). The spectrum of parental alienation syndrome (part II). *American Journal of Forensic Psychology, 15(4),* 39–92.
9. Balmer, S., Matthewson, M., & Haines, J. (2017). Parental alienation: Targeted parent perspective. *Australian Journal of Psychology,* 1–8. doi:10.1111/ajpy.12159
10. Hands, A.J., & Warshak, R.A. (2011). Parental alienation among college students. *The American Journal of Family Therapy, 39,* 431. doi:10.1080/01926187.2011.575336
11. López, T.J., Iglesias, V.E.N., & García, P.F. (2014). Parental alienation gradient: Strategies for a syndrome. *The American Journal of Family Therapy, 42,* 217–231. doi:10.1080/01926187.2013.820116
12. Bowlby, J. (1988). *A secure base. Clinical applications of attachment theory.* London: Routledge.
13. Bandura, A. (1979). Psychological mechanisms of aggression. In M. VonCranach, K. Foppa, W. LePenies, & D. Ploog (Eds.), *Human ethology: Claims and limits of a new discipline.* Cambridge: Cambridge University Press.
14. Baker, A.J.L. (2005). The long-term effects of parental alienation on adult children: A qualitative research study. *The American Journal of Family Therapy, 33,* 289–302. doi:10.1080/01926180590962129
15. Baker, A.J.L. (2005). Parental alienation strategies: A qualitative study of adults who experienced parental alienation as a child. *American Journal of Forensic Psychology, 23,* 1–23.
16. Baker, A.J.L. (2007). *Adult children of parental alienation syndrome: Breaking the ties that bind.* New York: W.W. Norton.
17. Henning, K., Jones, A., & Holdford, R. (2003). Treatment needs of women arrested for family violence: A comparison with male offenders. *Journal of Interpersonal Violence, 18,* 839–856.

18. Baker, A.J.L. (2005). The cult of parenthood: A qualitative study of parental alienation. *Cultic Study Review, 5,* 1–29. doi:10.1080/019261805 90962129

19. Baker, A J.L. (2006). Patterns of parental alienation syndrome: A qualitative study of adults who were alienated from a parent as a child. *American Journal of Family Therapy, 34,* 63–78. doi:10.1080/01926180500301444

20. Kopetski, L.M. (1998). Identifying cases of parental alienation syndrome – part I. *The Colorado Lawyer, 27,* 65–68.

21. Kopetski, L.M. (1998). Identifying cases of parental alienation syndrome – part II. *The Colorado Lawyer, 27,* 61–64.

22. Lorandos, D., Bernet, W., & Sauber, S.R. (2013). *Parental alienation: The handbook for mental health and legal professionals* USA: Charles C Thomas.

23. *Family Law Act, 1975 (Cth).* Retrieved from *www5.austlii.edu.au/au/legis/cth/consol_act/fla1975114/*

24. Clawar, S.S., & Rivlin, B. (2013). *Children held hostage: Identifying brainwashed children, presenting a case, and crafting solutions.* (2nd edn.). Chicago, IL: American Bar Association.

25. Godbout, E., & Parent, C. (2012). The life paths and lived experiences of adults who have experienced parental alienation: A retrospective study. *Journal of Divorce and Remarriage, 53,* 34–54. doi:10.1080/10502556.2012.635967

26. Baker, A.J.L., & Chambers, J. (2011). Adult recall of childhood exposure to parental conflict: Unpacking the Black Box of parental alienation. *Journal of Divorce and Remarriage, 52,* 55–76. doi:10.1080/10502556.2011.534396

27. Baker, A.J.L., & Ben-Ami, N. (2011). To turn a child against a parent is to turn a child against himself: The direct and indirect effects of exposure to parental alienation strategies on self-esteem and well-being. *Journal of Divorce and Remarriage, 52,* 472–489. doi:10.1080/10502556.2011.609424

28. Baker, A.J.L., & Ben Ami, N. (2011). Adult recall of childhood psychological maltreatment in adult children of divorce: Prevalence and associations with outcomes. *Journal of Divorce and Remarriage, 52,* 203–219. doi:10.1080/10502556.2011.556973

29. Baker, A.J.L., & Verrocchio, M.C. (2013). Italian college student-reported childhood exposure to parental alienation: Correlates with well-being. *Journal of Divorce and Remarriage, 54,* 609–628. doi:10.1080/10502556.2013.837714

30. Reed, C. (2019). *Parental Alienation: A qualitative investigation of the experience of targeted adult children* (Master's thesis, University of Tasmania, Hobart, Australia).

31. Ward, S. (2016). *Reunification of alienated parents and their adult children: A qualitative investigation.* (Master's thesis, University of Tasmania, Hobart, Australia).

32. Finzi-Dottan, R., Goldblatt, H., & Cohen-Masica, O. (2012). The experience of motherhood for alienated mothers. *Journal of Child, Family, and Social Work, 17,* 316–325. doi:10.1111/j.1365-2206.2011.00782.x

33. Reid, J.A., Haskell, R.A., Dillahunt-Aspillaga, C., & Thor, J.A. (2013). Contemporary review of empirical and clinical studies of trauma bonding in violent or exploitative relationships. *International Journal of Psychology Research, 8,* 37–73.

34. Poustie, C., Matthewson, M., & Balmer, S. (2018). The forgotten parent: The targeted parent perspective of parental alienation. *Journal of Family Issues, 39,* 3298–3323.

35. Baker, A.J.L., & Fine, P.R. (2014). *Surviving parental alienation: A journey of hope and healing.* Lanham, Maryland: Rowman & Littlefield.

36. Vassiliou, D., & Cartwright, G.F. (2001). The lost parents' perspective on parental alienation syndrome. *The American Journal of Family Therapy, 29,* 181–191. doi:10.1080/019261801750424307

37. Humphreys, C., & Thiara, R.K. (2003). Neither justice nor protection: women's experiences of post-separation violence. *Journal of Social Welfare and Family Law, 25,* 195–214. doi: 10.4324/9781351154246-17

38. Lowenstein, L.F. (2012). Child contact disputes between parents and allegations of sex abuse: What does the research say? *Journal of Divorce and Remarriage, 53,* 194–203. doi:10.1080/10502556.2012.663267

Part Two

The alienated family

Chapter Six

Alienating parents

Introduction

To have an effective means of identifying the alienation process and alienating parents, it is necessary to understand the characteristics of alienating parents. This will also assist with successful intervention. Although there may be individual differences in the ways in which alienating parents present, at least in terms of the combination of factors that are evident in any one individual, there are certain characteristics that are beginning to be understood. Before considering these characteristics, it is necessary to examine whether or not alienating mothers and alienating fathers are likely to present in similar ways.

It has been suggested that parental alienation is equally likely to be perpetrated by fathers and mothers (1). However, it may be the case that the selection of the tactics used to alienate the child from the targeted parent differs for alienating mothers and alienating fathers. This notion is beginning to be explored.

When considering alienating mothers, it is interesting to note that the psychological literature has highlighted the gatekeeping role of mothers, in general, and in parenting disputes (2). These mothers tend to be the parents who believe that they are best able to perform caregiving tasks and that they should be the parent who decides what is best for their children. There is a tendency for mothers functioning as gatekeepers to attribute less importance to the contribution of the fathers in their children's lives.

After separation, gatekeeping parents experience difficulty understanding why they should not be the person who decides the living arrangements for their children and how much time their children spend with the children's other parent. They resent the time a child is away from them when they do not have direct control over the child's circumstance and wellbeing.

When considering alienating fathers, there is a tendency for these fathers to be controlling. The alienation of the child from their mother is motivated by a need to continue to exert influence over the targeted parent despite the relationship that fostered the original imbalance of power being over (3).

It seems that it is not easy to know in advance who is likely to become an alienating parent. Some work has been done on trying to categorise alienating parents on the basis of shared characteristics, although this offers little to the understanding of why some parents will become alienating parents whereas others will not. Nevertheless, the categories of alienating parents are worth considering.

Categories of alienating parents

It has been suggested that there are three distinct parental alienation perpetrator groups (4). This categorisation is based on information provided by adults who were exposed to parental alienation tactics when they were children. These patterns have been identified as follows:

(a)   Narcissistic mothers in divorced families who alienate their children from the targeted parent.
(b)   Narcissistic mothers in intact families who alienate their children from the targeted parent.
(c)   Abusive and/or rejecting mothers or fathers who alienate their children from the targeted parent.

It is interesting to note from the above research that parental alienation can occur in intact families as well as separated/divorced families. Further, it was noted in this research that parental alienation can occur in non-litigious divorced families, so it is not solely the effect of a desire to 'win custody' in a legal process. It has been suggested that parental alienation is more strongly the result of parental conflict than the parents' marital/relationship status (5). In fact, parental alienation has been demonstrated to be related to the extent to which a hostile interpersonal relationship exists between the parents, with this affecting whether or not the child spends overnight time with the targeted parent (6).

The characteristics of alienating parents will be considered without making a distinction between those features that best describe alienating mothers and those that describe alienating fathers. Indeed, in all likelihood, there is greater overlap of characteristics between alienating fathers and mothers than there is distinction between them.

Characteristics of alienating parents

In addition to the categorisation of alienating parents, their characteristics have been investigated. Although there is variability between the presentation of one alienating parent and another, there are common themes when they are considered as a group. An individual alienating parent may demonstrate some of these characteristics but not necessarily all of them.

Problematic personality traits

The personality characteristics of alienating parents have been demonstrated to be associated with their drive to alienate their children from the targeted parents (7–8). This is not particularly surprising as personality traits do influence the way an individual's world is perceived and how they interact with others. A person's individual needs, at least to some extent, are determined by their personality characteristics. Let us consider, then, the nature of the personality characteristics most evident in alienating parents.

Research has indicated that narcissism is strongly evident in alienating parents, particularly alienating mothers (4). The DSM-5 (9) diagnostic criteria for narcissistic personality disorder include the following features:

•   An exaggerated sense of self-importance.
•   An expectation of being recognised as superior even in the absence of achievements that would warrant this recognition.
•   Exaggeration of one's achievements and talents.

- Preoccupation with fantasies of success, power, brilliance, beauty or the perfect partner.
- Belief of superiority that can only be appreciated by equally superior individuals.
- A need for constant admiration.
- A sense of entitlement.
- An expectation of special favours and compliance with these expectations.
- Advantage taken of others.
- An inability or unwillingness to recognise the needs or feelings of others.
- Enviousness of others and a belief that others are envious of them.
- Arrogant and haughty behaviour.

These traits seem severe. They are severe. Of course, it is not likely that alienating parents uniformly could be diagnosed with narcissistic personality disorder. Nevertheless, narcissism may still be evident in a sub-clinical presentation. In this way, you would expect alienating parents to present with self-aggrandisement and a sense of entitlement that interferes with interpersonal relationships but does not necessarily have a detrimental effect on overall functioning or life achievements.

The narcissism evident in alienating parents leads to behaviours that are consistent with parental alienation because the presence of the narcissistic personality traits makes it very difficult for these alienating parents to cope with the humiliation associated with abandonment experienced as a result of the breakdown of the relationship with the targeted parent, whether that abandonment is real or perceived. The narcissistic traits would make it exceedingly problematic for alienating parents to be rejected (4).

Box 6.1 Targeted parent: She acts like I have abandoned her but that's not what happened. The relationship hadn't been working for a long time … if it ever really worked. We talked about it and decided it was best for everyone if we accepted that the relationship had no future. She agreed. She said she had been unhappy for a long time. We agreed to work together to do what was best for the children. She seemed open to the idea of shared care of the children. But, then, she acted like I had harmed her in some way. She told everyone I had destroyed her life when I walked out without a word. She just can't cope with the fact that the relationship didn't work out the way she planned. The trouble is it was her plan, not mine.

Themes of abandonment and rejection can be evident in the presentation of alienating parents. Even when a more realistic view of the nature of the breakdown of a relationship can be held by alienating parents at some points in time, as the reality of the consequences of the end of the parental relationship are felt, the alienating parent will tend to interpret the dissolution of the relationship as evidence of abandonment and rejection. This causes the alienating parent to feel humiliated by relationship events and the perceived intentions of the targeted parent.

Box 6.2 Alienating parent: What am I supposed to do? I can't believe he left me. I did everything for him. I tried and tried to make the relationship work and he just threw it away. How can I face anyone? Everyone will know he walked out. I think about how worthless he is … It should have been me who left him, not the other way around. He doesn't realise what he is losing. Well, he will. I will make sure of that.

The humiliation seems to be more related to the alienating parent's perception of themselves and how the breakdown of the relationship will impact on other's perception of them than it being the result of enduring belittling experiences. In reality, relationships fail for many complicated reasons. Alienating parents tend to view the relationship breakdown as the type of failure about which a person should feel ashamed. It is perceived as something done to them. With the targeted parent blamed for the lack of success of the relationship, feelings of hostility develop.

It has been reported that children are likely to develop psychological difficulties when they are raised by a parent with a personality disorder that is characterised by hostility, such as Narcissistic Personality Disorder. It is also true that children are at risk of the development of psychological maladjustment when their parents have similar sub-clinical personality traits (10). It is not surprising, then, that these personality traits are associated with a process initiated by the parent that can be understood to be hostility-driven that has such a negative effect on the children involved, that is parental alienation.

It is certainly the case that alienating parents can present as hostile. Although the targeted parent is the main focus of their hostility, others may also bear the brunt of hostile interactions with the alienating parent. Consider the next example.

Box 6.3 Interviewer: Thank you for coming in today.

Alienating parent: I'm here because my lawyer told me I had to come. But, you should know, that I'm not happy about having to be interviewed.

Interviewer: I have been asked by the court to talk to everyone involved in this matter.

Alienating parent: Well, I'm fed up. I keep telling everyone that the children don't want to see their father and I keep being accused of stopping them seeing him. They don't like him! I don't know how many times I have to say it. Will no-one listen?

Interviewer: You have the opportunity here today to talk about your concerns about the children spending time with their father.

Alienating parent: With all due respect, I don't feel it's necessary to explain anything to you. No-one has ever listened before so I don't see why you would be the first. And, really, I have nothing more to say. The children don't want to see their father and I'm not going to force them to do something they don't want to do even if you or a judge says I have to!

The hostility experienced by this alienating parent is greater than is warranted and is greater than would be expected given the demands of the situation. Most people in this situation would attempt to 'win over' the interviewer. Of course, the hostility experienced by alienating parents may not always be openly expressed. The hostility may be masked by an act of seeming compliance and a presentation of reasonableness. However, this façade is superficial and the underlying hostility can be unmasked with appropriate questioning.

Even when it is not formally assessed, you are able to discern these personality problems or narcissism in alienating parents. They talk about their superiority, particularly in relation to the targeted parent. They see themselves and their families as better than the targeted parent and the targeted parents' families without there being any real justification for holding these views.

> **Box 6.4 Interviewer:** What was your relationship like at the beginning, when you first started seeing each other?
>
> **Alienating parent:** I don't know what I was thinking. I don't know why I started seeing him. I realise I have to accept responsibility for the choices I made but he was so far removed from the type of person I should have been dating that I can't explain it. His whole family is trash and so is he. I deserve so much more … I'm a better person than he could ever be. I could have easily done well in life if it wasn't for him holding me back. My family all did so much better than his family. My family are all well regarded in the community while his family is full of criminals and deadbeats. I don't know what I was thinking. You must think I am the most ridiculous person you have ever met for choosing such a partner.

The above example is not an uncommon presentation. The alienating parent will belittle the targeted parent and their family. This can reflect a genuine belief in their own superiority. Alienating parents are rejecting of the targeted parent's achievements in life and are dismissive of their needs.

Some alienating parents will talk about their need to make sure the activities of the targeted parent are curtailed. They tend to talk about it as if they have undertaken a crusade to protect the world. They describe the targeted parent as 'evil' and view themselves as without fault. Their hostility is very strongly evident.

> **Box 6.5 Psychologist:** For almost a decade, one alienating mother had plagued the targeted father by taking it upon herself to contact the women with whom the targeted parent tried to form relationships or these women's families to warn them about the faults the alienating mother perceived in the targeted parent. Despite there being every indication that she was an intelligent person, the alienating parent could not see that it was inappropriate for her to warn off the targeted parent's potential partners. When met with the inevitable rejection by some of these potential partners or their family members, this alienating parent would become hostile and express anger at their lack of appreciation of her efforts to protect them.

It is difficult to shift alienating parents' negative views about the targeted parent that are founded in their narcissism, even when they are directly challenged. Intellectually, alienating parents might see that it is not possible that all the targeted parent's actions are bad or that it is not possible that they always viewed the targeted parent so negatively given the fact that they pursued a relationship with this person, but, emotionally, they cannot abandon this view.

They do not even try to strongly justify their position. They tend to just state it as fact. The targeted parent is a bad person and others are expected to agree. There are cases of alienating parents becoming quite frustrated when others fail to agree with their view or continue to try to challenge their views, even mildly challenge their views. They do not really understand why the validity of their view is not apparent to others. Certainly, they often have an expectation that others will appreciate their importance. Consider this example.

> **Box 6.6 Alienating parent:** I look at my achievements compared with his and I wonder why I ever wanted to be in a relationship with him. I am an accountant. I have a university degree. He is a nobody. He didn't go to university and his earnings reflect that. I was the one who brought in the most money. I'm like you. Well educated. You must think I'm stupid for marrying someone who is not on the same level as me … intellectually. So, you can see that I can offer the children a better life than their father can. I'm sure you'll agree.

So, what is the link between narcissism and parental alienation? The explanation may be found in the way in which narcissistic individuals experience relationships. Narcissistic personality traits affect the quality and depth of interpersonal relationships. Rather than relationships being built on equality and reciprocity, they tend to have inherent power imbalances and superficial commitment. The narcissistic partner might want the relationship because it meets their own needs without really developing a sense of shared experience with their partner.

When the relationship ends, the need for the targeted parent no longer exists. Although the alienating parent may find it difficult to cope with what is lost, it is the relationship rather than the person they miss. With the need for the other person no longer evident and with a strong desire to reassert authority and order, the narcissistic alienating parent will act to eradicate the targeted parent from their lives. They must do this by severing the relationship between the targeted parent and the child.

Further, with a need to dominate as the superior parent, the narcissistic alienating parent poorly tolerates an ongoing relationship between the child and the targeted parent. In a sense, the targeted parent would present competition for the narcissistic alienating parent. With a lack of depth of feeling for the targeted parent, it would be an easy enough matter to act in a way that was hurtful for their former partner.

Abnormal grief reaction

Building on the notion that alienating parents cope poorly with perceived abandonment and rejection and experience humiliation at the loss of their relationship, it has been suggested that the problems experienced by alienating parents that drive them to alienate their children from the targeted parent reflect an abnormal grief reaction (7). The alienating parent cannot seem to come to terms with the failure of the relationship and feelings of distress and anger persist for extended periods of time.

Grief is a normal response to loss. This includes the loss of a relationship or the loss of a future that was planned. A person may struggle to cope with the change in their life circumstances. A grief reaction is considered to be abnormal when it is more intense than would be expected given the demands of the situation or continues for longer than expected. Although there are no hard and fast rules about how intense or prolonged a grief reaction should be, the severity and duration of a grief reaction is typically determined by the extent to which the person's daily functioning remains impaired. So, if a person continues to struggle to cope with the changes to their life course and this manifests in disrupted or disturbed functioning, then the grief can be considered to be abnormal.

Certainly, abnormal grief reactions have been experienced by alienating parents in response to the loss of the relationship with the targeted parent or the sense of family the intact family unit provided. The grief reactions can go on for many years without indication of resolution. The bitterness felt towards the targeted parent continues unabated despite the passage of time.

A conversation occurred between a lawyer and a psychologist about a case that was before the Family Court. The parents had been in conflict for many years despite the targeted father's quite moderate views about the alienating mother. When discussing the alienating parent, this lawyer asked how a person could stay angry for so long. In that case, the alienating mother was so disappointed by the breakdown of yet another relationship that she had considerable problem coping with the loss of the things she wanted in life – a husband, a father for her children, and the status she considered a marital relationship brought her.

The grief an alienating parent feels about the loss of the relationship may manifest in a variety of ways. It is often the case that alienating parents will talk about their feelings about the breakdown of the relationship with the targeted parent as if it occurred recently despite the relationship ending many months or years before. This can occur despite the fact that the targeted parent has moved on with their life.

Box 6.7 Interviewer: It's been about five and a half years since the divorce.

Alienating parent: Yes, that's about right. My husband left five years and four months ago, so it's not quite five and a half years.

Interviewer: During that time there have been a number of problems organising a suitable arrangement for the children to spend time with their father.

Alienating parent: The problem is that the children don't want to spend time with the bimbo he is sleeping with. And I don't want them going there when she is around. The thing with this woman won't last and then the children will be hurt again.

Interviewer: I understand Mr Smith has been with his current partner for the last three years or so and they recently married. Is that right?

Alienating parent: How would I know? That is what he says but how would I know what is happening with this woman. I still don't think it will last but he better not come crawling back to me when it falls apart.

It seems that this alienating parent has not come to terms with the loss of the relationship and the fact that the targeted parent has moved on with his life and formed another lasting relationship. Despite the fact that more than half a decade has passed, she continues to be dismissive of the fact that the targeted parent might be living a settled and satisfactory life.

Although alienating parents present as hostile, underlying this hostility is bitterness and regret at the failure of a relationship or the loss of the things they wanted. They are unable to accept that life can move on. They fail to deal with their emotional response to the breakdown of their relationship. It is sad for all those involved, including the children.

These problematic reactions to the loss of what they hoped for maintains their hostility and rage. There have been cases where the grief reactions of the alienating parents dragged out the conflict in court for more than a decade of disputes and legal challenges. In the centre of this conflict is a child who would be likely to benefit from a loving relationship with both parents. In some cases, the child knows no other circumstance than the one they find themselves involved in. All they can remember is their parents being in conflict.

> **Box 6.8 Alienating parent:** It's just not fair. He has everything. He has more money than me and a bigger house. And now he is in a new relationship. What about me? It's not fair he has everything and I have nothing.
>
> **Interviewer:** I understand, though, that there was a property settlement at the end of the marriage that you agreed at the time was fair.
>
> **Alienating parent:** Yes, but then how did I know everything would go so well for him. He has just moved on like I don't even count.
>
> **Interviewer:** Are you saying that you would prefer it if he wasn't happy?
>
> **Alienating parent:** Yes! No. Yes. I don't know. I just know that it's not fair that he has everything. He left me and now he's happy. He ruined my life! He is the one who should be unhappy. Well, he's not getting the kids, too. No way! He's not leaving me and taking everything!

The alienating parent's reaction to what she considers she has lost has caused her to use the children as a means of expressing her unhappiness. Her decision to deny the targeted parent time with the children seems to be based on her need to express her unhappiness rather than an action that is designed to offer the children what they need.

Alienating parents who are struggling to cope with the loss of a relationship will talk about the possibility of reconciliation. This can co-occur with other denigrating comments made about the targeted parent and despite an ongoing campaign to damage the relationship between the targeted parent and the children.

> **Box 6.9 Alienating parent:** I have pushed and pushed for Andrew to attend relationship counselling, but he keeps refusing. How are we supposed to solve our relationship problems if he doesn't agree to therapy?
>
> **Interviewer:** Andrew seems certain that the relationship is over, at least from his point of view.
>
> **Alienating parent:** Well, I can see us getting back together. It would be so much easier to be together as a family. Then he could see the children whenever he wanted. I just wish he would see sense.
>
> **Interviewer:** It's been three years since the end of your relationship, hasn't it?
>
> **Alienating parent:** He can't do this to me. Doesn't he realise how he is hurting me … and the children? Still, I don't know what I am expecting. He always was a selfish man. He never thought of anyone but himself.

It would be easy to assume that if a person was grieving the loss of a relationship then they would encourage the children to spend time with the other parent so that the connection with that parent could be maintained. However, the matter is more complicated than that. The alienating parent is unhappy and struggling to cope with the notion that the targeted parent can function independently of them or the relationship. The targeted parent's failure to do as the alienating parent wishes, by returning to the relationship or, at least, suffering away from the relationship, causes the alienating parent to feel overwhelming anger and hostility. It is an easy step, then, to use the children in a way that makes the expression of their unhappiness clear.

Externalisation of responsibility

As stated, alienating parents can find it difficult to cope with the loss of the relationship with the targeted parent, even if they claim that the relationship was problematic because of the targeted parent's allegedly poor behaviour. The unhappiness they feel is attributed to the targeted parent's actions or lack of action.

In fact, alienating parents tend to hold other people responsible for the problems they face (7). They seem unable to accept that they may have contributed to the problems that lead to the end of the relationship with the targeted parent or any conflict that developed after separation. Extending beyond their relationships, alienating parents tend to externalise responsibility in most domains of their life.

The externalisation mentioned here is evident in terms of their feelings, ideas, responsibilities and attitudes. Even when challenged, they refuse to see or are unable to see that they contributed in any way to the problems in their lives. They talk about the difficulties they face in terms of the burden of responsibility that must be borne by others.

Box 6.10 Interviewer: Tell me about what happened the last time you collected the children from their father.

Alienating parent: I was really upset. Their father wouldn't speak to me. I asked him to explain himself ... about the way he has been treating the children.

Interviewer: What did he say when you brought up these concerns?

Alienating parent: He said he wouldn't talk to me and turned his back on me.

Interviewer: When I interviewed him, he said he told you he wouldn't talk with you about these matters in front of the children. Is that how you remember it?

Alienating parent: Well, if I can't talk to him when I want then when am I supposed to talk to him? He won't answer my phone calls.

Interviewer: I understand things escalated.

Alienating parent: Yes, when he turned his back on me I became very upset. The children began to cry. They were upset, too.

Interviewer: What happened next?

Alienating parent: He just walked towards his car. He was just ignoring me like I didn't matter. How dare he do that? I won't be treated that way.

Interviewer: Do you think he was just trying to leave a situation that was getting out of control?

Alienating parent: It was only getting out of control because of him.

Interviewer: The police report said that you punched him on the back of the head.

Alienating parent: He was ignoring me! He was walking away. He was the one who was refusing to talk. What was I supposed to do? It wasn't my fault. He is the one to blame.

The escalation of this conflict seemed to be the responsibility of the alienating parent who did not cope well when the targeted parent would not comply with her demands. Despite the targeted parent trying to avoid conflict by leaving the scene, the alienating parent acted in a way that created a problem where one did not exist previously. Nonetheless, the alienating parent blamed the targeted parent and focused on what she perceived to be his wrongdoing.

In addition to avoiding responsibility for problem situations, alienating parents tend to avoid responsibility for resolving existing problems. They look to others to change their views or behaviour, but see little need to adjust their own point of view.

Box 6.11 Targeted parent: I don't know what to do. I seem to be the one who always has to make adjustments or give in to accommodate his wishes. I try to be reasonable and give him what he wants when he makes demands. But he still refuses to let me see the children. I think he believes that I am the one who has to jump through all the hoops, and he doesn't have to do anything. But that's the way it's always been. He never thinks he has done anything wrong and I am the one he always blames. But, this time, I don't know what else I can do to convince him I should see the children.

It is often the case that alienating parents absolve themselves of any responsibility for resolving problems or, indeed, changing their behaviour to avoid future conflict. It is not surprising, then, that alienating parents blame others for the negative emotions they experience. If they are not responsible for the problem situation, then the emotional costs must be caused by the other party to the dispute.

Box 6.12 Alienating parent: He makes me so angry. He does it deliberately, I'm sure. Every time I have to have anything to do with him, I become upset. So, I asked to sit in a separate room at the conference at the Family Court. I just didn't want to listen to him. Everything he has done to me has made me upset. He keeps taking me back to court, saying I have breached the orders again. Well, I wouldn't have to if he would just do the right thing and leave us alone. I would be fine if he would just back off and leave us alone.

Undoubtedly, this alienating parent is angry about the targeted parent's reluctance to do as she instructs and about the fact that she has to return to court to address the problem of her non-compliance with court orders. However, she fails to appreciate that her anger is the result of problems that had their genesis in her own actions and not those of the targeted parent, that is her contravention of court orders.

The failure of alienating parents to accept responsibility for their own actions can lead to frustrating exchanges when the alienating parent refuses to respond to questions that focus on their own wrongdoing or problems. Instead, the focus is shifted by the alienating parent back to the wrongdoing of the targeted parent.

Box 6.13 Interviewer: After your relationship broke down and Mr Smith moved out of the family home, there were reports that you weren't coping very well.

Alienating parent: It was his fault. The kids would have been fine if he had done what any father would do. I would give him money for groceries, and he would gamble with it. He could never handle money. I was the one who had to do everything.

Interviewer: I am talking about the four to six months after Mr Smith left your home and you had no contact with him. How were you coping during that period?

> **Alienating parent:** I was fine. He had the problems. He didn't get the kids off to school on time and there was never any food in the house. The kids know it was his fault.
>
> **Interviewer:** Can I ask you to consider that four to six months after Mr Smith left the home, when you and the children had no contact with him? Your mother told me that things were pretty bad for you and that you were struggling to cope with running the house and looking after the children.
>
> **Alienating parent:** I told him there would be problems if he didn't stop gambling, but he wouldn't listen to me. There were times when there wasn't much money but that was because of his gambling. He would say that he would bring home groceries, but he would waste the money on gambling and the kids would go hungry.

Unfortunately, although a seemingly extreme case of avoidance of responsibility, this exchange is based on an actual interview. Ignoring questions that were directed at examining the alienating parent's behaviour post-separation, the alienating parent instead chose to focus on the targeted parent's behaviour when they were still living in the same home. The alienating parent simply acted as if the questions were not asked.

Even though it is expected, the degree to which alienating parents reject the idea that they are in any way responsible for things going wrong can be startling. Even when you go through a process of logically challenging their views, they simply fail to accept that it is not someone else's fault, usually the targeted parent although the targeted parent's family or new partner also can be blamed.

Although these exchanges are psychologically interesting, we can also find them exhausting. This process of challenging the logic of their views is important because you need to determine the rigidity of their views and how amenable they are to change. However, they can be exhausting because, when you think you have got them to a point where they might agree that it takes two people to have a conflict, they then strongly revert to their position that they are fault free.

How does the externalisation of responsibility fit with the conceptualisation of parental alienation? If alienating parents hold the view that they are not responsible for the things that go wrong in their lives, they must identify the person who is responsible for their unhappiness. It is not a huge leap for the alienating parent to hold the targeted parent responsible. After all, the targeted parent is the one person who thwarted the alienating parent's needs and abandoned and humiliated them.

If the alienating parent is going to hold the view that the targeted parent is the person responsible for things going wrong, then the targeted parent must be viewed as a bad person. This view of the targeted parent as a bad person makes it easier for the alienating parent to explain why they are suffering. It also allows the alienating parent to act in a way that is hurtful to the targeted parent without the complication of feelings of guilt. It also justifies the alienating parent withholding the children from the targeted parent and supports their view that they are only acting in their child's best interests.

Family of origin

For alienating parents, problems often exist with their family of origin (7–8). Family relationships can be dysfunctional. The alienating parent's relationship with their own parents can be negatively influenced by unrealistic parental expectations, unhealthy dependence, or controlling or dominating parents. Family relationships can be overly enmeshed, and this produces difficulties when there is an expectation for the alienating parent to act independently of their family.

> **Box 6.14 Targeted parent:** Her parents hate me. I think they are contributing to these problems. If they had their way, I would never see my children again. And my ex-wife does whatever they say. Can you believe that her parents came on our honeymoon with us? She said she wasn't going if they didn't go, too. They spent the holiday doing touristy things together and I was left by myself. When I objected, a huge argument broke out. It's always been this way. Decisions that were made, like where we were going to live and what car to buy, were made by her and her parents. I was never consulted.

Alienating parents may offer an overly idealised account of their childhood experiences and their current relationships with their family members. Examination of this issue is likely to raise concern about the psychological health of the family of origin and cast doubt on the notion of the idealised view being presented.

> **Box 6.15 Interviewer:** Tell me about your childhood.
> **Alienating parent:** I had a wonderful childhood.
> **Interviewer:** In what way was it wonderful?
> **Alienating parent:** My parents were the best parents … so devoted to me and my brother. I couldn't have asked for a better childhood.
> **Interviewer:** What about school? Did you have friends at school?
> **Alienating parent:** Um … not really. But then I didn't need friends at school because I had everything I needed at home. My parents were always there for us.
> **Interviewer:** But it must have been harder at school with few friends.
> **Alienating parent:** Well … my parents more than made up for it. They did everything they could to support us. They never got angry with us and there were never any stressful times. Unlike his family. His parents were terrible. No wonder he can't parent his own children. He was never taught how to be a good parent. His family fought all the time. Mine never did. That's why I'm a better parent than him. My parents gave me everything. Whatever we wanted we got. That's the sort of childhood I want my children to have. Not the sort of childhood their father can give them.

It also is the case that the parents of alienating parents or the family of alienating parents often provide very poor examples for the alienating parents of how healthy families are supposed to function. Alienating parents tend to replay the problems experienced by the family of origin in their own adult relationships.

It has been our experience that the families of origin of alienating parents can be problematic or dysfunctional. However, we do not think it is the case that the family problems fall into a single category. For example, it occurs often enough to be noteworthy that alienating parents were raised by a single parent whose own relationship failed or by parents where there was one dominating individual and one passive parent. The alienating parents were raised in an environment where there was considered to be little need for the other parent to contribute to child-rearing efforts. Interestingly, alienating parents will see their own mother's child-rearing efforts without the assistance of the other parent as a virtue, even while they are also saying that they would not separate their child from his or her father because they were raised without their own father.

> **Box 6.16 Interviewer:** Were you raised by both your parents?
>
> **Alienating parent:** No, just Mum. My parents separated when I was about five years old. After that, I didn't see Dad much. Mum said he wasn't a very nice person to her or to me. My grandmother once told me that my father had tried to keep in touch, but he obviously didn't try hard enough. If he really had wanted to see me, he would have found a way. So, I can only assume that what Mum says about him is true. But I didn't need him. Mum did an excellent job. She gave me everything I needed, with the help of my grandparents, of course. We lived with them for a while … a long while. In fact, my grandparents were more like additional parents than grandparents. They are still really involved in my life and my daughter's life, of course. Mum never remarried. Why would she want to after all my so-called father put her through? She always said once was enough.

The conflict within the family of origin of alienating parents can be intense. Although desiring approval from their family members, alienating parents may not have been provided with that approval. This tends to distort how alienating parents see a working relationship.

The families of alienating parents can also be quite controlling. Alienating parents will struggle to go against the wishes of their own parent or parents. For example, if their parent disapproved of them facilitating a relationship between the child and the targeted parent, they would not facilitate the relationship. Their need not to alienate their parents is stronger than their need to do what is best for their child.

Certainly, alienating parents can be overly influenced by the negative views of their family members about the targeted parent. Also, the families of alienating parents can be enmeshed. They can seem to function as a single unit when standing up to the targeted parent who is pushed out. Rather than battling one alienating parent, the targeted parent ends up tackling a whole family.

> **Box 6.17 Alienating parent:** I should have listened to my parents. They never liked him. They used to warn me he was going to be trouble. And they were right. So now I have decided to pay more attention to what they have to say. Both my parents think it is a bad idea for him to have any contact with the children. They reminded me of times he growled at them. My Dad said that is a sign of a disturbed man and I tend to agree. I can see it clearly now. He shouldn't growl at the children, even if they have done the wrong thing. Mum said he should just explain to them why their behaviour is a problem. I think I must have been overly influenced by him when we were still together. I should have stood up for the children when their father growled at them, but I didn't. Dad said that is probably because I was worried that he would turn around and growl at me. I have thought about it and I think Dad is right.

We know that the way one conducts him or herself in adult relationships can be determined, in part at least, by the lessons we learn during our childhoods about how adult relationships work (11). The indication of dysfunction in the family of origin of alienating parents is likely to influence later choices with regard to the way in which relationship interactions are managed.

It is known that people who were alienated from a parent during their own childhoods are over-represented in groups of alienating parents (12). In this way, alienated children are likely to become alienating parents. Again, this is due to the fact that what we learn about how to conduct ourselves in adult relationships is partly determined by childhood experiences.

It seems to many that the alienating tactics of alienating parents are extreme. Certainly, most people would reject them because they are inappropriate ways of managing relationship disappointment or conflict. However, if our own childhood experiences are similar, those experiences have a normalising effect on our own behaviour choices.

The same is true of the current messages we receive from those closest to us. If our family members support a particular course of action, that support gives the actions we choose a sense of validation that our choices are good ones. It is easier to sustain a course of action if those around us are encouraging us and supporting the decisions we make.

It is easy, then, to see how problems related to the family of origin can influence parental alienation. The experience of relationship events or difficulties that mirror those of other family members and/or the support received for the courses of action taken, increase the chances that a parent will pursue a process of alienation if these events and experiences are consistent with the alienation message.

Deflection of attention from own problems

As already mentioned, alienating parents externalise their problems. It also is the case that the focus on the alleged wrongdoing of the targeted parent can be used to mask the alienating parent's own problems (8). The problems that are being avoided might include psychological symptoms, relationship problems, or a general inability to cope with life demands.

We have found that the tendency of alienating parents to blame others for their problems is quite marked. Mostly, they blame the targeted parent, but they may also blame family members, particularly the family members of the targeted parent. By focusing on the other parent's problems, the alienating parent diverts attention from their own problems, including those that might influence the way in which they deal with relationship breakdowns or how they parent their child.

When you examine the functioning of alienating parents, significant problems can be evident. For example, an alienating parent might focus on the drug use of the targeted parent to draw attention away from their own substance use problems. Or, an alienating parent with severe anxiety symptoms may focus on the problematic behaviour of the targeted parent as the source of distress, even though the symptoms predated their relationship. Indeed, when the focus is on their own problems, alienating parents can tend to talk about them as being the result of the targeted parent's actions, even in cases where the problems existed before the relationship with the targeted parent developed.

It is common enough to find alienating parents who refuse to acknowledge that their own problems are separate from the targeted parent's problems. That is, they will say they have had little choice but to respond in the way they have done because of the targeted parent's behaviour. Consider this example where the alienating parent tries to focus on the targeted parent's behaviour when directly questioned about their own violent actions.

Box 6.18 Interviewer: I see from these documents that you have been charged in relation to family violence episodes.

Alienating parent: The problem is his drug use. It was out of control. He would take anything he could get his hands on. And he did it around the children. That's disgusting. Letting children see all that sort of stuff. When he was using drugs, he didn't look after his kids. There was never any money because he spent it all on drugs. I will never forgive him for that.

> **Interviewer:** Can you explain the circumstances surrounding these family violence charges?
>
> **Alienating parent:** He said he used to look after the children, but it was his mother who used to look after them. She'd come around while I was at work and make sure the children's clothes were washed and they were fed. He's lazy. He would rather take drugs than look after his own children.
>
> **Interviewer:** But what about these charges you faced relating to family violence?
>
> **Alienating parent:** What do you expect me to do? I had to defend myself. If he's not going to do the right thing, what choice do I have?

It can be quite difficult to sort out what is the main source of existing problems and what issues existed before the relationship conflict contributed to them. For example, an alienating parent might blame the targeted parent for the breakdown of the relationship and the ongoing conflict. But, when you examine the evidence, it becomes apparent that the alienating parent has a history of similar problems with other partners that predate the relationship with the targeted parent.

It is interesting that alienating parents will tend to blame the targeted parent for the failure of the relationship, even in cases where their own actions determined the outcome. Consider this example.

> **Box 6.19 Alienating parent:** He didn't even try to fix the problems we were having. I suggested we go to counselling, but he said no.
>
> **Interviewer:** I understand your suggestion about counselling was made after the separation and after Mr Smith began a relationship with his current partner.
>
> **Alienating parent:** There was still some chance things could have worked if he just committed himself to trying to work things out. But he wouldn't. He just walked away from his family.
>
> **Interviewer:** Both your affidavit and Mr Smith's affidavit indicate that you were the one who left the relationship.
>
> **Alienating parent:** Well, what was I supposed to do? I had to make him see that he was making me upset by not doing what I asked. He just wouldn't listen. He said he was trying to make me happy, but he obviously wasn't trying hard enough. But I didn't expect him to walk away and not come back. That wasn't the plan. He was the one who gave up.

It may be the case that alienating parents experience conflict with people other than the targeted parent. Alienating parents tend not to be forthcoming with information that they have a pattern of interaction with others than results in interpersonal difficulties. Of course, the presence of the types of personality characteristics often displayed by alienating parents increases the chances of these types of interpersonal difficulties occurring. The focus on the conflict between the alienating parent and the targeted parent can allow the alienating parent to avoid discussing the potential pattern of interpersonal difficulty.

> **Box 6.20 Targeted parent:** She makes out that I am the only person she has trouble with but that's not true. She falls out with everyone ... except her parents, maybe. She is friends with people for a while and then they do something to annoy her and she cuts them out of her

> life. I couldn't keep up with who was in and who was out. It mostly happened if people dis-agreed with her. So, now she is cutting me out of her life, and she is making the same choice for our daughter. It seems that if I'm out of her life, I'm out of Amelia's life, too.

Focus on the conflict with the targeted parent also allows alienating parents to deflect attention away from a more general difficulty they might experience with coping with normal life demands and challenges. If this general pattern of failure to cope exists, then it is not surprising that the alienating parent would also fail to cope with the breakdown of the relationship with the targeted parent and the challenges that come with co-parenting after separation.

> **Box 6.21 Targeted parent:** He tells everyone he was a devoted husband and a dedicated father. That's not the case. He couldn't hold down a job. He'd become stressed whenever anyone at work told him what to do. That's what bosses do! He'd then drink too much and act like the world had done the wrong thing by him. He would become angry with me and ignore the children. Not exactly father of the year.

Attention needs to be paid to the link between a tendency to deflect attention from one's own problems and the adoption of parental alienation tactics. If consideration is given to the goals of parental alienation, they are to undermine the relationship between the child and the targeted parent. This is achieved, in part, by the alienating parent creating an impression of the targeted parent as an inferior parent to the alienating parent. It serves no purpose, then, for the alienating parent to highlight their own shortcomings. Indeed, if narcissistic personality traits are evident, then the alienating parent would struggle to admit that shortcomings existed.

Poor relationship history

A history of problematic romantic relationships is common among alienating parents. This may cause the recognised vulnerability to separation and loss identified in alienating parents (8). There can be a history of failed relationships and, as a consequence, the alienating mothers, in par-ticular, can be already raising children without the assistance of their children's fathers before they enter the relationship with the targeted parent. Indeed, there can be a history of the alienating parent actively trying to remove the fathers from these other children's lives prior to the conflict developing.

> **Box 6.22 Psychologist:** It is often the case that the alienating parent has a history of lack of success in romantic relationships. They either have experienced numerous short-term relationships or unstable and problematic long-term relationships. The negative relation-ship experiences can make the alienating parent less able to cope with the failure of the most recent relationship with the targeted parent. The animosity felt towards the targeted parent can reflect a sensitivity to relationship breakdown.

Alternatively, there can be a history of failure to form romantic relationships so that the alienating parent has a strong desire for the relationship with the targeted parent to have worked out. This can explain, in some cases, why alienating parents respond so poorly to the breakdown of the relationship with the targeted parent.

Box 6.23 Psychologist: In some cases, we find that the loss of the relationship with the targeted parent has such a big impact on the alienating parent because it is the only adult relationship the alienating parent has experienced. In these cases, you may find that the alienating parent pushed for the relationship despite the targeted parent's initial ambivalence. In this way, the relationship was always more important to the alienating parent than it was to the targeted parent, at least in the early stages. The loss of the relationship can have a profound effect on the alienating parent.

The failure of past relationships or the absence of relationships equates with a history of relationship disappointment. As a result, alienating parents tend to give a lot of weight to the importance of the relationship with the targeted parent. The failure of that relationship can be devastating and increases their anger that had its origin in other, past relationship failures or disappointments.

This history of poor relationships and the fact that the alienating parents are often already raising other children without the assistance of the fathers may create for the alienating parents the false expectation that this is what they can expect in relation to the current situation. They then resent the pursuit of time with their child by the current targeted parent.

Box 6.24 Psychologist: Although alienating parents tend to seek out a partner who can act as a parent for their child or children from previous relationships, the failure of the relationship often results in the alienating parent demonstrating a preference for returning to single parenting. They reject the notion that there is any advantage in having the other parent sharing the burden of parenting. They either prefer to parent alone or revert to their previous sources of support, such as family members.

Of all the characteristics of alienating parents, we have found a poor relationship history to be one of the most strongly evident. In particular, the alienating mothers may have older children who they have raised on their own. As a result, they seem to have little need for the involvement of the current targeted father, and they resent that father wanting to spend time with his child. In fact, we would say that they do not really see the point of his involvement. This has not been their experience and they resent his involvement.

Box 6.25 Targeted parent: She has two other children from previous relationships. She was raising these children on her own when I met her. She said their fathers were losers and hadn't helped out financially. She seemed to be managing ok. But now I wonder whether she really just isn't interested in having her children's fathers in her life. Once she is done with us there is no room in her life for our interference. I think she is turning our daughter against me so she can get rid of me.

During the evaluation process in a parenting dispute, if you ask the right questions, you can often find that others, including the targeted parent, have attempted to encourage the alienating parent to involve the older children's fathers in their children's lives. This tends to be met with a very strongly negative reaction from the alienating parent. Certainly, it is the case that all the attempts to invite the other children's fathers into the children's lives ends in failure. This seems to be because the alienating parent puts obstacles in the way of the relationship between their older children and the children's fathers.

Box 6.26 Targeted parent: I now know that Zoe's dad tried and tried to contact her but was stopped from doing so. My ex-wife said she wanted Zoe to be able to see her father and she blamed Zoe's dad for not bothering with Zoe. So, I thought I was doing the right thing by making it easy for him to spend time with Zoe. I even offered him somewhere to stay if he came to visit Zoe. When I spoke to him on the phone, he seemed really excited. He said he's wanted to see Zoe for years. But when I told Carol about my offer, she went off her head. I couldn't believe how angry she got. She had always told me that Zoe's dad had abandoned her and that she had wanted Zoe to spend time with her dad. But when I tried to help by arranging it and it seemed like it was all going to come together, Carol lost it completely. I have never seen anyone so angry. She said Zoe's dad was never going to see Zoe and she would do anything to stop him coming to see her. She didn't seem to have any logical reason for refusing. I was really shocked. She went from a really placid person to a mad woman. Of course, I understand now. She is treating me the same way she treated him.

In some cases, pregnancy occurs early in the ultimately unsuccessful relationship between the alienating parent and the targeted parent. The relationship may have been forced along by an accidental pregnancy. Without the natural development of the relationship between the couple, there is no real foundation on which the relationship is based that allows for stability when faced with relationship stressors. The relationship fails as a result.

However, it is also the case that some women deliberately become pregnant to force the development of the relationship. An indication of this having occurred can be found in discrepancies between the accounts given by the alienating parent and the targeted parent about the circumstances of the pregnancy. For example, the alienating mother may exaggerate the length of time after meeting the targeted parent before the pregnancy occurred and insist that the pregnancy occurred because of a contraception failure. In contrast, the targeted parent, often with collateral information to support their account, will speak of the brevity of the relationship before the pregnancy occurred and insist the alienating parent had been reassuring about either the reliability of their chosen method of contraception or about their inability to conceive because of a medical reason.

Box 6.27 Targeted parent: We had only gone out together a few times when she told me she was pregnant. I was shocked. I know it upset her, but I had to ask if the baby was mine. She wasn't happy. I didn't love her then … I'm not sure I ever did. But I couldn't bear the thought of there being a child out there that I didn't know, so I committed myself to the relationship. What a joke. I tried to make it work but I still don't get to see my child.

When examining the history of the relationship between the alienating parent and the targeted parent, it is often the case that the alienating parent strongly sought or encouraged the relationship at its outset. From there, a series of events can occur that results in the targeted parent being forced into a commitment about which they are not sure. The ultimate failure of the relationship may reflect the pressured but uncertain start.

> **Box 6.28 Targeted parent:** I was forced into this marriage. When she became pregnant after only dating a few weeks, I was really unsure about what to do. I told her I had to think about whether I wanted to continue with this relationship. Before I knew what was happening, she and her parents were organising the wedding. My head was spinning. I found myself getting married without ever saying that I wanted to marry her.

The history of relationship difficulties predating the relationship with the targeted parent sets the scene for the post-separation relationship between the alienating parent and the targeted parent to be affected. As a result of past experiences, the alienating parent can respond poorly to the failure of the relationship and feel a need for vengeance. Alternatively, the alienating parent can reject the need for the involvement of the targeted parent and revert to previously adopted single-parenting strategies.

Desire for control

Alienating parents like to be in charge. They demonstrate a need to control events and dominate others (3,8). This may reflect a genuine belief on their part that their status and views are superior to others, especially the targeted parent. This need for control can manifest in a number of ways and is not limited in its influence only in relation to the targeted parent.

> **Box 6.29 Psychologist:** It started with him being dissatisfied with the appointment times I offered him for my interview with him. He said he was a busy person and rejected all of the offered appointment times. So, I offered him alternative opportunities and he rejected those as well. I then suggested that he nominate a time and I would make arrangements to be available. I did this because I thought he was trying to avoid being interviewed. When we finally agreed on an appointment time and date, he then objected to me being the court-appointed expert because I was a woman and, therefore, would be biased against him. The judge said he could object on the basis of experience, qualifications or a genuine conflict of interest, but not on the expert's gender. So the appointment went ahead. Then, when he came into my room for the interview, he pulled his chair up close beside mine at the table. He kept putting his hand on my notepad. He refused to answer some questions although there seemed to be no rhyme or reason to which questions he answered and which he refused to answer. It seems that he was determined to be in charge of the situation even if it was not helping his cause. His behaviour supported what other people said about him being controlling.

This need for control or domination may partially be a reflection of the alienating parent's narcissism, believing that they can see more clearly than others the needs of their child. They talk as if the decisions they make are superior to the decisions made by others. This belief in the superiority of their decisions can influence how alienating parents respond to judicial decisions.

> **Box 6.30 Alienating parent:** I know what is best for my child and I don't need anyone else to tell me what to do. I'm an excellent parent. The judge said I'm going to have to come to terms with the fact that my son will be spending time with his father. Well, guess what? I don't agree that I have to come to terms with that. No-one knows my child better than me and no-one is able to make better decisions for my child than me. Maybe the judge needs to come to terms with the fact that she is not always right.

So confident are alienating parents that their decision-making in relation to their child is right and superior to others that alienating parents can become confused about why others do not see the sense of what they are saying or agree with their view of the situation. Alienating parents often struggle to understand why others would disagree with their conceptualisation of the situation.

> **Box 6.31 Interviewer:** I understand the judge suggested you come along to see me to try and resolve the stalemate that seems to exist.
> **Alienating parent:** I told the judge I'm happy to move forward with this so I don't know what the problem is.
> **Interviewer:** I think the problem relates to the conditions you want put in place before you will agree with the orders. I believe the judge isn't able to include these conditions in any orders.
> **Alienating parent:** Well, that's too bad for the judge. Look, I'm trying to be reasonable. Surely, you can see that the conditions I want to put in place are there to protect my child.
> **Interviewer:** I understand the problem is that the conditions you mention are outside the scope of parenting orders. For example, the judge has said that she cannot make an order denying the father permission to introduce your child to his new wife.
> **Alienating parent:** I just don't know what the problem is. I don't know this person and I don't trust her. How do I know how this person will treat my child? I am just taking reasonable steps to protect my child from harm.
> **Interviewer:** Would it make it easier for you to get a better idea about this person if you met her?
> **Alienating parent:** I don't need to meet her. I don't want to meet her. I just want to protect my son. I just don't understand why people think that is a bad thing.

This need to be in control, in combination with their personality characteristics, means that alienating parents may opt to disregard court orders because they believe they know best. They cannot tolerate having to abide by court orders if those court orders are contrary to their wishes. They may consent to orders but then contravene those orders as soon as they are in conflict with their own wishes or because it was always their intention to do so.

> **Box 6.32 Targeted parent:** She's done it again. Everyone worked so hard to get these parenting orders in place … ones that were going to work for everyone. But she goes and contravenes those orders again. Every time we think it is sorted out. she just refuses to abide by the agreement. She sat in that room and agreed to me spending time with Daniel … a little bit at first but building up over time. But then, the very first time she was supposed

to hand him over, she just didn't turn up. When my lawyer contacted her lawyer, we found out that she isn't happy with the way the orders are drawn up, so she isn't going to abide by them. When is she going to get into trouble for doing this all the time? Someone needs to tell her that she isn't the one who is in charge.

It must be really frustrating for the targeted parent and the court to have orders contravened by alienating parents, with these breaches occurring only because the alienating parent has changed their mind about what should happen. A process of negotiation, including lengthy negotiation, can lead to orders being agreed to by all parties, including the alienating parents. However, within weeks, even days, the alienating parents are disregarding the orders and doing as they wish. When you talk to alienating parents about their reasons, they tend to attribute these breaches of orders to the fact that they no longer agree with the orders and want things to be different. They then blame others for unsatisfactory orders, claiming they never wanted things to be that way. This occurs despite them signing off on the orders at the time they are made.

Box 6.33 Alienating parent: I know what's best for the children. I don't need anyone else to interfere and decide for me how much time they are going to spend with their father. I'm the one who knows when it is ok for them to go there. I've been reasonable about him seeing the children but I'm not going to send them there if he keeps changing girlfriends and he's not working. If he does what I ask he can see the children, otherwise he won't get to see them.

Interviewer: But I understand you agreed to the orders outlining when the children were to see their father.

Alienating parent: How was I supposed to know what was going on? I was pressured into it. My lawyer told me I had to sign so I did. If I'd known what I was agreeing to then I wouldn't have signed.

Interviewer: As I understand it, you were involved in the negotiation process before the orders were agreed to.

Alienating parent: I would have done anything to get out of there. My lawyer said I was being unreasonable, so I agreed. But it's only a piece of paper. How can a judge know what's best for my children? I have a right to protect them from their father if I think it's necessary, no matter what some piece of paper says.

It is not surprising that alienating parents present as controlling individuals who poorly tolerate things not being the way they like. Although often presenting themselves as the 'victims' of an unfair family law process or the parent who is most concerned with their child's wellbeing, they are driven by a need to be the person who determines how the child's life will evolve. This drive to be in control can result in alienating parents engaging in actions that are defiant of court orders, that result in increasing animosity felt towards them and, ultimately, that are not advantageous to the child.

Desire for vengeance

Alienating parents often want someone to pay for their unhappiness. The alienating behaviour is driven by a need for revenge (3,8). Of course, the person they want to pay is the targeted parent. Indeed, alienating parents often see the targeted parents as the only source of their unhappiness despite obvious indicators of other stressors in their lives or a history of such stressors.

> **Box 6.34 Alienating parent:** Everything would be fine if he would just leave me and the children alone. Nothing else is a problem. When it's just me and the children everything is fine. Really, life is good when he doesn't interfere. The children and I get along well, they do better at school, and we are all happier. He's the one who causes all the problems. Well, I've decided I'm not going to put up with it. I will do everything I can to stop him ruining our lives. He already tried to do that when he left us; so now he has to bear the consequences.

A need for vengeance can be a destructive force. The bitterness, frustration and anger can have a pervasive effect on parents' lives and, by association, their children's lives. The need for vengeance tends to blind alienating parents to the damage their attitudes and behaviours can do to their children. They fail to see that a more moderate view would improve their own quality of life and enhance the chances of the children being better adjusted.

> **Box 6.35 Interviewer:** This dispute with the children's father has been going on for a long time now.
>
> **Alienating parent:** It's his fault. He's to blame. If he would just back off everything would be all right.
>
> **Interviewer:** But it seems that there is a bit of a pattern in the way things have been going. You both go to mediation and reach an agreement about how to move forward so the children can have a relationship with both of you. You both consent to the parenting orders. Then you seem to change your mind and contravene those orders, or you take the matter back to court saying that circumstances have changed.
>
> **Alienating parent:** It's his fault. I think everything is going to be all right and then he does something stupid and I have no choice but to do what I think is right.
>
> **Interviewer:** Something stupid? What sort of things happen that make you change your mind?
>
> **Alienating parent:** Lots of things … most recently he started dating that cow who used to be our neighbour. He didn't think about how that might affect me. I used to know her. How dare he date someone I used to know?
>
> **Interviewer:** You continue to be upset about these sorts of things. You have been divorced now for five years and separated for a year before that. Do you think you would feel less distressed if you didn't put yourself through the stressful experience of returning to court to deal with the problems that develop? You've said before how stressful it is to be back in court.
>
> **Alienating parent:** How else is he going to know that he has done something to upset me … again? He won't even talk to me so it's the only avenue I have available to me to let him know he's done the wrong thing.

The bitterness alienating parents feel towards the targeted parent is often quite obvious, even in cases where they try to convey a more moderate view of the targeted parent. The need to express their unhappiness and make the targeted parent suffer can be all consuming. Alienating parents' thinking about these matters typically is not amenable to change through challenges to the logic of their views about the targeted parent. They will continue to try to exact revenge even when their actions directly or indirectly hurt their child.

> **Box 6.36 Interviewer:** It seems from what I've been told that Amber and her Dad used to have a good relationship. They used to do lots of things together … fun things that Amber enjoyed.
>
> **Alienating parent:** Not anymore. And it's his own fault. I told him that if he left his family to go and live with that bimbo, he would lose his daughter. And that's what happened. He's the one who is missing out.
>
> **Interviewer:** But it seems that Amber has gone from being a happy and well-adjusted child to being anxious a lot of the time.
>
> **Alienating parent:** Well, that's the price he has to pay for leaving his family. It's not my fault … it's his.

Alienating parents can talk about the targeted parents with such bitterness and hate. They can be quite irrational in their views of the targeted parent. Holding the view that the targeted parent is a bad person, they express a strong desire to see them suffer. Even those alienating parents who think they are presenting themselves in a more moderate light tend to find it difficult to hide their animosity. They can become quite upset when challenged to consider information that is contrary to their viewpoint.

> **Box 6.37 Interviewer:** Mr Smith seems to be doing much better now. His current partner says he's not drinking, and he has settled down.
>
> **Alienating parent:** That'd be right. He treats me like dirt and is then nice to someone else. I won't let him get away with it. He is only fooling her anyway. If she knew what he was really like, then she wouldn't stick around. She's probably as bad as he is anyway.
>
> **Interviewer:** If it is the case that Mr Smith has settled down and is doing well, do you see that as a better situation for the children?
>
> **Alienating parent:** It would be better if he regularly paid child support. I told the child support people that he wasn't paying regularly, and they set it up so that it comes out of his wages directly. That will embarrass him, but I don't care. He shouldn't have got behind in his payments. He said he wasn't getting much work and that's why he got behind but he was probably spending money on his new partner. If I find out that's the case, he will regret it.

Here, the alienating parent tends to be more focused on her negative feelings about the targeted parent and her need to have him suffer as a consequence of his actions than on the needs of the children. She cannot focus her attention on examining what would be advantageous for her children. Her discussion focuses only on how she expects things to play out if she catches him doing the wrong thing.

> **Box 6.38 Interviewer:** Mr Smith seems to go to some lengths to make sure the children are happy and well looked after when they are spending time with him.
>
> **Alienating parent:** He's a terrible father. Wait until his new girlfriend finds out what he's really like. I think it's my duty to contact her and tell her what he's like. I've warned his other girlfriends in the past. Not that they thanked me. But then they found out what he was like. They must have because the relationships never lasted.

The alienating parent has tried to ensure that the targeted parent's ongoing happiness is undermined by directly influencing the outcomes of relationships the targeted parent may try to form with others subsequent to the failure of the relationship between the alienating parent and the targeted parent. There is a link between the failure of the relationship and the alienating parent's desire to have the targeted parent's future relationships fail. However, it is the case that the alienating parent may hold the targeted parent responsible for all of their unhappiness, even those events over which the targeted parent had no control.

> **Box 6.39 Alienating parent:** Everything is terrible and it's his fault. I had to move out of my home because the house had to be sold in the property settlement. I rented a place but then my landlord decided to sell the property, so I had to find somewhere else to live. On top of that, I then lost my job because I had taken so much time off because I was so upset about the way my husband treated me. It's all his fault. He can't be allowed to get away with doing all this to me.

In response to these distressing feelings and driven by a desire for vengeance, the alienating parent uses time with the child as a means of punishing the parent. By withholding the child, the targeted parent suffers, and the alienating parent's feelings are assuaged.

> **Box 6.40 Targeted parent:** He is so angry that I left him. He took the children and wouldn't let me see them. He told me I would never see them again. He told me I'd made a mistake by leaving him and embarrassing him. He said there wasn't any point in getting a lawyer and asking the Family Court for help. He said if a judge told him he had to let me see the children he would just take off with the children and I would never find them.

Limiting the time the targeted parent spends with the child or undermining the relationship between the targeted parent and the child are ways in which alienating parents express their need for revenge. This need for revenge has its foundations in features such as the personality characteristics of the alienating parent, their need for control and their disappointment in the failure of the relationship with the targeted parent. The need for revenge overrides their obligations to care for their child in a way that does not harm the child. The targeted parent and the child become alienated because the alienating parent uses times with the child as a means of punishing the targeted parent.

Concluding comments

As a cautionary note, it should be mentioned that not all alienating parents are so blatant in the expression of their views. They may present as the reasonable parent who really just wants the best for the children and the targeted parent. It is only on further investigation that it becomes evident that the alienation process may be in operation. Consider the following.

> **Box 6.41 Alienating parent:** Look, I really want the children to be able to spend time with their father. They miss him when they don't get to see him. But he probably needs to address some issues before the children are comfortable going there. You know, I've tried to convince

the children to go and see their father, but they refuse. They tell me they're not comfortable there and I can see that they are unhappy about going. I tell them they don't have a choice because the court orders say they must go. But that doesn't work. I tell them they are going to have a good time, but they don't believe me. I've tried to address the problem with their father, but he can't see that I'm just trying to be helpful. I think the children just need a break from having to go there. We can restart the visits when they are more excited about going. Forcing them will just make things worse ... maybe when they are a bit older.

And from the other point of view.

Box 6.42 Targeted parent: I'm exhausted with this whole thing. I know that she comes across as charming and reasonable, but I have tried to explain to people that she has two sides. She said she does everything she can to encourage the children to come and see me, but I know it's not true. The kids have asked me why their mother hates me so much. I just try to reassure them that their mother and I don't hate each other. But, you know, I do hate her sometimes and I know she hates me. She took out a restraining order so I couldn't go to the kids' school events. I didn't do anything, but she made up all this stuff and convinced the court that I had threatened her. I go out of my way not to talk to her so I don't know how I could threaten her. I know the kids haven't received their birthday gifts I sent them. I didn't want to make a big issue about it with the kids, but they didn't receive their gifts. So, I took them shopping and bought them other stuff ... things I couldn't afford. She contacted my boss and told him I had been violent towards her and that's why she had to take out the restraining order. It's absolutely not true. My boss said he understands but his attitude towards me has changed. I can't blame him. As I said, she comes across as nice and reasonable. Why wouldn't someone who didn't know her well believe what she was saying.

References

1. Hands, A.J., & Warshak, R.A. (2011). Parental alienation among college students. *The American Journal of Family Therapy, 39,* 431–443. doi:10.1080/01926187.2011.575336
2. Pruett, M.K., Arthur, L.A., & Ebling, R. (2007). The hand that rocks the cradle. Maternal gatekeeping after divorce. *Pace Law Review, 27,* 709–739.
3. Clawar, S.S., & Rivlin, B.V. (2013). *Children held hostage: Identifying brainwashed children, presenting a case, and crafting solutions.* Chicago, IL: American Bar Association.
4. Baker, A.J.L. (2006). Patterns of parental alienation syndrome: A qualitative study of adults who were alienated from a parent as a child. *The American Journal of Family Therapy, 34,* 63–78. doi:10.1080/01926180500301444
5. Mone, J.G., & Biringen, Z. (2006). Perceived parent–child alienation: Empirical assessment of parent–child relationships within divorced and intact families. *Journal of Divorce and Remarriage, 45,* 131–156. doi:10.1300/j087v45n03_07
6. Altenhofen, S., Biringen, Z., & Mergler, R. (2008). Significant family dynamics related to postdivorce and adjustment in parents and children. *Journal of Divorce and Remarriage, 49,* 25–40. doi:10.1080/10502550801971280
7. Kopetski, L. (1998). Identifying cases of parental alienation syndrome: Part II. *Colorado Lawyer, 27,* 63–66.

8. Rand, D.C. (1997). The spectrum of parental alienation syndrome (Part I). *American Journal of Forensic Psychology, 15,* 23–51.
9. American Psychiatric Association. (2013). *Diagnostic and statistical manual of mental disorders* (5th edn.). Arlington, VA: American Psychiatric Publishing.
10. Berg-Nielsen, T.S., & Wichstrom, L. (2012). The mental health of pre-schoolers in a Norwegian population-based study when their parents have symptoms of borderline, antisocial, and narcissistic personality disorders: At the mercy of unpredictability. *Child and Adolescent Psychiatry and Mental Health, 6,* 19. doi:10.1186/1753-2000-6-19
11. Mikulincer, M. (2004). Attachment working models and the sense of trust: An exploration of interaction goals and affect regulation. In H.T. Reis & C.E. Rusbult (Eds.), *Close relationships: Key readings.* (pp. 175–191), Philadelphia, PA: Taylor & Francis.
12. Baker, A.J.L. (2005). The long-term effects of parental alienation on adult children: A qualitative research study. *The American Journal of Family Therapy, 33,* 289–302. doi:10.1080/01926180590962129

Chapter Seven

Targeted parents

Introduction

Considerably more information has been published about targeted parents compared with the attention given to both alienating parents and alienated children. This is because of the relative ease of accessing this population in comparison with the alienating parents and alienated children populations. This information will help with the understanding of the dynamics in separated families where parental alienation is a problem as well as identify any contribution targeted parents make to the alienation process.

Although there are features of the targeted parents' presentation that may add to the escalation of alienation (1–2), it should be noted that the characteristics of the targeted parent that might contribute to the alienation process should not invite the type of alienation response that is received in return. There seems to be nothing particularly extraordinary about the targeted parent's contribution that would warrant the personal attack and rejection that is experienced by the targeted parent (2).

Characteristics of targeted parents

The first noteworthy study examining the characteristics of targeted parents was reported in the 1990s (3). The information was obtained from the examination of parenting dispute evaluation data based on 600 cases. This information was obtained over a 20-year period. From these data, a profile of the typical presentation of targeted parents was developed. We will examine these characteristics. Other characteristics identified by other researchers will also be identified here (2,4).

History of passivity, emotional constriction and over-accommodation

When you look back over the course of the relationship between the alienating parent and the targeted parent, there is often an indication that the alienating parent had the greater power in the relationship, even in cases where they did not demonstrate greater emotional stability. Targeted parents have tended not to stand up for their rights in the relationship. Targeted parents have demonstrated a tendency over the course of the relationship to overly accommodate the demands made by the alienating parent or, perhaps, to fail to emotionally respond to their needs and demands (3–4). When targeted parents have a history of overly accommodating the wishes of the alienating parent, the alienating parent is then likely to have an expectation that their needs will be met. Certainly, this fits with the alienating parents' characteristic of needing to be in control.

Targeted parents can talk about their former partner being the demanding one and them trying to do all they can to accommodate the demands. Although they may have given up in the end because they realise there is little they can do to please their former partner or because they are simply fed up with having to do this over and over again, the general interaction pattern in the relationship is one where the alienating parent makes the demands and the targeted parent tries to please.

This fits with what we know about alienating parents, too. They tend to be sure of their position and determined to get their own way. And this has been evident throughout the relationship. In contrast, targeted parents have tried not to rock the boat.

> **Box 7.1 Psychologist:** I often hear targeted parents talk about them having little power in their relationship with the alienating parent. They say they were not involved in decision-making about important life choices, like getting married or where they will live. Therefore, the way alienating parents conduct themselves after the breakdown of the relationship is not unexpected.

Certainly, there appears to be a power imbalance in the relationship between the alienating parent and the targeted parent that existed prior to the end of the relationship. This power imbalance favours the alienating parent. Throughout the relationship, the partner who goes on to become an alienating parent tends to be the one who makes the demands and has an expectation that those demands will be met, even in cases where the foundation of the demands is an inherent insecurity. Targeted parents find themselves in a position where their needs are rarely considered. This may be because the alienating parent struggles to understand that the targeted parent's needs may be different from their own.

Alienating parents can have a history of asserting their wishes in their relationship with the targeted parent in ways that increase the relationship difficulties rather than resolve them. They can be demanding and manipulating while feeling their actions are justified. During their relationship, the targeted parent has had to learn to cope with the actions of the alienating parent that can shift the balance of power in their favour.

> **Box 7.2 Targeted parent:** During our relationship, everything had to be her way. And she knew how to make sure she got what she wanted. If I tried to offer an opinion that was different from hers, she would run to her parents and tell them I was being emotionally abusive. Then she got her counsellor to drag me in to tell me I was an abusive person. When I tried to explain, my ex-wife just started crying. Then, when I wouldn't agree to going on an expensive holiday, she called the police and told them I had threatened her. I felt like she was calling all the shots in a game when I didn't even know the rules.

Often, there is a history of failure on the part of the targeted parent to have met the needs of the alienating parent during their relationship. To be fair, this is likely to have been a result of the complex interaction patterns that existed between the two people involved. These interaction patterns are contributed to by factors such as the personality characteristics of the alienating parent, childhood experiences in families of origin, and the nature of the development of the relationship (e.g., rushing into a relationship without getting to know each other adequately).

Whatever the cause, the result is a history of emotional distance and disappointment in relationships. The alienating parent tends to have had complicated emotional needs during the relationship and the targeted parent tends to have few resources to deal with those needs.

Box 7.3 Targeted parent: She was a handful. I tried to make her happy but there didn't seem to be anything I could do. Nothing was ever right. She says now that I never helped out around the house, but that's not true. I used to do all sorts of things, including looking after the children, but she always criticised what I did. It was never good enough. But I tried and tried. And then tried some more. But, in the end, I couldn't take it anymore. She said I wasn't there for her emotionally. Well, that might be true. But it's hard to be criticised all the time and then still have loving feelings for someone.

When faced with the demands made by the alienating parent during their relationship, targeted parents will have tended to overly accommodate the alienating parents' wishes. They tend not to assertively stand up to unreasonable demands or to assert their own rights in the relationship. They often will not say no even if they recognise that the things being demanded of them are not what they want. This pattern sets the tone for the relationship while it lasts.

Box 7.4 Targeted parent: She wanted to get married, so I agreed even though I thought it was too soon. She wanted to live near her parents' home and I agreed, even though I can't stand them. She didn't like my best friend, so I agreed not to ask him to be my best man at the wedding, even though I know it hurt his feelings. She didn't like me playing sport, so I gave up even though I missed my friends and the fun we had on the team together. I even agreed to have another baby despite knowing that our relationship wasn't working. But, you know, in the end, no matter what I did it wasn't enough for her. And look where it got me. Now she says I can't see the children and she expects me to just get out of their lives.

Interestingly, the way in which the alienating parent and the targeted parent interacted during their relationship may be a reflection of the targeted parent trying to exert some influence. In an effort to avoid conflict, the targeted parent will accede to the alienating parent's demands and not challenge them. In the short term, this strategy may be effective in managing the relationship minefield by allowing the targeted parent to emotionally shut down but, in the longer term, it only leads to the targeted parent becoming resentful.

Box 7.5 Targeted parent: I think back over everything I put up with just to avoid an argument with her. I used to tell myself that by avoiding a fight with their mother I was protecting the children. But now I think I just didn't have it in me to keep arguing with her. She would say the most irrational things and I would try to give an alternative point of view. But, really, it wasn't worth it to argue. It just made things worse. So, in the end, I learned to just back down.

In the longer term, the targeted parent reaches a point where they can no longer tolerate the alienating parent's behaviour or tolerate their own unhappiness. At this point, they may choose to leave the relationship. Alternatively, the alienating parent may use their own withdrawal from the relationship as a way of forcing the targeted parent to abide by their wishes. They leave the relationship stating that they will only return when the targeted parent's behaviour changes. In these cases, the targeted parent may choose to remain separated and the alienating parent's strategy backfires. In either scenario, the targeted parent reaches a point where they opt out of the relationship.

Box 7.6 Targeted parent: In the end, I just couldn't take it any longer. I felt like I had lost myself somewhere along the way. I felt like I couldn't make a decision because I was anxious about whether or not she would object. It was terrible. After the relationship ended, things seemed clearer. I know what she was doing … trying to emotionally manipulate me and control me … but, at the time, I was just struggling to cope in a really bad relationship. But now I won't do what she wants, so she is punishing me by turning the children against me. She doesn't realise she is hurting the children as much as she is hurting me.

It is apparent how this type of relationship interaction sets the stage for the development of parental alienation after separation. The alienating parent started with an expectation that his or her needs would be met, and their demands would be accommodated by the targeted parent. However, the targeted parent's failures to provide the alienating parent with what they needed lead to relationship disappointments on both parts. As the alienating parent tries harder to have their needs met and the targeted parent tries harder to cope with the demands, the chances of successful resolution of relationship problems diminish.

Tendency to avoid self-assertion

In terms of the relationship dynamics, things do not markedly improve after the end of the relationship between the alienating parent and the targeted parent. For example, you will find that targeted parents seem to put up with more than the average person. It is not because they are particularly tolerant but because they tend not to assert themselves when the alienating parent acts in ways that clearly are detrimental to the targeted parent (3). This may be an extension of the interpersonal interactions that took place during the relationship. Once placed in a particular relationship role, targeted parents maintain this position.

Alternatively, this may reflect a more general tendency to lack self-assertion and what takes place in the relationship is one manifestation of this more general tendency. It also may be the case that targeted parents are reluctant to do anything that will make the situation worse and result in them seeing even less of their children than they already are or that will make it harder to resolve the situation so that the relationships with their children can be re-established if they have already broken down.

Sometimes we wonder why targeted parents put up with some of the things that are dished out to them. It is apparent that some seem to become paralysed into inaction when they are confronted with some of the tactics used by their former partner. It is like a form of learned helplessness. Indeed, that probably accurately describes what is going on. Their experience is that they cannot stand up to the demands made by their former partners, so they stop trying to do so.

Of course, it may be the case that they do not assert themselves because they are scared of losing their children altogether. They do not want to do anything to exacerbate the problem because they are fearful that this might happen … and probably with some justification. Certainly, any assertiveness or challenge by the targeted parent tends to be responded to by an escalation of alienation efforts by the alienating parents.

Box 7.7 Targeted parent: At least now I get to see my children every now and then. I couldn't bear to think about how it would be if they stopped coming to see me altogether. It makes me mad when I think about what their mother has done but what can I do about it? If I stand up to their mother, the children now see it as me picking on her. That's what she's told them. So, I just have to put up with it.

Certainly, it is often the case that targeted parents are cautious about taking any action that will upset the alienating parent. They fear the repercussions of any assertive action. They believe that asserting themselves will lead to an escalation of conflict and further alienation from their children.

Box 7.8 Targeted parent: People give me advice about what to do but I don't want to do anything that will rock the boat. It's hard to imagine how things could be worse, but I'm sure she'd think of something to do that would create more problems. So, I think I have to be careful about what I do so that she doesn't become even angrier with me. Who knows what she would do if she was angrier than she is now?

In this way the targeted parent is trying to control the alienating parent's behaviour by not doing anything to upset the alienating parent. In some way, their reasoning is logical. If the targeted parent is not doing anything to upset the alienating parent, the alienating parent should not be upset ... or so you would think. In situations where the targeted parent feels unable to resolve the problem of not seeing their children, it is not surprising that they will try to influence the situation in their favour by refusing to confront the alienating parent.

Box 7.9 Targeted parent: I figure if I don't do anything to upset her, she will eventually let me see the children. My brother disagrees. He said I didn't do anything in the first place and she still turned the children against me. But I'm hopeful that I can manage to get her to see reason if I don't do anything that causes her to become upset.

On top of this is the desire on the part of the targeted parent not to do anything that will further alienate their child or children. Although they may understand the conflict that exists between them and the alienating parent, it is harder for targeted parents to understand the negative reaction of their children to them. To try to avoid further deterioration of the targeted parent–child relationship, they will avoid actions that are likely to aggravate the situation or upset their child.

Box 7.10 Targeted parent: I would stand up to my ex-wife ... I really would. But I worry about how the children would react if I did that. They already believe everything their mother tells them about me ... all the lies. I think if I do anything ... even things I have a right to do given what she's done ... the children will just see that as confirmation of what their mother has said.

With concern about tackling the alienating parent and with reluctance to further alienate their child or children, targeted parents can seem to be paralysed into inaction by the alienating tactics used by the alienating parent. Even when pathways are available for them to take action, they may present as uncertain about whether or not they should take such action. Their fear of the situation worsening is enough to keep them in a state where they are unwilling to alter the status quo.

> **Box 7.11 Targeted parent:** My lawyer said she has contravened court orders and we have the right to take this back to court. I can see that he's right. She has contravened the orders … and not just once but lots of times. But I worry about how she would react to me taking her back to court. She wouldn't do what the court ordered her to do before, so I don't know what would be different this time around. I just can't decide what to do.

Without a clear pathway for them to follow to resolve the problem situation and when paralysed by uncertainty about what to do, it is not surprising that targeted parents often feel helpless when faced with the actions of the alienating parent. This feeling of helplessness makes it difficult for targeted parents to adopt a course of action that will allow them to assert themselves. This is especially the case when the actions they have taken have proven to be unsuccessful in resolving the problem of parental alienation.

> **Box 7.12 Targeted parent:** There is nothing I can do. I have tried everything. I have tried being reasonable, I have tried seeking help through the courts. I have tried to arrange mediation. Nothing works. She just keeps the children from me and tells them things that make them hate me. I don't know what to do. I don't think there's anything I can do. Nothing is ever going to make a difference.

The lack of self-assertion among targeted parents may be both a contributor to parental alienation and a consequence of parental alienation. As a contributor, an individual prone to unassertiveness is vulnerable to the tactics chosen by the alienating parent to alter the relationship between the targeted parent and the child. For example, an unassertive person may have no response to tactics such as denigration and vilification that the alienating parent chooses to undermine the targeted parent in the view of others. As a consequence of parental alienation, lack of self-assertion may be the result of the enduring campaign of alienation that is designed to undermine the parent–child relationship. For example, the targeted parent may choose not to act to challenge the alienating parent because of concern that the alienation may worsen.

Potential for distress in response to alienating tactics

Targeted parents can demonstrate a tendency to present with overt signs of distress that are related to the alienating strategies used by the alienating parent (3–5). In response to tactics such as vilification, targeted parents can become exceedingly distressed. The ongoing stress of the alienation process has the capacity to compromise the psychological adjustment of the targeted parent.

Undoubtedly, this distress can influence how the parent interacts with the child, confirming in the child's mind what has been said about that parent by the alienating parent. So, the targeted parent's distress can be used by the alienating parent in the alienation process.

Given how passive targeted parents tend to be in relation to their interactions with their alienating former partners, it sometimes seems that their psychological response is in marked contrast. Thoughts of what is being done to them consume them and they experience intense distress as a result. They focus on the unfairness of the former partner's actions and how others might view the claims made about them by the alienating parent. This distress can drive them to act in ways that clearly are not in their best interests.

> **Box 7.13 Targeted parent:** I'm devastated by the things she's said and done. All sorts of horrible things, ever since I started asking to spend more time with the children. But when she started making claims that I sexually abused her and my children I couldn't bear it. It's not true. I would never do such a thing. I don't know what to do. I want to clear my name, but I don't see how I can. I hate to think my children have been talked into believing that I've abused them. I can't sleep with worrying about all this. I can't concentrate at work. I just don't know what to do. She needs to pay for what's she's done. The courts need to know she lied.

It is apparent that the distress experienced by the targeted parent in response to the alienating parent's behaviour can have debilitating effects. The targeted parent's capacity to function becomes compromised. Their relationships with others suffer, their work performance is negatively affected and their ability to cope with normal life demands can be diminished.

> **Box 7.14 Targeted parent:** I have been feeling so stressed about all of this … you know, not seeing the kids and all the conflict with their mother … that I went to see my doctor. He suggested I should take an anti-depressant. I think he might be right. I can't think straight. I'm falling behind at work and can't seem to catch up. When I'm not at work, all I want to do is stay home. I can't seem to cope with anything. I was sent an overdue notice because I had forgotten to pay the phone bill and I felt like I wanted to burst into tears.

The distress experienced by the targeted parent tends to be exacerbated by the nature of the targeted parent's thinking. Targeted parents become consumed by the state of their relationship with their children and they struggle to focus on other things. It is because of the overwhelming nature of the experience that their ability to function is compromised. They can think of little else and their relationships with others change.

> **Box 7.15 Targeted parent:** I know my friends and family are sympathetic about my situation but, to be honest, I think they are fed up with me talking about it all the time. But I just can't think about anything else. No matter what I'm doing, thoughts about the children and the injustice of all this are not far from my mind. I realise I am not the same fun-loving person I used to be, but there is nothing I can do about it. I think if it was happening to them, they would feel the same.

The intensity of the targeted parent's feelings about the situation causes them to lash out at times. They feel angry and hurt, driving them to do unreasonable things some of the time. Targeted parents reach a point where they feel the need to retaliate in reaction to the tactics the alienating parent has used. The actions of the targeted parent that are caused by frustration, distress and a feeling of injustice are then used against them by the alienating parent as evidence of the more general claims of wrongdoing they are making about the targeted parent.

> **Box 7.16 Targeted parent:** Now I'm in trouble again. I tried to sit back and ignore what she was doing. But I heard from a friend that she questioned whether I had mistreated the children. How dare she! She knows it's not true, but she says it to attack me. Mud sticks, you know. If she says enough hateful things someone will believe it. So … and this is where I know I did the wrong thing … I sent her off a series of text messages telling her she is scum. Now she has some ammunition she can use against me in court. To be honest, I know I shouldn't have done it, but I felt so stressed I just had to do something.

The distress experienced by targeted parents in reaction to the alienating tactics used by the alienating parent can lead to the targeted parent threatening to take dire action to deal with the alienation. Threats to abduct the children, vilify the alienating parent, or take some other harmful action against the alienating parent can be made. In most cases, these threats reflect the distress and frustration experienced by the targeted parent rather than a well-formulated plan of action.

> **Box 7.17 Targeted parent:** I can't take it anymore. I don't know what to do. I can't think straight. I feel like I should just go to the children's school and collect them then disappear with them. I honestly believe they would be better off with me on the run than with their poisonous mother. Goodness knows what damage her attitude is doing to them. They would be better off if I just took them. I know I would be in trouble with the court, but they would have to find us first.

When consideration is given to the fact that parents are targeted in an alienation campaign because they want to spend time with their children, which is contrary to the alienating parents' wishes, it is not surprising that being alienated from their children is distressing for targeted parents. In addition to the distress caused by separation from their children, targeted parents are distressed as a direct result of the tactics used by alienating parents in the alienation process. Tactics that are directed at denigrating or vilifying the targeted parent are likely the greatest cause of distress although other tactics trigger difficult psychological reactions in targeted parents. These tactics will be discussed more fully in Chapter Twelve.

Possible willingness to justify alienating parent's strategies

Despite recognition of the nature of the alienating parent's intentions towards them and despite the distress they feel in relation to the alienating parent's actions, targeted parents may present with a willingness to justify the strategies used by the alienating parent (3). They try to inject reason into fundamentally unreasonable actions on the part of the alienating parent.

Many targeted parents try to explain the behaviour of the alienating parents. This is likely to be an effort to make sense of behaviour that generates feelings that are inconsistent with the feelings they used to have for each other. Alternatively, targeted parents are trying to make compatible pieces of information that really are not compatible. For example, targeted parents might try to link the fact that the alienating parent loves the children but then acts in a way that is detrimental to them.

Box 7.18 Targeted parent: I try to understand why he is doing this. I suppose he was hurt by my decision to leave and this is his way of expressing that hurt. He likes to be in control … that was the reason I left, mainly … and I suppose my leaving made him feel like he was losing control. Controlling what happens with the children might be his way of trying to get that control back. I don't know … I try to understand …

Targeted parents may try to make sense of the alienating parent's behaviour by considering the reasons why the alienating parent might feel motivated to act in the way they choose. In an effort to make sense of the alienating parent's behaviour, targeted parents may look for historical reasons why the alienating parent has chosen to undermine the targeted parent–child relationship.

Box 7.19 Targeted parent: I have gone over this and over this in my head. I have tried to figure out why he has done this. I know that he had a difficult childhood. His parents separated when he was a baby and he was raised by his father. He didn't know where his mother was for many years. And his father was a difficult man. Maybe he is trying to hang on to the idea of a family by keeping the children with him. Maybe he has coped so badly with me leaving him because his childhood was like it was … I don't know but I try to make sense of it.

As stated, targeted parents may try to reconcile two seemingly contrary pieces of information. That is, they try to make sense of the fact that the alienating parent loves their child or children but then acts in a way that is damaging to them. In doing this, the targeted parent is attempting to resolve a fundamental conflict. As the fact that the alienating parent loves the child is the irrefutable fact, the targeted parent will try to make sense of the decision by the alienating parent to adopt tactics that undermine the child's happiness and psychological adjustment.

Box 7.20 Targeted parent: I know he loves the children … I know he does. I would never say that he doesn't love the children. But he is harming them by keeping them from me, their mother. I can't imagine why he thinks this is a good idea. Maybe he truly believes I would harm them somehow, but I struggle to see why he would believe that. I would never do anything that was not in their best interests. Maybe someone has told him something that he has accepted as true but isn't really true. Maybe that is the reason. I just don't know what would cause him to do this.

In an effort to understand the alienating parent's behaviour, a targeted parent may try to explain the alienating parent's behaviour in terms of their mental health status. It is understandable that the targeted parent would try to do this. After all, the alienating tactics chosen by the alienating parent can seem to reflect a failure of reason, at least from the targeted parent's point of view.

Box 7.21 Targeted parent: I wish she'd get some help. She's obviously not coping. I worry about her. She can't be happy as a person, you know, in herself, if she has to do things like this. She has no reason to stop the kids from seeing me. The only reason I can think of is that she is depressed or something. Anyway, she needs help. This has to stop. She seemed so nice when I met her but that's changed. She seems so bitter and unhappy all the time. I worry about her, but I worry about the kids more. How is this affecting them?

In trying to process the meaning behind the tactics alienating parents choose to interfere with the parent–child relationship, targeted parents may try to make sense of the illogical nature of the alienating parent's actions. Difficulties arise when attempting to do this because the targeted parent tries to find a logical explanation for what are often unreasonable acts.

Box 7.22 Targeted parent: I think all the time about what would have caused her to make these claims that I have sexually abused the children. Maybe she has misinterpreted something the children have said, although I can't think what that would be. Or maybe someone else has put the idea in her head. She used to trust me with the children, and I would certainly never do anything to hurt them. But since the end of our relationship, she has been making these claims that I have been sexually abusing the children when they have been with me. She used this as the reason for why she stopped letting them come to see me. I don't understand why she would say such things. I try to look for an answer, but I just get more and more confused.

Even in face of strong indication of the unreasonableness of the alienating parent's actions, targeted parents may still express hope that the alienating parent will eventually 'see reason' and allow them to spend time with their child or children. The assumption is often made that it will become apparent to the alienating parent that their views are indefensible and that they will alter their behaviour as a consequence.

Box 7.23 Targeted parent: I try to think that this can't go on forever. He will see sense and then I will be able to have the children with me again. I have to believe that. Once he stops feeling hurt, maybe he will see that the children need to spend time with me. When he is thinking clearer about things, maybe everything will get better. He is an intelligent man. He must be able to see that what he is doing is hurting everyone, not just me.

It is possible to understand the targeted parent's attempts to justify the alienating parent's behaviour in the context of the hopefulness they hold on to that the problems they face will resolve.

With a strong desire to spend time with their children, the targeted parent must try to hold on to the hope that the situation will change, and the parent–child relationship will be restored. It is reasonable for targeted parents to assume that this is more likely to occur if there is a justifiable explanation for the alienating actions of the other parent. If there is a justifiable explanation, then there is a chance that the problem can be resolved.

Withdrawal from high conflict

Targeted parents may withdraw from the fight over spending time with their children. They stop pushing for contact and fail to attempt to communicate with their children. As a result of disappointment in the legal system they turn to for support, the lack of financial means to continue to pursue the matter through the courts, and/or the helplessness that develops after repeated failure of their attempts to resolve the problem, targeted parents reach a point where they feel too overwhelmed to continue. Unfortunately, the withdrawal of the targeted parent only tends to reinforce what the alienated child has been told about the parent's lack of commitment to them (2,4).

We have met alienating parents who know that if they keep the matter in court for long enough, especially if they have legal aid, the targeted parent will be forced to give up because they cannot afford the legal costs of fighting for their children. And that is what happens. Either because of financial concerns or because they become so worn down, the targeted parents give up. It is not that they do not care about their children or want to see them, they just cannot keep fighting.

> **Box 7.24 Targeted parent:** I can't keep doing this. I feel like I have done everything I can to make her see sense, but it hasn't worked. So maybe the best thing to do is to just walk away from it all. I never thought I would say this … that I would consider walking away from my children … but what choice do I have. I can't keep fighting. I have had about as much as I can tolerate.

As stated, the decision to withdraw or the idea that this might be an option for the targeted parent tends to reflect the emotional state that is a reaction to the overwhelming nature of the conflict in which they find themselves involved. When people feel this overwhelmed by events in their lives, their thinking tends to become constricted and they find it difficult to see ways that conflicts can be resolved. They reach a point where they believe that either they will continue to experience this high level of distress or they must opt out of the process that is causing the stress.

> **Box 7.25 Targeted parent:** I feel like I have to call a halt to this. I really can't keep fighting for something it looks like I will never get … that is, time with my children. It is killing me. I can't sleep. I can't work. I have no life outside of this fight with the children's mother. I don't want to give up, but I am no good to my children if I fall apart … that's what I feel is happening. I'm falling apart.

Also as stated, the financial burden that comes with prolonged conflict being played out in a legal context can prove to be too great for many people. The normal costs that come with separation of a family, such as housing costs and child support payments, are difficult enough to cover. On top of this can be ongoing and large legal expenses that are outside most people's capacity to comfortably pay, especially on an ongoing basis. As a result, some targeted parents feel forced to abandon the fight to spend time with their children because they simply cannot afford to continue to pay the costs involved.

Box 7.26 Targeted parent: There's nothing more I can do. I've tried everything. And it's broken me financially. I've gone from being financially quite ok but not anymore. The only people who have benefited from this are the lawyers and, I suppose, my ex-wife. Though who knows what she thinks she's getting out of this. I feel like I've been run over by a truck … like I have no control over my life anymore. I love my kids but, if I'm going to survive this, I have to let go. I have to find a way to get on with my life and get myself out of this financial mess. It doesn't seem right that it's come down to dollars and cents, but that is what has happened.

In the end, many targeted parents come to believe that there are simply no more avenues available to them to pursue their need to spend time with their children. Withdrawal from the conflict, or talk about needing to withdraw from the conflict, comes about because targeted parents feel they have exhausted all avenues for resolution of the problem and have no more coping resources available to them to deal with the challenges of the ongoing conflict.

Box 7.27 Targeted parent: I tried to convince her to be reasonable … but that didn't work. I went to mediation to sort this out … but that didn't work. I asked the courts for help … but that didn't work. I even approached her parents to convince them to help for the children's sake … boy, did that fail! I don't know what else to do. There is nothing more I can do. If the courts can't make her let me see the children, how can I?

Withdrawal from the conflict may take another form. Rather than withdrawing from the fight to spend time with their children, targeted parents may opt out of the interactions with the alienating parent that are characterised by high conflict as a means of managing the conflict with the alienating parent. In this way, targeted parents may manage the conflict by choosing not to compromise any further with regard to the demands made by the alienating parents. They refuse to involve themselves in the ongoing conflict while still maintaining their intention to spend time with their children.

Box 7.28 Targeted parent: I really have tried to be reasonable. I came up with plans that she might see as workable. I put off going to court in the hope that she would come around. When that didn't work, I sought legal advice and took the matter to court. I even won! The court said I could see the children … but she put all sorts of obstacles in the way of me spending time with the children. Well, enough! I have tried to be nice and reasonable, but enough is enough. The court says when I can see the children and, if she doesn't produce them, I am taking the matter back to court. I didn't want to rock the boat, but I am going to now. She has got away with saying horrible things about me for too long. I never retaliated. But maybe it's time the court knew about all her flaws. I won't be agreeable any longer.

At its most extreme, targeted parents may manage the conflictual situation in which they find themselves by refusing to communicate with the alienated child or children. Although this seems self-defeating, targeted parents will opt out of the conflict by deciding not to communicate with their child until such time as the matter is resolved and the child's attitude changes. In the absence of any other way of managing the conflict, targeted parents may come to believe that such a strategy is the only avenue left for them to feel some sense of control over what is happening to them.

Box 7.29 Targeted parent: I know why their mother is playing this game. She is bitter and angry about me leaving the relationship. But that doesn't excuse the children. I have never done anything to them to deserve being spoken to with such disrespect. They have no justification for making complaints about the way I have supposedly treated them. Well, now I don't want to speak to them until they are prepared to apologise for their behaviour. I deserve an apology!

Considering withdrawing from the conflict with the alienating parent is an extreme reaction of the targeted parent. Making a decision to withdraw or talking about the possibility of withdrawing is likely to be a reflection of the distress and helplessness felt by the targeted parent in response to prolonged conflict. In some cases, targeted parents feel they must learn to live without their children because they cannot cope with the disheartening nature of repeatedly fighting to spend time with their children without signs of progress or success

Rejection of the child in response to the child's rejection

In the face of repeated rejection by the alienated child, targeted parents can feel hurt and angry. As previously stated, they then may withdraw from their child (2,4). They develop an expectation that the alienated child should behave more respectfully, should show more gratitude and should apologise for their actions. Although aware that the source of the problem is the alienating parent, the urge to retaliate in response to the child's rejection can be strong. Of course, the targeted parent's rejection of the alienated child only makes the distance between them greater.

It is sad to see the deterioration of the parent–child relationship and then the breakdown of the regard the targeted parent has for their child. After long periods of disrespectful behaviour, the targeted parent finds themselves blaming the child rather than the real cause of the problem, especially with older children. There is a belief that the children should be able to understand the negative influence of the alienating parent or control their behaviour when they are around the targeted parent. Certainly, alienated teenagers can be disrespectful and this can be very difficult for a parent to accept. And, in many cases, it is hard to differentiate what is part of the alienation process and what is misbehaviour. Whatever the source of the rejection, that rejection by one's own child can generate hurt feelings.

Box 7.30 Targeted parent: I don't understand why the children are treating me like this. I have always tried to do the right thing for them. I have always tried to make them happy. I'm not like one of those fathers who disappears and doesn't care about their children. I like my children. I want to spend time with them. It breaks my heart that they don't want anything to do with me.

In coping with any life crisis, people's feelings can swing from sadness and hurt to anger. This also is true for targeted parents who feel rejected by their children. Feelings of anger can overwhelm them and, as a result, they are likely to respond to their child or talk about their child in ways that do not reflect the depth of positive feeling they have for the child. The expression of anger about the child's rejection can exacerbate the problems that exist in the targeted parent–child relationship.

Box 7.31 Targeted parent: How dare they treat me like this after all I've done for them. I gave up lots of things to give them what they wanted. They had all my time and attention when they were with me. What more do they expect from me? Ungrateful! They are ungrateful children. Most fathers would just walk away from them, but I have hung in there … and what do I get in return? They tell the psychologist that they don't like me and don't want to spend any time with me. How dare they treat me like that?

The hurt and anger targeted parents can feel about the rejection by their child can drive the targeted parent to retaliate. As a result, instead of only conflict between the targeted parent and the alienating parent, conflict also exists between the targeted parent and the child.

Box 7.32 Targeted parent: The children have made it clear that they don't want to spend any time with me. Well, I don't see why I should go out of my way to worry about them. I wonder what they would say if I stopped paying for all the things they want. Maybe that's what I will do. Then they can see what the consequences are for turning their back on me. That will show them. It can't be all their way. There has to be consequences!

The retaliation can take the form of criticism of the alienated child by the targeted parent. Targeted parents can talk about their children, emphasising their shortcomings and flaws. Also, importantly, targeted parents can interpret the alienated child's demonstration of the effects of the alienation process as indication of deficiencies in the child.

Box 7.33 Targeted parent: I thought I raised them to be better people than that. I certainly didn't raise them to be unsympathetic, selfish children who think it is all right to treat their father like he doesn't matter. Even if their mother is influencing them, they should be smart enough to see what she is doing. They should stop all this. They could if they tried. All they would have to do is insist that they want to see me. It's up to them.

Certainly, targeted parents often expect their children to act in a more respectful manner towards them than they do. Of course, the disrespect is likely to be a manifestation of the consequence of the alienation process instigated and maintained by the alienating parent. However, targeted parents tend to demand that their children behave in ways other than they do and despite the fact that the children's actions are influenced by the alienating parent.

> **Box 7.34 Targeted parent:** I've had enough. For a long time I was too scared to say anything about their behaviour. I didn't want to drive them away and I didn't want them to go back to their mother and say I'd been tough on them about their behaviour. That would have only made things worse. But I've had enough. They are so rude when I do get to see them. Well, the other day I read them the Riot Act. I told them that if they didn't want to behave in a decent manner, they weren't welcome in my home. We ended up having a huge argument and they went home to their mother. But I mean it. I don't think I've done anything that warrants them treating me like that. It got to the point where there was no pleasure in seeing them. I hope that one day they can clearly see what's been going on and that I'm not the enemy. But, until then, I don't think I can tolerate their offensive behaviour.

In the end, targeted parents may want their children to apologise for the children's treatment of them. They remain steadfast in their view that they cannot move forward without such an apology being given. The children, influenced by the alienation process, refuse to apologise to a parent they have been encouraged to see as flawed.

> **Box 7.35 Targeted parent:** I will be prepared to negotiate with the children but only after they apologise for the way they have treated me. Otherwise, what message am I sending them? If I let them off the hook, they learn that it is ok to treat people like dirt and get away with it. That's not the message I want to give them. So, they can apologise for their behaviour towards me and the bad things they have said about me. That's the only way things are going to get back on track.

In a way, it is understandable that targeted parents feel hurt and angry about their children's reaction to them, especially when the targeted parent feels the children's treatment of them is unjustified. As a result of this hurt and anger, targeted parents can criticise, reject and withdraw from their children. This reaction by the targeted parent reinforces the child's view of the parent that has been instilled in them by the alienating parent.

Also, it is unfortunately the case that this type of reaction to the alienated child by the targeted parent can be perceived as reflecting poorly on the targeted parent's parenting capacity. People trying to assist the targeted parent and those who are willing to believe the targeted parent has positive attributes can be frustrated by the targeted parent's lack of understanding about the child's position. The targeted parent can seem inflexible and unsympathetic.

Inflexible parenting style

Targeted parents can adopt or have adopted in the past a rigid parenting style (2). They will strongly enforce rules and set standards for the child's behaviour that can be hard to maintain. In contrast to the less rigid approach to parenting adopted by the alienating parent, the child can use the targeted parent's strict rules as evidence of an uncaring attitude.

There are a couple of examples of this that often are apparent. First is the targeted parent's insistence that parenting orders are followed, to the letter. If the order says the children should stay overnight, then the targeted parent insists on this even if the parent would have a better chance of seeing the children if they were more flexible.

Secondly, targeted parents can be quite insistent about what should take place when the children are with them. Often the children have to forfeit social activities with their friends because they encroach on the targeted parent's time. Of course, we can see why this occurs. With such limited time with their children, targeted parents tend not to want to share. However, from the child's point of view, this reinforces their view that their parent does not know them well enough or does not care about their happiness.

Let us start by considering the way in which targeted parents tend to enforce the rules they set for their child. These rules tend not to be open for negotiation. Although the rules cannot be criticised in terms of their parenting value, the extent to which they are strictly enforced tends to result in them being rejected by the child and used by the alienating parent as evidence of parenting incompetence on the part of the targeted parent.

> **Box 7.36 Targeted parent:** I don't care what they do at their other home, but when they are with me they have to follow my rules. I get tired of hearing that their mother doesn't make them go to bed so early or that she doesn't make them clean the table after dinner. My home, my rules! They say they can't sleep if they go to bed so early, but that's only because their mother lets them stay up late. They have to get used to the idea that I am the person calling the shots at my house.

Not only are the rules targeted parents set rigidly enforced, targeted parents also tend to set high standards for their children's behaviour. There is an expectation that children will always do the right thing and never make mistakes. In combination with a lack of flexibility, the demands on the children of targeted parents can be considerable. Although not necessarily detrimental to their wellbeing in a general sense, these high standards make it difficult for an alienated child to feel comfortable in the targeted parent's home so they can opt not to want to try to make the relationship with the targeted parent work.

> **Box 7.37 Targeted parent:** The children know I don't put up with any nonsense. There are rules in my house that they must abide by. I expect them to come home and do their homework straight away to get it out of the way. Their rooms have to be tidy at all times. They have to tidy up after themselves. No electronic devices at all hours … just half an hour a day. I don't think I'm being unreasonable, although the children act like I am some sort of tyrant.

As stated, targeted parents are often insistent that they determine what the child does when the child is with them. This is true even when it is contrary to the child's wishes. Here we are not referring to whether or not the child spends time with the targeted parent. We are referring to occasions when the targeted parent denies the child permission to engage in an activity that might take time away from the time they spend with the targeted parent. Although it is understandable that the targeted parent wants to spend their limited time with their child, their insistence that this occurs can reinforce for the child that the alienating parent was right to make negative comments about the targeted parent's unreasonableness.

> **Box 7.38 Targeted parent:** I don't think I'm being unreasonable to expect that the children spend their time with me when they are at my place. One of the complaints they made to the family counsellor about spending time with me is that I wouldn't let them spend time with their friends. Well, I don't get to see them very much, so I don't think it's unfair of me to want to spend my time with them. I arrange activities we can share, but then they say they don't want to do them. I can't win. I don't know what they expect of me. I want to be their parent. I don't want to just offer them somewhere to stay while they go off and do other things.

The targeted parent's inflexibility about matters relating to the parenting of their child or children can extend to their insistence that parenting orders are adhered to no matter the alienated child's circumstances. Targeted parents can refuse to take into account even special circumstances, such as alienating parent's family events, holidays or school events. The alienated child then finds themselves missing out on exciting activities they would normally enjoy. The child's resentment builds, and they then resist spending time with the targeted parent.

> **Box 7.39 Targeted parent:** The rules are the rules. The orders are clear about when the children should come to me. It's not fair that the children want to be excused from having to come and spend time with me just because they have other things they would rather be doing. They just need to learn to say no when they are invited to do things with their friends during my time. I don't care that there are family weddings or get togethers. Their time with me matters so I'm not going to give in on this issue.

As a result of the inflexible parenting strategies adopted by the targeted parent, the targeted parent–child relationship can be further diminished. The rigidity of the rules set by the targeted parent creates a situation where the alienated child feels less inclined to spend time with that parent. Also, the alienated child is inclined to believe the negative comments they have heard about the targeted parent are true.

Targeted parents will apply rigid parenting rules even though they are aware of the child's change of attitude towards them. They try harder to apply the strategies they have adopted that, in themselves, are not problematic. However, their application at times when a child is resisting time with the targeted parent can result in the child spending no time with that parent. So, despite their best intentions, the application of these rigid rules can be counterproductive for targeted parents.

Understanding targeted parents' characteristics

If these characteristics make the situation more problematic for targeted parents, one must question why they do not recognise this and change to meet the demands of the situation they find themselves having to endure. Kopetski (3) said these characteristics can be understood as survival strategies that are used by the targeted parent. They have developed in response to the power imbalance that typically exists in the association between the alienating parent and the targeted parent. Further, it has been suggested that the fear about the possibility of the alienating parents making allegations of abuse against the targeted parent or escalating the allegations cause targeted parents to fail to act in a way that might alter the course of the alienation in the targeted parent's favour.

The feelings of helplessness that must develop in response to a situation over which the targeted parent feels they have no control makes the psychological response of the targeted parent complicated. Anger and feelings of sadness in relation to the way in which the alienating parent has acted and the influence on the alienated child of these actions compete with the need to tolerate the situation because of the fear of reprisals as a result of the expression of these strong negative feelings.

The psychological response to this process of alienation is further complicated by the normal confusing emotions that are associated with the experience of divorce. Doubt about one's own actions and feelings of guilt at the separation of the family can lead to the targeted parent opting to justify the behaviours of the alienating parent.

Campaign of degradation of the parent–child relationships

In an effort to understand the alienation process from the targeted parents' perspective, Vassiliou and Cartwright (6) interviewed targeted parents to learn of their experiences. It was determined that targeted parents often face what has been described as a campaign of degradation of the targeted parents' relationships with their children. This campaign was identified to be progressive in nature and destructive in its effects.

Targeted parents reported a range of experiences that are characteristic of this campaign of degradation of the parent–child relationship. These characteristics included the following.

Gradual decrease in time spent with the alienated child

Targeted parents report that, over time, there is a gradual reduction in the amount of time they get to spend with their children (4,6). Although opportunities to spend time with their children may cease abruptly, it is more often the case that there are fewer and fewer opportunities to see their children as more obstacles are put in the way of these times together occurring. In this way, the consistency of the pattern of time the child spends with the targeted parent changes.

Box 7.40 Targeted parent: In the beginning he would bring the children to spend time with me on a regular basis. At the conference we agreed to me spending time with them three days and nights on the first week of the rotation and four days and nights on the second week of the rotation. In this way we had equal shared care of the children. But then, every so often, the children wouldn't come to spend their scheduled days with me. At first it was only occasionally that this would occur. I felt I didn't have any choice but to accept it, although I wasn't happy about it. But then it happened more often. Before long I was spending much more time without the children than I was spending time with them. Then it all stopped, and I haven't seen them for 11 months.

As the time the child spends with the targeted parent becomes disrupted, more and more excuses are made, or reasons given, for the child not attending. These reasons may relate to alternative events or activities that are reported to occur during time the child would normally spend with the targeted parent. Alternatively, the excuses may relate to claims by the alienating parent that the child is being punished for misbehavior, so they were denied permission to leave the home. Other excuses might relate to scheduled appointments.

> **Box 7.41 Targeted parent:** At first their father would say the children couldn't come to spend time with me because they had a school function they had to attend or a friend's birthday party they were invited to. When I pointed out that I could take the children to these events he just ignored me and didn't bring the children. Then the list of excuses just grew. There were dental appointments and doctors' appointments and scheduled museum trips and visits to his see their paternal family for some family function. Most of these things I could have handled, but they were used as excuses for the children not spending time with me. I'm not stupid. I do realise that he was scheduling appointments during my time with the children so he could keep them from me, but there was nothing I could do to stop him.

As the time between the targeted parent and the child becomes disrupted, there can be claims of increasing resistance on the part of the alienated child to spend time with the targeted parent. Most often, the alienating parent will claim that they did all they could to encourage the child to spend time with the targeted parent although it is doubtful this is the case. In all likelihood, the alienated child is given permission to refuse to attend time with the targeted parent and often rewarded for refusal. The resistance increases until it significantly interferes with the time the child spends with the targeted parent, often reducing it to the point where long periods of time can pass without any contact between the targeted parent and the child.

> **Box 7.42 Targeted parent:** Things got really bad when the children started saying they didn't want to come and stay at my house. Their father would tell me that he had tried to make them come, but he said he couldn't force them. More and more often they said they wouldn't come to see me. In the end, their father said they simply refused to spend time with me and there was nothing he could do to change their minds. He said he had tried and tried to convince them, but I don't believe that is true.

An indication that the relationship between the targeted parent and the child is breaking down can occur with a change in the pattern of visits. For example, after a period of time of spending overnights with the targeted parent, there can be reports of the alienated child refusing to spend overnights. Some children will continue to agree to spend time during the day with the targeted parent, but insist on being returned home to the alienating parent at the end of the day.

> **Box 7.43 Targeted parent:** The children used to spend overnights with me. They have their own bedrooms at my house. All their things are there. But they started saying that they would only come to see me during the day and didn't want to spend overnights at my house. It broke my heart to hear them say that they would rather be at home at night, that is their father's house, than at my house. It broke my heart that they didn't consider my house to be their home as well. Increasingly, they just refused to spend the night. If I tried to make it happen, they would become really angry and distressed and demand to be taken home. In the end, they said they couldn't trust me to allow them to go home when they wanted, so they refused to come to my home. For a while we met in public places like the park, but that didn't last long. Now I don't get to see them at all.

In addition to the change in pattern of the time the alienated child spends with the targeted parent, there can be a pattern of visits being cut short. After an increasingly shorter period of time with the targeted parent, the alienated child will ask to be returned to the alienating parent. Alternatively, they will make it clear they are unhappy until the targeted parent feels pressured to return them to the alienating parent.

> **Box 7.44 Targeted parent:** The children used to be happy spending time with me. They would come to my home and they treated it like it was their home too. And it was their home … But I noticed that, after all the problems started, the children started asking to go home early … you know, back to their father's home. It started with them wanting to go home half an hour early or an hour early, but it got worse and worse as time went on. The last few times I saw them, they would start getting fidgety after only about half an hour and they would start talking about wanting to go back to their father.

The end result of these changes to the time the alienated child spends with the targeted parent is that visits become infrequent or rare. Long periods of time pass without the targeted parent being able to spend time with their child or children. In the end, the visits cease.

Of course, in some cases, the cessation of visits will be abrupt. In some cases, an event will be used as an excuse for stopping visits. In other cases, the targeted parent never learns why the visits simply stopped.

> **Box 7.45 Targeted parent:** At the end, before they stopped coming to see me altogether, I would see them only infrequently. They would come to spend a small amount of time with me but only when I really insisted and, I suppose, kicked up about it. Their father would produce them, but the children were clearly unhappy about being there and were resentful. They wouldn't relax and I couldn't get them to communicate with me. Then it didn't make any difference if I kicked up or not, the children would still refuse to see me. Sometimes … hardly ever … I would get to see them for a few moments or talk to them on the phone for about a minute. But they were always so distant and wouldn't even make eye contact with me when I saw them.

The presence of court orders outlining the way in which time spent with the children is to occur does not prevent this reduction in time spent with the children. Alienating parents will defy court orders in an attempt to alienate their children from the targeted parent.

> **Box 7.46 Targeted parent:** We had these orders in place. I was supposed to see the children four nights a fortnight. But then things started happening. She would say the children were sick and couldn't come to my place. I don't know why I couldn't look after them if they were sick, but she said they couldn't come to me. Then she would say that the children had other activities to do. You know, friends' birthday parties, ballet classes, stuff like that. I tried to tell her that I could take them to these things, but she wouldn't listen. Also, things like ballet classes could have been scheduled at other times because I had such limited time with the children, but she wouldn't listen to that either. Then she would say that one of them couldn't

come because they were being punished for being naughty and the other one wouldn't come alone or couldn't come alone. I don't know which. I tried to explain that she couldn't punish the kids by taking away their time with me, but she didn't listen. Now, I haven't seen the kids in four months. She hasn't given an explanation and she won't answer my calls. Now she's going after a restraining order saying that I've been harassing her on the phone.

Gradual reduction in other forms of communication with the alienated child can occur. In addition to this reduction in time spent with the children, targeted parents also find that other means of communication with their children are reduced or prevented altogether by the alienating parent. Targeted parents are prevented from attending school functions and events, scheduled telephone calls do not take place, and letters are not handed on to the children.

> **Box 7.47 Targeted parent:** The court orders say that I can telephone the kids on Monday evenings and Thursday evenings on the weeks they are not with me. I am supposed to phone at seven at night and I'm allowed to talk with them for up to half an hour. But I would phone and nine times out of ten the phone wouldn't be answered. Sometimes she would answer the phone and when she realised it was me she would hang up. In any case, whenever I did get to talk with the children on the phone, she would put it on speaker phone, and I could hear her in the background putting her two cent's worth in. Then she'd offer the kids some activity that they wanted so they wouldn't be interested in talking with me. She would turn on a DVD and the kids would be distracted. It was so deliberate.

There are certain features that need to be present for a strong and healthy bond to exist between two people. These features are warmth, intimacy and continuity (7). Any disruption of the amount or quality of time one person spends with another will influence the strength of the bond between those two people. Parental alienation relies on the bond between the targeted parent and the alienated child being affected in this way. Alienating tactics that damage the targeted parent–alienated child relationship have an effect on this bond between these two people.

Ongoing sabotage of the parent–child relationship

Targeted parents report their relationships with their children being sabotaged by the alienating parent (4,6). It is considered that these actions on the part of the alienating parent are intentional and designed to significantly interfere with the quality of the relationship between the targeted parent and the child.

This sabotage can take a variety of forms. Some of these attempts are subtle but others are blatant actions that interfere with the targeted parent–child relationship. One tactic used by alienating parents is to reduce the opportunities the targeted parent has for seeing their child or children.

> **Box 7.48 Targeted parent:** She's done all sorts of things that have led to this situation where the children don't want to see me. I had a really good relationship with the school the children were attending. The principal was really supportive, and I could go to the school and help out at events. So, she just pulled them out of school and enrolled them in a different one. No discussion. She didn't even tell me. The school principal had to tell me. He was

> really apologetic, but it wasn't his fault. Now I can't even get copies of the children's school reports and the teachers there won't let me go to the school without their mother's permission. I hate to think what she's told them.

Another tactic used by alienating parents to sabotage the targeted parent–child relationship involves the alienating parent withholding information about the alienated child from the targeted parent. From the alienating child's point of view, the targeted parent then presents as knowing too little about their life. This can be interpreted by the alienated child as evidence of a lack of interest or care by the targeted parent.

> **Box 7.49 Targeted parent:** I don't get told anything. I don't get told when the children are sick or when they've seen the doctor. I don't get to hear about how well they are doing at school. I don't know when they are happy or when they are upset. I don't get to hear about the things they are interested in. Their mother keeps all this from me or makes sure I can't access it myself. She told the school I might abduct the children, so now I'm not allowed on school grounds. Abduct the children! That's just a lie she has made up. It's like my children live in a different country or different world to me. I just feel I know less and less about them.

False accusations of abuse

As discussed in relation to the strategies used by alienating parents, false allegations of child abuse have been reported to occur in the context of parenting disputes in general, and parental alienation in particular (8). These accusations of wrongdoing can relate to claims of sexual, physical or emotional abuse.

> **Box 7.50 Targeted parent:** First, she started by saying that I was violent towards her during our relationship. That's not true. I never even pushed her, let alone hit her. But that's what she claimed. Then she started claiming that I raped her during our marriage. That's rubbish. It never happened. It was after that she claimed I had threatened the kids. Then she started saying that she was concerned about how the kids were behaving and that I might have sexually abused them. She claims it isn't safe for them to be around me. But it's all rubbish. She's made up the lot. Nothing she's said is true. She's painted a picture of me as an abusive person who is a danger to our children.

Involvement of the alienating parents' extended family

In some cases, targeted parents report the involvement in the alienation process of extended family members of the alienating parent (6). This has been discussed in relation to the presentation of alienating parents. This involvement of the family members of alienating parents tends to take a form that is over and above normal support of a family members. In the following example, the involvement in the alienation process of the children's maternal grandmother is different from the typical support offered to that grandmother's daughter.

> **Box 7.51 Targeted parent:** Her mother is involved in this. When my ex-wife started making these hints that I had sexually interfered with the children, her mother jumped in and said she had seen all these concerning behaviours. She wrote in an affidavit that she had seen me behaving in a sexually inappropriate manner towards the children. But if she'd seen that back then, why wouldn't she have told someone? She reckons she has been concerned for some time, but she never acted like she was concerned. It was only after my ex-wife started making these claims that she jumped on board. Now she is just making up more and more stuff. She knows it's not true but she's doing it anyway. I know she wants to support her daughter, but I can't believe she's doing this to me. The woman is nasty.

Perceived reasons for the alienation campaign

From their perspective, targeted parents believe the intention to alienate a child from the targeted parent has its origins in three different factors (4,6). Firstly, the alienating parent is perceived to be driven by the hatred they feel towards the targeted parent. Secondly, the anger the alienating parent feels as a result of things not working out the way they wanted motivates them to interfere with the targeted parent–child relationship. Thirdly, a desire for vengeance is perceived to be the overriding force behind the alienating parent's actions.

> **Box 7.52 Targeted parent:** She's just so angry and bitter. It colours everything she does. She can't get past the fact that things didn't work out. I think she's embarrassed that she has another failed relationship. But she needs to consider her contribution to all the problems she faces. But she won't. She blames me for her unhappiness, and she is going to make me pay. And the way she does this is through the children. She's so tied up in her need to make me suffer that she doesn't even consider what this might be doing to the children.

Consequences of the alienation campaign

The consequences of the alienation of the child for the targeted parent are considerable and significant. As the result of the animosity expressed by the alienating parent, the targeted parent can experience life-altering consequences of the alienation process.

Loss of parenting role

As a function of the alienation process, targeted parents experience a loss of identity with regard to their parenting role. They end up not having a say in important decisions about their children's wellbeing. Their children do not view them as having a significant influence in their lives. Even if they get to spend some time with their children, the nature of the time they spend together, the limitations of when and how this takes place, and the influence the alienating parent has had on the children mean that these parents can rarely function as parents to their children (4–6).

We think this is one of the hardest aspects of parental alienation that targeted parents have to deal with beyond the separation from their children. The loss of the chance to parent their children pushes the targeted parents into a peripheral position in their children's lives. This is one of the purposes of the alienation process – to undermine the parenting role of the targeted parent to the point where this parent has little, if any, input in their child's life.

> **Box 7.53 Targeted parent:** I am their father, but you wouldn't know it from the way their mother behaves. She expects her own father to act like he is their father and not me. She has even said that the children don't need me because her father is a better parent to the children than I have ever been. This is part of her goal of cutting me out of the children's lives. She has replaced me with their grandfather.

When the role of parent is undermined, the targeted parent ends up being in a position where they cannot have any influence on the direction their child's life takes. Decisions are made by the alienating parent that might not be the decisions that would have been made if there had been joint input into the process of deciding what will happen to the child. It must be frustrating and disturbing for targeted parents to be aware that their child's life is evolving in a way that is contrary to their expectations.

> **Box 7.54 Targeted parent:** I don't get to have an opinion about where the children go to school or what they do outside of school. Those decisions are made by their mother. Even if she would talk to me, I doubt she would listen to what I had to say. She thinks she knows best and I don't get a look in. I feel like I am not contributing to the course of my children's lives. It's a horrible feeling.

As a result of these decisions about the child's welfare being made without reference to the targeted parent's input, it is likely that most targeted parents feel they have little control over events relating to their children. In addition, they often report feeling controlled by the alienating parent about when they can spend time with their child and about how that time is spent.

> **Box 7.55 Targeted parent:** It seems to me that the children's mother is the only one calling the shots about when I can and can't see the children. If she decides I can then I get to see them. But if she is annoyed about something I'm supposed to have done, then I don't get to see them. And she decides what happens when they are with me. She tells me how I am supposed to entertain them. She even goes as far as making arrangements for activities that I then have to agree to because she has told the children they are going to happen. If I say no, the children think I am the bad guy. If I don't do what she says, then I don't get to see the children for ages … months sometimes.

As a result of the time the targeted parent gets to spend with their child being determined by the goals of the alienation process, they are often unwilling to do anything that may make the situation worse. Targeted parents report they are too afraid to discipline their children or refuse unreasonable demands from their children because they fear further alienating their children. Also, they fear acting in a way that might reinforce the views the alienating parent has instilled in the child about the targeted parent.

Box 7.56 Targeted parent: I am in this bizarre situation where the children are calling the shots when I do get to see them. I know that if I try to apply any rule or ask them to do something they don't want to do, they tell their mother and I don't get to the see the children for a long time. And I don't want to do anything that will cause the children to reject me more than they already have rejected me. I'm stuck. I'm too scared to do or say anything that will upset them.

As well as being concerned about disciplining their child in case it further alienates them, targeted parents also fear the consequences of refusing to accede to the wishes of the alienated child, no matter how great the demand. Children are often encouraged by the alienating parent to make unreasonable demands, telling the child that they have the right to have all their needs and wants accommodated. The targeted parent learns that attempts to set limits are met with an escalation of conflict and the negative views held by the child about the targeted parent being reinforced.

Box 7.57 Targeted parent: Their mother keeps telling the children they should tell me what they want and insist they get it. So, the children make all sorts of demands … stupid demands! They tell me they will only eat certain things or insist that they don't have to go to bed until later than I would normally allow. But mostly, they insist I buy them things. Everything they lay their eyes on they want. And I am supposed to cough up and buy these things. Expensive things I can't really afford. Even the things that don't cost much add up because there are just so many of them. The trouble is that I don't know how to say no without upsetting them to the point where they refuse to come and see me again. I went for so long without seeing them and I don't want to go through that again. So, I give in to them and then I feel bad because I know they are taking advantage of me. It's a situation I don't feel I can easily escape.

The loss of a parenting role is particularly difficult for targeted parents when the alienating parent has a new partner. This new partner is the person who ends up making parenting choices and the targeted parent has to suffer seeing their children parented by a replacement. We think it would be different for them if they were not ready and able to parent their children themselves. But to see a replacement parent their children when they are prevented from doing so must be very difficult for targeted parents.

Box 7.58 Targeted parent: On the rare occasions I do get to see the children they go on and on about their mother's new partner. They call him Dad, which makes me very unhappy. 'Dad says this …' and "Dad does that …". I tell them I am their father but they just look away; so I know they don't see it that way. This has happened because their mother has encouraged them to see this person as their father. He gets to spend all his time with my children, and he gets to make decisions about what is going to happen to my children and I don't. It's not right! I'm their father!

Feelings of injustice

Targeted parents tend to feel let down by the legal system (5-6,9). The reasons for this are obvious. The court can determine that it is appropriate for the child to spend time with the targeted parent. Orders are made and there seems to be an agreement about how both parents are going to be able to spend time with the child. Then the alienating parent contravenes the order or breaches some other agreement that has been formulated and does so repeatedly. Despite seeking legal redress for these contraventions, the alienating parent refuses to comply and the relationship between the targeted parent and the child continues to deteriorate. The targeted parent looks to the court to fix the problem and the court seems to be powerless to do so.

> **Box 7.59 Targeted parent:** I really thought the family court existed to help families … parents and children. But the court has been no help at all. It's so frustrating. The thing I really don't get is how the court lets people get away with telling lies. The children's mother has told so many lies about me in her affidavits … and it has been shown in court that she has lied … but they do nothing. When is someone going to hold her accountable? And, really, if the court doesn't do it, who is going to hold her accountable?

It is particularly frustrating for targeted parents when they feel the alienating parent is not held accountable for contravention of parenting orders. They often report feeling that the court gives alienating parents more chances than they deserve to do the right thing and abide by the orders. Targeted parents report being distressed when no sanction is applied when an alienating parent defies court orders. They report feeling that if they were the one who was contravening the orders, they would be held accountable.

> **Box 7.60 Targeted parent:** It's just not fair. She keeps ignoring the orders. Time and time again she does this. She's supposed to let me see my daughter, but she just refuses to bring her or let me come and get her. If I try to go and get my daughter, she calls the police. So, I take the matter back to court. I tell them she has contravened the orders again, but they don't do anything. In fact, they have started to treat me as if I'm the problem. I keep bothering them with the same issue. She's the one breaking the rules and I am the one who misses out. Why won't they do something? Throw her in gaol or something. They have to be able to do something.

Targeted parents often feel misunderstood within the context of the legal system. They report concern that the lawyers and judges seem to know too little about parental alienation. They are often frustrated by the failure of the legal system to recognise that their problems in spending time with their children reflect parental alienation.

> **Box 7.61 Targeted parent:** The judge said there was nothing that could be done because my children didn't want to see me. I tried to tell her that this was the point … the fact the children didn't want to see me despite there being no reason for them behaving like this.

> I tried to get her to see that we were talking about parental alienation, but she really didn't seem to know much about it. She may have understood that this was parental alienation, but she acted like there was nothing that could change the situation. She kept asking me what I wanted, and I told her I wanted to see my children. She then kept asking me what I thought she could do about it if the children refused to see me. I tried to explain that there were ways to fix it, but she didn't want to listen.

There also have been reports of the frustration experienced by targeted parents over the relative lack of information about parental alienation known to the lawyers who act for them. In a sense, this is not surprising. Parental alienation reflects complex psychological processes and it is not reasonable for a lawyer to completely appreciate these psychological aspects of parental alienation. Nevertheless, targeted parents can feel let down by the failure of their lawyers to understand these processes. Research has demonstrated that almost all targeted parents asked expressed negative views about their lawyers (9).

> **Box 7.62 Targeted parent:** I really believe that my lawyer thinks I must have done something wrong for the children's mother to treat me this way or for the children to hate me so much. I try to explain it, but she doesn't seem to understand. I would get another lawyer if I could but I'm not sure that another one would understand any better. And I couldn't bear starting from scratch with another lawyer.

Targeted parents often express little faith in psychological interventions that might address the problems associated with parental alienation. This is likely to be a reflection of the fact that most attempts to resolve parental alienation do not use the strategies and techniques that have been demonstrated to be effective. It is often the case that alienated children are provided with individual therapy with the aim of altering the child's views about the targeted parent. Therapists will say that that the targeted parent can see the child when the children are ready. However, they typically never become ready because the nature of the individual therapy does not rectify the problems that are causing the children's rejection of the targeted parent. The drawn-out nature of ineffective interventions can be disheartening for the targeted parent who has little tolerance for the extended period when they do not get to spend time with their children.

It is recognised that the problem of parental alienation is difficult to manage. It requires a skilled practitioner to intervene using complex family therapy techniques to effect any real change for the families affected by parental alienation. So, targeted parents can have an expectation that change will occur once professional support is sought but then fail to discern any change in the alienating parent's behaviour or in the quality of the relationship with the alienated child because ineffective therapeutic techniques are applied.

> **Box 7.63 Targeted parent:** In the end the judge agreed that a psychologist could be appointed to fix the problem. The idea was that we would have family therapy so we could sort out the problems that were causing the children to not want to see me. But the children have been seeing the psychologist for six months or more and I have barely been involved. Twice I have

seen the psychologist – only twice – and never with the children. I saw the psychologist at the beginning and then heard nothing for months. Just last week he called me into his office to tell me the children didn't want to see me. I already know that! When I asked what he was planning on doing to address this problem, he said he would continue to work with the children to see if he could change their minds. Look, I don't know much about psychology, but I have investigated how to fix parental alienation and he is not doing it the right way. He doesn't know what he's doing. But who is going to listen to me? No-one, that's who!

In addition, alienating parents have been reported to deliberately sabotage intervention efforts, making it very difficult to achieve therapeutic gains. Again, the targeted parent is confronted with the knowledge that the alienating parent seem untouchable. From the point of the view of the targeted parent, it must seem like the alienating parent can do whatever he or she wishes without censure.

It is frustrating for targeted parents to experience the consequences of the alienating parents' attempts to sabotage the legal process or undermine psychological intervention efforts. Alienating parents will take actions that delay court proceedings, like making complaints that need to be investigated, such as complaints about the actions of lawyers or expert witnesses. Psychological intervention efforts can be undermined by the alienating parent's failure to engage or the placing of obstacles in the way of therapeutic efforts, such as demanding certain conditions apply. An example would be an alienating parent making unreasonable demands relating to being in the proximity of the targeted parent, making it almost impossible for therapy to progress. Targeted parents tend to feel that alienating parents are being given opportunities to derail attempts to rectify the damage done by the alienation process.

Box 7.64 Targeted parent: Why can't everyone see what she is doing? She causes hold ups in the court ... like last time when she made a complaint about the lawyer and the court-appointed psychologist on the Friday before the trial was due to start. The whole thing had to be delayed because of that. And all the mucking around she's done with the psychologist's appointments ... I can't believe she's been allowed to get away with it. It is so frustrating ... If I can see what she's doing, why can't everyone else?

It has been our experience that targeted mothers believe the legal system favours fathers, and targeted fathers believe the legal system favours mothers. The sense of injustice is likely to be fed by the frustration felt by targeted parents at the legal system's limited ability to manage parental alienation. When repeatedly confronted by disappointments and failures to effect change, an opinion is formed that the needs of the group to which the targeted parent belongs (e.g., targeted fathers or targeted mothers) are not being met.

Box 7.65 Targeted parent: It makes me so angry. I have to try to fight for my children in a system that always targets fathers. Fathers never get a look in. As far as the court is concerned, it is only mothers who can parent the children. Mothers always get what they want, and fathers are left out in the cold. No-one cares about fathers! Judges don't even seem to understand that children need their fathers too.

It is not surprising that targeted parents feel a sense of injustice. They turn to the legal system or seek psychological support to deal with a problem situation that is beyond their capacity to fix. In an absence of a straightforward pathway to resolution of the problems they face, they feel let down by the systems that are available to support and assist them.

Personal costs

Of course, the personal costs of the alienation process for the targeted parent can be substantial. Targeted parents grieve for the children they do not get to see. The loss is made more difficult by the fact that there is no real barrier to them seeing their children apart from the actions of the alienating parent. The grief experienced by targeted parents can be profound and enduring (4–5).

Box 7.66 Targeted parent: I've lost my children. I don't think I could feel any worse if they had died. I know that sounds dramatic, but it is so painful to know they are out there and I can't see them or hold them … or parent them. Do they even know I love them? I cry all the time. I cry when I see parents I don't even know with their children. I can't bear to be around my friends who have children. I feel this huge hole inside me that nothing will fix.

Targeted parents also can suffer psychologically in other ways. They have to deal with the effects on their lives of the absence of their children. They are often exhausted by having to fight for time with their children. They are angry, distressed and, sometimes, traumatised as a result of the separation from their children and their need to fight for their parental rights.

The effects of being separated from their child, coupled with the hopelessness they feel about the resolution of the problem of parental alienation can lead to targeted parents feeling traumatised by their loss. Contributing to these feelings is the fact that the cause of the separation is perceived by targeted parents to be malicious human intent, a factor known to exacerbate traumatic reactions (4–5).

Box 7.67 Targeted parent: I feel like the children have been ripped away from me. I have nightmares where something awful is happening to the children and I can't reach them in time to save them. I wake up in a sweat. I will be doing something else … like at work … and they jump into my mind. Not the good stuff … the horrible stuff. I see their faces in my mind … their frightened faces. Frightened of me! I would never hurt them. I can't go near the places we used to go because it is so upsetting. I go out of my way to avoid driving past their old school. It is just too painful.

As stated, targeted parents can become increasingly angry about the failure to resolve the conflict that is parental alienation. Although anger is a normal enough reaction to a life crisis, and being separated from one's children can be viewed as such a crisis, the anger itself is often misinterpreted by others. The more the targeted parent expresses angry feelings, the more likely they are to be seen as aggressive and uncontrolled. This encourages others to view the targeted parent as unstable and provides the alienating parent with the means of using this perceived instability against them in the alienation process.

> **Box 7.68 Targeted parent:** I have done absolutely everything I can. I have followed all the rules and done what has been asked of me. I've tried not to rock the boat or cause any trouble. But look where it's got me … nowhere! Now, I'm just so angry that nothing has fixed this problem and I still don't get to see my children. This has been going on for four years … four years! How many more years of my children's lives am I going to lose?

It is not really surprising that targeted parents can experience intense distress. After all, their needs are being frustrated and they can find no resolution to the problem they face. At times, this distress is expressed as volatility, with targeted parents acting in threatening ways or communicating it is their intention to act in threatening ways.

> **Box 7.69 Targeted parent:** If I get my hands on her, I will rip off her head. How dare she tell the children I don't love them anymore! The damage she does … and she doesn't care! I'm so angry with her … I can't even think straight. Well, she is going to pay. I don't know how … I don't know what I will do … but I will do something!

For most people, navigating a legal system is challenging. The demands placed on a targeted parent to operate within a legal context can exceed their capacity to cope, especially when they are feelings distressed and overwhelmed.

> **Box 7.70 Targeted parent:** My affidavit has to be done by the end of the month. I know I have to do it but every time I think about starting, I begin to feel really anxious. It's so confronting to have to go over all the documents again. I get really anxious thinking about all that has happened and how I don't get to see the children. I know I have to do it, but I don't know how I am going to manage to get it done. It's just too much …

Last, but not least, targeted parents can find themselves facing financial ruin because of the prolonged legal fight to spend time with their children (5). The costs of legally fighting against parental alienation can be crippling. This is due to the length of time it takes to resolve parental alienation, the cost of legally challenging the alienating parent's repeated contravention of parenting orders, the need to cover the cost of psychological evaluations and interventions, and the need to take time away from work to attend court, lawyers' appointments, mediation and psychologists' appointments. It must be difficult to be financially drained without there being any identifiable improvement in the circumstances that gave rise to the legal fight, that is, separation from their children.

> **Box 7.71 Targeted parent:** This legal fight has wiped me out financially. I've lost everything trying to cover the legal bills. It doesn't matter to her. Her father is wealthy, and he is paying her legal costs … I think that is part of their plan. I think they believe that if they drag this out long enough then I will run out of money and she will win. Sometimes I worry that is

> exactly what is going to happen. Every time she takes this back to court or delays things, I think about how much it is costing me. I would much rather have spent that money on the children and not on lawyers. She doesn't think of that. The children could have had more of what they need if she would just be reasonable and let me see the children.

The personal costs of parental alienation for the targeted parent can be considerable. These costs can impact on other aspects of the targeted parent's life, making it difficult to function. Deterioration in functioning can then be interpreted as demonstrating deficiencies in the targeted parent and their capacity to fulfil parenting roles. A spiralling effect then occurs that results in a decrease in the chances of both time with their children being granted and parental capability being demonstrated.

Concluding comments

It seems inconceivable that a parent who was actively engaged in their child's life, had a loving relationship with their child and who viewed that child as an integral part of themselves is then faced with a situation where they are banished from the child's life. The importance of their role in their child's life is dismissed as if the relationship between that parent and the child does not matter. It is not surprising, then, that targeted parents struggle to cope.

References

1. Baker, A.J.L. (2006). Patterns of parental alienation syndrome: A qualitative study of adults who were alienated from a parent as a child. *The American Journal of Family Therapy, 34*, 63–78. doi:10.1080/01926180500301444
2. Kelly, J.B., & Johnston, J.R. (2001). The alienated child: A reformulation of parental alienation syndrome. *Family Court Review, 39*, 249–266. doi:10.1111/j.174–1617.2001.tb00609.x
3. Kopetski, L. (1998). Identifying cases of parental alienation syndrome: Part II. *Colorado Lawyer, 27*, 63–66.
4. Baker, A.J.L., & Fine, P.R. (2014). *Surviving parental alienation: A journey of hope and healing.* Lanham, MD: Rowman and Littlefield.
5. Poustie, C., Matthewson, M., & Balmer, S. (2018). The forgotten parent: The targeted parent perspective of parental alienation. *Journal of Family Issues, 39*, 3298–3323. doi:10.1177/0192513x18777867
6. Vassiliou, D., & Cartwright, G.F. (2001). The lost parents' perspective on parental alienation syndrome. *The American Journal of Family Therapy, 29*, 181–191. doi:10.1080/019261801750424307
7. Bowlby, J. (1988). *A secure base. Clinical applications of attachment theory.* London: Routledge.
8. Lowenstein, L.F. (2012). Child contact disputes between parents and allegations of sex abuse: What does the research say? *Journal of Divorce and Remarriage, 53*, 194–203. doi:10.1080/10502556.2012.663267
9. Baker, A.J.L. (2010). Even when you win you lose: Targeted parents' perceptions of their attorneys. *American Journal of Family Therapy, 3*, 292–309. doi:10.1080/01926187.2010.493429

Chapter Eight

Alienated children

Introduction

When you consider that the major focus of the situation that gives rise to parental alienation is the care of the child, it is surprising that more attention has not been given to the impact of this process on the child. Nevertheless, it has come to be understood that a campaign of parental alienation can have a significantly negative psychological effect on the children involved in this process. Examination of the short- and long-term effects on children often is undertaken by considering the reports of adults who have been exposed to parental alienation tactics when they were children (1–2). The nature of the influences of this process on the child at the various stages of a child's development still needs to be determined.

The identified problems that develop as a consequence of exposure to parental alienation tactics and the subsequent breakdown of the parent–child relationship with the targeted parent can be attributed to the parental alienation process. The problems that have been demonstrated to be a consequence of exposure to parental alienation exist even when other forms of child abuse and maltreatment have been taken into account (3). The genesis of these problems may reflect the competing demands of loving their parents and being encouraged to give a false account of the actions of one. It has been suggested that this conflict sets the stage for lifelong problems (4).

Parental alienation is considered to be a form of abuse or maltreatment by the alienating parent because of the impact on the child. It has been suggested that negative consequences for the child of parental alienation and maltreatment are similar in nature. That is, it has been suggested that exposure to either leads to children feeling like they are flawed, worthless and unloved (5).

Children at risk of alienation

There is no consistent support for the notion that there are child characteristics that increase the chances of parental alienation occurring. In this way, there is nothing about a child's presentation that will make them more vulnerable to the alienation process than any other child. Further, there has been insufficient attention given to whether there are child characteristics that protect children from being influenced by parental alienation attempts.

There is an indication that the children most at risk of being alienated are females during early adolescence (6). Some understanding of the reasons for this may come from the literature about children's experiences post-divorce and literature related to shared care of children after family breakdown. For example, information that might be relevant to alienating mother–alienated daughter relationships can be found in the literature relating to the communication styles that exist between mothers and daughters. Particular communication styles can present an obstacle to improvement or maintenance of the father–daughter relationship (7).

Mothers who demonstrate a tendency to be overly emotionally dependent on their daughters have a tendency to inappropriately disclose to their daughters negative information about their daughter's father (7). Daughters' trust in their fathers is then compromised because they begin to doubt their fathers' expressions of love resulting in them being more likely to form an allegiance with their mother against the father in any interparental conflict (8). This role of ally to their mother increases the risk for the development of depressive symptoms and more severe levels of stress (9). In the absence of any catalyst for change, these unhealthy alliances can be maintained through to adulthood (10), resulting in an enduring relationship distance between father and child.

This enduring allegiance may result in daughters being provided with information from the mother that reflects the mother's views about the father's competence that may not be an accurate account (7). In particular, daughters are likely to hear that their fathers did not adequately parent pre-divorce and have little desire to parent post-divorce (7). Of course, in reality, it is exceedingly unlikely to be true in all cases. Fathers may agree to a lives with/spends time with parenting agreement in favour of the mother, but the majority report being dissatisfied with the arrangement because it does not allow them enough time to maintain a meaningful relationship with their child (11–12).

In all likelihood, similar processes occur in any cases of parental alienation. The relationship between the alienating parent and the alienated child has unhealthy characteristics that cause the interactions between these parents and children to foster the change in the relationship between the child and the targeted parent.

Psychological consequences

Given the nature of parental alienation, it is not surprising that exposure to alienating tactics can have a negative psychological impact on children. It has been suggested that the psychological symptoms that develop as a consequence of exposure to parental alienation tactics can be either internalised (e.g., anxiety) or externalised (e.g., oppositional behaviour, conduct problems) (13). With the psychological impact of exposure to alienating tactics being varied in nature, it is necessary to consider the effects of parental alienation on children's adjustment both in terms of its immediate impact and its longer-term impact.

Poor self-esteem

As adults, people exposed to parental alienation strategies as children reported experiencing or having experienced poor self-esteem and feelings of self-hatred (1). There are a number of reasons for the influence of parental alienation on children's self-esteem.

Low self-esteem and feelings of self-hatred have been understood to be a reflection of the child internalising the hatred towards the targeted parent felt by the alienating parent. That is, it has been argued that if the alienating parent demonstrated animosity towards the targeted parent and said unfavourable things about the targeted parent, the child, who understood themselves to be linked to the targeted parent on a psychological or biological basis, believes they, too, should receive some of those same negative feelings because of that connection with the targeted parent (1–2).

In addition to this, alienating parents often choose to tell alienated children that the targeted parent does not love them and does not want them. Undoubtedly, this would have an impact on the child's feelings of self-worth (1).

It would be easy to reach the conclusion that alienated children would not care if the targeted parent rejected them because they are so dismissive of the need to have the targeted parent in their lives and lack empathy for the targeted parent's situation. However, that is not the case. While still dismissing the targeted parent, children can become very distressed at the slightest hint of rejection by the targeted parent. Even a stern word can cause some of these children to react like they are deeply hurt. Alienated children develop a way that allows them to comfortably reject the targeted parent, but they are unable to protect themselves from the psychological impact of being rejected. So, alienated children can do the rejecting, but they do not want to be rejected.

Certainly, the impact on self-esteem of believing that a parent, even a rejected parent, does not love you is well established (14). A child will assume responsibility for a parent holding negative views about that child (15), or believe that the parent holds these negative views because they have been told this is so by the alienating parent. From an attachment theory framework, it is evident that a child's interactions with a parent or caregiver will determine the way in which their internal view of their own worthiness develops (16). Simply put, a child will believe that if a parent does not love them, they are unlovable.

Further, it is well understood that alienating parents can make their love of their child contingent on the alienated child's rejection of the targeted parent. The child comes to understand that the alienating parent's negative feelings towards the targeted parent are stronger than the positive feelings the alienating parent feels for the child (17). An acceptance of this message, whether or not the message was intentional, reduces the child's feelings of self-worth.

Depression

Adults who were alienated from a parent during their childhood were asked about the effects of this process on mood (1). About 70 percent of the people interviewed had experienced depressive episodes that had interfered with their capacity to function.

The depression seemed to be linked to the loss of the relationship with the targeted parent (18), with anxiety also being linked to this loss. Further, it was evident that the children had been given no opportunity by the alienating parent to mourn the loss of the relationship with the targeted parent. Indeed, the alienating parent tended to express the opinion to the child that the loss was a positive experience.

The inability to openly grieve for the loss of the targeted parent means that feelings about the loss would be likely to remain unresolved. A process known as disenfranchised grief can be applied here. Disenfranchised grief is where a person feels the loss but is unable to express that grief because it is not societally sanctioned or permitted in other ways. An example would be a child in foster care being unable to express the grief they feel at separation from a parent (19). Such would be the case for an alienated child in relation to the loss of the targeted parent. The alienating parent's failure to acknowledge the loss would limit the extent to which the alienated child could express their grief openly.

In addition, the child would need to deal with confusion that would be generated by the conflicting feelings of grief and the negative feelings towards the targeted parent that are encouraged by the alienating parent. The conflicting feelings also would make it difficult to express feelings of grief even in the absence of clear signals from the alienating parent that grief for the lost targeted parent is unwarranted and unnecessary.

Feelings of guilt and shame

The adults who were alienated from a targeted parent during their childhood have been reported to experience feelings of guilt and shame. These feelings are linked to the experience of parental alienation and, in particular, the active role the children were encouraged by the alienating parent to take in the rejection and betrayal of the targeted parent (1).

Certainly, it is well understood that an alienated child is encouraged by the alienating parent to actively participate in the process of alienating their targeted parent (20). The child receives considerable reward, in the form of a positive response from the alienating parent, for joining in the targeting of the parent who is being excluded from the child's life. The young person's understanding of these influences on their own choices may be limited. As a result, guilty feelings develop at a time when the young person gains additional insight into their contribution to the rejection of the targeted parent.

Alcohol and drug use

Given the psychological difficulties experienced by people who have been alienated from a parent, it is not surprising that they would seek a means of coping with the distress they feel. It has been identified that there is a tendency for the adults who were alienated from a parent during their childhood to use drugs and alcohol as a means of dealing with the other psychological consequences of the loss they experience and the process into which they were drawn (1).

Relationship consequences

In addition to the psychological consequences of exposure to parental alienation tactics, there is a range of relationship or interpersonal consequences. These develop as a result of the alienation process and the loss experienced as a consequence of this process. This can affect attachment relationships, even into adulthood (17–18).

Lack of trust

An alienated child has to try to make sense of confusing information. Firstly, they believe they have been rejected by the targeted parent because they are encouraged by the alienating parent to hold this view. The belief that the targeted parent has rejected them would seem like a normal enough conclusion if the information about the targeted parent's attitude towards the child is accepted by the child. And there would be no real reason why the child would not accept the alienating parent's viewpoint. The alienating parent presents this information while also telling the child that he or she has a special relationship with the alienating parent.

In addition, the information being provided by the alienating parent to the child may have some elements of truth, making the story they tell more convincing. For example, the development of a friendship or new relationship by the targeted parent after the alienating parent has told the child that the targeted parent had abandoned the family and the child in favour of another relationship will confirm for the child that the alienating parent is telling the truth. The failure of a targeted parent to contact the alienated child will confirm the alienating parent's account of the targeted parent's rejection of the child and lack of feeling for the child, even if it is the alienating parent who is preventing the communication.

The result of this process is that the targeted parent, with whom the child is likely to have had a loving relationship in the past, is now perceived by the child to be untrustworthy. Despite the fact that the alienated child may have rejected the targeted parent, the perceived rejection by the targeted parent is likely to be interpreted as a betrayal. This sets a foundation for lack of trust and suspiciousness with regard to other relationships.

Compounding this problem can be the effect on the alienated child of the realisation that their trusted parent, the alienating parent, also has betrayed them by deliberately interfering with their relationship with the targeted parent. This realisation may occur much later in life, but can still have a profound effect on the way in which relationships are viewed.

The lack of trust that develops as a consequence of the actions of the alienating parent can have a significant effect on the development of future relationships. The impact of this foundation of mistrust can influence the way adult relationships are viewed and experienced (17).

Subsequent alienation from own children

There is evidence of an intergenerational transmission of the phenomenon of parental alienation. Some people who were alienated from a parent as a child will go on to alienate their own children or be alienated from them (1).

Certainly, experience would indicate that there can be a pattern of alienated children becoming alienating parents. As previously mentioned, some alienating parents have been raised by an alienating parent. These people do not have contact with their father, typically, and have a domineering mother who seems to have determined the nature of the relationship between their child and their child's father. These alienating parents seem to hold the view that if their mother could raise her children without assistance of a partner, then so can they. For these people, it seems normal to reject the targeted parent and this might be why they do the same thing to the next generation of children.

As mentioned, people who were alienated from a parent when they were a child also can be alienated from their own children. Contributing to this outcome may be a distorted view about parent–child relationships, in general, that developed as a consequence of their own childhood experiences of being alienated. Without a good template for the way in which parent–child relationships should function, the alienated child fails to adequately connect with their own children.

Partner selection

The likelihood of alienation from one's own child may be contributed to by a reported tendency for adults who were alienated as children to select partners who share similar psychological characteristics as their own alienating parent (1). By selecting partners with the same characteristics, there is an increased chance that the alienated child will end up being the targeted parent.

Relationship breakdowns

It has been reported that the divorce rates for people who were alienated from a parent during their childhood are higher than average (1). This may be a reflection of the poor partner selection or the lack of trust experienced by people who were alienated as children. It also has been reported that some chose not to have children because of an expectation that marital relationships will fail, and their children will reject them.

Other problems

Of course, the negative consequences of being alienated as a child are not limited to those mentioned above. Other problems have been identified.

School-related difficulties

It is not surprising that the difficulties experienced by an alienated child, including the psychological effects, the disruption to family life and the stresses associated with the tactics used by the alienating parent, affect other areas of functioning. One of these areas is academic performance, although it is likely that other aspects of the school experience may be affected, such as social/peer relationship development (13).

Search for identity

It is interesting to note that many adults who had been alienated from the targeted parent as children also reported that they experienced a poor relationship with the alienating parent, even while maintaining the view that the targeted parent had rejected them (21). So, parental alienation can have a negative influence on relationships with both parents during adulthood.

It is worth noting that even very badly maltreated children who are not in the care of their parents throughout their childhoods will be allowed to maintain some well-managed contact with their parents. This is allowed for identification purposes. This means that a child has the opportunity to establish their identity by knowing and interacting with their parents.

Consideration has to be given to the damage that can be done to a person's understanding of their identity as a result of alienation from a parent and the realisation that the previously trusted parent had acted in a way that would cause them harm. A person who was alienated from a targeted parent during their childhood may search for an understanding of who they are and where they fit in the world.

Self-sufficiency failure

Following on from this loss of identity, it has been reported that people who were alienated as children often find it difficult to become self-sufficient in the adult world (2). It has been argued that, as children, they have the alienating parent's world view forced upon them. As part of this process, alienated children are encouraged not to think of their own needs because this might lead to them questioning and, presumably, rejecting the alienating parent's views. Therefore, compliance and obedience rather than self-determination and independent thinking would be encouraged by the alienating parent (17).

Concluding comments

It would seem from the available research that the impact of parental alienation on the alienated child can be enduring in nature and pervasive in its effects. It is important to gain a better understanding of this impact as this might encourage greater effort in terms of finding ways to help resolve parental alienation. Further, greater understanding of the impact of parental alienation on children as they experience it and into their futures may encourage courts to recognise the importance of protecting children from the risk of harm in the same way that the courts protect children from the risk of harm from other forms of abuse.

References

1. Baker, A.J.L. (2005). The long-term effects of parental alienation on adult children: A qualitative research study. *The American Journal of Family Therapy, 33,* 289–302. doi:10.1080/01926180590962129

2. Baker, A.J.L. (2007). *Adult children of parental alienation syndrome: Breaking the ties that bind.* New York: Norton.
3. Baker, A.J.L., & Ben-Ami, N. (2011). To turn a child against a parent is to turn a child against himself: The direct and indirect effects of exposure to parental alienation strategies on self-esteem and well-being. *Journal of Divorce and Remarriage, 52,* 472–489. doi:10.1080/10502556.2011.609424
4. Summers, C.C., & Summers, D.M. (2006). Parentectomy in the crossfire. *The American Journal of Family Therapy, 34,* 243–261. doi:10.1080/01926180600558349
5. Binggeli, N.J., Hart, S.N., & Brassard, M.R. (2001). *Psychological maltreatment of children. The APSAC study guides 4.* Thousand Oaks: Sage Publications.
6. Balmer, S., Matthewson, M., & Haines, J. (2017). Parental alienation: Targeted parent perspective. *Australian Journal of Psychology,* 1–8. doi:10.1111/ajpy.12159
7. Nielsen, L. (2011). Divorced fathers and their daughters: A review of recent research. *Journal of Divorce and Remarriage, 52,* 7–93. doi:10.1080/10502556.2011.546222
8. Koerner, S.S., Kenyon, D.B., Rankin, L.A., & Williams, L.R. (2006). Growing up faster? Post-divorce catalysts in the mother-adolescent relationship. *Journal of Divorce and Remarriage, 45,* 25–41. doi:10.1300/J087v45n03_02
9. Silverberg Koerner, S., Wallace, S., Jacobs Lehman, S., & Raymond, M. (2002). Mother-to-daughter disclosure after divorce: Are there costs and benefits? *Journal of Child and Family Studies, 11,* 469–483. doi:10.1023/a:1020987509405
10. Jurkoic, G.J., Thirkield, A., & Morrell, R. (2001). Parentification of adult children of divorce: A multidimensional analysis. *Journal of Youth and Adolescence, 30,* 245–257. doi:10.1023/a:1010349925974
11. Bonach, K., Sales, E., & Koeske, G. (2005). Gender differences in perceptions of co-parenting quality among expartners. *Journal of Divorce and Remarriage, 43,* 1–28. doi:10.1300/j087v43n01_01
12. Spillman, J.A., Deschamps, H.S., & Crews, J.A. (2004). Perspectives on nonresidential parental involvement and grief: A literature review. *Family Journal, 12,* 263–270. doi:10.1177/1066480704264347
13. Godbout, E., & Parent, C. (2012). The life paths and lived experiences of adults who have experienced parental alienation: A retrospective study. *Journal of Divorce and Remarriage, 53,* 34–54. doi:10.1080/10502556.2012.635967
14. Khalique, A., & Rohner, R.P. (2002). Perceived parental acceptance–rejection and psychological adjustment: A meta-analysis of cross-cultural and intracultural studies. *Journal of Marriage and Family, 64,* 54–64. doi:10.1111/j.1741-3737.2002.00054.x
15. Briere, J. (2004). Psychological assessment of child abuse effects in adults. In T.M. Wilson & J.P. Keane (Eds.), *Assessing psychological trauma and PTSD* (pp. 538–564). New York: Guildford Press.
16. Bretherton, I., Ridgeway, D., & Cassidy, J. (1990). Assessing internal working models of the attachment relationship. In M.T. Greenberg, D. Cicheetti, & E.M. Cummings (Eds.), *Attachment in the preschool years* (pp. 273–310). Chicago: University of Chicago Press.
17. Ben-Ami, N., & Baker, A.J.L. (2012). The long-term correlates of childhood exposure to parental alienation on adult self-sufficiency and well-being. *The American Journal of Family Therapy, 40,* 169–183. doi:10.1080/01926187.2011.601206
18. Baker, A.J.L., & Verrocchio, M.C. (2016). Exposure to parental alienation and subsequent anxiety and depression in Italian adults. *The American Journal of Family Therapy, 44,* 255–271. doi:10.1080/01926187.2016.1230480
19. Mitchell, M.B. (2018). "No one acknowledged my loss and hurt": Non-death loss, grief, and trauma in foster care. *Child and Adolescent Social Work Journal, 35,* 1–9. doi:10.1007/s10560-017-0502-8
20. Warshak, R.A. (2000). Remarriage as a trigger of parental alienation syndrome. *The American Journal of Family Therapy, 28,* 229–241. doi:10.1080/01926180050081667
21. Mone, J.G., & Biringen, Z. (2006). Perceived parent–child alienation: Empirical assessment of parent-child relationships within divorced and intact families. *Journal of Divorce and Remarriage, 45,* 131–156. doi:10.1300/j087v45n03_07

Chapter Nine

Other family members

Introduction

Families are more than a parent–child triad. They consist of a wider network of siblings, grandparents, uncles, aunts, cousins and step-parents. Therefore, it is reasonable to assume that members of the alienated child's extended family either can be involved in facilitating parental alienation or can be alienated from the child. Not only is the alienated child–targeted parent relationship damaged, so is the relationship the alienated child has with any extended family members who are believed to be aligned with the targeted parent (1). Any extended family member who is not in support of the alienating parent's agenda becomes a potential target for the alienation campaign.

Despite this, little is known about the role extended family members play in the alienation process. How extended family members are affected by being alienated from the alienated child also is unclear. The role of other family members in the alienation process has generated little attention in academic literature. However, the role of extended family members is evident in clinical practice and the importance of these members should not be dismissed.

This chapter describes the role extended family members can play in facilitating parental alienation. Consideration is given to the ways extended family members can reinforce parental alienation by actively engaging in alienation tactics or passively allowing it to occur. Indeed, some extended family members can be the primary alienator. Also, this chapter will explore how extended families can help prevent the alienation process from occurring and can help to lessen the negative consequences of parental alienation and facilitate the reunification process.

Other targeted family members

The new partner

The targeted parent's new partner almost inevitably becomes a target of the alienating parent's campaign of denigration and vilification. By virtue of commencing a relationship with the targeted parent, they are showing their allegiance to the targeted parent. We saw in Chapter Six that alienating parents tend to hold the view that the targeted parent abandoned and rejected them regardless of how the relationship ended. This interpretation results in feelings of humiliation, which are compounded further by the introduction of the targeted parent's new partner.

When the alienating parent has not come to terms with the loss of the relationship with the targeted parent, the alienating parent inevitably struggles to come to terms with the presence of the new partner. To the alienating parent, the new partner is the 'other woman' or 'other man' and, consequently, they view this new relationship as evidence of further betrayal. This exacerbates the alienating parent's hostility and rage. It is unsurprising that the introduction of a new partner can lead to an increase in the intensity, severity and frequency of alienating behaviours (2-3).

The alienating parent will compare themselves to the targeted parent's new partner. When the alienating parent presents with narcissistic personality traits, the new partner will never measure up or be good enough in their eyes. The alienating parent will struggle to understand why the targeted parent chose the new partner over them and will interpret the new relationship with reference to self.

Box 9.1 Alienating parent: How dare he do this to me and the children! Hasn't he hurt us enough? It's bad enough he turned his back on his family. Now he's gone and shacked up with another woman. You should see her. I have no idea what he sees in her. She's not particularly attractive. He can't be choosy about who he gets involved with. He's certainly come down in the world …They deserve each other, I reckon. If he can't choose a suitable partner, then how can I trust him to make appropriate choices when it comes to the children. And I wouldn't trust her around my children. Definitely not!

Here, the alienating parent expresses her disgust at what she perceives as the targeted parent's audacity to re-partner. She sees the targeted parent's new relationship as a deliberate choice to betray her and the children. She compares herself to the new partner and concludes the new partner will never meet her standards. The alienating parent considers herself to be the superior option and is outraged the targeted parent cannot see this. Her revenge for not being chosen is to alienate the children from their father. She uses the existence of the new partner and her belief that the targeted parent's decision-making abilities are faulty to justify her actions.

In the centre of this conflict and narcissistic rage is a child who would likely benefit from a loving relationship with both parents as well as a loving step-parent. However, the alienating parent demands loyalty and will act to convince the child that the targeted parent's new partner is a villain, unsafe and cannot be trusted. The alienating parent will ensure the child comes to believe the new partner is the reason why their parents will never get back together again. For these reasons, any hostility the child directs towards the targeted parent will also be directed towards the new partner.

Box 9.2 Adult targeted child: I hated my step-mother for years. I thought she was the reason my parents separated. That's what my mother led me to believe. When I got older, I started thinking about the timeline of events. I realised my parents separated three years before my dad met my step-mother. She couldn't have been responsible for my parents splitting up. Mum hated her. She always spoke of her like she was the other woman. She still talks about my step-mother as though she's my dad's mistress. It's been over a decade and my mum still isn't over the fact she and dad are no longer together and he's moved on. I wish my mum could move on. It would make it easier for me to enjoy spending time with dad and my step-mother. Next year I'm getting married and I'm unsure I can invite mum, dad and step-mother to be there at the same time. I can't trust my mum to not make a scene.

Becoming part of an alienated family is an enormous undertaking for a new partner. Their life will be catapulted into a world where they will be accused of all kinds of wrongdoings. This inevitably takes its toll on their psychological wellbeing and the relationship they have with the targeted parent. It takes a brave and compassionate person to commit to a relationship with a targeted parent and join them in a never-ending battle to hold on to the targeted parent–alienated child relationship against the will of an alienating parent.

Forgotten grandparents

Ample research has shown that grandparents play an important part in children's lives (4-5). Children who report being close to their grandparents during family separation also report fewer adjustment problems following family separation (6). This is because grandparents can provide comfort and a sense of security and stability during a time of significant change and emotional upheaval. Parental separation or divorce in the middle generation (i.e., alienating parent and targeted parent generation) and family feuds are two important reasons the grandparent–grandchild relationship can be damaged (5).

In instances of family separation and family feud, withholding children from seeing their grandparents can be used to punish grandparents for perceived wrongdoing. Within the context of parental alienation, grandparents are collateral damage (7) as the alienating parent's and alienated child's hostility towards the targeted parent is extended to the targeted parent's parents (8).

Grandparents effectively grieve for the loss of their grandchildren twice. They grieve for the loss of their grandchildren because of parental alienation while coming to terms with the fact that, due to their age, they may never see the alienated grandchildren again. Grandparents fear for their grandchildren's wellbeing as a result (5,7-8). In addition to this grief, grandparents fear for their own children's wellbeing. When their child is the targeted parent, grandparents feel helpless and at a loss with regard to improving the situation for their child and grandchildren. Sometimes, grandparents will meet their own child's legal costs, which is a serious financial burden for them (8). These financial costs on grandparents have far-reaching consequences for the comfort of their retirement and their ability to leave a financial legacy to their family. All of these burdens have serious psychological impacts on alienated grandparents.

Some grandparents can be completely alienated from their grandchildren, knowing it is unlikely they will ever see their grandchild again. Other grandparents try to maintain a relationship with their grandchildren by juggling a difficult relationship with the alienating parent while preserving the relationship with their own child, the targeted parent. This juggling act is stressful and can take a toll on the alienated grandparent's relationship with their own child as well as their own psychological wellbeing. Alienated grandparents can become caught in a particularly perverse triangle (10) between the alienating parent and alienated child as well as the alienating parent and targeted parent.

Box 9.3 Alienated grandparent: It's a terrible thing. I see my daughter suffering every day because of the abuse she's suffered from her ex-husband and their son. My grandson refuses to see my daughter and now me. We both grieve for that little boy every day. I feel my daughter's pain, I feel mine and I really feel for my grandson. He was such a sweet little child and now he's unrecognisable. So full of vitriol. I don't understand why my grandson is so vile towards his mother. She never hurt him. She wouldn't hurt a fly. After my daughter left her ex-husband, I tried to keep in contact with my grandson, but his father made it increasingly difficult. It became clear that I had to choose. As far as he was concerned, I had to reject my own daughter or reject my only grandson. I couldn't have both in my life. What kind of person thinks like that?

Just as the alienating parent forces the child to choose between them and the targeted parent, their demand for loyalty means the alienated child has to choose between the alienating parent and any significant other whom they consider to be 'not with them'. Moreover, significant others, such as grandparents, must also choose if they are with the alienating parent or against them. If a significant other is unable to align with the alienating parent, the consequence is the loss of the relationship between the significant other and the alienated child. This includes the parents of alienating parents. It cannot be assumed that only the parents of targeted parents can be alienated from their grandchildren. If alienating parents form the view that their parent is disloyal, the alienating parent will have no qualms in alienating the child from their own parents. In this instance, perceived disloyalty is likely to include maintaining a relationship with the targeted parent.

Other family members as alienators

The new partner in crime

As we saw in Chapter Six, alienating parents often have a history of poor romantic relationships. They tend to have histories of multiple failed relationships or a history of failure to form romantic relationships. When the alienating parent does re-partner and an allegiance develops between that partner and the alienating parent, the two can form a formidable alienating force.

The new partner in crime quickly becomes the alienating parent's confidant. The new partner will enter a distorted world created by the alienating parent and, subsequently, come to believe their view. When the new partner takes on the alienating parent's distorted view, at best they will support the alienating parent's behaviours and, at worst, actively participate in the alienation or become the primary alienator (8).

When the alienating parent's new partner shares similar personality characteristics as the alienating parent and is adept at alienating behaviours, they can quickly insert themselves as a replacement parent for the alienated child. This manoeuvre will be supported and encouraged by the alienating parent.

Box 9.4 Targeted parent: My children have started calling me by my first name. Apparently, I'm not a mother to them now. My children told me their step-mother is more of a mother to them than I ever was. Apparently, she's shown them what a real mother is like. I feel so powerless. I fear for my children's wellbeing. They have no idea they've been manipulated. I miss my children so much. My ex-husband is so proud of himself. He thinks he's replaced me with a newer model and has a perfect family of his creation with his new partner. I don't know how long this one will last. Regardless of how long she stays around, the children continue to suffer.

The alienating parent now has their new family until the new partner no longer serves a purpose to them or the new partner can no longer stay a member of an alienated family. When the new partner becomes the primary alienator or actively participates in the alienation campaign, the impact of their behaviour is just as serious and destructive as the behaviour of alienating mothers and fathers.

Grandparents in arms

Just as step-parents can become complicit in the alienation process or become the primary alienator, so can grandparents. We saw in Chapter Six that often problems exist in the alienating parent's family of origin. The alienating parent's relationship with their own parents can be overly enmeshed. Sometimes, the alienating parent's best teacher of alienating behaviour is their parent.

The alienating parent's parents can be supportive of the alienating parent's behaviour. They can support it by reinforcing the alienating parent's cognitive distortions and fuelling the fire that feeds irrational and dramatic reactions to events and situations. As families of alienating parents can be quite controlling, it is not unusual for the alienating parent's mother or father to be the primary alienator.

Box 9.5 Targeted parent: My ex-wife's mother loads the gun and my ex-wife pulls the trigger. If it wasn't for my ex-mother-in-law I could probably have a half decent co-parenting relationship with my ex-wife. I was never good enough for my ex-mother-in-law's daughter. She made it clear I wasn't welcome in her family from day one. I thought at the time I wasn't marrying her, I was marrying my now ex-wife. I had no idea then how wrong I was. My ex-wife can't do anything on her own. Every choice, every opinion has to be approved by her mother. If my ex-mother-in-law disapproves, then watch out. The kids fear her. In the end they had no choice. Obey her or suffer the consequences. Obeying her means believing their dad is a bad man and keeping away from him. I think the only way out of this for my children is when their grandmother passes away. That might sound awful, but her reign over people will only end when she goes.

The alienating grandparent has not been described in the literature; however, the influence of an alienating grandparent should not be underestimated in clinical and legal practice. It is reasonable to assume the behaviours and processes used by alienating grandparents are the same as those used by alienating parents and alienating step-parents. Also, it is important to acknowledge that alienating grandparents can be the targeted parent's grandparents. Parental alienation tends to run in families (1,10). Alienated children can go on to become targeted parents and their parents (the alienating parent) can become alienating grandparents.

How can other family members help?

Extended family members can make a difference in reducing the impact of parental alienation on the child or even facilitating reunification (1). Parental alienation is a poorly recognised counter-intuitive phenomena most extended family members are unlikely to understand or fully appreciate. As a result of their limited understanding, extended family members can give well-meaning but unhelpful advice or commentary. Extended family members may struggle to understand why everyone cannot "just get along" and make naïve attempts to reconcile the targeted parent and alienated child. The naïve extended family member may even attempt to confront the alienated child or alienating parent with poor outcomes, such as strengthening the alienation while becoming a target of the alienating parent's denigration and vilification.

Often, extended family members focus on the behaviour of the alienated child without understanding it to be a consequence of alienating behaviours by the alienating parent. Extended family members can blame the alienated child for the alienation and come to resent their behaviour. Extended family members can help by becoming knowledgeable about parental alienation, alienating behaviours and the experience of alienated children. Extended family members need to avoid becoming complicit in the alienation. Being aware of the processes and behaviours underpinning parental alienation can help prevent extended family members from unwittingly reinforcing the alienation and becoming part of a perverse triangle. Instead, extended family members can act as a bridge between the alienated child and targeted parent. Extended family members can help to build this bridge by providing alienated children and targeted parents with ongoing, unconditional support. Also, they can provide the alienated child with a supportive environment that counteracts the distorted world of the alienating parent.

Concluding comments

Families are complicated and the alienated family exemplifies this. Research has provided insight into the complexity of the triangulation between the alienating parent, alienated child and targeted parent, but little is known about the experience of extended family members in the alienated family. The impact of being alienated from an entire social support network has not been fully understood and acknowledged in the literature. When a child is alienated from a parent, they also are alienated from significant others. Not only can they be taught to fear and hate a parent, they also can be taught to fear and hate the extended family members at the alienating parent's discretion. Extended family members can provide children with considerable psycho-social support throughout their lives as well as during the stress of family separation, but this support is taken away from the alienated child.

Little is known about the experience of alienated and alienating siblings. Siblings can form an alliance with the alienating parent and reject their other siblings if they choose to have a relationship with the targeted parent. There is no known literature exploring the psychological impact of sibling rejection within the context of parental alienation. However, legal and mental health practitioners should not ignore the fact that alienated children are members of a wider family system. Within this wider family system there are family members who are complicit in the alienation process or even active participants. When a child is alienated from a parent, they are alienated from other supportive family members.

References

1. Baker, A.J.L. (2007). *Adult children of parental alienation syndrome: Breaking the ties that bind.* New York: W.W. Norton.
2. Sauber, R. (2006). PAS as a family tragedy: Roles of family members, professionals, and the justice system. In R. Gardner, R. Sauber, & D. Lorandos (Eds.), *The international handbook of parental alienation syndrome: Conceptual, clinical and legal considerations* (pp. 12–32). Illinois: Charles C Thomas.
3. Warshak, R.A. (2000). Remarriage as a trigger of parental alienation syndrome. *The American Journal of Family Therapy, 28,* 229–241. doi:10.1080/01926180050081667
4. Drew, L.A., & Smith, P.K. (1999). The impact of parental separation/divorce on grandparent–grandchild relationships. *The International Journal of Aging and Human Development, 48,* 191–216. doi:10.2190/xyx5-tr6y-tgh5-eyn9
5. Kruk, E. (1995). Grandparent–grandchild contact loss: Findings from a study of "grandparent rights" members. *Canadian Journal on Aging/La Revue canadienne du vieillissement, 14,* 737–754.
6. Lussier, G., Deater-Deckard, K., Dunn, J., & Davies, L. (2002). Support across two generations: Children's closeness to grandparents following parental divorce and remarriage. *Journal of Family Psychology, 16,* 363–376. doi:10.1037/0893-3200.16.3.363
7. Golly, C.H. (2016). Pruning the family tree: The plight of grandparents who are alienated from their grandchildren. *The International Journal of Aging and Society, 7,* 21–31. doi:10.18848/2160-1909/CGP/v07i02/21-31

8. Gardner, R. (2006). Parental alienation syndrome and the corruptive power of anger. In R. Gardner, R. Sauber, & D. Lorandos (Eds.), *The international handbook of parental alienation syndrome: Conceptual, clinical and legal considerations* (pp. 33–48). Illinois: Charles C Thomas.

9. Haley, J. (1977). Toward a theory of pathological systems. In P. Watzlawick & J. Weakland (Eds.), *The interactional view* (pp. 31–48). New York: Norton.

10. Baker, A.J.L. (2005). The long-term effects of parental alienation on adult children: A qualitative research study. *The American Journal of Family Therapy, 33,* 289–302. doi:10.1080/01926180590962129

Chapter Ten

Outside forces

Introduction

The ways in which outside forces contribute to parental alienation is particularly important to explore. This is because systems such as education systems, child protection services, courts and the professionals who work within or in collaboration with these systems and services can unintentionally facilitate parental alienation. When these systems and services facilitate and perpetuate parental alienation, the consequence is socially sanctioned parental alienation and unwitting acceptance of an insidious form of abuse.

When an alienating parent seeks support from these services and systems, they can appear as a well-meaning parent concerned for their child's welfare and safety. Any professional hearing such concerns would be negligent if they did not take them seriously. However, the challenge for these professionals is to recognise emerging evidence of parental alienation and act appropriately in response to it.

This chapter provides an overview of how systems such as courts, education systems and professionals can facilitate parental alienation. How systems and professionals can be manipulated by alienating parents is considered.

The legal system as an outside force

Time is of the essence

The essence of parental alienation is one parent determined to prevent the other parent from having an involved relationship with their child. For this reason, parenting disputes characterised by parental alienation are rarely resolved quickly and easily. The legal system has been described as often slow and ineffective in addressing parental alienation (1).

In Australia, anyone applying for resolution of their case through the family court system must attempt family dispute resolution (FDR). FDR involves bringing parents together to discuss their differences to provide them with an opportunity to resolve their dispute themselves with the assistance of a family dispute resolution practitioner. If the matter cannot be resolved through FDR, the family dispute resolution practitioner can issue what is known as a section 60I certificate (2).

Section 60I of the *Family Law Act, 1975* legislates for FDR to occur before an application can be submitted to the court and defines the reasons family dispute resolution practitioners can issue a certificate to allow an application to proceed. There are five types of section 60I certificates a dispute resolution practitioner can issue: (a) The person did not attend FDR because they refused or failed to attend; (b) The person did not attend FDR because the practitioner considered the matter inappropriate for FDR, such as in cases of reports of family violence; (c) All parties involved attended FDR, all parties made a genuine effort to resolve their dispute, but the dispute remains unresolved; (d) All parties attended FDR, but one or more of them did not make a genuine effort to resolve the dispute; and (e) All parties began FDR, but the practitioner came to realise the matter was inappropriate for FDR during the course of FDR. Family dispute resolution practitioners must consider issues such as the safety of the parties involved, reported histories of family violence, child abuse and issues associated with coercive power and control that could affect a party from freely engaging in the process. The number of section 60I certificates being issued is increasing and the most common type of certificate being issued is the 'inappropriate for FDR' type (3).

There is little research examining the efficacy of FDR and there is no research into its capacity to change the course of cases of parental alienation. When the nature of the alienating parent's behaviour is considered, it is reasonable to assume that FDR is unlikely to offer a resolution for moderate to severe cases of parental alienation. This is because the goals of FDR are likely to be counter to the alienating parent's goals and motivations. Additionally, an alienating parent using false allegations of abuse as an alienating tactic will likely trigger an 'inappropriate for FDR' section 60I certificate.

Once an application to the Family Law Court has been made, the length of time from application to final hearing varies depending on the nature of the application and the number of applications before the court at that time. The longest known case in the Family Law Court of Australia took approximately ten years before a final determination was made. This case is available for viewing on the Australasian Legal Information Institute (AustLII) database, and their names were changed in the judgement; however, the name of the case will not be identified here in order to further protect the anonymity of the family involved.

In this case, parental alienation was considered as a possible reason for the ongoing parenting dispute and behaviours typically associated with parental alienation were identified. Specifically, the mother made allegations of child sexual abuse against the children's father. The allegations could not be substantiated, and it was determined that the father posed no particular risk of harm to the children. In addition, it was determined that the children's perception of their father had been negatively influenced by their mother. In 2014, it was ordered that the children should remain in the primary care of the mother because a change of primary care may be confusing and stressful for the children. In the final judgment in 2017, it was determined that the children remain in the primary care of the mother because they had adjusted to life without their father and remaining in the care of their mother was consistent with the children's wishes.

This case exemplifies the length of time complex family law matters involving possible parental alienation can take to come to a resolution. In this case, time and court orders sealed the fate of the children and their relationship with their father. The court sanctioned the removal of a parent from the lives of the children when that parent posed no risk of harm to the children. This case was also complicated by the involvement of many single expert witnesses, with very little consensus among these experts as to the exact nature of the problem.

Time is of the essence in cases of parental alienation. These cases need to be identified earlier than is currently the case. Once identified, the alienated family needs to be case managed in a coordinated way. Clear and concrete orders should be made quickly, and the judiciary must follow up on orders and sanction non-compliance (4–6). This also means providing some judicial oversight after final orders have been made to ensure long-term compliance. Of course, the ramifications of this additional workload on an already over-burdened system are recognised.

Family court consultants and single expert witnesses

Family Court consultants are psychologists or social workers who specialise in assessing child and family issues after separation and divorce. The role of a Family Court consultant is defined by the *Family Law Act, 1975*. Their role involves assessing families involved in parenting dispute proceedings to assist and advise the court in relation to these proceedings. They do this by way of conducting an assessment of the family and providing the court with a report of their findings and recommendations. The evidence provided by a family consultant is considered expert evidence. Other expert witnesses in family law proceedings, for example, can include psychologists, social workers, psychiatrists and medical specialists. Expert witnesses may be appointed by an order of the court or directly engaged by the parties to the case. The evidence given by Family Court consultants and single expert witnesses may or may not be relied up by the judge when making their determination.

By the time a family is ordered to participate in an interview process allowing an expert to formulate an opinion, the issues these families face are typically quite complex. The challenge of single experts is to disentangle and make sense of the complex family dynamics and dysfunction occurring in the family system. When a parent and a child are engaging in alienating behaviours, the expert's capacity to accurately identify this is compounded by a lack of psychometrically sound assessment procedures for parental alienation as well as prevailing biases and ideologies that can blinker an expert to the existence of parental alienation dynamics in a family (7).

Undoubtedly, court-appointed experts take their role seriously and conduct their assessments with non-malfeasance at the core of what they do. In parental alienation matters, court-appointed experts can fall into a trap of misinterpreting a child's reasons for rejecting a parent because missed opportunities for hypothesis testing during interview and biases can prevent objective evidence-based decision-making (7).

Common mistakes seen in expert opinion in cases of parental alienation include:

- Focusing on the targeted parent's flaws and giving insufficient weight to the ways alienating parents contribute to the problem.
- Failing to examine alternative explanations for the child's rejection and negative view of the targeted parent.
- Using a single ideology of family violence to guide assessment and decision-making
- Being influenced by gender biases and stereotypes.
- Relying on the alienating parent's accusations about the targeted parent as a reference point for the assessment and decision-making.
- Conflating the best interests of the child with their expressed wishes.

These mistakes lead to selectively attending to information that confirms initial impressions about the family (7–8). Expert witnesses need to be aware of the influence of confirmation bias and actively protect against it. This will be discussed further in Chapter Sixteen.

What can be done?

Expert witnesses must avoid making assumptions about a child's reasons for rejecting a parent. Experts need to remain impartial and observant to all factors that could contribute to this (9–10). Begin with a null-hypothesis and test alternative hypotheses as evidence emerges.

The outcomes of assessments conducted by court-appointed expert witnesses have serious ramifications for the individuals they assess. Any single expert cognisant of the weight of their work on children's lives would be highly motivated to engage in strategies that minimise the undue influence of biases and assumptions on their work. Participation in continual professional development and education programmes is one obvious way of addressing this problem (9–10). Single experts should become knowledgeable in contemporary understanding of parental alienation and current scientific literature in this area. Cross-disciplinary collaboration and training exposes single experts to alternative opinions, practices and perspectives (11). Such collaborations can also ensure alienated families receive the thorough assessment they deserve. For example, social workers, psychologists and psychiatrists should work together to ensure thorough assessment of the family system, risk assessment and diagnostic mental health assessment.

The role of education systems

Parental alienation in schools

It is common for alienated children to develop school-related problems. Alienated children can experience fluctuations in school performance, disruptive behaviour and social withdrawal (12). Truancy is common because alienated children are unable to attend to the demands of school while they are in the midst of family turmoil. Furthermore, some alienating parents prioritise their own needs over their children's educational needs and fail to ensure regular school attendance.

> **Box 10.1 Formerly alienated child:** Now I'm with Dad I go to school every day. It's not a choice. He expects me to be up at 7 o'clock, showered, dressed. He makes me breakfast and then he takes me to school. When I was with Mum, I went to school when she didn't need me. I had to stay at home to look after my younger brothers and sisters. I got sick of being the weird kid at school who was hardly ever there, and I was sick of being so behind. Mum always made sure I missed school when it was Dad's turn to have me. She also told the school that Dad was a bad and violent man to try and stop him from going there. It's much better now I live with Dad. I go to school like normal kids and the teachers don't believe Mum anymore. I feel like a normal kid again.

In this scenario, the alienated child was a 12-year-old boy whose mother tried to alienate him from his father. The boy's mother kept him at home on school days because she prioritised her needs over her son's need for an education. She also used school to perpetuate her distorted view of the boy's father and attempted to damage the relationship between the school and the targeted parent. In the end, this boy could no longer cope with the emotional turmoil created by his mother. After intervention to reunify father and son, the boy decided to live with his father full-time. The boy's mother rejected him for making this choice.

Alienating parents not only manipulate their child, they also manipulate school teachers, principals and other school personnel. Alienating parents will ask school staff to limit their contact with the targeted parent. They will refrain from providing the school with the targeted parent's contact details, list a step-parent as a contact instead of the targeted parent and refrain from providing the targeted parent with information from the school (13).

Alienating parents will make allegations of wrongdoing about the targeted parent to school staff. Just as they manipulate their children into believing the other parent is dangerous in some way, they can convince school staff of the same. Alienating parents will use the process of triangulation and other manipulative techniques to elicit school staff to be cautious of the targeted parent and to become hostile towards them. When this occurs, the outcome is the breakdown of communication between the targeted parent and school staff. The alienated child sees school staff behaving in a cautious or hostile way towards the targeted parent, and this perpetuates the lies and reinforces belief in the lies. Consequently, the alienating parent's control over the child and targeted parent is strengthened.

What can be done?

Staff in educational settings need to become aware of parental alienation and the ways in which alienating parents and alienated children can present in the school setting. It is not in the child's best interest for a teacher or any school staff to become hostile towards a child's parent solely on the basis of one parent's descriptions of that parent. Unless a court order prohibits a parent from engaging with their child's school, schools should ensure they know the names and contact details of both parents. They should ensure both parents are kept informed of school matters pertaining to their child and their child's progress in school. Both parents should receive school newsletters and invitations to parent–teacher information sessions. School staff need to avoid becoming personally involved in a family's problems and set clear professional boundaries to avoid being caught in a game of triangulation.

Child protection services

Being seduced by the story or evidence-based opinion

Child protection services are vitally important for ensuring children are kept safe from abusive and neglectful parents. In Australia, child protection services are the responsibility of state and territory governments and, therefore, are subject to legislative differences. This is different from the Family Law Court of Australia, which is governed by federal law. What this means is the legal obligations of child protection workers, the practices of child protection workers and legal mandates for reporting child abuse differ from state to state. Nonetheless, the central function of all child protection services is to intervene when a child is being abused or neglected by a parent or legal guardian.

As a result of the role child protection services play in society, they are an obvious service for alienating parents to use as an outside force. Alienating parents can make reports to child protection services about the targeted parent. They can try to use child protection services as a means of obtaining legitimacy for their beliefs that the targeted parent poses a risk of harm to the child and as a means of stopping the child from spending time with the targeted parent. Therefore, alienating parents can involve child protection services in a process of triangulation just as they do with other services and systems.

The challenge for child protection workers is to distinguish an alienating parent from a protective parent. This is not an easy task in the absence of psychometrically sound assessment techniques for doing this. However, there are interviewing strategies that should be used and others that should be avoided when assessing allegations of child abuse from a parent, particularly when they occur during the course of parenting dispute proceedings.

The judge in the lengthy parenting dispute case referred to earlier in this chapter was particularly critical of the manner in which child protection services responded to the mother's allegations of child abuse against the father. The judge was critical of the manner in which the child protection workers interviewed the child, highlighting the use of leading, suggestive and repetitive style of questioning that was only going to result in one outcome – the child disclosing being the victim of an abusive act perpetrated by the father regardless of whether or not that act happened. The actions of the child protection workers were found to be sufficiently harmful in this case that an injunction was successfully sought to prevent these workers from having further involvement with the family.

When distinguishing between reports of abuse from an alienating parent from those of a protective parent, child protection workers need to ensure they follow a standard interviewing protocol that encourages children to provide a free narrative of events without the use of leading and suggestive questions. Children should not be verbally or non-verbally rewarded for giving answers that support any allegation (14).

When child protection services is the alienator

Unfortunately, in their efforts to keep children safe, there are times when some child protection workers can alienate children from a parent who no longer poses or never did pose a risk of harm to their children. This is a form of parental alienation perpetrated and sanctioned by the state. Research exploring this form of parental alienation has shown that child protective services can place many unnecessary barriers to reunification (15–16).

Research has demonstrated that child protection services, at times, have failed to define for parents the criteria used to label them 'unfit' and continually changed the rules and standards parents need to meet in order to see their children (15–16). Some child protection workers failed to form a working relationship with parents and then used the poor relationship as evidence for supporting no contact. These parents felt excluded and powerless to help their children (17–18). Parents reported that child protection workers focused on their weaknesses and ignored their capacity to care for their children (16). None of the parents who participated in this research had been convicted of any crime and were deeply disturbed about the way in which they and their children were being treated.

What can be done?

Child protection workers need to ensure their assessment and intervention procedures are free from biases and stereotypes. Child protection workers need to ensure they interview the parent making the allegations, the child at the center of the allegations and the parent who is the subject of the allegations. Effort should be made to collect collateral evidence that can assist with hypothesis testing. Child protection workers need to be knowledgeable of the patterns of behaviour seen in parental alienation. They should become knowledgeable in contemporary understandings of parental alienation and current scientific literature in this area. To ignore the existence of parental alienation is to become complicit in an insidious form of abuse. This constitutes state sanctioned parental alienation.

Concluding comments

Alienating parents determined to obtain legitimacy for their opinion of the alienating parent and motivated to sever the relationship between the alienated child and targeted parent will seek support from sympathetic services and systems. They will exploit the very nature of these services and systems to maintain control over the alienated child and targeted parent. The challenge faced by professionals working within these systems and services is to avoid being drawn into the distorted world of the alienated parent. It is recommended here that all professionals working with children and families become knowledgeable about parental alienation and the manipulative behaviours of alienating parents. To be forewarned is to be forearmed. When state and federal systems and services fail to recognise parental alienation, they are engaging in legally sanctioned abuse and normalising the experience of growing up without a loving parent.

References

1. Poustie, C., Matthewson, M., & Balmer, S. (2018). The forgotten parent: The targeted parent perspective of parental alienation. *Journal of Family Issues, 39,* 3298–3323. doi:10.1177/0192513x18777867
2. *Family Law Act, 1975* (Cth). Retrieved from *www5.austlii.edu.au/au/legis/cth/consol_act/fla1975114/*
3. Smyth, B., Bonython, W., Rodgers, B., Keogh, E., Chisholm, R., Butler, R., Parker, R., Stubbs, M., Temple, J., & Vnuk, M. (2017). *Certifying mediation: A study of section 601 certificates.* Canberra: ANU Centre for Social Research and Methods.
4. Bala, N., Hunt, S., & McCarney, C. (2010). Parental alienation: Canadian court cases 1989 2008. *Family Court Review, 48,* 164–179. doi:10.1111/j.1744-1617.2009.01296.x
5. Martinson, D.J. (2010). One case–one specialized judge: Why courts have an obligation to manage alienation and other high conflict cases. *Family Court Review, 48,* 180–189. doi:10.1111/j.1744-1617.2009.01297.x
6. Templer, K., Matthewson, M., Haines, J., & Cox, G. (2017). Recommendations for best practice in response to parental alienation: Findings from a systematic review. *Journal of Family Therapy, 39,* 103–122. doi:10.1111/1467–6427.12137
7. Warshak, R.A. (2015). Ten parental alienation fallacies that compromise decisions in court and in therapy. *Professional Psychology: Research and Practice, 46,* 235–249. doi:10.1037/pro000003
8. Martindale, D.A. (2005). Confirmatory bias and confirmatory distortion. *Journal of Child Custody, 2,* 31–48. doi:10.1300/j190v02n01_03
9. Fidler, B.J., & Bala, N. (2010). Children resisting postseparation contact with a parent: Concepts, controversies, and conundrums. *Family Court Review, 48,* 10–47. doi:10.1111/j.1744-1617.2009.01287.x
10. Warshak, R.A. (2003). Payoffs and pitfalls of listening to children. *Family Relations, 52,* 373–384. doi:10.1111/j.1741-3729.2003.00373.x
11. Beck, C.J.A., Holtzworth-Munroe, A., D'Onofrio, B.M., Fee, W.C., & Hill, F.G. (2009). Collaboration between judges and social science researchers in family law. *Family Court Review, 47,* 451–467. doi:10.1111/j.1744-1617.2009.01267.x
12. Clawar, S.S., & Rivlin, B.V. (2013). *Children held hostage: Identifying brainwashed children, presenting a case, and crafting solutions.* Chicago, IL: American Bar Association.
13. Baker, A.J.L., & Darnall, D. (2006). Behaviors and strategies employed in parental alienation: A survey of parental experiences. *Journal of Divorce and Remarriage, 45,* 97–124. doi:10.1300/J087v45n01_06
14. Bernet, W. (2006). Sexual abuse allegations in the context of child custody disputes. In R. Gardner, R. Sauber, & D. Lorandos (Eds.), *The international handbook of parental alienation syndrome: Conceptual, clinical and legal considerations* (pp. 242–263). Illinois: Charles C Thomas.
15. Harris, N. (2008). Family group conferencing in Australia 15 years on. *Child Abuse Prevention Issues, 27,* 1–19.
16. Healy, Y., Darlington, K., & Feeney, J.A. (2011). Challenges in implementing participatory practice in child protection: A contingency approach. *Children and Youth Services Review, 32,* 1020–1027. doi:10.1016/j.childyouth.2010.03.030
17. Kapp, S.A., & Propp, J. (2002). Client satisfaction methods: Input from parents with children in foster care. *Child and Adolescent Social Work Journal, 19,* 227–245. doi:10.1023/a:1015580015223
18. Thorpe, R. (2007). Family inclusion in child protection practice: Building bridges in working with (not against) families. *Communities, Families and Children, 3,* 4–1.

Part Three

Assessment of parental alienation

Chapter Eleven

Assessing alienating parents

Introduction

Despite the interest in parental alienation and the potentially life-changing influence it can have on alienated family members, surprisingly little attention has been given to assessment. Methods for determining the presence of strategies that define parental alienation have not received the research attention that would be expected given the issues about the validity of the concept that have plagued the examination of parental alienation. As a result, few standardised assessment processes for parental alienation exist. Indeed, the complex nature of parental alienation leads some to suggest that it is not possible to assess for the presence of parental alienation using a psychological questionnaire designed for this purpose although others disagree (1).

Nevertheless, some assessment instruments have been developed to meet the needs of specific research approaches (2). However, the target of these questionnaires often are adults who experienced parental alienation during their childhood; they do not assist the clinician wanting to establish support for suspected cases of currently occurring parental alienation.

Other assessment attempts have compared groups with and without the experience of parental alienation (3–4). However, in the absence of any valid method of identifying the presence of parental alienation, the soundness of group allocation is limited. It is not wise to allocate participants to a group on the basis of one's belief that they belong in that group and then identify the variables that distinguish the groups and use these results as evidence of the presence of the phenomenon you used as the basis of the group allocation in the first place. Do you see the problem?

To explain further, you might believe a child has been exposed to a parental alienation process and allocate them to a group of alienated children. You might then compare the experiences of these children with those you believe were not alienated. You may even choose to interpret the results as definitive statements about the experience of parental alienation. However, if you cannot be sure that the parental alienation group members have been exposed to parental alienation, then the house of cards collapses.

Further, this approach examines differences between groups. However, it is not really possible to apply the results of this type of research directly to single cases of parental alienation (or any other variable you are examining). This is because it is unlikely that any single case of parental alienation would demonstrate all the characteristics of parental alienation you could identify. So, you then have to consider whether your single case fits with the parental alienation group you have identified or whether the single case is different enough to make you uncertain about whether or not you can say that parental alienation has occurred.

Of course, as a starting point for the development of an assessment instrument a group differences approach is a useful strategy. However, if the allocation of participants to groups is not based on something other than professional opinion, then the end result is rightly open to question. After all, as good as clinical opinions may be, they are open to biases that influence decision-making.

This problem could be overcome if there was some definitive means of determining the presence of parental alienation. For example, we can identify the characteristics of children with obsessive-compulsive disorder and research the factors that are associated with the disorder because the diagnostic criteria for obsessive-compulsive disorder have been established. You can, with considerable accuracy, diagnose the condition and, therefore, group allocation is sound. However, this is not the case with parental alienation.

So, what do we do? Do we just abandon the whole notion of parental alienation because it is too hard to determine if it has taken place or is taking place? Of course not. Researchers in psychology have more backbone than that. We do accept the limitations that we currently face and work at clarifying the issue so that we can have confidence in our understanding of a particular phenomenon.

So, we need to consider what is available to use at present. We also need to consider what else we need to know to be able to gain that confidence. This process will direct future research and adequately focus research attention.

What do we know so far? Let us consider this from the point of view of alienating parents, targeted parents and alienated children. The purpose of this chapter, considering ways to identify alienating parents, focuses on those aspects of a parent's behaviour that are characteristic of parental alienation. It is not the intention here to cover what would normally be addressed in an evaluation of a parent's functioning in a parental dispute, such as parenting capacity.

Identifying alienating parents

It is important to be able to properly identify parental alienation. This is particularly the case when consideration is given to circumstances that are likely to give rise to parental alienation, that is parenting disputes, and the trap of triangulation.

You need to consider that most of the cases of parental alienation take place in the context of parenting order disputes. This is not always the case, but most of the examples of parental alienation have to be understood within the demands of a legal system. It is the case that alienating parents can be pressured to undertake therapy because the courts insist that the problem of parental alienation be addressed before parenting decisions are made.

The issues associated with parental alienation increase the likelihood that you will be drawn into a situation where one parent is trying to gain your support for their case so that your support can be used as evidence that they are the superior parent and there is a problem with the other parent. The information you receive from the alienating parent is distorted by the views held by that parent and the tactics used as part of the alienation process. Without conducting an adequate assessment, you may find yourself supporting a situation that, fundamentally, is detrimental to the child you are intending to help.

The assessment of parental alienation is approached in at least two ways. Firstly, consideration is given to the tactics being used by the alienating parents. Secondly, examination is made of the ways in which the child presents. You may also give reference to the presentation of the targeted parent although their identifying behaviours more often tend to be reactions to the alienation process rather than contributors to this process. In this chapter, we will examine the alienating tactics used by alienating parents and how these tactics might be identified.

Tactics of alienating parents

It is evident from information provided by adults who were exposed to parental alienation tactics by one parent when they were children that parental alienation is a diverse construct (2). A range of tactics used by alienating parents has been identified. Although there is overlap with regard to these tactics, researchers have identified a variety of specific behaviours that constitute the strategies used by alienating parents to change the relationship between their child and the child's other parent. These alienating tactics are used by the alienating parents to alter or terminate the relationship between the child and the targeted parent.

Tactics associated with the targeted parent

The strategies used by alienating parents may be directly focused on the targeted parent. These tactics provide a good measure of the animosity felt by the alienating parent towards the targeted parent. When identifying the presence of these strategies, you are looking for the way in which the alienating parent responds to the targeted parent or how they react to discussions about the targeted parent.

Denigration of the targeted parent

Outside of the context of parental alienation, denigration of one's partner or former partner can occur. There is evidence to suggest that denigrating comments made by one parent tend to be reciprocated by the other, with the child being exposed to both parents saying detrimental things about the other parent. Further, there is a tendency for each parent to under-report their own denigrating comments and over-report the denigration by the other parent (5). In the context of parental conflict in the absence of parental alienation, exposure to the denigrating comments made by parents about each other damages both parents' relationships with their child (5).

Denigration in the context of parental alienation is known to occur. In particular, alienating parents make denigrating comments about the targeted parent (6–7). Even if they are interspersed with more general comments that grudgingly support a particular behaviour (e.g., "I suppose he always packs her lunch for school", "She wants to be a good mother"), there is a predominant theme of denigration. This relates to the way the targeted parent is talked about and the views held about him or her by the alienating parent.

Denigration can be evident in how the alienating parent labels the targeted parent or in the way their views about the targeted parent, their actions and achievements are expressed. You will notice the denigrating comments appearing in conversations with the alienating parent even when this parent is denying animosity towards the targeted parent or when they claim that they support the relationship between the targeted parent and the child.

Consider the following examples. Some alienating parents will refer to the targeted parent using a pejorative label (8). Notice in this first example how the alienating parent refers to the targeted parent. Bear in mind that the way this parent is talking about the other parent occurred in the context of an interview when the alienating parent was trying to defend herself against an assertion that she was alienating her children from their father.

> **Box 11.1 Interviewer:** Concern has been raised that you might be having an influence on the children's reluctance to spend time with their father.
> **Alienating parent:** That's rubbish. I don't stop them seeing Idiot. They make up their own minds about whether they go and see Idiot. I don't have to tell them what Idiot is like, they already know. The man is a fool. He can't do anything right.

Here you can see that the alienating parent is quite blatant in her denigration. Based on an actual interview, the use of the term 'idiot' when referring to the targeted parent during an interview when the alienating parent was trying to deny alienating the children indicates how little control this parent had over the animosity she felt towards the targeted parent. This parent cannot moderate the denigrating tone of her discussion of the targeted parent despite it probably being in her interest to do so.

Some alienating parents simply refuse to use the targeted parent's name. Although not as obvious as labelling a person an 'idiot', it is evident when interviewing parents at length that some alienating parents never refer to the other parent by name. Even when you challenge their tendency to do this, they will continue to refuse to use the person's given name.

> **Box 11.2 Alienating parent:** He tried to take out a restraining order.
> **Interviewer:** Who did?
> **Alienating parent:** He did.
> **Interviewer:** I'm sorry, who do you mean?
> **Alienating parent:** Him. He tried to take out a restraining order.
> **Interviewer:** Are you referring to John?
> **Alienating parent:** [Silence]
> **Interviewer:** I'm just trying to clarify who you are talking about. Do you mean the children's father?
> **Alienating parent:** Their father tried to take out a restraining order.

You can notice here that the alienating parent both refuses to use the targeted parent's name and refuses to respond to questions when his name is used. She is able to refer to him as the children's father. Whole conversations can take place where an alienating parent refuses to use the targeted person's name. Indeed, this refusal can extend to any context. As a result, the children never get to hear one of their parents refer to their other parent by name. The children are then likely to form the opinion that the targeted parent is unworthy of respect.

Let us consider another example. Here the alienating parent sets out to make her views about the targeted parent clear by pointing out his faults. Although it is likely that this person would deny alienating the children from their father, notice how it is apparent that the alienating parent has not shielded the children from her views about their father.

> **Box 11.3 Interviewer:** The children told me they can't rely on their father, but I couldn't really get a clear idea of why they hold this view.
> **Alienating parent:** They have figured it out for themselves. Of course, I don't hide it from the kids, either. They know what their father is like. He tries, I suppose, but he can't seem to do anything properly. The children can't even rely on him to pick them up from school on

time. That day he was late, I had to explain to the kids that their father just can't be relied on. They know that now. It's not my fault he can't do what he needs to do to look after the kids. That's his fault.

Although perhaps not as blatantly denigrating as calling the targeted parent 'Idiot', the end result is the same. The children are exposed to denigrating comments about the targeted parent's capacity as a parent. The underlying message is that the targeted parent is incompetent and unreliable, and this message has been integrated into the children's view of the targeted parent.

Of course, not all denigrating comments are overtly stated. It may be the case that the denigration is implied in what is said by the alienating parent. Consider the following example.

> **Box 11.4 Alienating parent:** You can't blame her for not knowing how to raise the children. Look at her own childhood. Her own parents were terrible at parenting. So, it's no wonder she never learned how to be a good parent. She is just replaying what she learned. My own parents sacrificed everything for me and my brothers. They set a good example. But the way she parents was set in stone even before she had kids. It's not really her fault. But it's not the kids' fault either. I don't think they have to suffer because of their mother's childhood experiences.

In a way, this alienating father is making it clear that he holds the targeted mother in low regard despite making a suggestion that he is somewhat sympathetic about the targeted mother's circumstance. However, the sympathetic overtone is barely covering the underlying denigration. Of course, the end result is the same. The view is formed that the targeted parent is deficient whether the denigration is direct or implied.

When challenged during an interview, you will find that it is difficult for alienating parents to accept any positive statement you present about the targeted parent. Presenting evidence that supports the positive statement being made about the targeted parent will not make them any less reluctant to acknowledge a positive attribute in the targeted parent. It seems that the animosity that drives the alienating parent's denigration of the targeted parent is not amenable to change through rational discourse.

> **Box 11.5 Interviewer:** The children's father seems to be doing much better.
> **Alienating parent:** [Humpf]
> **Interviewer:** His drug tests have been clear for over 18 months and he has taken positive steps to live a more settled life.
> **Alienating parent:** He has you bluffed.
> **Interviewer:** Well, I am relying on objective signs of his improvement.
> **Alienating parent:** He's fooling everyone.
> **Interviewer:** If it can be shown that John is doing better, do you consider that to be a good thing for the children?
> **Alienating parent:** No, because I don't believe it and I won't ever believe it. Anyway, even if it's true, why would he change things for the better only after we split up? All the problems I had to put up with throughout the time we were together and then, suddenly, I'm supposed to believe things have improved. If things were going to improve, why wouldn't it have happened when we were together as a family. He is who he is, and he will always be that way. With all due respect, if you believe otherwise then you are being fooled by him.

It could be argued that it is this parent's experience with her former partner that has made her pessimistic about the likelihood of positive change. That may be the case. However, it is the rejection of the objective indicators of improved behaviour and the reluctance to acknowledge they have meaning that can be interpreted as indicating rigidity of thinking that comes with the drive to denigrate a targeted parent. This parent is expressing the view that the targeted parent's behaviour is as problematic as it always has been and will never change.

Alienating parents also will demonstrate difficulty in admitting that the targeted parent is capable of adequately caring for the child or children. This is especially the case when the parenting styles of the alienating parent and the targeted parent differ. However, the rejection of the targeted parent's capacity to adequately care for the child is not only limited to situations where the way the parents care for the child is in conflict. It can occur even in cases where there is fundamental agreement about parenting practices.

Box 11.6 Alienating parent: I'm worried that Bella doesn't get to have any lunch at school after staying overnight with her father.

Interviewer: Why is that? I understand from Bella's teacher that her father packs her a good lunch.

Alienating parent: I don't think that's true. I know she doesn't like the lunches he packs. Her teacher says she eats her lunch, but she doesn't.

Interviewer: How do you know she doesn't eat her lunch?

Alienating parent: I know. I know what she likes and doesn't like.

Interviewer: So, what do you consider to be wrong with the lunch her father packs for her?

Alienating parent: Well, he cuts her sandwiches in triangles and she prefers them to be cut in squares. Also, he puts bananas in her lunch box that have those dark marks on the skin.

Interviewer: Apart from the shape of the sandwiches and the fact that he has included a ripe banana in her lunch, is the actual content of her lunch similar to what you would provide for Bella?

Alienating parent: Well, yes … but the lunch I give her has the things she likes. This is just an example of how her father doesn't know her well enough to look after her properly. He never was a good parent. He just does what he wants and doesn't pay attention to what Bella wants. He's always been the same, so I don't know why I'm surprised.

Here the alienating parent has no real reason to speak negatively about the targeted parent. Even if he did not make school lunches for his daughter before the separation, he seems to be doing so now. In addition, it seems that, fundamentally, the targeted parent is providing a lunch that is similar to the lunch provided by the alienating parent, with the exception of the shape of the sandwiches. However, the alienating parent is rejecting of the father's efforts, is dismissive of his parenting capabilities and wishes to paint a picture of ongoing failure to meet their child's needs.

The denigration of the targeted parent reflects the low regard with which they are held by the alienating parent. The animosity they feel for the targeted parent drives them to make negative comments about the targeted parent, even in situations where it would serve their purpose to do otherwise, such as when they are trying to claim they do not denigrate the targeted parent. Even if interspersed with claims that they do not hold negative views about the targeted parent, many alienating parents cannot control the urge to make these denigrating comments.

Alienating parents tend to explain their denigrating comments as statements of truth or fact. They claim they are merely giving an account of the way things are or have been in the past. Their views cannot be shifted by offering alternative frames of reference or through logical challenge.

In advancing the goals of interfering with the targeted parent–child relationship, denigration of the targeted parent is influential in at least two ways. Firstly, denigrating comments in front of or to the child can influence the way the child sees the targeted parent. Secondly, making denigrating statements about the targeted parent may influence others to adopt negative views about the targeted parent, leading to the alienating parent having a larger support base for their views.

Vilification of the targeted parent

The vilification of the targeted parent is a tactic used by the alienating parent to advance the alienation process (6,9). This tactic is considered separately from denigration because of the seriousness of the allegations that are made about the targeted parent. The consequences of vilification can be severe. A child will refuse to spend time with a targeted parent because they have been encouraged to hold the view that the parent is a dangerous person (11). The threat the targeted parent is claimed to present is often to the child (e.g., sexual abuse of the child) but may be to the alienating parent (e.g., family violence) or others (e.g., sexual assault of other women, criminal behaviour).

This vilification can take the form of labelling the targeted parent as an abuser or suggesting that it may be the case that the targeted parent has abused the child or children. Blatant allegations of wrongdoing by the targeted parent can be made by the alienating parent in the absence of any evidence to support these allegations.

Box 11.7 Alienating parent: I can't let the children spend time with their father. He has sexually abused my daughter and I will not put her in the position where she will be abused again.

Interviewer: I am aware that the police and child protection conducted investigations, including interviewing your children, and could not substantiate the claims that have been made about their father sexually abusing your daughter. So, tell me about your ongoing concerns.

Alienating parent: I know he did it. He is a pervert and a paedophile. I know what sort of person he is, and I know what he is capable of doing to the children.

Interviewer: So, are you saying you are concerned that abuse has occurred, but you can't say what the indications are that it happened?

Alienating parent: I know he did it. I'm their mother. I know. Anyway, I know he takes my daughter into bed with him.

Interviewer: Except he denies that is the case and your daughter reported that she has never been in her father's bed with him.

Alienating parent: I don't care. I asked my daughter when her father had touched her on her private parts, and she said that happened when she stayed over at her father's house. I asked if that had happened in his bed and she said yes. So, I know it's true.

This parent is making a blatant allegation of sexual wrongdoing by the other parent. Her view is not swayed by the findings of various investigations or denial on the part of her daughter. Of course, it is possible that the child did agree with statements made by the alienating parent.

For example, the alienating parent reported using the types of leading questions that confound the investigation of sexual abuse allegations. The answers she may have received from the child would have supported her pre-formed opinion that the child's father had done something wrong. She formulated the questions to support her opinion, so it was not surprising her opinion was supported.

In addition to blatant statements alleging wrongdoing by the targeted parent, alienating parents may make statements that seem to allege wrongdoing without directly accusing the targeted parent. The suggestion that it is possible the targeted parent has acted in an abusive manner can be difficult for the targeted parent who is not in a position to be able to defend themselves against innuendo.

Box 11.8 **Interviewer:** Jenny seems to have a very negative view of her father.

Alienating parent: What do you expect? She knows he is the most untrustworthy person ever born. I think he's dangerous. He could do anything to hurt Jenny so why shouldn't she be scared of him. I warned her to be careful. It's my job as a mother to protect my child, so it's no good pretending to her that everything is ok. What if he hurts her?

Interviewer: I haven't seen any information suggesting that he has physically hurt Jenny.

Alienating parent: So what? She knows he might hurt her and then it will be too late.

The alienating parent has indicated that the targeted parent is a dangerous person who intends to harm the child. Even without any experience of wrongdoing on the part of the targeted parent, the targeted parent comes to be viewed as potentially dangerous by the alienated child. An unspecified allegation of wrongdoing can be as damaging to the targeted parent–child relationship as a specific allegation because it creates anxiety in the child.

Box 11.9 **Interviewer:** Jenny talks about her father as if he has a history of bad or criminal behaviour, but I have seen his police record and read the various documents and can find no indication that this might be the case.

Alienating parent: Jenny and I have talked about this. Even if he's never been caught, I wonder sometimes if he has done terrible things.

Interviewer: What sort of terrible things?

Alienating parent: Well, it's not for me to say. But I can tell you, I know the sorts of people he hangs around with. They're the sort of people who don't think twice about breaking the law.

Here the alienating parent is implying that the targeted parent is a bad person. There is no burden of proof for the alienating parent. She only needs to say that she has concerns for the views of the child to be influenced.

Parental alienation also has been reported to be related to high rates of false claims of abuse by the alienating parent, including sexual abuse (6). Although it is vital that true cases of sexual abuse are managed in the appropriate way that protects the child, it is also important to identify and appropriately respond to knowingly false accusations of child sexual abuse (11). It has been suggested that making false claims of sexual abuse by the alienating parent against the targeted parent is the most severe parental alienation tactic. Also, in the absence of blatant accusations of abuse, the alienating parent may allude to indicators or suggestions of abuse with the aim of undermining the targeted parent's standing or credibility (9).

Box 11.10 Interviewer: I understand you are concerned that Mr Smith may have sexually abused Bethany. I read that this has been investigated by the child protection services and the police with no support for this being found. What are your concerns?

Alienating parent: I don't really know if he has done anything or not, but I wouldn't put it past him. And there have been some things he's done that disturb me. He likes to have Bethany sit on his lap and I don't like that. He also lets her get into bed with him when she wakes up in the morning. I just don't trust him. I told Bethany to be careful.

Here the alienating parent is taking normal events (e.g., a young child sitting on her father's lap) and making the suggestion that the targeted parent's motive is abuse of the child. The child then becomes concerned about normal loving parental behaviours and withdraws from the targeted parent. This withdrawal can be used by alienating parents as 'evidence' of wrongdoing.

Box 11.11 Alienating parent: Jenna doesn't want to go near her father. She is reluctant to be around him and won't give him a hug. She freaks out if her father tries to give her a hug and a kiss on the cheek.

Interviewer: Is it possible, though, that Jenna is reacting to the things she has heard said about her father rather than reacting to things he has actually done?

Alienating parent: If she reacts that strongly, something must be wrong. Everybody knows that if a child reacts like that to a parent something must be wrong. I'm her mother. Even if no-one else pays attention, it's my job to do the best for her. And the best thing I can do is protect her from her pervert father.

This parent fails to see that she may have contributed to the fear response demonstrated by the child when she is around her father and the child's reluctance to experience physical contact with him. Instead, she is using the child's reaction as the 'evidence' she needs to 'prove' that the father has sexually abused his child. In her mind, her intention to prevent the father from spending time with the child can be justified.

Also, having others support the views of the alienating parent can lead to him or her feeling their actions of keeping the child from the targeted parent are warranted. Their support then can be used by the alienating parent as 'evidence' that the targeted parent is dangerous or abusive (e.g., "My friends and family don't trust him, and I trust their opinion").

The timing of the allegations of wrongdoing by the targeted parent should be considered. Often, it is the case that there is an increase in allegations at times when changes to parenting arrangements are imminent. For example, at a point when the time the targeted parent spends with the child is due to increase, an alienating parent may make allegations that the targeted parent has acted in a way that threatens the child.

> **Box 11.12 Targeted parent:** Every time things are supposed to progress, she accuses me of doing something else. When it was supposed to go from supervised time to unsupervised time, she claimed I had used drugs. Not true. I proved that in the end. I did drug tests and got a letter from my doctor and psychologist. But the whole thing was slowed down, and it was months before we moved to unsupervised time. Then when we moved to overnight time, she accused me of sexually abusing the children. I was investigated by the police and I didn't get to see the children for almost a year. In the end, it was shown that I hadn't done anything wrong, but it was really stressful to be accused of something so horrible. Now we are supposed to move to two nights, and she has claimed the children are scared of me because of my temper. How many times does she get to do this before someone stops her?

These allegations are timed to disrupt the progress of parenting order arrangements. Indeed, repeated allegations can drag out the process of resolving parenting matters for years. There are often extended periods of time when the targeted parent does not get to spend time with the child as allegations are investigated.

It seems that the purpose of the vilification of the targeted parent is to advance the alienation process and to turn the parenting dispute in the favour of the alienating parent. With allegations often made in the context of legal proceedings, vilifying comments are made to convince the decision-makers that the alienating parent is the preferred parent and the risk of placing the child with the targeted parent is too high.

It is worth noting that allegations of serious wrongdoing are often made at a point in legal proceedings when they are likely to influence the course of those proceedings. When considering the timing of the allegations, it is often the case that the allegations could have been made before that point in the legal proceedings when they were made. When questioned about their failure to report their concerns before that point in time, alienating parents state that they have only recently interpreted the targeted parents' behaviours as indicating wrongdoing. Alternatively, they tend to be dismissive of the question about the timing of the allegations and fail to adequately answer the question.

Interference with time spent with the targeted parent

In an effort to sabotage the relationship between the targeted parent and the alienated child, the alienating parent will put obstacles in the way of the targeted parent spending time with the alienated child. This goes beyond not encouraging the targeted parent–child relationship. Here we are referring to the deliberate refusal to facilitate the relationship by engaging in behaviours that interfere with that relationship (7,9,12).

This interference in the time the targeted parent can spend with their child can be achieved in a variety of ways. The alienating parent may simply put obstacles in the way of the child spending time with the other parent by numerous means. Consider this account by a targeted parent.

> **Box 11.13 Targeted parent:** It seems that three visits out of four there are problems. She says he can't come to see me because he has to visit his grandmother or because he has a cold or because he is tired after a busy week at school. Things like that. But, let's face it, he can visit her mother any time, not during his time with me. And she must know that I can look after him when he has a cold or when he's tired. These are not good enough reasons to cancel my son's time with me. This is part of her plan to stop him spending time with me.

The consistency with which there are problems that interfere with the targeted parent spending time with the child should raise suspicion that the interference is deliberate. It is also the case that alienating parents will use discipline or punishment as an excuse for failing to send the child to spend time with the targeted parent. That is, they will say that they stopped the child from spending time with the targeted parent because the child had misbehaved. Withdrawal of time with a parent should never be used as a form of punishment.

As another way of interfering with the time the targeted parent spends with the child, the alienating parent may schedule appointments for the child. All the appointments are probably important for the child to keep, such as dentist or counsellor, but it is unlikely that it is necessary that the appointments are made during the limited time the targeted parent has to spend with the child. An expression of displeasure by the targeted parent when this occurs is then used by the alienating parent as evidence the targeted parent is unconcerned about the wellbeing of the child.

Box 11.14 Interviewer: I understand there have been some issues about the organisation of time Jessica's father spends with her.

Alienating parent: Brett's been complaining about the fact that Jessica has to go to some appointments, like her doctor and dental appointments. He doesn't seem to care about her health. He would rather she miss the appointments just so he gets more time with her.

Interviewer: But, then, Brett only gets to spend limited time with Jessica. Is it possible to schedule these appointments at times other than during his midweek time with Jessica?

Alienating parent: No, why should I do that? Anyway, I'm not in charge of when appointments are available.

Interviewer: It does seem, though, that most weeks Jessica has an appointment on Wednesdays after school at the time when Jessica is scheduled to spend the afternoon and evening with her father.

Alienating parent: What is your point?

Interviewer: The point is that it is being claimed that you have been deliberately interfering with the time Jessica spends with her father.

Alienating parent: That's not true.

Interviewer: If that's the case, then you won't mind scheduling Jessica's appointments on days other than Wednesdays.

Alienating parent: As I said, I'm not in charge of when appointments are available, so I can't agree to scheduling her appointments on other days.

Alienating parents will entice children to engage in alternative activities that they offer instead of spending time with the targeted parent. When the child elects to engage in the alternative, offered activity, the alienating parent holds the child responsible for the disruption to the time the targeted parent gets to spend with the child. The alienating parent then will say they tried to convince the child to spend time with the targeted parent, but the child refused.

Box 11.15 Targeted parent: She does it all the time. She knows the scheduled times I get to see Michael, but she then arranges for him to play soccer during my time. She invites his friends over and then says that Michael can't come to see me. She has arranged visits from his cousins and weekend trips. There are just too many times this happens for me to believe she isn't deliberately doing this to cause a problem and stop Michael from coming to spend time with me. I am so frustrated. I can't blame Michael for wanting to do the things his mother arranges. She makes sure she offers him something better than I can offer him.

This is a good example of the alienating parent offering the child alternative activities that compete with the arranged time with the targeted parent. The child is put in the position of engaging in a desired activity or missing out and spending time with a parent whose relationship with the child has already been undermined by the alienation process.

The alienating parent also will interfere with the time the targeted parent spends with the child by insisting on contacting the child while the child is with the targeted parent. The alienating parent will insist on contacting the child in the morning and at the end of the day, as well as during the day. The child may be provided with the means for staying in touch with the alienating parent when the targeted parent objects to the interference and refuses to respond to the alienating parent's attempts to contact the child. In this way, a child will be given a phone so they can remain in touch with the alienating parent.

In addition, the alienating parent may interfere with the relationship between the targeted parent and the child by overseeing and directing the telephone contact the targeted parent is allowed to have with the child. The alienating parent will insist on the use of the speaker phone so that they can listen in on the conversation between the child and the targeted parent. Further, they will cut the time short by insisting the child attend to another activity so that the amount of time the targeted parent has to talk with their child on the telephone is reduced.

> **Box 11.16 Targeted parent:** I get so angry. I can't spend any time with the boys without her interfering. I am allowed to call the boys twice a week, but she always listens in. I can hear her in the background telling the boys what they can say and what they can't say. And then, when the boys are with me, she phones them non-stop. Some days she will call them 20 times. It's ridiculous. How am I supposed to have a relationship with them if she keeps interfering?

In its most extreme form, the alienating parent will simply fail to produce the child for scheduled time with the targeted parent. If the targeted parent is supposed to collect the child from school, the targeted parent may take the child from the school prior to the end of the school day or keep the child at home so the child is not present when the targeted parent turns up to collect the child.

> **Box 11.17 Targeted parent:** I turn up to the place where I'm supposed to pick up the boys and she just doesn't show up. When I try to call, her phone is turned off, so I don't know whether she is just running late or doesn't intend to show up at all. I spend ages just hoping she will turn up.

Although often clearly in breach of court orders, alienating parents may repeatedly fail to produce the child for scheduled time with the targeted parent. The reasons given for this failure may range from a misunderstanding about the arrangements to the parent's insistence that they are protecting the child from harm by not exposing the child to the targeted parent's abuse or maltreatment.

With the goal of parental alienation being the termination of the targeted parent–alienated child relationship, the less time the child spends with the targeted parent the greater the chances are of this being achieved. If the attachment relationship between a parent and a child, in part, is determined by continuity of time spent together, any disruption to this will undermine the parent–child relationship.

Eradication of the targeted parent from the child's life

Alienating parents take action to eradicate the targeted parent from the child's life (6–7). With the alienating parent having no further need for the targeted parent and no desire to have the targeted parent in his or her life, the alienating parent chooses the same thing for their child.

This process of eradication can take the form of the alienating parent engaging in actions that prevent communication between the targeted parent and the child. For example, the alienating parent may not pass on cards or messages meant for the child or fail to give the child gifts offered by the targeted parent.

> **Box 11.18 Targeted parent:** I don't know what to do. The cards and gifts I send aren't getting through to Ben. I stopped sending them because a friend said they were just being thrown away by his mother. When I did see Ben, he didn't seem to know anything about the games I sent him for his birthday. He just shrugged it off. It's like he doesn't believe I sent them or doesn't care.

The view that the targeted parent does not care is an obvious one for the child to reach if many of the normal indicators of care and concern are absent. However, the eradication also may be more symbolic in nature. For example, the alienating parent may refuse to mention the targeted parent's name or, indeed, refuse to mention the parent at all. Alternatively, the alienating parent may encourage the child to refer to the targeted parent by their given name, thus eroding their parental role (8).

> **Box 11.19 Interviewer:** I met your father and had a talk with him …
> **Alienated child:** You mean John?
> **Interviewer:** You call him John?
> **Alienated child:** That's his name. My Dad is Mum's new partner. I call him Dad.
> **Interviewer:** You used to call your father 'Dad'.
> **Alienated child:** He doesn't deserve to be called Dad. Mum said Dad, my Mum's partner, Dad, has been more of a father to me in the last three months than John ever was. I reckon that's true. Dad is my father now. John isn't my father anymore. Mum said I should call her boyfriend Dad.

This is an example of the symbolic removal of the targeted parent from the child's life. We have found it is often the case that alienating parents will encourage or expect their children to identify their new partner as a replacement parent even within a few days of the start of the new relationship. The effect is to remove or diminish the targeted parent's importance for the child.

Commonly, alienating parents will prevent telephone contact from occurring by simply refusing to answer the telephone or turning off their phone so that the targeted parent's calls repeatedly go through to voicemail. Even when the contact is court ordered, the refusal to allow telephone contact causes the child to go for longer periods of time without connecting with the targeted parent.

Box 11.20   Targeted parent: And she won't let me have any telephone contact with him. I am allowed to phone every Wednesday and Sunday evening, but the phone is either not turned on or is never answered. I have tried calling from another phone but when she answers and realises it is me, she just pretends the phone connection has been cut off.

In an effort to eradicate the targeted parent from the child's life, alienating parents also may make it difficult for the targeted parent's extended family to spend time with the child. Relationships with grandparents, aunts, uncles and cousins are not encouraged by the alienating parent or obstacles are deliberately put in place to prevent such contact occurring.

Box 11.21   Targeted parent: The children haven't seen their grandparents, my parents, for over two years. Two years! It's not fair. Even if she is angry with me, she is only hurting the children by not letting them see their grandparents. And their aunts and uncles and cousins. My parents try to contact her to make arrangements to see the children but she either refuses to take their calls or she makes up excuses about why the children can't spend time with them. I doubt my youngest would even remember her grandparents. It's sad.

When not embedded in that family unit, the child feels disconnected from the members of their family. Consequently, the child thinks of them less often and the family members become less important to them. For an attachment relationship to be maintained, it is necessary to have three elements: warmth, intimacy and continuity. By moving to eradicate the targeted parent from the child's life, these elements are affected, and the attachment relationship is damaged. Therefore, even if an attachment relationship once existed, it is unlikely that the bond will survive the attack on these elements.

Information gatekeeping

Labelled 'information gatekeeping', this tactic involves the alienating parent managing the flow of information about the child to the targeted parent (7). The alienating parent can interfere with the targeted parent being able to access information about school performances or the dates and times of school events, such as sports carnivals. Information about medical appointments can be withheld. The alienating parent also may interfere with the child's counselling by failing to inform the targeted parent, failing to produce the child for scheduled appointments, or limiting the information provided during sessions.

> **Box 11.22 Targeted parent:** I don't get told anything. I never know if Bec has been sick. I usually find out through someone else if she's been to the doctor. I never get told when there are events at school. The court has given me permission to attend these events, but I'm never told when they are happening. She is supposed to send me Bec's school reports, but they never arrive. I don't get any photos of her birthday parties. It's like I'm being cut out of her life.

By managing the flow of information about the child, the alienating parent is systematically removing the targeted parent from the child's life. This can occur even when the targeted parent may have useful input that would assist the child.

> **Box 11.23 Targeted parent:** I'm so frustrated and angry. I didn't even know Josh was seeing a psychologist. I don't know why he is seeing someone. Then, when I found out about it, I contacted the psychologist. It seems that the psychologist had formed the opinion I wasn't a part of Josh's life. Well, that's not true. When I asked her what Josh was seeing her for, she told me she needed to get his mother's permission to tell me things about Josh. What am I supposed to do? No-one will tell me anything. I don't even know if I need to be worried about Josh.

Information gatekeeping certainly advances the alienation goals of the alienating parent. It is not only the withholding of information that is problematic. The impact of withholding information on the targeted parent–alienated child relationship should be considered. When the targeted parent does not attend important events, is never there to comfort the child when he or she is ill or even asks after their wellbeing, or seems to have little knowledge about the child's achievements, the child must develop a belief that the targeted parent is disinterested or does not care about the child. Also, the child learns to do without the targeted parent's praise, concern and interest. As a result, the targeted parent becomes less necessary in the alienated child's life.

Tactics associated with the alienated child

Some of the tactics used by alienating parents are focused on the child. In most cases, the goal of the alienating parent is to alter the way the child views the targeted parent and, indeed, the alienating parent so that a stronger allegiance exists between the alienating parent and the child.

Interrogation of the alienated child

The child can be interrogated by the alienating parent on return from the targeted parent (9). The alienating parent wants to know, in detail, what occurred while the child was with the targeted parent. The type of questioning used sets up an expectation in the child that the targeted parent has done something wrong. Certainly, the child must come to believe that the alienating parent is concerned about the possibility of wrongdoing on the part of the targeted parent.

> **Box 11.24 Interviewer:** What happens when you get back home to Mum after spending time with Dad?
>
> **Alienated child:** Mum usually asks me what I did while I was with Dad. She likes to make sure he hasn't done anything wrong. She wants to know what Dad has said about her, so I tell her otherwise she gets mad.
>
> **Interviewer:** What happens if you don't want to talk about it when you get home?
>
> **Alienated child:** She gets a bit mad if I tell her I'm too tired or don't want to talk. It's easier just to tell her … to get it over with. I don't mind though.

The pressure placed on a child by this type of interrogation can be considerable. The child learns that it is easier to give in to the interrogation tactics and give the alienating parent what they want than to resist. Of course, anticipation of the interrogation can cause the child to feel anxious.

> **Box 11.25 Targeted parent:** When the kids are with me, I don't say bad things about their mother. If the kids say anything about her, I just say, "Oh, that's nice". If they complain about her, I tell them they have to do what she tells them to do when they are with her. But I know that the kids are questioned when they get home. Andrew once asked me about what he was supposed to say when their mother asked them about something that happened – Jake fell off the swing. He wasn't hurt but it frightened him a bit. I just told Andrew to tell the truth, but he seemed worried that his mother would be angry. I didn't want to tell him not to tell his mother. It's too confusing for a child to have to remember what he should and shouldn't say all the time. But it makes me really mad that the kids get interrogated when they get home. Jake asked me the other day if I have a girlfriend. It seems he wanted to know because his mother kept asking him if he had seen any evidence laying around that I had a girlfriend. She needs to back off.

In the early stages, the child will try to navigate their way through the competing demands of just wanting to have a nice time while they are with the targeted parent and the alienating parent's requirement that they disclose every aspect of their time with the targeted parent. However, as time goes on and the pressure mounts, the child is forced to take a course of action that is likely to damage the relationship with one parent.

Indeed, the child can be put under so much pressure that it is easier to appease the alienating parent by providing information that is an exaggeration or fabrication of events that took place while the child was in the targeted parent's care. The child learns that the alienating parent is pleased when such information is supplied, so the relating of such information is rewarded and reinforced.

> **Box 11.26 Psychologist:** In the context of a difficult parenting order dispute, the alienating father reported that his six-year-old daughter had told him that there were problems when she stayed overnight at her mother's home with her mother and stepfather. He said his daughter told him that her stepfather would force her to eat things that made her ill and that she was forced to stay sitting at the dining table and eat her meal, even after she had

vomited. He said his daughter told him that her mother would smack her when she couldn't sleep, and she would cry herself to sleep. These were serious allegations. However, on examination of the evidence, it became apparent that the child seemed to be making up these events to please her father. When the child returned from spending time with her mother, she would be questioned by her father about events that had occurred at the child's mother's home. The questions put to the child were quite leading and the child soon learned what she had to say to make her father happy.

Undoubtedly, the interrogation of a child on return from the targeted parent can advance the goals of parental alienation. It is exceedingly difficult for a child to disclose, embellish or fabricate negative experiences with the targeted parent when pressure is placed on the child to do so and still maintain a close relationship with the targeted parent. Withdrawal from the targeted parent is likely to protect the child from the internal conflict they experience from loving a parent but saying bad things about them. For the child, it would be easier to distance themselves from the targeted parent as a way of managing that conflict. The child then uses as a logical explanation for their own withdrawal the fact that the targeted parent must have done what the child said they have done. The alienating parent's tactic of interrogation then has the outcome of creating distance between the child and the targeted parent.

Damage to the loving connection with the targeted parent

The alienating parent can tell the child things about the targeted parent or what the targeted parent said that damage the loving connection between the targeted parent and the child (6). The things that are relayed to the child might be things that have occurred, exaggerations or embellishments of things that have occurred or things that never occurred. It makes little difference. Any challenge by the targeted parent of the alienating parent's story creates suspicion in the child because of what he or she has been told by the alienating parent. The damage to the loving connection between parent and child can occur even if the quality of the relationship previously had been good.

> **Box 11.27 Alienating parent:** I have every right to tell Rosie that her father never wanted her. When I got pregnant so soon after we met, he wanted me to have an abortion. Rosie knows her father wanted to kill her before she was even born. It's a terrible thing for a child to know, but then Rosie should know what sort of person her father really is.

No matter what your personal views are about this sensitive topic, it is the case that consideration of whether to progress with a pregnancy can be understood to be separate from the loving feelings for a child that develop after the child has arrived. However, this distinction may not easily be made by a child. A child might reach the conclusion that ambivalence about an important life decision equates with a lack of loving feeling towards the child. As a result, damage to the loving connection between the targeted parent and the child is achieved by the alienating parent who disclosed the information to the child.

> **Box 11.28 Alienating parent:** I told Amber that her father never cared about her even when we were together as a family. It's not like he ever looked after her properly. He hardly ever changed her nappy and I was the one who used to get up to her during the night when she was a baby. He used to say that he was working and needed his sleep but that was just an excuse. He never cared enough to bother getting out of bed when she cried. And then, when he came home from work, he would play with her for a minute and then not bother with her. She knows. She should know what her father is like. I don't think she should expect him to be any different now. I don't want her to be disappointed. I am protecting her by making it clear that her father has never cared and won't ever care for her.

It is not unusual, in a traditional family structure, for one parent to adopt a greater role in child caring while the other parent works to meet the family's financial/ economic needs. However, the interpretation that is being placed on this division of duties by the alienating parent is likely to influence the way the child perceives the commitment to them by each parent. The targeted parent is then viewed as uncaring or unfeeling despite there being other explanations that might better account for the situation that existed prior to separation.

> **Box 11.29 Alienating parent:** I warned the children their mother would run around with other men and it's been proven to be right. I heard she has a new partner just like I predicted. This man has two children and she spends time with them. So, my children know their mother has abandoned them. She is a mother to his children she doesn't even know but doesn't care about her own children. What sort of person is she?

This notion of the targeted parent finding a replacement family is often fed to alienated children. Superficially, there seems to be evidence to support what the alienating parent is saying. The targeted parent may have formed a new relationship and that person may have children. Of course, this most often does not alter the targeted parent's feelings for their own child. However, the 'spin' placed on the situation by the alienating parent encourages the child to view the targeted parent as dismissive of the child's needs, disinterested and unconcerned. This is likely to result in damage to the loving connection the targeted parent and the child previously enjoyed.

> **Box 11.30 Alienating parent:** My children know we are struggling financially and that it's their father's fault. He refuses to pay child support. He says he won't pay until I let the children come to see him, but they don't want to see him because he won't pay the money he owes us. I don't think I have to cover up for him and pretend that he is a nice man when he isn't. When the children ask for something, I have to tell them they can't have it because their father hasn't paid any child support.

Problems related to failure to financially support the alienating parent and the child can be used to damage the loving connection between the targeted parent and the child. The alienating parent's account provided to the child can misrepresent the nature of the situation or can be used to highlight the targeted parent's reported lack of concern for the child's wellbeing. In reality, disputes about child support payments should be considered to be adult concerns. Children should be protected from such matters whenever possible.

It is evident that, in most cases, a loving connection between the targeted parent and the alienated child existed prior to the end of the parents' relationship. An alienating parent then must alter that relationship to meet the goals of a parental alienation process. Attacks on the connection the child feels with the targeted parent widens the emotional gap between the targeted parent and the child. With emotional distance comes lack of empathy for the targeted parent and ease of rejection. With the connection to the targeted parent either diminished or severed, the child will hold onto the connection with the alienating parent. Therefore, the importance of the alienating parent for the child increases and the child is much more likely, then, to align themselves with that parent.

Inappropriate disclosure about the targeted parent

The alienating parent can influence the child's view of the targeted parent by telling the child negative things about the targeted parent (6). In particular, the alienated parent will disclose negative information about the targeted parent that relates to the parental relationship or relates to events that occurred before the child was born.

Box 11.31 Alienated child: My father is a drunk.

Interviewer: When I spoke to your father, he said he hadn't drunk any alcohol for many years.

Alienated child: Well, he's a drunk.

Interviewer: Have you ever seen him drink or have you seen him when he's been drunk?

Alienated child: No, he stopped by the time I was born. How could I have seen him drinking?

Interviewer: Then why do you call him a drunk?

Alienated child: Mum told me how much he used to drink when they first got together. She said he was drunk all the time. She told me he would choose to drink rather than doing something nice for her. She said she tried to fix him, but she couldn't.

Here the alienating parent has disclosed to the child negative information about the targeted parent that has no real impact on the child. Although the experience of the targeted parent's drinking history may have been meaningful for the alienating parent, it was not relevant to the child. The information must have been presented to the child in a way that caused the child to accept the negative view of the targeted parent despite that not being the child's experience of that parent.

The information disclosed to children by alienating parents can exceed the bounds of what normally would be discussed with children. The disclosure also may be about concepts that are beyond the child's capacity to understand because of their developmental stage.

Box 11.32 Alienating parent: I told my daughter about her father's treatment of me in our sexual relationship. I had to tell her about the times he forced me to have sex and how perverted he is. How could she protect herself from him otherwise? His behaviour disgusts her. It disgusts me. I know he says sexual intercourse in our marriage was always consensual but, you know, when I look back on it now, I can see that it wasn't. Not always. Hardly ever. My daughter should know this. She should know what her father is like. She has a right to know.

Unfortunately, the disclosure of this type of information to a child is not an uncommon occurrence in the context of parental alienation. The child is exposed to information and concepts from which he or she should be protected. Undoubtedly, being provided with this information is likely to alter the way the child views the targeted parent.

The child may be exposed to negative information about the targeted parent by being given access to information contained in court documents. Invariably, the information that reaches the child is filtered. That is, the alienating parent will expose the child to selected information from court documents that shows the targeted parent in a poor light but withholds information that offers a more benign interpretation or is more positive in nature. Of course, the child does not have access to information that gives a more concerning view of the alienating parent's behaviour.

Box 11.33 Interviewer: Amelia told me that she knew all about what a liar her father is. She said she knew this because she had seen the lies he tells in court documents.

Alienating parent: Well, it's true.

Interviewer: I listened to what Amelia told me about her father and it is apparent that the issues she raised are ones that are disputed. That is, her father has offered other explanations for the issues you listed in your affidavits that Amelia identifies as evidence of his lying.

Alienating parent: So what? He's a liar.

Interviewer: And how did Amelia come to see the court documents?

Alienating parent: What do you mean?

Interviewer: Well, children aged eight years don't normally have access to legal documents. So, how did Amelia get to see them?

Alienating parent: Well, she may have seen them on my computer, or she may have seen them on my desk. I have had to spend so much time working on this case and there are always documents lying around. Maybe she saw them then.

If it had been the case that the child had inadvertently viewed court documents, then it would be unlikely that the child would have seen only those documents that placed the targeted parent in a negative light and not all court documents. It is a common parental alienation strategy to involve the child in legal matters from which they should be protected. An alternative strategy is for the alienating parent to complain to the child about the negative impact of the court process on the alienating parent. The message received by the child is that the targeted parent has done this to the alienating parent.

A child's view about the targeted parent may be influenced by the disclosure that other people he or she loves think poorly of the targeted parent. This is a common strategy. Even if it is not overtly stated that other family members dislike the targeted parent, the way in which the targeted parent is discussed by family members when the child is within earshot is enough to influence the child's view of the targeted parent.

Box 11.34 Alienated child: Grandma hates my mother.

Interviewer: Why?

Alienated child: She said my mother is a tramp. I think she's a tramp, too.

Interviewer: A tramp? What's a tramp?

> **Alienated child:** I don't know, but it's something pretty bad. Grandma said so. She said my mother is nothing but a tramp and she deserves everything she gets.
> **Interviewer:** Did Grandma tell you this about Mum?
> **Alienated child:** No, Grandma was talking to Dad and Aunty Jenny. Dad said my mother was sleeping with lots of men … he reckoned she was. Grandma said that was because she was a tramp. Then Aunty Jenny and Dad laughed about Grandma hating my mother. I hate her, too … because she's a tramp and Grandma hates her. I think Aunty Jenny hates her, too. And Dad. We all hate her.

It would be difficult for this child to hold a view that was contrary to the view being expressed by the rest of the family. By not shielding the child from negative opinions, the child is going to be influenced by that information. The child must either accept that other family members are correct in their view or assertively stand up to everyone who shares the negative view.

The result of exposing a child to negative information about the targeted parent is clear. The child comes to see the targeted parent as flawed. A strong allegiance is formed between the alienating parent and the child because the child comes to see the alienating parent as the victim of the targeted parent's wrongdoing.

Encouraging child defiance

The alienating parent will encourage the child to act in a defiant manner when he or she is with the targeted parent (12). This action is likely to create conflict in the relationship between the targeted parent and the alienated child. The connection between the targeted parent and the child is further eroded by this type of interference on the part of the alienating parent.

> **Box 11.35 Targeted parent:** She doesn't openly defy me but it's like there is this campaign of resistance. I will ask her to do something and she'll either not do it or do the opposite. I know her mother's put her up to this. She used to be such an obliging child. Now I can't get her to do anything. Everything is a problem. It's exhausting.

Here the child is demonstrating passive resistance to the parenting strategies adopted by the targeted parent. Without being openly defiant, the result is still erosion of the relationship between the targeted parent and the child. This ongoing, unspoken conflict results in there being few positive interactions between the targeted parent and the child. It is not unreasonable, then, for the child to claim that he or she is not comfortable when they are at the home of the targeted parent. Of course, it is also the case that defiance can be openly expressed.

> **Box 11.36 Targeted parent:** Things are getting worse. Now it's open warfare. She argues with me about everything. I reckon if I said it was daytime, she would argue that it's night. She tells me she doesn't have to do what I say. I know she's been told this by her mother. She gets such a defiant look on her face. I can't reason with her. I can see she's upset by all the arguing, but she won't see sense. I don't know what's going to happen. It can't keep going on like this.

As is the case with passive resistance, open defiance can result in there being few, if any, positive interactions between the targeted parent and the child. Although the source of the problem is the decisions made and the actions taken by the alienating parent to encourage child defiance, the alienated child responds to the alienating parent as a source of comfort and the targeted parent as a source of conflict.

When questioned about what the child is resisting, an alienated child may complain about the demands being made on them by the targeted parent, even when these demands are normal enough or typical of the requests parents make of their children. When talking with the child it becomes clear that the alienating parent has encouraged the child to defy these normal parental requests.

Box 11.37 Alienated child: I don't want to see my father anymore.
Interviewer: Why not?
Alienated child: Because he's always telling me what to do.
Interviewer: Like what?
Alienated child: Well, he said I had to wait until dinner and I couldn't have a snack. Mum said I should have had a snack anyway if I was hungry.
Interviewer: Was it nearly dinner time?
Alienated child: Um … well … I was hungry.
Interviewer: Had Dad started cooking dinner?
Alienated child: Yes, but he's slow. Mum's a much faster cooker. Anyway, Mum said if I want a snack, I can have one. So I took a biscuit and then Dad got mad.
Interviewer: What happened then?
Alienated child: I told him I was allowed to have a biscuit because Mum said so … so I ate the biscuit.

An alienating parent may encourage the child to view as unreasonable the rules the targeted parent sets. Without directly telling the child to defy the targeted parent, the alienating parent offers implicit encouragement for the child to reject the rules the targeted parent sets.

Box 11.38 Alienating parent: My daughter doesn't want to go to her father's home anymore. I try to encourage her, but she just doesn't want to go. And I can't blame her. We've talked about it and the rules he sets are too rigid. She has to be in bed by 8pm when she is there. I'm more flexible. If she's not tired, then I don't make her go to bed. She has to pack her own schoolbag when she is there, whereas I do that for her when she's with me. There are so many rules to remember there it's no wonder she gets fed up. I told her that at least she doesn't have to put up with that when she's home with me.

Child defiance contributes to the process of parental alienation by fostering emotional deprivation in the targeted parent–child relationship. When the child is encouraged by the alienating parent to defy the targeted parent, problem behaviours develop. The child misbehaves and is rebellious, and their behaviour is difficult to manage. The targeted parent then responds to these behaviour problems and attempts to rectify them. This usually involves the targeted parent trying to apply more rules or strongly enforce the rules that already exist.

As a result of the increase in problematic child behaviour and the targeted parent's struggle to enforce rules, there is an increase in the number and intensity of the negative interactions that take place between the targeted parent and the child. The alienated child responds poorly to the increased demand placed on them by the targeted parent and resists the targeted parent's effort to control the child's behaviour. These negative interactions reinforce the views that have been expressed by the alienating parent to the alienated child. That is, the alienating parent had warned the child that the targeted parent was not a good parent and the conflict experienced because of the child's defiance proves the alienating parent to be right, at least in the mind of the alienated child.

If the defiance continues and negative interactions increase in frequency and intensity, the targeted parent tends to become angry and frustrated. As a consequence, normally affectionate behaviour by the targeted parent towards the alienated child reduces in frequency. Warm interaction between the targeted parent and the alienated child becomes contingent on the child not being defiant. Of course, this rarely occurs because the alienating parent continues to encourage the defiance and the child has developed hostility towards the targeted parent because of the difficult interactions they have experienced.

The outcome of this process is an emotional distance between the targeted parent and the alienated child. Physical displays of affection stop occurring and the closeness that existed before the alienation process began to influence the relationship is no longer apparent. The child then stops feeling empathy towards the targeted parent's position. It is in this way that encouragement of the child's defiant behaviour advances the goals of the parental alienation process.

Tactics associated with the alienating parent

Finally, alienating parents use tactics that reflect changes to their own behaviour and the way they manage situations so that they turn out in their favour and against the targeted parent. We will examine these strategies.

Forcing loyalty to the alienating parent

Alienating parents make it clear to their children that they have to choose a side, even if they do not overtly say so. Of course, the expectation is that the child will choose the side of the alienating parent. It is made clear to the alienated child that relationships with both parents will not be tolerated by the alienating parent and that the consequences of non-compliance would be unpleasant for the child (6–7).

Interestingly, it is not necessary to inspire loving devotion in a child by good quality parenting, a warm relationship and a sense of closeness for a strong connection to exist between a parent and a child. It can be the case that the threat of unpleasant consequences for the child is sufficient for the child to take the side of the alienating parent.

Box 11.39 Alienated child: Dad said if I decided to go and see Mum then I wouldn't be able to live with him. He said I wouldn't see Milo, my dog. He said I wouldn't be able to see Nan and Pop. He reminded me of the reasons why I don't see Mum … you know, like she has a new boyfriend and she told lies about Dad. He said I could see Mum if I wanted but I'm not sure. I think I'd rather only see Dad and not Mum. Dad looks after me and takes me to school. Who would take me to school if I stayed at Mum's?

Although the child is being encouraged to believe that the decision about whether to see the targeted parent is their own, it also is made clear to the child that a decision in favour of seeing the targeted parent is likely to bring about outcomes that are intolerable for the child. The child then takes the less challenging pathway of complying with the alienating parent's wishes.

A child also may be encouraged by the alienating parent to express their loyalty towards them by reporting to others their commitment to the alienating parent. This is likely to occur when the child is interviewed in the context of a parenting dispute.

Box 11.40 Alienated child: I don't want to see my mother at all. She isn't a very good mother. Dad said so. Anyway, if I do see Mum then Dad would think I wasn't on his side. He said he has been fighting for me in court. It cost him a lot of money to fight for me. He told me that it didn't cost my mother anything because she got legal aid. I'm not sure what legal aid is but Dad said it is free, so it didn't cost my mother anything to cause lots of problems for Dad. So, I want to show Dad I am happy he spent all his money getting me. So, I only want to see Dad and not my mother.

Clearly, the child's understanding of the legal process is limited. Nevertheless, aspects of the parenting dispute process are being used to provide an argument for the child about why they should be loyal to the alienating parent. The argument the child then provides to the interviewer about why they are committed to the alienating parent seems logical to the child.

However, this loyal devotion to the alienating parent can occur in the absence of a logical argument. The influence placed on the child to demonstrate this loyalty can occur without the child understanding that influence is being exerted. In these cases, interviewers are likely to notice a child's stubborn adherence to a point of view without the child being able to provide a justification for the point of view.

Box 11.41 Alienated child: I only love my father. I don't love my mother.
Interviewer: Why do you only love Dad?
Alienated child: Because my Dad is the best father in the world, and he loves me the best.
Interviewer: Mum told me she loves you, too.
Alienated child: No, only Dad does. I only want to be with Dad. I will run away if I have to go to stay at Mum's house.
Interviewer: Tell me why you love Dad so much.
Alienated child: It's because he's the best father in the world. I only love him. I will run away if I have to see Mum.
Interviewer: Yes, you told me that. I was just asking about Dad.
Alienated child: He is the best parent. I only need him. You can't make me go and see my mother. Dad said I could choose, and I choose Dad.
Interviewer: What about if you didn't have to choose? What about if you could see both Dad and Mum?
Alienated child: I only want to be with Dad. He is the best.

By establishing a sense of loyalty towards the alienating parent from the child, the alienating parent is protecting their position from others, including the targeted parent, trying to influence the child to adopt a more moderate view towards the targeted parent. The feelings of loyalty the child has towards the alienating parent cause the child to reject efforts to be more accepting of the targeted parent. It would feel like a betrayal of the alienating parent if the child adopted a more moderate view towards the targeted parent, such is the strength of the loyalty generated by the actions of the alienating parent.

Encouraging an unhealthy alliance

An unhealthy alliance between the alienating parent and the child develops because of the actions of the alienating parent (7). A relationship based on dependence is encouraged. In this way, the child comes to believe that they cannot function without the alienating parent. In a sense, the child comes to believe the targeted parent is not to be trusted.

> **Box 11.42 Targeted parent:** This is getting to be ridiculous. I can't parent my child. She won't go to bed without calling her mother. She wants to phone her mother to decide what to wear in the morning. If she's in a bad mood, or grazes her knee, or has a disagreement with her friends, she demands to be taken back to her mother. This is her mother's doing. My daughter told me the other day that her mother should be allowed to come to my house to tuck her in when she goes to bed. She said her mother is the only person who can tuck her into bed properly. She has also told me that her mother is the only person who can cook properly and iron her clothes properly. From what she's said, it's pretty clear that these ideas have been put in her head by her mother.

It would seem here that the child has been encouraged to be overly dependent on the alienating parent. The child's inability to function independently of the alienating parent diminishes the influence the targeted parent has on the child. So, this process undermines the parental role for the targeted parent.

However, the most important manifestation of this unhealthy alliance is the combined effort on the part of the alienating parent and the alienated child to achieve a common goal of rejecting the targeted parent. The alienated child will be expected to engage in activities that foster or cement the alliance. Indeed, the child will often be rewarded by the alienating parent for participating in the activities that undermine the targeted parent–alienated child relationship.

> **Box 11.43 Targeted parent:** I was shocked to find out that her mother has told my daughter to spy on me. I caught her going through some things in my bedroom. When I asked her what she was doing, she told me Mummy had told her to look to see if I had a girlfriend. She told her to look at the things beside the bed for 'girl things' and to look in the wardrobe and the bathroom. If she wants to know if I am in a relationship with anyone, she should just ask me instead of sending our daughter to spy. It's like my daughter and her mother have turned into this sneaky spy ring with me being the target. What on earth is she teaching my daughter?

The development of this unhealthy alliance between the alienating parent and the alienated child advances the goals of parental alienation in several ways. Firstly, it strengthens the relationship between the alienating parent and the child. Working together towards a common goal makes the child feel a stronger connection with the parent whose side they are taking.

Secondly, engaging in behaviours that support this unhealthy alliance normalises the rejection of the targeted parent for the child, particularly when these activities are supported by the alienating parent. Knowing that the parent on whom you rely is pleased with your actions is strongly motivating for a child.

Thirdly, the strength of the unhealthy alliance legitimises the rejection of the targeted parent by the child. The closer the relationship with the alienated parent, the easier it is for the child to reject the targeted parent. The child is then likely to engage in activities, such as conspiring with the alienating parent against the targeted parent, that they would not otherwise feel comfortable doing.

Emotional manipulation

Alienating parents can emotionally manipulate their children (6–7). This is a disturbing aspect of parental alienation and should be viewed as a specific form of emotional abuse. Emotional manipulation is used by people to get others to do things they would not otherwise agree to do or would be reluctant to do. The target of the manipulation feels psychological pressure to do what is being expected of them because the cost of non-compliance is typically something greater than the person feels comfortable losing.

This emotional manipulation can take a number of forms. It may take the form of a demand of an expression of loyalty along with the threat of negative consequences for failure to provide that expression of loyalty. Alternatively, the manipulation can manifest as a withdrawal of love and affection as a punishment for supporting the targeting parent or expressing a positive view about that parent.

Box 11.44 Paternal grandmother: It's heartbreaking to watch what my daughter-in-law, ex-daughter-in-law, does to that child. She expects her to be completely loyal. If Gemma says one thing against her then her mother screams at her. She tells Gemma that she obviously doesn't love her so she should go and live with her father. The arguments mostly happen when Gemma asks about her father or mentions his name. Gemma ends up apologising to her mother so that the fight can be over. As I said, it's heartbreaking to watch. Gemma practically begs her mother to forgive her and she hasn't done anything but ask after her father.

Here the alienating parent is threatening rejection and the threat is being presented in an emotionally volatile manner. The alienated child would be left in little doubt about the seriousness of the threat and the impact the child's decision would be likely to have in terms the alienating parent following through with the predicted outcome of non-compliance. To alleviate the felt anxiety, the child must act to avoid the threatened change related to the child's perceived defiance.

Of course, the alienating parent does not need to act in an emotionally volatile manner to make it clear to the alienated child that the child's wellbeing is at risk if he or she does not comply with the alienating parent's wishes.

> **Box 11.45 Paternal grandmother:** The other thing Gemma's mother does is sulk. She refuses to talk to Gemma, sometimes for days on end, if Gemma mentions her father or sticks up for him. I have seen the sad look on Gemma's face when she tells me her mother's not talking to her. And I don't think it's just not talking. I think things get very frosty at their house. Gemma said her mother wouldn't come to her dance recital after she asked her if she could send her father a photo of her in her costume. You're either on my daughter-in-law's side or you are frozen out. I have to be careful what I say if I want to be able to see Gemma.

The alienated child has learned by her mother's reactions that certain decisions or behaviours result in the withdrawal of her mother's positive regard. As a parent–child relationship is supposed to foster closeness and warmth, this type of parental behaviour is likely to be deeply disturbing for a child. Alienated children will do what is necessary to have that closeness and warmth returned, bearing in mind that the child has already rejected one parent, so the alienating parent is the only one with whom they have this close relationship. In more extreme cases, the alienated child may face threatened abandonment. Of course, real abandonment is unlikely given the goals of the alienating parent to terminate the relationship between the child and the targeted parent although the child would not know this was the case.

> **Box 11.46 Alienated child:** Mum said that if I decide to go and live with Dad, I will never see her again … ever. She said she will move to another house and I won't know where she lives … and I'll never get to see her ever again. I don't want to see Dad. I don't like him. I just want to stay with Mum.

The alienated child is being faced with an untenable situation. She either has to support her mother's wishes or she will have to go and live with the father she has rejected and terminate her relationship with the parent with whom she has aligned herself. The consequence of rejecting the targeted parent, with the psychological costs for the child that are inherent in this process, would make it difficult for the child to cope with this threatened change in circumstance.

It is not difficult to appreciate how effective emotional manipulation could be in advancing parental alienation goals. Consider the effect of emotional manipulation on the alienated child. A demand for allegiance and compliance is made on the alienated child. The potential costs of non-compliance with the alienating parent's wishes are made clear, either directly or indirectly. These costs are sufficiently disturbing for the alienated child that a possible follow-through by the alienating parent on the threats that have been made increases the child's anxiety. The degree to which a child is disturbed by the potential costs of non-compliance relates to the extent to which the alienation process has affected the child. That is, the more the child has rejected the targeted parent because of the influence of the alienation process, the more troubling the threats must seem to the child.

The anxiety felt in relation to the alienating parent's threats would be sufficiently strong to drive the child to avoid the situation that is triggering the anxiety. That is, the child is strongly driven to oblige the alienating parent's demands to avoid the outcome that has been predicted or implied by the alienating parent.

Utilising outside forces

Alienating parents will use outside forces to bolster the alienation process (12). They will make notifications to child protection services or to the police claiming wrongdoing on the part of the targeted parent in relation to the care of the child. They will seek and obtain restraining and family violence orders claiming the targeted parent represents a significant threat to themselves and the child. The aim of the alienating parent is to put another obstacle in the way of the targeted parent being able to spend time with their child.

Further, alienating parents will seek out psychological or counselling support for their child to legitimise their decision to cut the targeted parent out of the child's life. They will identify the child as being distressed about spending time with the targeted parent and will seek therapeutic support. However, typically, there is an expectation that the psychologist will support the alienating parent's position and, often, produce a report that can be used to support the alienating parent's case in a legal context.

Box 11.47 Targeted parent: I got the shock of my life when I was served with papers that my ex-wife was seeking a family violence order preventing me from contacting her. Our daughter was named on the application so I wouldn't be able to see her either. What family violence? It's a lie. And she knows it's a lie. They gave her an interim order so I can't see my daughter, but I'll fight this. She's listed all these awful things I'm supposed to have done. I never laid a finger on her.

The targeted parent is faced with a problem. In many situations such as this, it is often the case of one person's word against the other's word. Without witnesses to the abuse and in the absence of medical or police interventions, the targeted parent may find themselves in a position where it is necessary for them to prove something did not occur. This is a difficult undertaking.

The agenda of the alienating parent may not be hidden when they approach a helping professional. It may be quite clear that the only reason help is being sought is because a change in court orders is being sought.

Box 11.48 Alienating parent: I've brought my child along to see you because she's not coping very well spending time with her father. We separated about 12 months ago and the court has forced her to spend four nights a fortnight with him. But she really isn't handling it very well. She is exhausted when she comes back to me and takes ages to settle down. She's upset for ages as well. He just doesn't get it. He thinks I'm the one responsible for these problems but it's him. I know he wants to be a good father, but he needs to handle himself better. I think a period of time when my daughter doesn't have to go and spend time with her father would be good for her. It would allow her to settle down and be happy for a while. I can't keep sending her to her father's knowing that she is going to be upset because she's not looked after well enough.

It is easy to see why the parent has sought help. Although it is not clear that parental alienation is occurring, the goal of help seeking is to obtain support for a change in orders. However, the approach made by the alienating parent to the helping professional may not be blatant regarding the request for the type of assistance they actually want. The alienating parent, on the surface, may present as reasonable and concerned, offering an argument for the management of the situation that would be beneficial for the child.

> **Box 11.49 Alienating parent:** Thank you for seeing Billie. She is having a hard time separating from me when she has to go and spend overnight time with her father. She is struggling to sleep the night before she has to go and takes ages to settle down when she comes back. I have tried to encourage her to go but she insists she doesn't like it there. I think it is just being away from me that she finds difficult. Her father doesn't like me contacting Billie when she is with him so I can't monitor how things are going or offer Billie support while she is there. Last time she had to go she simply refused. I had to come down harder than I would have liked. I told her that the judge said she has to go. In the end, she went with him, but it was very upsetting.

On the surface, it seems that the parent is concerned about the child's wellbeing and she is seeking assistance in managing the child's separation anxiety. However, in cases of parental alienation, this therapeutic appeal is a precursor to a greater demand to support the withdrawal of the child from the targeted parent's life. The challenge is to recognise emerging evidence of parental alienation when it occurs and act appropriately once it has been recognised. It is important to adhere to therapeutic goals and do not be drawn into a parenting dispute because of the alienating parent's agenda. Of course, you can be involved in a parenting order matter when you can offer a useful professional opinion.

It is easy to see why alienating parents utilise outside forces to support their cases. Professional support gives their agenda legitimacy it might otherwise lack. In this way, it is not only the parent who is saying that the relationship between the targeted parent and the child should be terminated, but professionals as well who may have more standing in a legal context. It is sometimes the case that an alienating parent will shop around for a professional who will support their case. If at first you don't succeed, try and try again.

Concluding comments

From this chapter, it is evident that there are a broad range of behaviours by the alienating parents or strategies used by them to influence the relationship between the targeted parent and the alienated child. Of course, it may be the case that not all alienating parents will use all strategies to advance their goals. In addition, there are clearly going to be other manifestations of these strategies than the ones listed here as the indicators of each alienation tactic.

It is important to familiarise yourself with these strategies so that you are able to recognise them when presented with the indicators. You then need to use your judgment about whether parental alienation is occurring. It is unlikely that alienation is occurring if one tactic is evident. If multiple tactics are evident, then you need to consider whether the targeted parent–child relationship is being influenced by a process of alienation.

However, it is not only the way in which the alienating parent behaves that can assist you in assessing the presence of parental alienation. Also, you can focus on the child's behaviour and, to a lesser extent, the way in which the targeted parent is reacting to the pressures and demands placed on them.

References

1. Bernet, W. (2016). Children of divorce: Breaking news for clinicians and forensic practitioners. *Journal of the American Academy of Child and Adolescent Psychiatry, 55,* S27. doi:10.1016/j.jaac.2016.07.538
2. Mone, J.G., & Biringen, Z. (2012). Assessing parental alienation: Empirical assessment of college students' recollections of parental alienation during their childhoods. *Journal of Divorce and Remarriage, 53,* 157–177. doi:10.1300/j087v45n03_07
3. Gordon, R.M., Stoffey, R., & Bottinielli, J. (2008). MMPI-2 findings of primitive defences in alienating parents. *American Journal of Family Therapy, 36,* 211–228. doi:10.1080/01926180701643313
4. Siegel, J.C., & Langford, J.S. (1998). MMPI-2 validity scales and suspected parental alienation syndrome. *American Journal of Forensic Psychology, 16,* 5–14.
5. Rowen, J., & Emery, R. (2018). Parental denigration: A form of conflict that typically backfires. *Family Court Review, 56,* 258–268. doi:10.1111/fcre.12339
6. Baker, A.J.L. (2005). Parent alienation strategies: A qualitative study of adults who experienced parental alienation as a child. *American Journal of Forensic Psychology, 23,* 1–23.
7. Baker, A.J.L., & Darnall, D. (2006). Behaviors and strategies employed in parental alienation: A survey of parental experiences. *Journal of Divorce and Remarriage, 45,* 97–12. doi:10.1300/J087v45n01_06
8. Warshak, R.A. (2015). Poisoning parent–child relationships through the manipulation of names. *The American Journal of Family Therapy, 43,* 4–15. doi:10.1080/01926187.2014.968066
9. Vassiliou, D., & Cartwright, G.F. (2001). The lost parents' perspective on parental alienation syndrome. *The American Journal of Family Therapy, 29,* 181–191. doi:10.1080/019261801750424307
10. Bernet, W., von Boch-Galhau, W., Baker, A.J.L., & Morrison, S.L. (2010). Parental alienation, DSM-V, and ICD-11. *The American Journal of Family Therapy, 38,* 76–187. doi:10.1080/01926180903586583
11. Lowenstein, L.F. (2012). Child contact disputes between parents and allegations of sex abuse: What does the research say? *Journal of Divorce and Remarriage, 53,* 194–203. doi:10.1080/10502556.2012.663267
12. Turkat, I.D. (1994). Child visitation interference in divorce. *Clinical Psychology Review, 14,* 737–742. doi:10.1016/0272-7358(94)90039-6

Chapter Twelve

Assessing targeted parents

Introduction

The approach to assessment of targeted parents is different to the assessment of alienating parents and alienated children. When conducting an assessment of targeted parents, the goal is not to identify the presence of behaviours that indicate alienation or the ways in which it manifests. There are two assessment goals when dealing with targeted parents. The first is the way in which the targeted parent has responded to the alienation process, such as the targeted parent's current mental health and risk of self-harm. The second goal relates to the assessment of the validity of allegations made about the targeted parent's behaviour by the alienating parent.

Assessing psychological wellbeing

It is not the intention of this book to provide instruction on how to conduct a psychological assessment. Rather, the aim here is to highlight the importance of evaluating the current psychological functioning of the targeted parent being assessed and how that current functioning might impact on a number of important points.

Firstly, it is recommended that current psychological functioning is assessed to determine the targeted parent's adjustment. From the point of view of the individual, assessment results may indicate a real need to seek therapeutic intervention if the person's adjustment is negatively affected by the parental alienation campaign. Given the potential seriousness of the impact on targeted parents of parental alienation, a measure of how an individual is coping with the demands being placed on them is likely to guide therapeutic recommendations.

Secondly, it is important to assess a targeted parent's current psychological functioning to determine whether any maladjustment would influence parenting capacity. In the context of any parenting evaluation, the targeted parent's current parenting capacity is important to determine. Here, attention is drawn to the need to determine the potential impact on that capacity, such as current psychological state affected by the alienation campaign itself.

Thirdly, it is important to determine a targeted parent's current psychological state if therapeutic intervention to combat parental alienation is undertaken. The targeted parent's psychological readiness to engage in what can be a difficult and challenging therapeutic process is important to determine.

The focus of an assessment of psychological functioning should include an evaluation of the presence of psychological symptoms. In addition, it may be wise to investigate the types of distortions in thinking that might make a person more rigid in their approach to problem solving and less flexible in negotiation if family therapy is to be undertaken.

Assessing suicide risk

As a result of the challenges that are inherent in parental alienation, it is imperative that consideration be given to the risk to the targeted parent of suicidal ideation and behaviour. The duty to protect a person from self-harm exists irrespective of whether that individual is engaging in ongoing therapy or is taking part in a parenting dispute evaluation process. Any action taken to protect a person from harm from suicidal actions has its foundation in a proper suicide risk assessment.

Suicide risk factors

In undertaking a suicide risk assessment, it is necessary to consider the factors that have been identified in the psychological literature as being associated with higher suicide risk. In addition, the way in which parental alienation might exacerbate these risk factors should be considered.

Past psychiatric history

A history of psychiatric problems has been associated with increased suicide risk (1–5). Such a history indicates psychiatric vulnerability that may make it difficult for an individual to cope with life demands. Also, it may relate to the experience of severe psychiatric symptoms, such as auditory hallucinations, that can drive a person to engage in suicidal behaviour.

In relation to the assessment of suicide risk in targeted parents, a history of psychiatric illness may make it difficult for the targeted parent to cope with the considerable psychological demands that are evident in parental alienation. The impact of previous psychiatric difficulties on the current functioning of targeted parents should be considered.

Current mental illness

In general, the presence of a current mental illness contributes to suicide risk (1,4,6-10). This includes a broad range of psychiatric disorders, such as psychotic illnesses, mood disorders, substance use disorders and eating disorders.

In the case of targeted parents, the presence of current psychopathology should be investigated. This not only is to determine the current capacity of the targeted parent to cope with the demands being placed on them that might increase suicide risk, but to determine how symptoms might affect capacity to parent.

Comorbidity

Considered as a separate risk factor to the presence of a current mental illness, comorbidity, that is the presence of more than one psychiatric or medical condition, independently increases the risk of suicide (6,9-10). The presence of more than one condition increases the psychological burden on the individual, making it more difficult to cope with life events.

For targeted parents, the additional burden that is experienced as a function of a poor and multi-determined mental state needs to be considered. In combination with the challenges that are experienced as a function of separation from one's child, involvement in the legal system, and other demands such as financial strains, the additional effects of multiple influences of mental health problems can make it difficult for any person to cope and suicide may be considered.

Family relationship disturbance

There is a range of family-related factors associated with disturbances in the family unit and with family dynamics that increase suicide risk (7). These include high conflict, parental psychiatric disturbance and a family history of suicidal behaviour.

Family relationship disturbance is at the very heart of parental alienation. The conflict that exists and that is central to parental alienation tends to be unrelenting in its nature and pervasive in its effects on other domains of the targeted parent's life. As a risk factor for suicidal behaviour, the extent of family relationship disturbance and the way it manifests should be examined.

Recent suicide of somebody close

A contagion effect associated with suicidal behaviour has been well-reported (7). Knowledge of a significant person who suicided as a means of dealing with the problems they faced increases the chances that the same coping choice will be made by another person close to the person who suicided because they identify with the person who suicided.

An assessment of the increased risk of suicidal behaviour caused by the recent suicide of someone close could extend beyond close relationships in the case of targeted parents. These parents often seek information and support from other people in similar situations, either in person or through the Internet. In sharing the psychological effects of their own experiences, other targeted parents often discuss suicidal thoughts and behaviours. It is important to consider the increased risk caused by exposure to the suicidal experiences of others in a similar position to their own.

Childhood physical/sexual abuse

A history of childhood sexual or physical abuse has been reported to increase the risk of suicidal behaviour (3,11). Although most commonly reported to be a trigger for suicidal behaviour during adolescence and young adulthood, the effect on suicide risk of childhood abuse can continue throughout adulthood.

In the case of targeted parents, a history of childhood abusive experiences should be investigated when determining suicide risk. Given that allegations of abusive behaviour towards their own children may be levelled at targeted parents by alienating parents, a history of the targeted parent's own experience of such abuse may trigger a strongly negative psychological reaction akin to re-traumatisation that is likely to further increase suicide risk.

Unipolar depressive disorder

Although not all people who suicide will have been experiencing depressive symptoms at the time of death, depressive disorder is still a significant risk factor for completed suicide (1,3,5,8,10,12).

The enduring nature of the fight to spend time with their children can cause targeted parents to suffer from changes in mood and to develop depressive symptoms that impact on capacity to function. An assessment of current symptomatology should be conducted, with special attention paid to mood symptoms because of the link to increased suicide risk.

Hopelessness

A sense of hopelessness that is a reflection of the constricted thinking of suicidal individuals is a risk factor for suicidal behaviour (3,12). The suicidal individual's distorted and constricted thinking encourages the belief that their life circumstance will never improve and they either have to suffer or end their life.

For targeted parents, the development of a sense of hopelessness is hardly surprising. The experiences of ongoing separation from their child, continuing conflict with the alienating parent, repeated breaches of orders by the alienating parent, and dealing with a legal system that is perceived to be unresponsive to their needs, leads to targeted parents feeling hopeless about the future. This sense of hopelessness may increase the suicide risk of targeted parents.

Worthlessness

Feelings of worthlessness have been associated with suicidal risk (12). These feelings, which are a reflection of the distorted thinking that comes with low mood and suicidal ideation, result in the suicidal individual seeing little point in fighting suicidal urges.

It is not surprising that parents who are rejected by their own children would develop feelings of worthlessness. The suicidal risk associated with feelings of worthlessness would be likely to be higher for targeted parents whose parenting role is central to their understanding of their status in life. For parents who hold this point of view, the rejection by their children would have a profound effect on how they view themselves and their worth.

Drug/alcohol abuse/dependence

Substance use problems are associated with increased suicidal risk (1-4,7,12). Significant substance use problems are linked to difficulties coping with life demands. Also, substance intoxication is associated with disinhibition and increased impulsivity that increase the risk that an individual will engage in impulsive suicidal actions.

Targeted parents experience the type of life stressors that cannot easily be resolved. When other problem-focused coping strategies fail, targeted parents may adopt substance use as a means of managing difficult emotional reactions to the problems they face. With drugs and alcohol having disinhibiting effects, targeted parents are at risk of impulsive suicidal behaviour because they experience sufficiently powerful triggering events.

Impulsivity

Many suicidal actions are impulsive in nature. Moreover, an inherent impulsive tendency increases the risk for suicidal behaviour (7,12). In the face of life stressors, an impulsive individual may act on suicidal thoughts in a way that would not happen in a less impulsive individual.

As previously stated, targeted parents experience the types of difficult life stressors that are likely to trigger impulsive suicidal behaviour in vulnerable individuals. The vulnerability is contributed to by the life circumstances faced by targeted parents, such as separation from children and vilifying alienation tactics used by alienating parents.

Self-injury

Non-suicidal self-injury, also known as self-harm, is not considered to be a suicidal behaviour (13). Nevertheless, the suicidal risk in people with a history of self-injury is considerable (2,4,10,14). The risk of suicide is particularly high in the six months after the first self-injury episode but can persist throughout the course of a person's life.

Non-suicidal self-injury is generally understood to be a maladaptive strategy for coping with intense distress. A person will engage in self-injury when in a state of distress, triggering a reduction in tension and a return to a feeling of equilibrium (15). Undoubtedly, targeted parents can experience intense distress as a result of the events they experience. Non-suicidal self-injury should be viewed as increasing the risk of suicidal behaviour in targeted parents.

Suicidal ideation

Although many more people have thoughts about suicide than ever end their lives, it is evident that people who commit suicide have experienced suicidal thoughts (3,12). Any thoughts about suicide should be taken seriously, including when reported by targeted parents. The inability to resolve problems relating to their separation from their children is likely to restrict the thinking of targeted parents so that thoughts of suicide strongly manifest.

Prior suicide attempt

Not surprisingly, a prior suicide attempt increases the risk that an individual will again engage in suicidal behaviour (2,5,7,12). A prior suicide attempt reflects a pattern of difficulty coping with demanding life circumstances.

In targeted parents, look for a pattern of failure to cope that includes a prior suicide attempt. This is true whether or not the suicide attempt relates to the problems of parental alienation.

Stressful life events

Stressful life events can act as a precipitant to suicidal behaviour. In addition, the experience of stressful life events can contribute to increased risk of suicide, especially in combination with other factors that indicate vulnerability (2,4). That is, with the presence of pre-existing vulnerabilities, the individual can fail to cope with the additional stressful life event and the likelihood that the person will engage in suicidal behaviour increases.

The nature and duration of the life stressors faced by targeted parents in relation to parental alienation are likely to increase the risk of suicidal behaviour by targeted parents. In combination with a sense of hopelessness, it is likely that targeted parents would see little chance of a resolution of their difficulties, especially after seemingly unsuccessfully exploring avenues for resolution that are available to them.

Social isolation

Social isolation is recognised as a significant contributor to suicide risk (2,12). Social support is a known buffer, assisting people to cope with demands and life challenges. In the absence of this social support, suicide risk increases. Further, in the absence of social support, the constricted thinking of suicidal individuals has greater strength because it is not countered by more rational thought that can be offered by others.

In estimating the suicide risk for a targeted parent, it is important to consider the extent to which that parent has access to social support. With parental alienation being associated with feelings of rejection, the further isolation that would occur with limited social support would be enough to increase suicide risk.

Suicide risk assessment

When assessing targeted parents, it is essential to consider suicide risk and to work through a checklist for increased suicide risk indicators. Such a list might include the following:

- Is this person in a high-risk suicide category?
- Does this person have a history of suicidal thoughts or actions?
- Does this person currently experience thoughts of suicide?
- Does this person have a suicide plan?
- Does this person have the means to carry out their suicide plan?
- Does this person have one strongly evident or multiple suicide risk indicators?
- Does this person have protective factors that might ameliorate the suicide risk?

Risk of child abuse offending

As stated, an assessment of a targeted parent may move beyond factors that impact on that individual's wellbeing. With allegations being made about wrongdoing on the part of the targeted parent, it may be necessary to consider the indicators of these claims being true.

In the face of claims of child abuse made by the alienating parent, it is necessary to consider the risk factors present for the perpetration of child abuse by any targeted parent. There are a number of offending risk assessment instruments available as a guide to clinical judgment. In addition, there are certain features of the perpetration of child abuse that should be considered when formulating an opinion about the likelihood that any one individual has abused a child.

For example, it has been reported that, apart from child sexual abuse, a child is more likely to be abused by a parent or caregiver than by other individuals (17). Parents also may perpetrate sexual abuse against a child but there is greater diversity in the relationships of the perpetrator and the child in the case of child sexual abuse.

When considering the characteristics of people who abuse their children, there is a general view that abusive parents were abused themselves as children. However, there are many more parents who were abused as children who do not harm their children than there are parents with a history of abuse who do harm their children. Nevertheless, there is some evidence for the intergenerational transmission of physical abuse and neglect of children (17–18). The research results relating to the transmission of sexual abuse are less clear with some reporting high rates of transmission (19) and others low rates (20).

Consideration of the recognised characteristics of people who engage in child abuse will assist in the assessment of targeted parents when allegations of abuse have been made. This is necessary if there is to be a differentiation made between alienated children and those who reject a parent for justifiable reasons.

Perpetrators of physical abuse

It is evident from the available research that both mothers and fathers may physically abuse their children. Australian data (21) indicated that physical abuse is more likely to be perpetrated by fathers than mothers. However, a large British study demonstrated that mothers were more likely than fathers to perpetrate physical abuse of their child (22). This study did find that the more serious or severe physical abuse was more likely the result of actions by fathers, with these findings supported by research from the US (23).

Perpetrators of neglect

Neglect, by definition, is perpetrated by a person whose role it is to provide care for a child. As a result, it is often parents who fail to adequately provide that care. In many states of Australia, neglect is the most frequently reported form of maltreatment of a child (24) although the lower rates in other states may reflect the lack of focus on neglect as a form of maltreatment of children. Certainly, many studies of the prevalence of forms of maltreatment do not focus on neglect (25).

Based on the available data, it is apparent that biological parents are the adults most likely to neglect a child (16,24) because of their role as primary carers of their own children. Also, mothers are more likely than fathers to neglect their children (23), with this likely to reflect the predominance of primary care roles for mothers.

A combination of parental psychopathology (e.g., substance use problems), family violence and more general social issues, such as socioeconomic status and the consequent factors of health, housing and employment, have been identified as contributing factors for the neglect of children by their parents. The neglect may be a consequence of the stressors that occur that detract a parent from being able to focus their attention on their child's need (25).

Perpetrators of sexual abuse

More research attention has been devoted to the examination of perpetrators of child sexual abuse than any other form of child maltreatment. There is strong support for the view that the vast majority of child sexual abuse offenders are male (26–27). However, although it is recognised that a small proportion of child sex offenders are female, it has been suggested that the actual proportion of female offenders is higher than reported (26). This is likely due to under-reporting of female perpetrated sexual abuse of children. Child sexual abuse is less likely to be perpetrated by parents than by other adults (23).

Perpetrators of emotional abuse

Although emotional abuse is one of the most commonly reported forms of abuse of children in Australia (24), less research attention has been paid to the perpetrators of emotional abuse than sexual abuse. This is despite the fact that emotional abuse has been associated with a range of significantly negative psychological outcomes for victims (28).

The major problem that has interfered with researching the characteristics of the perpetrators of emotional abuse has been related to problems of definition (29). There is little agreement about whether acts of omission, that is emotional neglect in the form of ignoring and emotional withdrawal, should be distinguished from acts of commission, such as verbal abuse, and shaming and humiliation.

Nevertheless, it has been reported that the majority of perpetrators of emotional abuse of children are parents, with more fathers than mothers engaging in emotional abuse (16). However, it is still evident that a significant proportion of emotional abuse cases are perpetrated by mothers.

Fatal child abuse

Given the claims made by alienating parents about the alleged dangerousness of targeted parents, it is worth examining the characteristics of people who cause their children's deaths from abuse and neglect. The children most at risk of death at the hands of their parents or through neglect by their parents are younger children (30).

Males are more likely to fatally assault their children than females. It has been demonstrated that non-biological caregivers are considerably more likely than biological parents to cause a child's death from assault (31). However, a problem exists with this research. Most data are obtained from homicide records and deaths caused by neglect may not be identified in these records (32–33).

Assessing violence risk

If violence on the part of the targeted parent is alleged by the alienating parent, it is necessary to assess the risk of violent behaviour. If the conclusion reached is that the targeted parent does not pose a notable violence risk, then it is necessary to back up this opinion with a reason why it was formulated.

Approach to violence risk assessment

There is no definitive way of determining the risk of violent behaviour. Risk assessment instruments are available to assist in the process of estimating violence risk. These typically guide clinical judgment when attempting to determine the risk of future harm. They remind you of the factors to be considered and instruct you in the way in which the information you have available to you can be interpreted so that a judgment can be made about the likelihood that violent behaviour will occur in the future.

It is worth keeping in mind that there is no such thing as 'no risk of violence'. We are all capable of violent behaviour even if the likelihood that violent behaviour will occur is low.

In using clinical judgment to determine violence risk, it is necessary to consider three types of factors. These include static factors, dynamic factors and risk management/speculative factors (34).

Static factors

Static factors are the relatively unchanging features or experiences of a person, some of which are based on actuarial information. They are the factors that have occurred and are recorded as having been present for an individual.

An established history of violent behaviour is the best predictor of future violent behaviour. This is not to say that a person who has been violent cannot change their behaviour. It does indicate that a history of violence increases the risk that violence will occur again in the future. Added to this is a history of antisocial behaviour that increases the risk of violence in the future. Further, the presence of violent attitudes suggests a propensity to violent behaviour in the future.

Other static factors relate to a history of instability in a variety of life domains. These include relationship and employment instability. This might include a failure to comply with intervention or supervision directives, suggesting a pattern of instability with regard to help seeking and acceptance of advice given.

In addition, static factors that should be considered include a history of psychological problems. These include a substance use history, the experience of a major mental disorder, and the presence of personality disturbance or disorder. The history of psychological problems may include traumatic experience in the individual's past.

Dynamic factors

Dynamic or clinical factors refer to those features of an individual's experience that may alter across time and circumstance. While present, these factors increase the risk of violent behaviour but that increase in risk diminishes when these factors resolve.

Not surprisingly, thoughts of violence or an intention to engage in violent behaviour increases violence risk. A lack of insight into the risk of violent behaviour also increases the risk of violence.

Some factors that impact on violence risk when evident in the person's history also may increase violence risk if currently influencing the individual. These include currently experiencing the symptoms of a major mental disorder, instability experienced in various life domains and lack of compliance with intervention efforts.

Speculative factors

Speculative or risk management factors refer to situations for the person that might either destabilise them in the near future or protect them from violent behaviour. These include factors such as whether professional services can be accessed, the person's living situation and how much personal support they have available to them, whether they are likely to avail themselves of intervention options and situations that may cause them stress or challenge their coping resources.

Risk factors associated with family violence

There is additional information available about the risk factors that are associated with family violence, in particular, and not just a general risk of violent behaviour. This is important information to know as most of the accusations of violent behaviour made about targeted parents by alienating parents relate to domestic/family violence.

There are some general risk factors that have been identified as being associated with family violence (35). These include factors such as poor academic achievement, low income, social disadvantage and problematic adolescent behaviour that was characterised by aggressiveness. All of these factors increase the risk of family violence, along with excessive alcohol use and generally aggressive and controlling behaviour. However, none of these factors by themselves or as a group have good predictive power so the chances of falsely identifying an individual as a family violence perpetrator based on these features alone is high.

The prediction of re-assault among family violence perpetrators can be made to a more confident degree when consideration is given to a range of re-offending risk factors (36). These include the following:

1. As past behaviour is the best predictor of future behaviour, a history of previous family violence assaults, whether against the identified victim or others, increases the risk of future family violence. Also, the risk is increased by a history of suicide or homicide attempts or threats of the same, along with prior arrests for these types of actions.
2. Instability of employment and the resultant instability of income have been associated with a higher risk of family violence re-offending.
3. Drug and alcohol misuse increase the risk of family violence. This is not surprising as substance use is likely to have a disinhibiting effect on an individual's behaviour making actions less constrained and more vulnerable to impulsive urges.

4. With regard to relationship or interpersonal characteristics, the risk of family violence re-offending increases when the identified or suspected perpetrator has traits of jealousy, has a well-developed sense of entitlement, and is possessive. In combination with a lack of empathy for others, the risk of family violence increases in the presence of these factors.

5. The childhood histories of family violence perpetrators can influence risk of re-offending. Childhood abuse experiences and other types of problematic childhood experiences, such as neglect, have been demonstrated to increase risk.

6. A pattern of relationship instability has been identified as a risk factor for future family violence. This might include multiple short-term relationships or problematic and unstable longer-term relationships.

7. The termination of a relationship and separation can act as a trigger for family violence re-offending. With few ways of coping with the challenges of relationship breakdown, family violence perpetrators revert to previously adopted and aggressive ways of dealing with life challenges.

8. Interestingly, the risk of family violence re-offending by the identified perpetrator is likely to increase if there is a pattern of escalating violent behaviour on the part of the identified victim. The same risk increase is evident with regard to suicidal behaviour on the part of the identified victim. In both cases, these factors increase the volatility of the relationship dynamics and, therefore, increase family violence risk.

9. Factors related to an individual's psychological state can affect family violence risk. These have been identified as depressive symptoms, personality disorder and poor self-esteem.

10. Violent behaviour towards animals, including pets, has been associated with increased risk of family violence.

11. Finally, a male family violence perpetrator's attitude towards women can influence the risk of re-assault. Misogynistic attitudes are the most problematic.

These are the factors that have been associated with increased family violence re-offending risk and, if evident in relation to the targeted parent, would increase suspicion that the allegations being made by the alienating parent have their foundation in truthfulness. However, some caution is recommended. It has been suggested that there is a fundamental difference between abusive relationships and the interpersonal difficulties that occur during high conflict divorce (37). It is advised that the situational nature of any problematic interpersonal experience between the alienating parent and the targeted parent be considered, rather than immediately labelling these difficulties as an indication of longer-term relationship problems. Below, in Table 12.1, is a list of the factors that are characteristic of abusive relationships in contrast to those associated with high conflict divorce.

Concluding comments

As stated, the assessments of targeted parents tend to take a different form from the approach to the assessment of alienating parents and alienated children. Taking two different pathways, the assessment of targeted parents and their behaviour should focus more on their current psychological state that has developed as a consequence of involvement in the parental alienation process, and the testing of the allegations made about the targeted parent by the alienating parent. The purposes of these assessments includes:

Table 12.1 Indicators of relationship difficulties.

Abusive relationships	High conflict divorce
Physically violent behaviour or threats of physically violent behaviour; inducing fear in the victim.	Ongoing difficulties in agreeing to parenting strategies caused by lack of trust and blaming.
Emotionally abusive behaviour; actions that target the victim's self-esteem.	High levels of hostility that can deteriorate into verbally abusive behaviour or, on occasion, physically violent behaviour.
Sexually coercive behaviour; rape within the relationship.	Rejection of the rules or demands imposed by the other party.
Unilateral decision-making with regard to financial and other matters affecting the victim.	Greater equality of power in the relationship.
Insistence of control or authority in relation to child-rearing decisions.	Failure to reach agreement, even in a legal context, that is contributed to by both parties.
Isolation of the victim from social contacts and interactions with others.	
Using legal options to punish the victim or harass them.	

1. The testing of the allegations made by the alienating parent about the targeted parent is an effort to determine how much weight is going to be given to the accounts provided by both parties.
2. The psychological health of the targeted parent.
3. The effect of the stresses of parental alienation on the targeted parent's parenting capacity.
4. The readiness of the targeted parent to deal with the significant challenges associated with any therapeutic intervention directed at improving family relationships.

References

1. Arsenault-Lapierre, G., Kim, C., & Turecki, G. (2004). Psychiatric diagnoses in 3275 suicides: A meta-analysis. *BMC Psychiatry, 4*, 37. doi:10.1186/1471-244x-4-37
2. Cooper, J., Kapur, N., Webb, R., Lawlor, M., Guthrie, E., Mackway-Jones, K., & Appleby, L. (2005). Suicide after deliberate self-harm: A 4-year cohort study. *American Journal of Psychiatry, 162*, 297–303. doi:10.1176/appi.ajp.162.2.297
3. Evans, E., Hawton, K., & Rodham, K. (2004). Factors associated with suicidal phenomena in adolescents: A systematic review of population-based studies. *Clinical Psychology Review, 24*, 957–979. doi:10.1016/j.cpr.2004.04.005
4. Neeleman, J. (2001). A continuum of premature death. Meta-analysis of competing mortality in the psychosocially vulnerable. *International Journal of Epidemiology, 30*, 154–162. doi:10.1093/ije/30.1.154
5. Tidemalm, D., Langstrom, N., Lichtenstein, P., & Runeson, B. (2008). Risk of suicide after suicide attempt according to coexisting psychiatric disorder: Swedish cohort study with long-term follow up. *British Medical Journal, 337*, 2205. doi:10.1136/bmj.a2205
6. Agerbo, E., Nordentoft, M., & Mortensen, P.B. (2002). Familial, psychiatric, and socioeconomic risk factors for suicide in young people: Nested case-control study. *British Medical Journal, 325*, 74–77. doi:10.1136/bmj.325.7355.74
7. De Leo, D., Cerin, E., Spathonis, K., & Burgis, S. (2005). Lifetime risk of suicide ideation and attempts in an Australian community: Prevalence, suicidal process, and help-seeking behaviour. *Journal of Affective Disorders, 86*, 215–224. doi:10.1016/j.jad.2005.02.001

8. Harris, E.C., & Barraclough, B. (1997). Suicide as an outcome for mental disorders. A meta-analysis. *British Journal of Psychiatry, 170,* 205–228. doi:10.1192/bjp.170.3.205

9. Hawton, K., Sutton, L., Haw, C., Sinclair, J., & Deeks, J. (2005). Schizophrenia and suicide: Systematic review of risk factors. *British Journal of Psychiatry, 187,* 9–20. doi: 10.1192/bjp.187.1.9

10. Nock, M.K., & Kessler, R.C. (2006). Prevalence of and risk factors for suicide attempts versus suicide gestures: Analysis of the National Comorbidity Survey. *Journal of Abnormal Psychology, 115,* 616–623. doi: 10.1037/0021-843x.115.3.616

11. Brown, J., Cohen, P., Johnson, J.G., & Smailes, E.M. (1999). Childhood abuse and neglect: Specificity of effects on adolescent and young adult depression and suicidality. *Journal of the American Academy of Child Adolescent Psychiatry, 38,* 1490–1496. doi:10.1097/00004583-199912000-00009

12. Rogers, J.R., Lewis, M.M., & Subich, L.M. (2002). Validity of the Suicide Assessment Checklist in an emergency crisis center. *Journal of Counselling and Development, 80,* 493–502. doi:10.1002/j.1556–6678.2002.tb00216.x

13. Klonsky, E.D. (2007). The functions of deliberate self-injury: A review of the evidence. *Clinical Psychology Review, 27,* 226–239. doi:10.1016/j.cpr.2006.08.002

14. Hawton, K., Houston, K., Haw, C., Townsend, E., & Harriss, L. (2003). Comorbidity of axis I and axis II disorders in patients who attempted suicide. *American Journal of Psychiatry, 160,* 1494–1500. doi:10.1176/appi.ajp.160.8.1494

15. Haines, J., Williams, C.L., Brain, K.L., & Wilson, G.V. (1995). The psychophysiology of self-mutilation. *Journal of Abnormal Psychology, 104,* 471–489. doi:10.1037//0021-843x.104.3.471

16. Sedlak, A., Mettenburg, J., Basena, M., Petta, I., McPherson, K., Greene, A. et al. (2010). *Fourth National Incidence Study of Child Abuse and Neglect (NIS-4): Report to congress.* Washington DC: US Department of Health and Human Services, Administration for Children and Families.

17. Kim, J. (2009). Type-specific intergenerational transmission of neglectful and physically abusive parenting behaviors among parents. *Children and Youth Services Review, 31*(7), 761–767. doi:10.1016/j.childyouth.2009.02.002

18. Pears, K.C., & Capaldi, D.M. (2001). Intergenerational transmission of abuse: A two-generational prospective study of an at-risk sample. *Child Abuse and Neglect, 25,* 1439–1461. doi:10.1016/s0145-2134(01)00286-1

19. Simons, D., Wurtele, S., & Durham, R. (2008). Developmental experiences of child sexual abusers and rapists. *Child Abuse and Neglect, 32,* 549–560. doi:10.1016/j.chiabu.2007.03.027

20. Salter, D., McMillan, D., Richards, M., Talbot, T., Hodges, J., Bentovim, A. et al. (2003). Development of sexually abusive behaviour in sexually victimised males: A longitudinal study. *Lancet, 361*(9356), 471–476. doi:10.1016/s0140-6736(03)12466-x

21. Australian Bureau of Statistics (2005). *Personal safety survey.* Canberra: ABS.

22. May-Chahal, C., & Cawson, P. (2005). Measuring child maltreatment in the United Kingdom: A study of the prevalence of child abuse and neglect. *Child Abuse and Neglect, 29,* 969–984. doi:10.1016/j.chiabu.2004.05.009

23. US Department of Health and Human Services. (2005). *Male perpetrators of child maltreatment: Findings from NCANDS.* Author.

24. Australian Institute of Health and Welfare. (2014). *Child protection Australia 2012–13.* Canberra: AIHW.

25. Scott, D., Higgins, D., & Franklin, R. (2012). *The role of supervisory neglect in childhood injury* (CFCA Paper No. 8). Melbourne: CFCA information exchange.

26. McCloskey, K., & Raphael, D. (2005). Adult perpetrator gender asymmetries in child sexual assault victim selection: Results from the 2000 National Incident-Based Reporting system. *Journal of Child Sexual Abuse, 14,* 1–24. doi:10.1300/j070v14n04_01

27. Peter, T. (2009). Exploring taboos: Comparing male- and female-perpetrated child sexual abuse. *Journal of Interpersonal Violence, 24,* 1111–1128. doi:10.1177/0886260508322194

28. Tonmyr, L., Draca, J., Crain, J., & MacMillan, H.L. (2011). Measurement of emotional psychological child maltreatment: A review. *Child Abuse and Neglect, 36*, 767–782. doi:10.1016/j.chiabu.2011.04.011

29. Black, D.A., Smith Slep, A.M., & Heyman, R.E. (2001). Risk factors for psychological abuse. *Aggression and Violent Behavior, 6*, 189–201. doi:10.1016/s1359-1789(00)00022-7

30. Asmussen, K. (2010). *Key facts about child maltreatment* (NSPCC Research Briefing). London, UK: NSPCC.

31. Yampolskaya, S., Greenbaum, P., & Berson, I. (2009). Profiles of child maltreatment perpetrators and risk for fatal assault: A latent class analysis. *Journal of Family Violence, 24*, 337–348. doi:10.1007/s10896-009-9233-8

32. Finkelhor, D. (1997). The homicides of children and youth. In G.K. Kantor & J. Jasinski (Eds.), *Out of the darkness: Contemporary perspectives on family violence* (pp. 17–34). Thousand Oaks, CA: Sage.

33. Lawrence, R., & Irvine, P. (2004). *Redefining fatal child neglect* (Child Abuse Prevention Issues No. 21). Melbourne: AIFS.

34. Guy, L.S., Wilson, C.M., Douglas, K.S., Hart, S.D., Webster, C.D., & Belfrage, H. (2013). *HCR-20 Version 3: Item-by-item summary of violence literature*. HCR-20 Violence Risk Assessment White Paper Series, #3. Burnaby, Canada: Mental Health, Law, and Policy Institute, Simon Fraser University.

35. Morgan, A., & Chadwick, H. (2009). Key issues in domestic violence. *Research in Practice Summary Paper No. 07*. Australian Institute of Criminology.

36. Campbell, J.C., Webster, D., Koziol-McLain, J., Block, C., Campbell, D., Curry, M.A., Gary, F. et al. (2003). Risk factors for femicide in abusive relationships: Results from a multisite case control study. *American Journal of Public Health, 93*, 1089–1097. doi:10.2105/ajph.93.7.1089

37. Johnston, J., Roseby, K., & Kuehnle, V. (2009). *In the name of the child: A developmental approach to understanding and helping children of conflicted and violent divorce* (2nd edn.). New York: Springer.

Chapter Thirteen

Assessing alienated children

Introduction

The effects on children of the alienation process are varied. Although the outcome is degradation of the targeted parent–child relationship, the ways in which the alienation can manifest need to be considered. The presentation of the children, the ways in which they conduct themselves during interview, and their actions both inside and outside the interview setting are worthy of attention.

Although not all alienated children will demonstrate all indicators of parental alienation, you should be aware of all the ways this process may influence a child's behaviour. Identifying alienated children may require that you access collateral information because it is not possible to observe all features when interacting with an alienated child.

Identifying alienated children

When undertaking parenting dispute evaluations and/or when acting as a court-appointed expert witness, it is necessary that a robust opinion is reached about the presence or absence of parental alienation. Also, in the role of therapist, it is necessary to be able to recognise signs of parental alienation in the children with whom you work.

Ellis (1) has suggested a step-wise process of assessment of the presence of the indicators of parental alienation in affected children. In doing this, she identified the features of parental alienation that should be able to be identified if parental alienation has occurred. There is one other indicator, referred to as the independent thinker phenomenon, that is rightly placed in a consideration of the child-related indications of parental alienation.

Expression of negative views about the targeted parent

When interviewed, the child may express negative views about the targeted parent. These negative views are often accompanied by a belief that the targeted parent is persecuting the alienated child. In this way, the child will provide accounts of how the parent is deliberately acting in a way that will upset the child or interfere with their happiness or quality of life.

What makes the evaluation of the source of these negative views challenging is that the views being expressed often are not unreasonable. It is easy to dismiss clearly distorted accounts of the wrongdoing of a targeted parent. In contrast, when the accounts possibly may be true, a decision must be made about how much weight is going to be given to the views expressed by the alienated child.

In most cases, the initial point of consideration is that you are presented with information from the child to the effect that a parent has engaged in behaviours or has treated the child in a particular way that is detrimental to the child. Also, you are presented with information from the targeted parent that no such negative behaviour has occurred. It is necessary to consider, then, collateral information that would support the account given by the alienating child or the targeted parent.

In the case of the expression of negative views as an indicator of parental alienation, this collateral information will not be available to support the child's account. Alternatively, some collateral information will be available to support a considerably more moderate view than the one expressed by the child (e.g., information about the way the targeted parent treats the child from other observers). The alienated child (and, presumably, the alienating parent) is embellishing experiences to make them seem more negative. In the absence of sufficiently supportive collateral information, acceptance of the account provided by the child should be done cautiously.

Box 13.1 Interviewer: Tell me what it's like when you go to Dad's place.

Alienated child: It's horrible. He's angry with me all the time and never lets me do anything. He sends me to my room for even little things. I have to stay in my bedroom for ages and ages. He picks on me all the time. Everything I do is wrong. I don't think he likes me much. He cooks me things I don't like and then makes me eat them even though I remind him I don't like them. He never talks to me. He just watches TV all the time and I have to just sit there and not disturb him otherwise I'll get into trouble. He's mean to me on purpose.

The account this young person is providing is not so extreme that it is outside the realms of possibility. However, in light of other material that may support the notion of a better relationship between the targeted parent and the child or more effort on the part of the targeted parent, the account starts to take on an excessively negative character.

Notice that this young person does not say that her father is angry with her some of the time or even much of the time. She claims he is angry all of the time. He is reported to pick on her all the time. Everything she does is wrong in his eyes. He never talks to her. So, the encompassing nature of the account is one feature to consider.

Not only will alienated children state that the targeted parent engages in behaviours that are detrimental to them, they will also make statements to the effect that the targeted parent is a bad person on a more fundamental level. That is, an alienated child will tend to undertake a character assassination of the targeted parent when asked to express a view about that parent.

Box 13.2 Interviewer: Tell me about your father.

Alienated child: He's a horrible person. He is really mean and doesn't care about people. He does mean things on purpose.

Interviewer: That sounds serious.

Alienated child: Yes, and he is mean to everyone he knows. I don't know anyone who likes him. He just thinks up mean things to do to people. And he doesn't care about people … even his own children.

In the context of the expression of negative views about the targeted parent, an alienated child may indicate that they hold the belief that the targeted parent is deliberately undermining their happiness. Rarely would a reason for their persecution be provided. From the alienated child's point of view, it is enough to say that the targeted parent's goal is to cause them unhappiness. In many cases, the alleged persecution extends to the alienating parent, most likely because of the strong alliance between the alienating parent and the alienated child.

Box 13.3 Interviewer: You said you are worried about what Dad has been doing. Tell me what has been worrying you.

   Alienated child: Well, he has been deliberately taking Mum to court just to make her upset.

   Interviewer: Why do you think he is doing that?

   Alienated child: He just wants to make things hard for Mum … and for me. He does it on purpose. Everything is going fine and then he makes Mum go back to court. He should just leave us alone.

   Interviewer: Maybe Dad doesn't think everything is fine … at least from his point of view.

   Alienated client: He does know everything is fine and he just makes Mum go back to court so that she will be upset. He does it on purpose.

So, whatever the reason for the targeted parent's alleged attack on the alienated child and the parent with whom they share this strong alliance, the goal of the attack is to make the alienated child and the alienating parent unhappy. Again, no reasonable account is provided by the child for why a parent who is seeking to spend time with them and who wishes to maintain the parent–child relationship would want their child to be unhappy.

Box 13.4 Alienating child: Dad just wants me to be unhappy.

   Interviewer: Why would he want you to be unhappy?

   Alienated child: I don't know but it's true. If he wanted me to be happy, he would just leave me alone. I'm only happy when I am with Mum and not when I am with him. He knows that. So, if he wanted me to be happy, he would just leave me alone.

When pushed, the alienated child might provide an account of ways in which the targeted parent acted that caused them to be upset or unhappy. Most often, the malicious intent on the part of the targeted parent that is implied by the alienated child is not present. At least, the actions of the targeted parent can be interpreted in more moderate ways.

Box 13.5 Interviewer: You said Dad just wants to make you unhappy.

   Alienated child: That's right.

   Interviewer: Give me some examples of things he does that make you unhappy.

   Alienated child: Well, he keeps asking to see me. That makes me unhappy. And when I do see him, he makes me do things I don't want to do.

   Interviewer: Like what?

> **Alienated child:** Well, he makes me go and see my cousins and my grandmother. And he takes me with him when he goes to the supermarket. And he makes me do my homework. Um ... and he cooks things that are not my favourites anymore.
> **Interviewer:** These don't sound like really terrible things.
> **Alienated child:** Well, they are, and they make me unhappy.

Not only will you notice exaggerations or misinterpretations of events and behaviours by the alienated child, the child also may provide accounts of negative experiences with the targeted parent that lack any supporting evidence that they ever occurred. The degree of certainty with which these accounts are provided does not differ from the accounts about events that did occur but have been misinterpreted in terms of the targeted parent's intention.

> **Box 13.6 Alienated child:** Dad has done lots of mean things.
> **Interviewer:** Tell me about some of these things Dad has done.
> **Alienated child:** Well, he took me around to his friend's house and he got drunk and had a fight with his friend. That happened the last time I saw him. I said I didn't want to see him again after that.
> **Interviewer:** I'm a little bit confused because Dad said he only had a cup of coffee when you visited his friend and he didn't have a fight with him.
> **Alienated child:** He did get drunk and he did have a fight with Simon.
> **Interviewer:** I'll tell you why I am still confused. I read a note from Simon that says Dad wasn't drunk and they didn't have a fight. I also read a note from your Grandma saying that you both visited her house after going to Simon's and Dad wasn't drunk and he seemed happy ... not like he had just had a fight.
> **Alienated child:** They are telling lies.
> **Interviewer:** After seeing Grandma, I understand you then went to visit Aunty Beth and you stayed there for the afternoon while Dad went to work. She said you seemed happy and Dad wasn't drunk.
> **Alienated child:** I don't care. He does mean things all the time.

When assessing the presence of this indicator of parental alienation, that is the expression of negative views about the targeted parent, consideration may need to be given to available collateral information. Determine whether there is external, collateral information that the targeted parent and child engage or have engaged in activities together. Determine whether they have been observed interacting in their home or in each other's company. Evaluate what others have to say about the responsiveness of the targeted parent to the child's needs.

Also, it is worth considering how your views about this possible indicator of parental alienation fit with other indicators. It is a mistake to form an opinion about this indicator that then may influence how you interpret other indicators. If, early on in the evaluation process and before all material has been considered, you choose to hold the view that the negative account provided by the child is an accurate one, it is likely to colour how you see other information that is provided to you. You then are influenced by a confirmation bias – you look for information that supports your original supposition. This process can take you so far from the truth that your final opinion becomes worthless. In the end, you need to be able to formulate an opinion that takes into account all the information you have available to you. Our advice is to withhold judgment about any one indicator until all information is collected and then go back and make a determination about whether individual indicators are present.

Extreme and opposite views about parents

Human beings tend to strongly desire internal consistency in relation to their thoughts, views, attitudes and behaviours. Cognitive dissonance refers to the feeling of intense mental distress or discomfort experienced when there is contradiction between a person's ideas and beliefs. The individual then feels driven to reduce that dissonance by resolving the internal conflict.

This can be applied to an alienated child's situation. It often is the case that the targeted parent is someone with whom the alienated child once had a positive relationship. Even in the absence of a strongly positive relationship, the alienated child, at one time, may have strongly desired a close and loving connection with that parent. Now, the child is expressing negative views about the parent, is rejecting of the parent and is demonstrating little empathy for the targeted parent's situation. Potentially, a state of cognitive dissonance develops.

Further to this, the alienated child's other parent, that is the alienating parent, is someone who has held a position of trust, has been loving and supportive and has offered a positive and consistent relationship. This parent also is encouraging the child to develop negative feelings about the targeted parent. Potentially, the child is being encouraged to lie, to engage in behaviours that are harmful or damaging to the once loved targeted parent, and to alter their views. Again, a state of cognitive dissonance is likely to develop.

The psychological distress that is likely to be experienced as a result of these conflicts would need to be resolved so that the child can function well and remain well adjusted. When experienced, people will try to reduce cognitive dissonance. One way for the alienated child to do this is to adopt extreme views about the alienating and targeted parents. A child may avoid some of the conflict if the view is adopted that the alienating parent is the perfect parent who is devoted to the child and that the targeted parent is a terrible person who wishes to harm the child and the alienating parent. If the child can maintain this view, even when faced with evidence to the contrary, the child can avoid the discomfort and distress that is likely to return if the extreme attitudes towards the parents are examined.

Alienating children will make strongly positive statements about the alienating parent and strongly negative statements about the targeted parent. This lack of ambivalence is more evident in alienated children than in children estranged from a parent for other reasons (2). They will do this even in the absence of objective evidence of wrongdoing by the targeted parent.

Box 13.7 Interviewer: Tell me about your Dad.

Alienated child: He's great. I love him and he loves me. He never growls or gets angry.

Interview: What, never?

Alienated child: Hardly ever and then only when I have done something naughty which is hardly ever.

Interviewer: What about Mum? What's she like?

Alienated child: I don't like her. She's grumpy all the time. She complains about everything. She's never happy. She does mean things to Dad and I don't like it when she does that.

Interviewer: But you used to do some nice things together.

Alienated child: No, I didn't. I hate her. I don't ever want to see her again.

The extreme nature of these views actually allows the child to experience a degree of psychological comfort. It is acceptable to reject her mother if her mother is a terrible person and it is acceptable to support her father if he is a consistently kind and loving parent.

In addition to stating that the alienating parent is a better and nicer person than the targeted parent, the alienated child will translate that superiority of one parent over the other into an examination of the relative parenting strengths of the alienating parent compared with the targeted parent. In this way, the alienated child is likely to identify specific behaviours on the part of the alienating parent that indicates the targeted parent is the inferior parent.

Of course, the alienated child is still vulnerable to the effects of the conflict that exists between what they are thinking and saying about the targeted parent, and what they know to be true. However, even when gentle challenge elicits evidence of that conflict, the alienated child is likely to revert to the stronger statement of support for the alienating parent and rejection of the targeted parent.

Box 13.8 Interviewer: I met your Mum yesterday. She said she hasn't seen you in seven months.

Alienated child: I don't care. I hate her. She is a terrible mother. She runs around with other men and does whatever she likes. She doesn't care about us. She doesn't care about Dad.

Interviewer: Mum said she would like to see you.

Alienated child: Well, I don't want to see her. Dad looks after me now. He makes me apple pie because he knows I love it. He looks after all of us really well. He doesn't run around with other women. He stays at home and looks after us.

Interviewer: Are you sure you don't want to see Mum? She told me that you used to cuddle up on the couch and watch television together. She said you used to sit in the kitchen while she cooked tea and chat about what happened at school.

Alienated child: [Silence – then overt signs of distress] Please don't make me remember! I can't ... [Pulls himself together] I hate her anyway.

This alienated child coped poorly with even the mildest challenge to his extreme position about his parent. To cope with his current situation, he maintained his negative views. Failure to do that would cause him even more distress.

Alienating parents work to establish a strong alliance between themselves and the alienated child. As a result of this influence, an alienated child may view the alienating parent as the most trustworthy of the two parents. In contrast, the targeted parent is viewed as a bad person who is untrustworthy.

Box 13.9 Alienated child: My Dad always does the right thing. He told me I can always trust him, and I think that's true. My Dad never does anything wrong.

Interviewer: What about Mum?

Alienated child: Well, she's the opposite! She never does anything right. Dad said I can't trust her and that's true, I can't. She tells lies and does sneaky things to Dad.

As a result of these opposite views about the alienated child's parents, it makes sense to the child to want to spend time only with the loving, trustworthy and skilled parent. The rejection of the unloving, untrustworthy and unskilled parent is then much easier for the alienated child than would be the case if the child held a more moderate view about the targeted parent.

Box 13.10 Alienated child: I only want to see Dad. I never want to see Mum ... ever. I only want to live at Dad's house and I only want Dad to take me to school. I never want Mum to take me to school. I only want Dad to take me shopping and never her. I don't want her to take me anywhere.

    Interviewer: What about visiting Mum at her house?

    Alienated child: I never want to go to her house. I don't want to go there. I hate it there and I don't like her. I have told everyone that I don't want to see her. I don't know why people keep trying to make me like her when I don't.

It is easier for the alienated child to align him or herself with the alienating parent if the view is held that the unhappy situation experienced by the family is entirely the fault of the targeted parent. As a result, the alienated child often will hold the targeted parent responsible for the breakdown of the parents' marital relationship. Without adequately understanding the complexities of adult romantic relationships, the alienated child categorises parents as villain and victim, with the targeted parent being the villain.

Box 13.11 Alienated child: I feel sorry for Dad.

    Interviewer: Why do you feel sorry for him?

    Alienated child: I feel sorry for Dad because he was a good husband, but my mother ran off with another man. If it wasn't for her, then Dad would be fine, and he wouldn't be sad.

    Interviewer: I heard that your mother and father had lots of problems that made it difficult for them to stay together.

    Alienated parent: Not Dad. He didn't have any problems. They aren't together anymore because my mother did something horrible to Dad. No wonder Dad is sad after what she did to him.

The negative views expressed about the targeted parent and the positive views expressed about the alienating parent by the alienated child can influence how the child responds to extended family members. The family of the targeted parent can be rejected and the family of the alienating parent can be warmly embraced by the alienated child.

Box 13.12 Interviewer: Do you get to see your grandparents?

    Alienated child: I get to see Nan and Pop all the time. We visit them all the time.

    Interviewer: Are Nan and Pop your father's parents?

    Alienated child: Yes. Dad takes me to their house all the time to visit them.

    Interviewer: What about your other grandparents? Do you get to see them?

    Alienated child: No. Why would I want to see them? I don't like them. They are on my mother's side, so I don't like them. Anyway, they are mean and grumpy all the time, so

I don't want to go there. Dad said I have good grandparents, so I figure I don't need any more. I only like Nan and Pop. The others are horrible and make me do things I don't like.
Interviewer: Like what?
Alienated child: Well, I don't remember. But I know I don't like them.

The strongly contrasting views about the alienating parent and the targeted parent are an effect of the alienation process. That is, these contrasting views developed because the child was exposed to alienation strategies by the alienating parent. Also, it is the case that the more strongly these contrasting views are endorsed, the more effective the alienation process.

Situationally determined changes in the child's behaviour

Given the very negative nature of an alienated child's account of the relationship with the targeted parent, a conclusion could easily be reached that this represents a well-entrenched position. However, it is a mistake to assume that an alienated child's behaviour is consistent across time or circumstance.

In fact, there is likely to be some inconsistency across situations in relation to the alienated child's behaviour towards the targeted parent. The alienated child will maintain a negative response to the targeted parent when the alienating parent is present or when an evaluator is observing. A more moderate response in the presence of the targeted parent alone or in the presence of others who are not evaluating the interaction can be reported.

Further, we have observed a change in behaviour as soon as the alienating parent's immediate influence is removed. Young children who express negative feelings about a targeted parent can be observed to physically and positively respond to the targeted parent's presence even when an evaluator is present. These children will reach out and touch the targeted parent and will refuse to move out of arm's reach of the targeted parent they have not seen for some time even if they do not verbally engage with the parent. Children who have expressed negative views about targeted parents in other situations will lean into that parent even when they are being observed. Children have been noted to be anxious and need to be reassured that the targeted parent will still be present when they return if they leave the room during the observation period.

This particular manifestation of parental alienation can be confusing for the parties involved. The alienating parent will claim that the child is dismissive of spending time with the targeted parent, that they do not discuss or mention the targeted parent, and they express distress at the suggestion that they spend time with the targeted parent. All of these manifestations of seeming rejection are likely to be accurate representations of how the child behaves. The targeted parent will report warmth of contact, good quality interaction and good child adjustment as long as the influence of the alienating parent is removed. These are likely to be accurate representations of how the child behaves when he or she is with the targeted parent.

Box 13.13 Targeted parent: I just don't understand it. Honestly, when we are together, everything's fine. She's happy to give me a hug and we laugh and have a good time, mostly. At least, we used to until recently when things have been weird, and she takes longer to settle. But when I drop her off at her mother's she acts like she's miserable and like she had a terrible time. I say goodbye and tell her that I'll see her soon and she just shrugs and walks away. I feel like she's Jekyll and Hyde.

This person's confusion is likely to be genuine. In a general sense, it is assumed that if there is a stark difference in the accounts being provided by the alienated child and the targeted parent, or the alienating parent and the targeted parent, then one of the parties must be distorting the truth. However, rather than there being any real conflict between the views expressed, the differences may simply reflect this phenomenon of alteration of the expression of negativity towards the targeted parent depending on the situation being described.

Certainly, the behaviour of an alienated child when they are with the targeted parent may be inconsistent with the child's stated reluctance to spend time with the targeted parent. The child may be insistent they do not wish to spend time with the targeted parent but then appear to enjoy the time they do get to spend with that parent.

Box 13.14   Targeted parent: She says she doesn't want to see me. I would say it's probably the case that she tries to get out of coming to spend time with me. She has told everyone who will listen that she doesn't want to come to my house or see me. But, you know, when I am in a position to force her mother to let my daughter come to see me, my daughter is fine. All right, I suppose it takes her a little while to settle down, but then she seems to enjoy herself and it is never as terrible as she predicts it will be. I would even say she has fun. It's like she has to prove to her mother she doesn't like me, so she refuses to come and see me. I know that if she was forced to come, she would be ok.

This variation in the way a child responds to the targeted parent is an interesting phenomenon. Their stated rejection of the targeted parent is not always consistent with their actions. Also, it is interesting to note that while the child may repeatedly be rejecting of the targeted parent, they can express considerable distress if they perceive that the targeted parent is rejecting them. It is natural enough for a targeted parent to feel frustrated by their child's repeated rejection. In response, targeted parents can be critical of their child's behaviour. In response to this criticism, alienated children can react as if they have been hurt by the loss of the targeted parent's good will. We have observed children who have adamantly stated they want nothing to do with the targeted parent and become tearful when the targeted parent expresses displeasure about the child's behaviour or, indeed, accepts the rejection and withdraws.

Box 13.15   Alienated child: I hate my father. I don't like him, and I never want to see him again … ever.

Interviewer: I'm sorry to hear you feel that way. I think Dad would be sorry to hear that, too.

Alienated child: I don't care. I don't care what he thinks.

Interviewer: Dad said you used to do lots of nice things together and he is disappointed that you don't seem to remember how things used to be.

Alienated child: Well, it's all his fault. He's the one to blame. I hate him. He just says mean things about me.

Interviewer: Like what?

Alienated child: Like he is disappointed in me … like you just said.

The rejection by the alienated child of the targeted parent may be accompanied by claims of fearfulness about being in the targeted parent's presence or observable indicators of anxiety and distress. However, it can be the case that if time with the targeted parent does occur, the alienated child will not demonstrate the fear and distress that anticipation of time together evoked.

Box 13.16 Targeted parent: I know her mother claims that Chloe is upset about spending time with me and is frightened of me for some reason, but when she is with me, she seems fine. She might be a little bit frosty to begin with, but it doesn't take long for her to settle down. We do nice things together and she seems relaxed. I do notice, though, that as the time for her to return home comes closer, she becomes more stressed. But rather than being frightened of me, it seems like she is frightened about returning home to face her mother.

It can be confusing when an alienated child, who claims they have definite, negative views about the targeted parent, then behaves as if they are unsure of their feelings for the targeted parent or reports positive feelings. Alienated children may backtrack on statements they have made rejecting a targeted parent or they may moderate their statements to express a less definitive point of view.

Box 13.17 Psychologist: I have interviewed children who are very insistent that they do not have any positive regard for their targeted parent but then will act as if that is not the case. For example, one eight-year-old girl told me there was no way she intended to see her father. She blamed him for her mother's unhappiness and was insistent she didn't like him. However, she seemed concerned that her father would learn that she had said negative things about him. As insistent as she was that she didn't care what her father thought, she also was insistent that her father never learn that she did not have positive things to say about him.

As a result of the alienation process, children can spend extended periods of time without seeing the targeted parent. During that time, the child may simply not talk about the targeted parent or may actively make negative statements about that parent. It is interesting, then, that these same children can respond to the targeted parent as if they are yearning for a connection with them after contact is re-established.

Box 13.18 Psychologist: I have observed alienated children act very differently from the way you would expect when they are with the targeted parent after an extended period of separation. Despite claims by the alienating parent that the child fears the targeted parent, and despite claims by the alienated child that they do not wish to spend any time with the targeted parent, I have observed children sit close to the rejected parent, to insist on being within touching distance from the parent and to experience distress on separation from the targeted parent. These behaviours are inconsistent with the claims made about and by the alienated child regarding their rejection of the targeted parent.

It is the case that alienated children will make strong statements about the rejection of the targeted parent and act in a manner that supports this expressed view. For example, they may refuse to go with the targeted parent, become distressed at changeovers or hide in their bedrooms. However, these children also may respond more positively than expected under certain conditions and in particular circumstances. When other indicators of parental alienation are present, this variation in response should not be taken as evidence that parental alienation has not occurred.

Denial of positive regard for the targeted parent

When interviewed, alienated children will often deny any degree of positive regard for the targeted parent. This view will be maintained even when contrary information is presented. When presented with objective evidence supporting the notion of a previously positive and loving relationship or variation in the feelings towards the targeted parent across time and circumstance, the alienated child will tend to rationalise their position, minimise the depth of their previous positive feelings or the meaning behind the more positive reaction to the targeted parent, or simply deny that any positive feelings ever existed.

Box 13.19 Interviewer: How did you go at your Dad's yesterday?
   Alienated child: I didn't want to go. The judge said I had to.
   Interviewer: I understand Dad put some effort into making sure you'd have a nice day.
   Alienated child: I didn't ask him to. That's his problem.
   Interviewer: He wanted you to have a nice time.
   Alienated child: Look, I don't care what he wanted. I don't care if he's happy and I don't care if he's sad. I just don't care. I went to see him because the judge made me go.

Alienated children may go so far as to refuse to acknowledge any positive aspect of the targeted parent's behaviour. This occurs even when evidence of the targeted parent's positive actions exists. The child will continue to insist that they do not have positive regard for their targeted parent.

Box 13.20 Interviewer: From what Dad said, it seems he has set up a bedroom at home for you that has everything you will need.
   Alienated child: I bet it's horrible.
   Interviewer: I think Dad has made sure your room has everything in it that you will like. He knows you like pink, so he got lots of pink things.
   Alienated child: I only like pink things that Mum buys for me.
   Interviewer: And he told me he got all your favourite books.
   Alienated child: He didn't buy them to make sure I am happy. He only bought them to make him happy.
   Interviewer: It sounds like he has done lots of things to make your bedroom nice for you.
   Alienated child: I bet everything is stupid. I know I will hate everything. He can't trick me into thinking he is nice just because he got me things I like.

In an effort to make it clear that they have no positive regard for the targeted parent, an alienated child may present 'evidence' of the parent's wrongdoing. In this way, they will often interpret positive or neutral parenting events by the targeted parent as negative in nature.

Box 13.21 **Interviewer:** Dad said you didn't eat the school lunch he made for you.
  Alienated child: That's because it was horrible. I hated the lunch he made me.
  Interviewer: What made it horrible?
  Alienated child: He put a banana in my lunchbox.
  Interviewer: Don't you like bananas?
  Alienated child: I only like the bananas that Mum puts in my lunchbox.
  Interviewer: Was the lunch Dad made ok except for the banana?
  Alienated child: No, I hated everything about it. He made a horrible lunch. I hated it all, so I didn't eat it.
  Interviewer: Dad told me he made you a sandwich and put some strawberry yoghurt in your lunch. Don't you like sandwiches and strawberry yoghurt?
  Alienated child: I just don't like it when he makes my lunch. It tastes funny.
  Interviewer: It tasted funny? So, you tried it and didn't like it?
  Alienated child: No, I didn't eat any of it. It looked funny. I just didn't like it because he made it.

It is not surprising that the alienated child will deny that they love the targeted parent. Somewhat more confusing is that they will insist that they never loved that parent, even when there is evidence to the contrary. In this way, the denial of positive regard for the targeted parent can be retrospective in nature.

Box 13.22 **Interviewer:** Dad told me he loves you very much.
  Alienated child: I don't love him.
  Interviewer: Grandma said you used to love your Dad. She said you used to want to be with him all the time. She said you were happy when you spent time together.
  Alienated child: I don't love him. I didn't love him before. I wasn't happy when I was with him.

The denial of positive regard expressed by the alienated child can be so severe that the child is unable or unwilling to identify any redeeming characteristic of the targeted parent. An unwillingness to shift their view can be strongly evident. They will insist that there is nothing good about the targeted parent and never was anything good about them.

Box 13.23 **Interviewer:** Tell me something about your Dad.
  Alienated child: Like what?
  Interviewer: Tell me some nice things about him.
  Alienated child: There isn't anything nice about him.
  Interviewer: Nothing at all?
  Alienated child: No, nothing. Just horrible things. There isn't one single nice thing about him. Just yucky stuff.
  Interviewer: Most people have some good things about them and some not so good things about them.
  Alienated child: Not him. He's completely horrible.

The alienated child will say it always has been the case that they had little positive regard for the targeted parent. Attempts to shift the alienated child's point of view to a more moderate one is usually met with little success. When evidence is presented that suggests the nature of the targeted parent–alienated child relationship may have been more positive in the past than the child is admitting, the child may simply state that their current feelings are the true ones and previous expressions of positive regard were pretence on their part. Alternatively, an alienated child may indicate a belief that they were naïve in the past when expressing positive regard and suggest that they now know better.

Box 13.24 Alienated child: He is a horrible father and I don't care that he misses me.
Interviewer: But lots of people have told me that you used to love your Dad and you used to do lots of fun things together.
Alienated child: That's not true. People are lying.
Interviewer: What about when you used to go bike riding together?
Alienated child: I just pretended to be happy and to like him.
Interviewer: Dad said you used to like to read books together.
Alienated child: I was younger then and didn't know what I was doing.

In aligning themselves with the alienating parent, it becomes easier for the alienated child to feel comfortable with the rejection of the targeted parent if the child can convince him or herself that no positive feelings for the targeted parent are felt. It would be difficult for a child to continue to openly reject the targeted parent if they also expressed positive feelings for that parent. The reported absence of positive regard may quieten any internal conflict the child may experience.

Distorted views about the targeted parent

As previously mentioned, alienated children may express negative views about the targeted parent that possibly could be true although they probably are not because of a lack of collateral confirmation. It also may be the case that alienated children's views about the targeted parent are so distorted that the concerns being expressed are unlikely to be true or are without merit.

Box 13.25 Alienated child: I don't want to see Mum.
Interviewer: Why not?
Alienated child: She's a hippie and that's why she doesn't look after us properly.
Interviewer: She's a hippie?
Alienated child: Yes, she wears dresses with flowers on them and puts her hair in a pony-tail. People who look like that can't look after their children properly.

The distorted thinking about the targeted parent may be evident in the negative stories told by the alienated child about the targeted parent. These stories typically are characterised by a high degree of improbability that they could ever be an accurate account of events that occurred. This might be because it is unlikely that anyone would engage in such behaviour or because it can be proven that the events did not take place. Pointing out the improbability of the statement being true will not correct the distortions in the child's view.

Box 13.26 Alienated child: My father kept driving up and down our street on Monday night.

Interviewer: How do you know it was Dad?

Alienated child: I saw him. It was definitely him.

Interviewer: Why would he be driving up and down your street?

Alienated child: He wanted to stick a knife in the tyres on Mum's car. We were frightened.

Interviewer: And you say it was definitely him.

Alienated child: Yes, it was him. He got out of the car and yelled at us from the path leading up to the front door. Mum turned on the outside light so we could see it was him. It was 8.30 on Monday night.

Interviewer: My problem is that Dad has been away this week. He went to a work meeting that lasted all week. He had to give a talk at the meeting. After the meeting he went out to dinner with the people he works with. That was on Monday night.

Alienated child: Well, he must have flown back and yelled at us then flew back to the dinner with his friends.

The chances of a targeted parent attending a dinner, flying home, driving up and down a street and yelling at the child, then flying back and resuming dinner are low. Of course, some of the accounts provided by the alienated child about the targeted parent might seem like they could be true despite the fact there is no evidence to support the claims being made.

Box 13.27 Alienated child: It is dangerous for me to go to my father's house.

Interviewer: Why is it dangerous?

Alienated child: It is dangerous because I will probably starve to death.

Interviewer: Starve to death? Why would you starve to death?

Alienated child: I would starve to death because my father never gives me anything to eat. He has food and his girlfriend has food, but he doesn't give me any … ever. He gives food to his girlfriend's children but never to me.

Interviewer: Dad said he made your favourite chicken dish last time you were there.

Alienated child: Well, he still didn't give me any. I've never ever had anything to eat when I've been there so I will probably just starve to death.

It is possible that this targeted parent never fed the alienated child, but it seems unlikely that it would be true. In the absence of evidence to support the claim, consideration would have to be given to the possibility that the account reflected a distorted view by the alienated child of the targeted parent's actions. In any case, the distortions in the accounts about the targeted parent by the alienated child often attribute ill intention on the part of the targeted parent. The interpretation of the targeted parent's behaviour as indicating ill intention tends not to be the interpretation that others would place on the action.

> **Box 13.28 Alienated child:** I don't want to have anything to do with my mother. She is so embarrassing. She does stupid things that I hate.
> **Interviewer:** Like what?
> **Alienated child:** Well, she had an argument with the lady from across the road and they didn't talk to each other for a while. And then she made up with her and that just makes her a hypocrite.
> **Interviewer:** Isn't it a good thing for people to sort out their problems?
> **Alienated child:** She just did it because she's dishonest. She also said she's going to get a job and that just makes her stupid. How does she think that will affect me? How can I go to school and face everyone if Mum gets a job?

Although this seems extreme, this is based on an interview that was conducted with a 13-year-old girl. Clearly, this alienated child is interpreting the targeted parent's behaviour in a more negative light than would other people. It is not unusual for alienated children to misinterpret normal parenting activities on the part of the targeted parent as being motivated by a desire to aggravate the child or cause harm.

> **Box 13.29 Interviewer:** What's it like when you go to stay with Dad?
> **Alienated child:** It's horrible. Dad is so mean.
> **Interviewer:** How is he mean?
> **Alienated child:** He does mean things. He doesn't let us use the swimming pool without him there watching us all the time. He makes us do our homework before dinner.
> **Interviewer:** Does Mum make you do your homework?
> **Alienated child:** Yes, but not in a mean way. She makes us do our homework because she cares about us. Dad doesn't care about us. He's just being mean.

Insisting that a child does their homework and supervising the use of the swimming pool are not unusual parenting activities. The problem here is that the alienated child is misinterpreting the parent's behaviour to indicate ill intent. Indeed, alienated children often talk about the targeted parent in extreme and negative terms that reflect a distortion in their thinking about that parent.

> **Box 13.30 Alienated child:** My father is the worst father in the world.
> **Interviewer:** Why is he the worst father?
> **Alienated child:** He is the worst father because he always does things on purpose to make me unhappy. And he always argues with me. He doesn't look after me properly and he never talks to me. He just watches television all the time … and drinks beer. He drinks a lot of beer. He makes me eat things I hate. He does it on purpose because he is mean and horrible. That makes him the worst father in the world. He always growls at me and never says anything nice.

In this case, the alienated child talks about the targeted parent in a way that is both extremely negative and likely to reflect a distortion in their thinking. Using words like 'always' and 'never' when describing events should lead you to further investigate whether or not the child's account is an accurate one.

Let us consider one more way an alienated child can distort their views of the targeted parent. In this case, the child may reinterpret previously pleasurable experiences with the targeted parent as if they were negative in nature. This usually is accompanied by a denial that the child ever experienced the event as pleasurable. Alienated children tend to be more likely to deny positive experiences with the targeted parent that adopt the view that a retrospective examination of the shared activities with the targeted parent has resulted in them seeing their experiences differently.

Box 13.31 Interviewer: Dad said you used to go camping a lot together and you always had a good time.

Alienated child: I didn't have a good time.

Interviewer: Dad said you used to play with your cousins and go swimming and fishing. It sounds lovely.

Alienated child: Well, it wasn't lovely. I was sad all the time I was camping.

Interviewer: Why would you have been sad all the time if you were doing the things you like to do?

Alienated child: That's because I don't like doing them with my father. I only like going camping when I go by myself.

Interviewer: Have you ever been camping by yourself?

Alienated child: Um, I don't remember.

The distorted views may be a reflection of a need to justify the position they have taken about the targeted parent. In the absence of reasonable examples of wrongdoing on the part of the targeted parent, the alienated child must rely on the information they have available to them. They then take this information and reinterpret its meaning to better fit with their current view of the targeted parent.

False memories or accounts of events not experienced

In order to support his or her negative views about the targeted parent, an alienated child may provide an account of events about which the child has no first-hand experience or events that occurred before a time when the child would be expected to accurately recall the event, or events that are unlikely ever to have occurred.

The child may maintain the memory is of events directly known to the child. This is because the events have become integrated into their understanding of what has happened. It can be a very simple matter to create false memories in a child. The child needs only to be exposed to discussions about events even when they are not actively involved in the discussion. So, a child may develop a false memory because they hear the alienating parent talking to other adults about the events in question. In fact, a child is more likely to develop a false memory from passive learning if the source of the information is a trusted adult, like the alienating parent (3).

Of course, false memories also develop through an active pathway. Alienating parents will discuss with the child events that have occurred in an effort to sway the child's views about the targeted parent. The child then comes to believe that they experienced or witnessed the events or that they can recall the events because the information about the events has been presented to them repeatedly.

Even when the information the alienated child uses to develop a belief in the account they are provided about the targeted parent is obtained from the alienating parent, the child may not identify the source. Certainly, the alienated child's tendency to protect the alienating parent decreases the likelihood that the child will willingly identify the alienating parent as the culprit. So, the child may provide an account of an event they could not have witnessed but insist that their knowledge of it is something directly known to them or 'magically' known to them.

Box 13.32 Interviewer: Mum told me that you don't want to spend any time with Dad.

    Alienated child: Yes. I don't want to see him anymore.

    Interviewer: Why don't you want to spend time with Dad?

    Alienated child: I don't want to see him because after he dropped me off last time he went home and got drunk.

    Interviewer: Who told you Dad got drunk that day?

    Alienated child: No-one. No-one told me.

    Interviewer: Then what makes you think Dad got drunk after he dropped you off.

    Alienated child: I just know it happened. He got really drunk and he fell over and couldn't get back up again. He got angry and yelled.

    Interviewer: Who did he yell at?

    Alienated child: No-one. He just yelled.

    Interviewer: How do you know he yelled?

    Alienated child: I just know. He got drunk and then he fell over and he yelled at himself.

As stated, the events about which the child provides an account do not have to be current events. Alienated children will give knowledgeable accounts of events that occurred before they were born or that occurred at a time when the child was too young to remember. It should be remembered that events that occurred before language developed are unlikely to be remembered (4). Despite this, children will talk about these events as if they have direct knowledge.

Box 13.33 Alienated child: My Dad is an alcoholic. He pushes Mum around and falls over all the time. One time he pushed her against the fridge and Mum hurt her head.

    Interviewer: People have told me that Dad stopped drinking alcohol before you were born. Did you see him push Mum against the fridge or did someone tell you about it?

    Alienated child: I remember him doing it. He's an alcoholic.

    Interviewer: I think Mum said that Dad pushed her against the fridge before you were born.

    Alienated child: I don't care. I remember that he did it. I know he did it.

You will notice that even when presented with information that supports the notion that the child could not have witnessed these events, the child still maintained that she could recall this happening. The child cannot discriminate between events they witnessed and those that were related to them. To them, the memories have the same character or sense of realness. As a result, alienated children will have a strong belief in the veracity of the account they are providing about the wrongdoing of the targeted parent even when it is pointed out that the child could not have known what they are claiming to know.

Box 13.34 Interviewer: You said before that after Dad dropped you off at home after you saw him that last time that he went home and got drunk. You said he then fell over and was yelling at no-one in particular.
Alienated child: That's what happened.
Interviewer: And you said that no-one told you this happened.
Alienated child: That's right. No-one told me about it … I just know.
Interviewer: But how can you know if no-one told you and you were at Mum's house and not with Dad.
Alienated child: I just know. Dad always gets drunk and that day he dropped me off and got drunk then fell over.
Interviewer: You seem pretty sure that happened.
Alienated child: Yes.
Interviewer: But I was just wondering how you know that is what happened.
Alienated child: I just know … It really happened.

Despite the confidence with which they claim the accounts they provide are true, alienated children are able to provide few details of the specifics of the event about which they are talking. Of course, this is because they have no real experience of that event. It is unlikely that, when forming the false memory, they learn of and process sufficient information to allow them to provide an account of an event as they would be able to do if they actually experienced it.

Box 13.35 Interviewer: So, tell me what happened when Dad got drunk after he dropped you off at home.
Alienated child: He got drunk, then he fell over and he yelled.
Interviewer: Whereabouts was he when he fell over?
Alienated child: At his house.
Interviewer: Whereabouts at his house?
Alienated child: Just at his house.
Interviewer: Was he inside or outside his house?
Alienated child: Um …
Interviewer: Did he hurt himself?
Alienated child: Um … I don't know.

In attempting to determine whether or not a memory of an event relayed by the alienated child is an accurate one, or as accurate as any memory can be, it may be necessary to consider whether the child has been exposed to information other than direct experience that could have formed the basis of the 'memory'. Often, this can be achieved by interviewing the child.

Box 13.36 Interviewer: Remember you were telling me about the time that Dad pushed Mum against the fridge?
Alienated child: Yes, I remember.
Interviewer: Do you remember I told you that Mum said that happened before you were born.

> **Alienated child:** Yes.
> **Interviewer:** That sounds like a bad thing to happen to Mum.
> **Alienated child:** Yes, it was. She was very sad about it. It made Mum cry.
> **Interviewer:** Do other people in your family think it was a bad thing to happen to Mum?
> **Alienated child:** Yes! Grandma said Dad was nothing but a wife-basher.
> **Interviewer:** Gosh, that sounds like Grandma was upset about what happened.
> **Alienated child:** Yes, she is very upset. When she was talking with Mum about it, she said Dad should have been locked up in gaol for doing that.
> **Interviewer:** And what did Mum say to that?
> **Alienated child:** Mum said Dad was a wife-basher and all wife-bashers should be locked up. She said because Dad pushed her against the fridge the police should have arrested him.

Even if you are not able to determine from interviewing the child whether or not a child has been exposed to information that would have formed the basis of a suspected false memory, you may have available information that supports the notion that the child has not been shielded from negative views about the targeted parent. Such information may come from a variety of sources including the targeted parent.

> **Box 13.37 Targeted parent:** I have tried and tried to have my ex-wife stopped from talking about these types of things around our daughter. The judge even put it in the orders that she wasn't allowed to do it, but it keeps happening. All my ex-wife's family share their views about me when my daughter is around. None of it is good. So, her head gets filled with all this negative stuff about me and I never get the chance to defend myself. My ex-wife says she doesn't tell our daughter these things, but she really doesn't have to tell her directly. Talking with her family while my child is around is enough. She's a smart little girl. She knows what they are saying. But she never hears my side. She never hears the other side of the story. If I tried to stand up for myself and tell my daughter what actually happened, I would be in trouble so fast my head would spin. My ex-wife and her family just keep getting away with it.

It is worth remembering that a child's confidence in their recollections of an event does not necessarily relate to veracity of the account. Some interviewers hold the view that a child should always be believed when they provide an account of events that negatively affected them. However, this discounts the extent to which children's recollections can be influenced. The strength of the child's belief in his or her recollections of past events to which they could not have been exposed is a reflection of the extent to which that child is influenced by the information provided to them, either directly or indirectly. In the context of parental alienation, it advances the alienation cause if the alienating parent exposes the child to negative information about the targeted parent that the child then integrates into what they believe they know about the rejected parent.

Lack of concern about internal inconsistency of information provided

As a result of a range of factors, such as reliance on false memories, distorted views about the targeted parent, and the strongly negative views the child wishes to express about the targeted parent, the accounts provided by an alienated child may be internally inconsistent. That is, because much of what is related may not be objectively the case, an alienated child will tend to make illogical leaps in what they tell you.

When this lack of internal consistency is pointed out to the alienated child, he or she may simply alter their account so that it has a more logical flow. Alternatively, the child may ignore the challenge and carry on as if the query was not made.

Box 13.38 Alienated child: My father was so mean to Mum the other day.
Interviewer: What happened?
Alienated child: Well, he came around to our house and upset Mum. He was shouting and wanted to come inside.
Interviewer: Tell me more about what happened.
Alienated child: Dad just turned up without Mum knowing he was coming. He's not allowed to do that. The court said he has to stay away.
Interviewer: What happened when Dad turned up?
Alienated child: He got out of his car and stood at the gate. He yelled at Mum to come and talk with him.
Interviewer: Then what happened?
Alienated child: Dad just stayed by the gate.
Interviewer: And what did Mum do?
Alienated child: Mum just stayed inside and didn't say anything. She stayed inside the whole time and hid from him.
Interviewer: What did Dad do then?
Alienated child: Dad said mean things to Mum and said he would hit her. And then he did … then he hit her. Just like that. Mum didn't say anything. She just stayed inside and didn't say anything.
Interviewer: How did he hit her? You said Mum stayed inside and Dad was out by the gate.
Alienated child: Oh yeah. Dad came up to the house and then he hit Mum.
Interviewer: And where was Mum?
Alienated child: Mum was on the front porch.
Interviewer: So, Mum did come outside?
Alienated child: Um … yes but only after Dad said he would hit her.
Interviewer: Why did Mum go outside if Dad was going to hit her?
Alienated child: Well, Dad came up to the house and then Mum pushed him … just to get him to go away. He made her call him a rude name.
Interviewer: And then Dad hit Mum … after she pushed him?
Alienated child: Yes, but it wasn't her fault. He made her push him and then he hit her.

Even when the inconsistencies in a child's account are pointed out to them, alienated children can respond with indifference. Although you may expect the child to correct themselves or feel embarrassed at being caught out telling an untruth, this may not occur.

Box 13.39 Interviewer: Just let me get things right. I wasn't there so I don't know so I will have to ask you to help me get it right. You said Dad stayed by the gate, but you also said he was up near the porch.

> **Alienated child:** Um … yes.
> **Interviewer:** You also said Mum stayed inside the whole time but then you said she was out on the porch.
> **Alienated child:** Yep.
> **Interviewer:** You also said that Mum didn't say anything, just stayed inside and stayed quiet. You then said Mum called Dad a bad name and pushed him to make him go away.
> **Alienated child:** So?
> **Interviewer:** Well, I'm a bit confused about whether Mum stayed inside or not and whether she called him a name or stayed quiet.
> **Alienated child:** Both.
> **Interviewer:** How can both things be true?
> **Alienated child:** They just are.

Challenges to the child's account of what occurred can be ignored by the child. The child will act as if they were never confronted with the discrepancies in their account. Alternatively, the child will become angry and try to rectify the situation in their favour. This may involve becoming angry with the interviewer or it may involve an expression of frustration at those who provided the account that was different from their own. The latter can be the case when a child has been coached to provide a particular account.

> **Box 13.40 Interviewer:** So, what happened next?
> **Alienated child:** Dad came around and threatened Mum. She wanted him to go away but he was shouting from outside in the front yard.
> **Interviewer:** Mum said your father was inside the house.
> **Alienated child:** Oh, that's right. I forgot. He came inside and was shouting at Mum. He threatened to hurt Mum. He came inside because he broke in through the back door.
> **Interviewer:** Mum said she let him in.
> **Alienated child:** I want to go to the bathroom, and I need Mum to come with me.
> **Alienated child:** [On her return] As I said, Dad was shouting at Mum and then she went to let him in but he was already breaking in through the back door but then he realised that Mum was opening the door for him so he came around the front again and she let him in. She only did that because she was scared.

If the alienated child is challenged to address the inconsistencies in their story, they may provide different and inconsistent answers to the questions being posed. The child adapts to the content of the new question by treating it as if is separate to the ongoing conversation. In this way, the answers to the new questions may contradict the answers to previous questions. Over the course of a single interview, there may be several changes of account.

> **Box 13.41 Interviewer:** So, what happened next?
> **Alienated child:** Dad grabbed Mum around the throat so she couldn't call out. I saw him do it.

> **Interviewer:** I thought you said you were out in the backyard with Ben and couldn't see what was going on.
> **Alienated child:** That's right. I was in the backyard but I could hear Dad put his hands around Mum's throat so she couldn't call out?
> **Interviewer:** What did that sound like?
> **Alienated child:** I could hear Mum call out when Dad put his hands around her throat.
> **Interviewer:** Then how did you hear your Mum call out?
> **Alienated child:** My brother saw it and told me what happened.

Notice that there are several shifts to adjust to new questions being asked. The inconsistencies in an alienated child's account are a function of the fact that they are attempting to provide information about matters that do not have factual basis or about which they have no direct experience. The lack of concern that is noted when these discrepancies are pointed out to the alienated child reflects the focus of the child. That is, the child is focused on presenting their position or supporting the alienating parent and not on the way they are doing this.

The errors in consistency made by an alienated child are likely also to reflect their age and developmental stage. Keeping track of exaggerations, embellishments and fabrications in a conversation comes with a high cognitive demand. Put simply, this is often too difficult for a young child to do.

Relating targeted parent's faults as a litany

When discussing the shortcomings of the targeted parent or the negative views about this parent, the alienated child may provide information almost in the form of a litany. The account provided seems like a well-rehearsed or practised account. In fact, in all likelihood, that is exactly what has happened. The alienating parent will encourage the child to 'remember' to tell the interviewer certain things. When you question children about the events they relate, there is often little detail forthcoming, suggesting that what is being said is not the child's account of what occurred.

It should be kept in mind that questioning the child about what they had been told to say does not always clarify whether or not the child has been coached. Some children will be insistent that the ideas are their own. Further questioning that is appropriately targeted can usefully provide some indication of whether or not coaching and rehearsing has occurred.

As stated, the account provided by the alienated child of the targeted parent's shortcomings can seem rehearsed or practised. When questioned about details about the complaints, alienated children will tend to revert to listing the complaints and not provide the details requested. So, they will state and re-state the list of shortcomings, no matter what question is posed.

> **Box 13.42 Alienated child:** Dad's done lots of things wrong. He smacked Jacob with a ruler, pushed Mum against the wall, yelled at Nan when she tried to stop him, was rude to my teacher, lost his driver's licence, got drunk at Pop's barbecue, was arrested by the police and cheated on Mum. Did I remember to say he yelled at Mum?
> **Interviewer:** Yes, you mentioned that.
> **Alienated child:** [Counting wrongdoings off on her fingers] So, as I said, Dad smacked Jacob with a ruler, pushed Mum against the wall, yelled at Nan when she tried to stop him,

was rude to my teacher, lost his driver's licence, cheated on Mum and, um, got drunk at Pop's barbecue. Did I say he had been arrested by the police?

Interviewer: You did the first time.

Alienated child: Good.

This gives the impression of a well-rehearsed account by the child. Of course, you could not rule out that these events occurred based on this information alone, but it is worth taking into account the fact that rehearsing or coaching is likely to have occurred.

Sometimes, but not always, an alienated child will let slip that coaching has taken place. This is likely to occur when the targeted parent's shortcomings are being listed. They will give an indication that they were reminded to relay information to the interviewer.

Box 13.43 Interviewer: It's my job to help families so I thought we could talk about your family.

Alienated child: Mum told me to remember that Dad forgot to pick me up from school one day.

Interviewer: Did he?

Alienated child: [Nod]

Interviewer: Well, we can talk about that later. Now I just want to talk about all the people in your family.

Alienated child: Dad left me in my cot to cry when I was a baby.

Interviewer: Did he? Do you remember this, or did someone remind you about it?

Alienated child: Mum reminded me.

It is certainly evident in cases where children are coached to provide information about which they know very little that they are unable to provide much detail about the events about which they are speaking. The child will usually start with a definitive statement of wrongdoing. However, when questioned about the event, little information is forthcoming.

Box 13.44 Interviewer: You told me a whole list of things that Dad had done. Let's talk about one of those things. You told me that Dad smacked Jacob with a ruler.

Alienated child: Yes, he did.

Interviewer: Where were Dad and Jacob when this happened?

Alienated child: Um … at home.

Interviewer: Where at home? What room where they in?

Alienated child: Um … they were at home … in the kitchen, I think.

Interviewer: And where on Jacob's body did Dad hit him with the ruler.

Alienated child: Dad hit Jacob with a ruler.

Interviewer: Where on Jacob's body did Dad hit him?

Alienated child: He just hit him.

Interviewer: What was Dad upset about?

Alienated child: Um …

> **Interviewer:** Dad must have been upset about something. What happened to make Dad decide to smack Jacob with a ruler.
> **Alienated child:** He just did … no reason.

When relaying information about which they were coached, an alienated child will often use language that reflects the coach's language and not their own. In this way, coached children will often use language not commonly used by a child of that age.

> **Box 13.45 Alienated child:** Dad's not very nice. He doesn't respect me.
> **Interviewer:** Doesn't he? In what way doesn't he respect you?
> **Alienated child:** He doesn't respect me.
> **Interviewer:** What does respect mean?
> **Alienated child:** Um … My father doesn't respect me.

This seemingly well-rehearsed stream of information about the wrongdoings of the targeted parent is commonly used by an alienated child to drive home the point that they view the targeted parent negatively. It is certainly indicative of coaching although this will not always be the case. When occurring in combination with other indicators of parental alienation, consideration must be given to this litany being a reflection of the alienation process, even in cases when it is not possible to obtain collateral information to support all the claims being made about negative actions on the part of the targeted parent.

Fear response

An alienated child's reaction to the imminence of time with the targeted parent can be extreme in nature. In this way, the child demonstrates a severe fear response, sometimes in combination with regressive behaviour.

However, on examination, often there is no obvious indicators of what had occurred in past interactions with the targeted parent that would warrant such a severe response to the thought of spending time with that parent. It is understandable if consideration is given to the fact that the child is likely to have been repeatedly told that the targeted parent is a threatening or dangerous person, or that the targeted parent intends to take the child and not return him or her to the alienating parent.

> **Box 13.46 Alienating parent:** Every time it gets close to me dropping Jamie off, she gets really anxious and upset. She cries and cries and doesn't want to go to visit her father. She wets the bed the night before she has to go. When we get there, she screams when I hand her over. As a mother, I can't allow this to happen. If she is that upset about spending time with her father something is wrong. She needs to stay with me where she is safe.

This is not particularly surprising in young children. If a child is told that the targeted parent is a dangerous person and they come to believe this is so, a fear response to the presence of the targeted parent would be expected. However, this fear response does not only occur with younger children. Adolescents may also react with a seemingly unwarranted fear response to the targeted parent's proximity or anticipation of time with the targeted parent.

In many cases, the alienating parent will report that the alienated child is distressed or frightened when faced with the knowledge they are to spend time with the targeted parent. However, the fear response by the alienated child may be observed by others. The child may hide from the targeted parent and refuse to come out of their hiding place despite being reassured that they are safe.

Box 13.47 Psychologist: I have observed children to react with fear when they come face to face with a parent they used to have a good relationship with but from whom they are now alienated. I remember one boy climbed under my receptionist's desk and refused to come out. Another child, a girl, sat with her face buried in a cushion and would not raise her head despite becoming hot and bothered. I have had children grip my hand and refuse to let go. All of these children had one thing in common. They were alienated from a parent with whom they used to have a warm and loving relationship.

The most noteworthy aspect of this fear response is that, although the response seems to genuinely reflect fear, it is out of proportion to the actual threat the child faces. Typically, there has been no experience that can be identified that would have caused the child to fear the targeted parent. As a result, targeted parents can be shocked by the intensity of the child's response to them.

Box 13.48 Targeted parent: I'm so upset about what happened. I pulled up to pick up the kids and Tom came running out of the house and threw himself down onto the footpath. When I tried to approach him, he jumped up and ran out into the road. I was terrified he was going to be run over. I tried to reason with him. He's 14 for goodness sake. But he wouldn't listen. He was sobbing and carrying on like I was going to hurt him. I'm devastated. We used to have such a good relationship.

In some cases, an alienated child will refuse to attend school because of their fear that the targeted parent will come and collect them from the school premises. In some cases, the fear that has developed in relation to the targeted parent generalises to other circumstances, like school attendance.

Box 13.49 Alienating parent: My daughter is now refusing to go to school because she is frightened her father is going to come to the school and take her away. I am investigating home schooling her because she simply refuses to go to the school. There is nothing I can do to make her. I have always tried to encourage her to go to school. I told her that I have talked to the teacher and the principal and they know not to let her father take her. Unfortunately, it doesn't make any difference. She is still so frightened of him that she refuses to go there.

It would be easy to form an opinion that the fear response demonstrated by a child must reflect a genuine reaction to the degree of threat the parent represents. Indeed, in cases of identified abuse, a fear response may be expected. However, when a strong fear response occurs in the absence of identifiable triggers, and in combination with other indicators of parental alienation, it must be considered whether this fear response reflects a process of alienation.

Dependent or symbiotic relationship with alienating parent

The alienated child's relationship with the alienating parent may be symbiotic in nature or the child may become excessively dependent on the alienating parent. A symbiotic relationship occurs when one parent, usually the mother, links her identity or sense of self to the other person, typically the child, and the relationship becomes interdependent.

Box 13.50 Alienating parent: I'm an excellent mother. My whole life is dedicated to my children. That's the difference between me and their father. The quality of their childhood experiences is so much more enriching with me. You only have to come into my house to see that. My dining room walls are covered with their artwork and the craft we have done together. The lounge room is set up for fun and craft activities. Every moment of the day I dedicate to the children. I don't know how you can suggest that I should be separated from them. And the children now know this is what they should expect from a parent. Their needs are central to my existence and they know that. They don't get that level of parenting at their father's.

When this type of relationship develops, the alienating parent has difficulty functioning separately from the child. It would be difficult, then, for the parent to tolerate a situation where the child spent time with the targeted parent and away from them. In addition, the child would find it difficult to be away from the parent on whom they depend so completely.

Certainly, the alienated child may develop an overly dependent relationship with the alienating parent. In these cases, the child finds it difficult to function in the care of the targeted parent because they cannot tolerate being separated from the alienating parent. The alienated child will seek out the alienating parent to meet even the simplest of their needs.

Box 13.51 Alienated child: I hate Dad. He stops me from calling Mum when I want her. I need to ask her things. He says I should ask him, but he doesn't know the answers. Only Mum does. I hate going there. I would rather be with Mum. Then I could ask her what I wanted whenever I wanted to. How am I supposed to know what to do if Mum's not there and I can't call her?

These types of relationships between the alienating parent and the alienated child make it very difficult for the alienated child to be separated from the alienating parent. Certainly, the child finds it difficult to spend any time with the targeted parent without being in contact with the alienating parent.

Box 13.52 Targeted parent: The situation is ridiculous. When I do manage to have my daughter at my house, she insists on calling her mother all the time. And I mean, all the time. She won't decide what she wants for lunch or what games she wants to play without consulting her mother. When she stayed overnight, she had to phone her mother to say goodnight and again in the morning as soon as she woke up. She wouldn't eat breakfast until she spoke with her mother. If I said she couldn't phone her mother, she would have a huge meltdown.

The depth and nature of the relationship between the alienating parent and the alienated child extends beyond having limited ability to function when the child and parent are separated. At a more fundamental level, the alienated child will see him or herself as aligned to or connected with the alienating parent. This will cause the child to protect the alienating parent and the relationship they share in whatever way is necessary.

Box 13.53 Interviewer: Let's talk about Dad for a minute.
   Alienated child: I don't want to talk about him. I don't like him. I only need Mum. She knows what I want so I don't need anyone else. Mum said I make her happy. Dad used to make her sad. I don't like him because he made Mum sad. Mum said she and I will be ok as long as we have each other. We don't need anyone else. I don't want Mum to be sad, so isn't it good I make her happy? Dad was mean to Mum, so I don't like Dad.

The types of relationship that develop between the alienating parent and the alienated child can create difficulties in relation to the behaviour of the child. The alienated child can present as overly demanding, at least in relation to the alienating parent. The child develops an expectation that the alienating parent will do as they request, no matter how unrealistic the demand.

Box 13.54 Interviewer: Tell me something about your Mum.
   Alienated child: Mum gives me everything I want and that's why I love her. I don't love Dad because he doesn't give me anything.
   Interviewer: Mum gives you everything you want?
   Alienated child: Yes. I think she is the best parent because she gives me everything. Mum said Dad is a terrible parent.
   Interviewer: So, what sort of things does Mum give you?
   Alienated child: She let me spend lots of money at the toy shop. She said she didn't really have any money, but she used her credit card.
   Interviewer: So, what did you buy at the toy shop?
   Alienated child: I got lots of stuff. I got a new painting set and a princess costume. I got new furniture for my doll's house and lots of other stuff.
   Interviewer: But Mum had no money. Do you think it was a good idea to buy so much stuff when Mum didn't have any money?
   Alienated child: But I wanted it. I told Mum I wanted it. She said she'd think about it, but I knew she would buy it for me. She always buys me what I want.

Certainly, it is the case that the alienated child will come to hold the view that it is only the alienating parent who can meet their needs. They will reject attempts by the targeted parent to undertake even normal parenting tasks. This rejection increases the emotional distance between the alienated child and the targeted parent.

Box 13.55 Targeted parent: My daughter won't let me do the things her mother does for her. She says that only her mother can get her ready for school and only her mother knows how to cook her favourite meals. She won't let me brush her hair and she doesn't want me to read her a story at night because, apparently, only her mother knows how to do these things. And I know it's not true. She stays overnight with her grandmother and her aunt without any problems. It's when it comes down to either her mother or me, I am the one who misses out. She only wants her mother to do things for her … It never used to be this way.

So, not only does the alienated child believe that the alienating parent is the one who can meet their needs, attempts on the part of the targeted parent to negotiate for change cannot be conducted with the alienated child without the child referring to the alienating parent. In this way, negotiation attempts are doomed to fail because the alienating parent will not encourage the child to resolve difficulties with the targeted parent. Indeed, the opposite is likely to be the case.

Box 13.56 Targeted parent: My daughter won't do anything I ask of her without first checking with her mother to see if it is ok. Even the simplest of things has to be run by her mother before she will agree to do it. This includes things she would like to do like going to the beach. She simply refuses to budge until she calls her mother to see if they both agree that my suggestion is a good one.

A symbiotic or dependent relationship between the alienating parent and the alienated child serves to exclude the targeted parent from the child's life. The unhealthy strength of the relationship with the alienating parent leaves the child little emotional space to maintain a strong relationship with the targeted parent. When attempts to establish, or more correctly re-establish, the targeted parent–child relationship are made by the targeted parent, they are undermined by the nature of the relationship that has developed between the alienating parent and the child and the behaviours that foster this unhealthy relationship.

Compliant with adults other than targeted parent

An alienated child may become more disobedient, more resistant and more disrespectful in the presence of the targeted parent. In contrast, the child may behave in a compliant, responsive and respectful manner when with other adults. The alienating parent will then use the child's defiant behaviour as evidence of parenting incompetence on the part of the targeted parent or as evidence of a fundamental breakdown of the targeted parent–alienated child relationship. As the child does not behave poorly when around other adults, the alienating parent will say that the source of the problem must be the targeted parent.

There are many ways in which the discrepancy between the way an alienated child will behave with the targeted parent and around other adults will manifest. A child who is disrespectful towards the targeted parent may not be so when interacting with other adults. Reports of the child being defiant and difficult when with the targeted parent are not matched by observations of the child when they are with others.

Box 13.57 Targeted parent: I am really struggling to cope with Phoebe. She is so defiant. Whenever I ask her to do anything, she tells me I have no right to tell her what to do. She's impossible to handle. But when I speak to her teacher or talk with my sister and mother who spend time with her, they all say she is very polite and well-behaved. She always does what she's told. I don't understand why she is so disobedient with me but is so well-behaved with everyone else. It makes me question my abilities as a parent. What am I doing wrong?

Certainly, when you have a discussion with an alienated child outside of the context of their relationship with the targeted parent, that child can seem polite and well-mannered. There can be little evidence of behavioural disturbance and no strong indication of maladjustment, at least in some cases.

Box 13.58 Psychologist: It is easy to form an opinion about a child being difficult and defiant if you consider only what the targeted parent tells you. However, it is often the case that when you meet the child, they are polite and well behaved. I do not doubt that the targeted parent's description is accurate, at least from their experience. I accept that the behaviour of alienated children can be different when they are around the targeted parent.

The defiance demonstrated by an alienated child has been generated by the alienating parent. The message the child receives from the alienating parent, that may be explicitly stated or implied, is that they should disregard the wishes of the targeted parent. The alienated child comes to believe they have no real need to obey the targeted parent.

Box 13.59 Alienated child: I don't have to do what Mum says.
Interviewer: Why not?
Alienated child: Because she's not the boss.
Interviewer: Then who is the boss?
Alienated child: Dad … Dad is the boss … No, me … I'm my own boss.
Interviewer: So, what do you do if Mum asks you to do something?
Alienated child: I just don't do it. Dad said Mum isn't the boss of me and I can choose what I want to do. And I don't want to do the things Mum wants me to do.
Interviewer: Why not?
Alienated child: Just because …

The problems with defiant behaviour experienced by the targeted parent when the child is with them are not consistent with recorded accounts of the child's behaviour. For example, school reports will describe behaviourally appropriate, socially appropriate and compliant behaviour by the alienated child.

> **Box 13.60 Targeted parent:** I read her school reports and it's like they are talking about a different child. I read things like 'She is helpful in the classroom' and 'She likes to please others' and I wonder who they are talking about. She used to be like that, but she hasn't been like that with me for a long, long time. When she is with me, she is sullen and refuses to do what I ask. She picks a fight about everything. The simplest request is met with full-scale war every time.

The defiant behaviour of the alienated child experienced by the targeted parent may extend to the family members of the targeted parent. Also, it is likely to extend to the partner of the targeted parent. The child rejects the notion that they should behave in other than a defiant way towards the people close to the targeted parent.

> **Box 13.61 Targeted parent:** The way my daughter speaks to my partner is terrible. She is so rude. My partner tries hard to make friendly conversation but my daughter brushes her off. If my partner asks her to do anything, like come to the dinner table, my daughter tells her she doesn't have to do what my partner tells her. When I ask my daughter to behave, she just refuses. My partner is a patient and loving person, but this is really testing her. I think that my daughter feels that if she is rude enough then my partner will leave. I'm convinced she is trying to break us up.

There is probably more than one reason for an alienated child behaving in a defiant manner towards the targeted parent but not towards other people. Firstly, it could be argued that the alienating parent has such a level of authority over the child that it is expected that he or she behave in the presence of others who are considered by the child to have some authority. In contrast, they have been led to believe that the targeted parent has no role in their lives so there is no imperative need to behave well when around the targeted parent.

Secondly, the encouragement from the alienating parent to behave in a disrespectful and defiant manner is focused solely on the targeted parent. The child learns that this is expected behaviour around the targeted parent but sees no need to be non-compliant around other adults, expect perhaps those who support the targeted parent.

Thirdly, it serves the purposes of the alienating parent to have the child behave in a defiant manner when around the targeted parent but be compliant around others. The alienating parent can then point to this discrepancy as evidence of wrongdoing on the part of the targeted parent or an inability to adequately parent the child. Therefore, the child could be strongly encouraged by the alienating parent to behave well when around other adults.

Believes alienating parent persecuted by targeted parent

An alienated child may hold a view of the alienating parent as a long-suffering victim of the persecuting targeted parent. This view tends to be strongly held by the child and is not easily amendable to change. The child believes the alienating parent is the victim of the targeted parent's 'abuse'. The alienated child will talk about the harm the targeted parent has done to the alienating parent and the threat the targeted parent represents to the alienating parent.

Box 13.62 Alienated child: My mother has always treated Dad really badly. She has hit Dad lots of times, ever since they first met. And Dad wouldn't hit her back because he doesn't hit women. Dad would come home from work and Mum would yell at him and say horrible things. She's always done that, even since before I was born. Dad said he only stuck it out because of me. He said he wanted me to have two parents. But he said it got so bad he needed to leave and take me with him. He said Mum is crazy and dangerous.

As stated, the alienated child's view that the alienating parent is the victim of the targeted parent's abuse is difficult to sway. It is not amenable to normal challenge. The child remains convinced of the targeted parent's wrongdoing even if evidence to the contrary is presented.

Box 13.63 Alienated child: Dad said there was nothing he could do about Mum.

Interviewer: What do you mean? Nothing he can do about what in particular?

Alienated child: Well, he can't do what he wants otherwise Mum will dob him in to the Child Support Agency, just like she did before.

Interviewer: I don't think Mum has ever done that. Mum said the only time she had ever contacted the Child Support Agency was when Dad asked her to.

Alienated child: She's lying!

Interviewer: I can't find any reason why Mum would have done what you say she did. Why would she have done that?

Alienated child: Because she hates Dad.

Interviewer: But Mum said that she and your Dad made an arrangement about child support that they both agreed to.

Alienated child: She's a liar, she's a liar, she's a liar!

The alienated child will believe the accounts of alleged wrongdoing by the targeted parent that have been provided to them by the alienating parent. They will continue to hold the view that the targeted parent has treated the alienating parent poorly despite such behaviour by the targeted parent not being in the child's own experience.

Box 13.64 Alienated child: Mum hits Dad all the time. She gets really mad and loses her temper. She shouts and screams and calls Dad bad names. Every time she sees Dad she does that.

Interviewer: Have you ever seen Mum do that?

Alienated child: She does it!

Interviewer: But have you seen her do that?

Alienated child: No, but she does it. She can't control herself.

Interviewer: What about when she is with you? Does she behave like that when she is with you?

Alienated child: No, but that's just because she's pretending.

Interviewer: Pretending what?

Alienated child: Pretending to be nice when I'm around.

The views the alienated child forms about the targeted parent can be reinforced by the alienating parent selectively exposing the child to court documents. These extracts from court documents will seem to support the view that the targeted parent is the aggressor and the alienating parent is the victim. For example, the alienating parent may show the child their affidavit but not the targeted parent's rebuttal that might cause the child to adopt a more moderate view about the targeted parent's intentions.

Box 13.65 Alienated child: I don't want to spend time with a parent who has been so horrible to my father. If she cared about us, she wouldn't treat Dad like that. And she keeps taking him back to court. Dad gets really upset when more court papers arrive. And she tells lies in the court papers. I know she is telling lies because she makes stuff up about Dad. She does that just to hurt Dad. I hate her.

This is a good example of this process. The alienating parent has allowed the child to have access to information about court proceedings that should be of adult concern and should not influence a child. Of course, the views about the court proceedings to which the child is exposed are filtered. The alienating parent allows the child to have access to information that supports the view that the targeted parent is doing the wrong thing and hurting the alienating parent.

Of course, the alienating parent has encouraged this view of the child that the targeted parent is persecuting the alienating parent. The disclosure of relationship events or information about the targeted parent or exposure to fabricated information about the wrongdoings of the targeted parent by the alienating parent fosters the child's view that the targeted parent has acted in an inappropriate, threatening or harmful way towards the alienating parent. Wanting to support the alienating parent who is perceived as the victim will encourage a child to reject the targeted parent.

Lack of empathy for plight of targeted parent

The alienated child demonstrates little empathy for the targeted parent and little concern for their wellbeing. They seem not to care that the targeted parent is hurt by their rejection of that parent. The targeted parent can be perceived by the child as someone to exploit for money or personal gain. Such a view is encouraged by the alienating parent.

This lack of empathy for the targeted parent exists even if a previously positive and loving relationship between the targeted parent and the child existed prior to the commencement of the alienation process. The distress felt by the targeted parent at the change of circumstance resulting in them spending little time, if any, with the alienated child will not move the child to express concern.

Box 13.66 Interviewer: Dad said he misses you.
   Alienated child: So?
   Interviewer: He wants you to know that he thinks about you all the time.
   Alienated child: I don't care. Saying things like that won't make me go and see him. I don't care if he misses me. I don't care if he's sad. That's his problem, not mine.

As stated, the child may view the targeted parent as someone who should be exploited for financial gain. This view is likely to have been instilled in them by the alienating parent. Certainly, alienating parents often discuss child support arrangements with the child.

Box 13.67 Interviewer: Dad seems a bit confused about why you stopped going to see him.
  Alienated child: I don't care. He doesn't deserve to spend time with me. It's his own fault. He can rot for all I care. And he wouldn't pay up for my school trip. He should pay. He has a responsibility to pay but he won't. So, too bad that he misses me. Too bad that he wants to see me.

With little feeling for the plight of the targeted parent, the alienated child will fail to make contact with the targeted parent on important dates. Father's or Mother's Day, birthdays and other celebrations can go by with the targeted parent not receiving any communication from the child. The child will not ask to contact the targeted parent and reject the notion they should have cared.

Box 13.68 Interviewer: Dad said he didn't hear from you on Father's Day.
  Alienated child: I don't care.
  Interviewer: Tell me why you didn't call Dad on Father's Day?
  Alienated child: I didn't call him because I didn't want to. It doesn't worry me if that upset him. It is like I don't have a father, really, so why would I call him on Father's Day. I don't want him to be my father so I will never call him on Father's Day … or any other day.

The alienated child can adopt a harsh attitude towards the targeted parent. However, expected feelings of guilt for treating the targeted parent in this way are rarely expressed by the child. The child continues to fail to have an empathic response to the targeted parent's situation and distress. Attempts to elicit an empathic response in the child are usually unsuccessful.

Box 13.69 Interviewer: It must be pretty tough for Dad not to ever see you.
  Alienated child: That's his problem.
  Interviewer: You and Dad used to have a nice time together so it's a bit sad that has changed.
  Alienated child: No, it's not sad at all. It's good for me. My father just needs to get over it and get used to the idea I don't want to see him.

If attention was only paid to the way the child responded to the targeted parent's distress it would be easy to assume that the lack of empathy demonstrated in that circumstance reflected a more general problem of lack of empathy. However, that is not typically the case. An alienated child is likely to demonstrate an appropriate level of empathy in relation to the dilemmas faced by people other than the targeted parent or those close to the targeted parent, such as grandparents.

> **Box 13.70 Interviewer:** I understand your friend, Jack, doesn't get to see his father.
>   **Alienated child:** Yes, his father moved away for work and he doesn't get to see Jack much anymore.
>   **Interviewer:** How does Jack feel about that?
>   **Alienated child:** Jack is a bit sad about that. He misses him.
>   **Interviewer:** And what about Jack's dad? Do you think he's sad, too?
>   **Alienated child:** I reckon he is a bit sad. He lives far away so he can't see Jack much.
>   **Interviewer:** Do you think your Dad feels the same about not being able to see you?
>   **Alienated child:** I don't care.

This lack of empathy for the targeted parent demonstrated by the alienated child may reflect the stance the child has taken in rejecting this parent. That is, the strongly negative view they have developed for the targeted parent must then be supported by a lack of empathy. If an alienated child felt empathy for a parent's position, it would be difficult to maintain the strongly negative view they have adopted.

Targeted parent holds no important position

The targeted parent holds a position of very little significance in the alienated child's life. This may be demonstrated as a preference to call the parent by their given name. They may insist that they are the decider of whether time is spent with the targeted parent. They do not see the targeted parent as contributing to their own sense of wellbeing or important to a good quality of life.

> **Box 13.71 Alienated child:** I know Dad wants to see me, but I don't want to see him. I would rather do other stuff. I'm too busy anyway. I will let you know when I'm ready to see him. Maybe in a few months. Maybe.

As stated already, an alienated child may opt to refer to the targeted parent by their given name or with no reference to a name at all. Many do not call the targeted parent 'mum' or 'dad'. To refer to the targeted parent as mum or dad gives that parent greater status in the child's life than the alienated child has come to believe they deserve. So, it is easier, and more dismissive of that parent's role, to refer to the parent by their given name.

> **Box 13.72 Interviewer:** I was talking to your Dad the other day …
>   **Alienated child:** You mean John?
>   **Interviewer:** You call your Dad John?
>   **Alienated child:** That's his name.
>   **Interviewer:** Most kids don't call their parents by their given names.
>   **Alienated child:** Well, he's not really my father … not really. I know he is my birth father, but he isn't a 'dad'. So, I call him John … if I have to talk about him at all, that is.

Indeed, the level of warmth or sense of connection they afford the targeted parent often is equivalent to what would be offered by the alienated child to an acquaintance or stranger. The closeness that is necessary to maintain a sense of emotional attachment to the targeted parent is deliberately rejected by the alienated child. As a result, an alienated child will often express no interest in sharing with the targeted parent important news about events that happen in the child's life.

Box 13.73 Interviewer: Is there anything you would like Dad to know about how things have been going for you? He might be interested to know that your team won the premiership.

Alienated child: No. Mum knows and so do Nan and Pop so that's enough.

Interviewer: But you are really proud of your win. Wouldn't you like Dad to know?

Alienated child: No. Why would I tell him?

Not only do alienated children express little interest in sharing important news with the targeted parent, they often communicate a wish not to share important occasions with them. They will reject the suggestion of shared celebrations or inviting a targeted parent to an important event, such as a recital or a sporting event in which the child is involved.

Box 13.74 Interviewer: Have you thought about whether you are going to see your Dad at Christmas?

Alienated child: No, thanks. I don't want to.

Interviewer: Families normally catch up and spend time together at special times of the year.

Alienated child: I don't want to. Mum is organising Christmas things.

Interviewer: Most kids from separated families spend some time with one parent and some time with the other parent on important days like Christmas Day.

Alienated child: Well, I don't want to. Mum is handling it. She's doing everything so I don't need to see my father.

In addition to showing little interest in telling the targeted parent about important events in the child's life, alienated children present as disinterested in events in the targeted parent's life. They do not seek information about the targeted parent's life and reject such information, or passively accept it, when it is offered.

Box 13.75 Interviewer: A couple of good things have happened for Dad.

Alienated child: You don't have to tell me. I don't want to know.

Interviewer: Don't you want to know that Dad has a really good new job?

Alienated child: No, I'm not interested. Don't tell me stuff about him. I don't care.

In many ways it must be easier for an alienated child to view the targeted parent as someone of little importance to them. This view is more consistent with their overall rejection of the parent and, thus, less confusing for them than if faced with the need to reconcile the importance of the role a parent plays and their rejection of that parent.

Rigidity of belief system regarding targeted parent

The belief system of an alienated child related to the targeted parent can be rigid. It is not easily altered and not amenable to change through a normal process of challenge. The alienated child's negative views about the targeted parent tend to remain rigidly in place despite more moderate explanations for that parent's actions being offered. When presented with such information, the alienated child simply dismisses the evidence that does not support their own views about the targeted parent and the targeted parent's behaviour.

Box 13.76 Alienated child: I don't ever want to see Mum. She runs around with other men. She had one boyfriend and now she has another.

Interviewer: Mum told me she hasn't had a new boyfriend since she and your Dad broke up. Other people have said the same thing.

Alienated child: I know she has. I saw her outside the supermarket, and she was talking to some man I've never seen before. Dad said that was her latest victim.

Interviewer: Maybe she was talking to a person she knows, and that person isn't her boyfriend.

Alienated child: I don't think so. If she's talking to a man, I bet he is her boyfriend. Dad said I was right.

Interviewer: How can you tell?

Alienated child: I just know what sort of person she is. She just wants some man, any man, to pay the bills for her. She will rip him off just like she ripped off Dad.

Presenting evidence to support a contrary point of view will do little to change the alienated child's view of the targeted parent. When their views about the targeted parent are challenged, the alienated child will present an argument in favour of their position. They will persist with this argument no matter how illogical the argument becomes.

Box 13.77 Alienated child: You can't tell me Mum doesn't have a new boyfriend because I know it's true.

Interviewer: How do you know?

Alienated child: Well, the last time I saw her car there was a hand print on the passenger side window.

Interviewer: A hand print?

Alienated child: Yes. And I knew it wasn't her hand print.

Interviewer: It could have been anyone's hand print.

Alienated child: I know it belonged to her new boyfriend.

Interviewer: How do you know?

Alienated child: Well, it's obvious, isn't it?

This argument sounds illogical … and it is illogical. However, it is also an argument that was presented by an alienated child during an interview. Not only will an alienated child defend their illogical position on a matter, they will continue to adhere to their point of view even when it is clearly demonstrated that it is based on incorrect information. The alienated child will simply reject the notion that it is possible they may be wrong about the issue that forms the basis of their argument or that their views about the targeted parent may be flawed.

Box 13.78 Alienated child: Mum is just a criminal. She gets arrested all the time.

Interviewer: That's not true. I know that's not true.

Alienated child: Yes, it is.

Interviewer: I was given the police records of your mother and your father and those records say your mother has never been arrested.

Alienated child: She's just lied on the police record.

Interviewer: It's not possible for her to do that. She cannot access those records to change them.

Alienated child: All I know is that she has been arrested lots of times.

This seeming inability to shift their view about the targeted parent does not reflect a more general problem in this area. That is, an alienated child can readily accept that others who engaged in similar behaviours to the targeted parent did so with benevolent intentions. However, they cannot apply this understanding to the targeted parent's actions.

Box 13.79 Alienated child: I hate my mother. She makes me eat vegetables I don't like, and she makes me go to school when I don't want to because I don't feel well. She always makes me do my homework as soon as I get home. It's not fair.

Interviewer: Do you think it is the job of parents to look after their children?

Alienated child: Yes.

Interviewer: Do you think that parents should make sure their children are healthy by getting them to eat the right things?

Alienated child: Yes.

Interviewer: Do you think it's the job of parents to make sure their children get a good education, so they have good futures?

Alienated child: Yes.

Interviewer: So, do you think it's possible that Mum is just doing her job as a parent when she makes you do these things?

Alienated child: No, she's just being mean. She does it because she hates me, and she is mean.

The rigidity of the alienated child's belief system reflects the seriousness of the impact of the alienation process on the child. In this way, the child's ideas present as beyond reason, not amenable to change, and detrimental to the child's world view.

Independent thinker phenomenon

The term 'independent thinker phenomenon' was coined by Gardner (5) and the phenomenon was included as one of the indicators of his syndrome. However, quite separately from the notion of a syndrome, it is evident that children will demonstrate this characteristic. The independent thinker phenomenon refers to children, who have been alienated from a parent, insisting that their decision to reject the targeted parent was theirs alone and not influenced by any other person, including the alienating parent. They dismiss the notion that their decision must have been influenced by others or by information others have provided. They will continue to do this despite evidence being provided that contradicts their story.

> **Box 13.80 Alienated child:** My father is a dangerous man so I'm not going to see him again.
> **Interviewer:** Who decided that?
> **Alienated child:** I did. I decided that.
> **Interviewer:** Has Mum ever talked about that with you?
> **Alienated child:** No, never. She never talks to me about my father … not ever.
> **Interviewer:** I was talking with your Grandma who told me that she has heard Mum tell you that Dad is dangerous person and you don't have to see him.
> **Alienated child:** That's not true.
> **Interviewer:** And then, when I talked to your Mum, she agreed that she had told you this.
> **Alienated child:** I decided for myself. It was my idea and not anyone else's idea.

When questioned about the views they hold of the targeted parent, an alienated child will state that their negative views are a result of their own, direct experience. They will cite these experiences as the reason why they hold such negative views about the targeted parent. They will refute the notion that the alienating parent influenced their view, even in cases where it can be demonstrated to the child that they could not possibly have experienced the events they claim are their own.

> **Box 13.81 Alienated child:** My father is a druggie and a drunk. He's been fired from every job he has ever had, and he has no friends.
> **Interviewer:** Who told you these sorts of things about Dad?
> **Alienated child:** No-one. I just know myself.
> **Interviewer:** We can talk later about whether or not these things are true. At the moment, I am interested how you would know about things that you wouldn't have seen yourself.
> **Alienated child:** No-one told me anything about my father. Mum never talks about him. I just know these things. I didn't need anyone to tell me because I already know.

Even when an alienated child recognises that the views held by the alienating parent about the targeted parent are negative in nature, they will continue to deny that the alienating parent's attitude influences their own. This 'independent thinker' point of view will be maintained even when there is acknowledgement that they have been exposed to negative information about the targeted parent.

> **Box 13.82 Interviewer:** Some of the things you have told me today about your father are the same as the things your mother told me.
> **Alienated child:** That's because they are true.
> **Interviewer:** The trouble is that lots of things you have told me about your father are things that happened before you were born.
> **Alienated child:** They are still true.
> **Interviewer:** I was wondering who told you about these things involving Dad.
> **Alienated child:** No-one.
> **Interviewer:** Someone must have told you about these things because they happened before you were born.
> **Alienated child:** No, no-one told me. I just know. It is my own idea that I don't want to see my father.

If a suggestion is made that the alienating child has been influenced in their views by the alienating parent, the child will act in a protective manner towards the alienating parent. They will stubbornly insist that the alienating parent had no impact on their own attitude towards the targeted parent and would never behave in such a way.

> **Box 13.83 Interviewer:** I think that it must have been Mum who told you about the things that happened with your Dad before you were born.
> **Alienated child:** That's not true.
> **Interviewer:** I think this because what you have told me and what Mum told me are exactly the same and most people, when they tell you about something that happened, have their own point of view that makes their story a bit different from other people's stories.
> **Alienated child:** My mother would never say anything bad about anyone. She is a nice person. She has never told me anything about my father … not one word. She would never do that.

An alienating child will insist that they be the one who decides whether or not they spend time with the targeted parent. They see their role in deciding what should happen as a natural consequence of them 'independently' deciding not to spend time with the targeted parent.

> **Box 13.84 Alienated child:** The judge has decided that I have to spend two nights a fortnight with my father. Well, I'm not going to do that. It's not up to the judge, it's up to me. I decide what I want to do. It's my choice.

As this example indicates, an alienated child who holds the view that they should be the decider of whether or not they spend time with the alienated parent will reject the notion that a court should make orders that, in effect, direct them to see a parent. In many cases, an alienated child will insist that they will defy court orders if they are made contrary to their 'independent' wishes.

> **Box 13.85 Interviewer:** The judge is going to make a decision about whether or not you will spend time with Dad, and he will decide how much time you spend with Dad.
>
> **Alienated child:** I don't want to see my father and I won't. The judge can't decide that, only I can. I am the one who decides. No-one can tell me what to do. They keep saying that Mum has stopped me from seeing Dad, but I am the one who doesn't want to see him. If the judge tells me I have to see Dad then I will tell him I won't see him. He can't make me.

Encouraging a child to hold the view that they are the person who has reached the conclusion that the targeted parent is someone they wish to reject makes it easier for the alienating parent in this alienation process. The child then becomes the person who needs to be convinced to have contact with the targeted parent and the alienating parent can present themselves as supporting a child's relationship with the other parent. Alienating parents often claim they try to encourage their child to see the targeted parent but that the alienating child is insistent that no contact take place. This allows alienating parents to present themselves as more reasonable in their views than is actually the case.

Concluding comments

A cautious approach should be taken when determining the presence of the indicators of alienation in a child being assessed. In approaching any evaluation, the starting point should be that the evaluator does not know the nature of any problem or even if one exists. A process of hypothesis formulation and testing should then be undertaken based on the information that becomes available during the assessment period and from collateral information sources. The final opinion should account for all information and not just the information that supports a preconceived notion of the problems faced by the family.

There are a multitude of reasons, other than parental alienation, why a child might resist spending time with a parent (6). These need to be examined. These include:

- Behaviours associated with normal development, such as, difficulties experienced by a young child in separating from a parent.
- The child's inability to cope with poor parental behaviour during high conflict situations, such as during changeover of the child from one parent's care to the other parent's care.
- The influence of parenting style on the child's capacity to cope with spending time with one parent.
- The child's worry about what will happen to a poorly coping parent in the child's absence.
- Issues arising from the re-partnering of parents, such as the child's reaction to the introduction into the child's life of a person with a parenting role.

When examining visitation resistance in a child, it has been suggested that consideration should be given to alternative explanations other than alienation. In particular, it has been recommended that it be determined whether the following are evident (7):

- The child has a tendency to provide the questioner with responses the child perceives are expected.
- The child generally has a problem with separating from the 'sending' parent.

- The child generally resists spending time with the 'receiving' parent.
- The receiving parent more rigidly or less rigidly applies rules and boundaries for the child.
- The receiving parent is able to recognise the child's needs and respond to them.
- The sending parent indicates support of the receiving parent.
- The sending parent has the capacity or inclination to foster the child's sense of security when the child spends time with the receiving parent.
- The receiving parent is able to act in a way that counters the child's views that underlie the resistance to spend time with that parent.
- It is feasible or necessary to alter the amount of influence the sending parent has on the child by limiting the time s/he spends with the child.
- It is feasible or necessary to limit the amount of time the receiving parent spends with the child.

At the end of this process, parental alienation may be determined to be evident based on appropriate evaluation procedures.

References

1. Ellis, E. (2008). A stepwise approach to evaluating children for parental alienation syndrome. *Journal of Child Custody, 4,* 55–78. doi:10.1300/j190v04n01_03
2. Bernet, W., Gregory, N., Reay, K., & Rohner, R.P. (2017). An objective measure of splitting in parental alienation: The Parental Acceptance–Rejection Questionnaire. *Journal of Forensic Sciences, 63,* 776–783. doi:10.1111/1556–4029.13625
3. Principe, G.F., & Schindewolf, E. (2012). Natural conversations as a source of false memories in children: Implications for the testimony of young witnesses. *Developmental Review, 32,* 205–223. doi:10.1016/j.dr.2012.06.003
4. Uehara, I. (2015). *Developmental Changes in Memory-Related Linguistic Skills and Their Relationship to Episodic Recall in Children. PLoS ONE 10,* e0137220. doi:10.1371/journal.pone.0137220
5. Gardner, R.A. (1998). Recommendations for dealing with parents who induce a parental alienation syndrome in their children. *Journal of Divorce and Remarriage, 28,* 1–23. doi:10.1300/j087v28n03_01
6. Kelly, J.B., & Johnston, J.R. (2001). The alienated child: A reformulation of parental alienation syndrome. *Family Court Review, 39,* 249–266. doi:10.1111/j.174–1617.2001.tb00609.x
7. Garber, B.D. (2007). Conceptualizing visitation resistance and refusal in the context of parental conflict, separation, and divorce. *Family Court Review, 45,* 588–599. doi:10.1111/j.1744-1617.2007.00173.x

Chapter Fourteen

Assessing dysfunctional family interaction patterns

Introduction

When working with the alienated family, it is essential to remember that each member of the family, whether it be the alienating parent, alienated child or targeted parent, is one part of a wider family system that is intrinsically intertwined. No one member of the alienated family can be completely understood without an understanding of the behaviours of other family members and how they mutually influence each other.

Family assessment is a process of gathering and organising information about how families function and dysfunction. When working with the alienated family, it is important to obtain a full, unbiased view of the family. Although the alienated family is fractured in many ways and may no longer resemble what is traditionally considered a family, it is important to remember that it is still a family system.

When working with the alienated family, it is easy to focus on family dysfunction, discord and difficulties. When conducting a family assessment, it is important also to explore the family's strengths, values and goals. This chapter reviews prevailing models of understanding the family system. It explores how these models can be applied to understanding the alienated family and how they can be used to guide the assessment of family interaction patterns. Consideration is given to assessment tools therapists can use to conduct these assessments. Recommendations for best practice in family assessment with the alienated family are provided. This chapter focuses on family assessment needed for intervention. However, reference will be made to recommendations for best practice when examining family functioning for the court.

Approaching family assessment for intervention purposes

Before deciding on the best way to intervene with the alienated family, it is essential practitioners conduct thorough assessments to obtain a clear and unbiased opinion of the family and each of its members. A good family assessment requires astute observation and listening skills.

When first meeting with the alienated family, it is inappropriate to meet with the family members together in the same room. Initially, it is best practice to meet individually with each member of the family involved in the alienation. This will ensure the psychological safety of all family members. Meeting with each parent separately first can provide the clinician with a wealth of information. Not only does it provide information about the presenting problems, it also gives practitioners information about discrepancies in the parent's perceptions of the problems.

Once the practitioner has met with the parents, it is important to meet with the children. Even when a child is very young, the practitioner should still meet with them to assess if the child or infant appears to be well looked after. For children who are old enough, hearing their perception of the problems will provide valuable insight into their experience. Children's reports also can demonstrate their alliance with one parent over another, as seen in Chapter Thirteen.

Family assessment focuses on the relationships and interactions between family members while being aware of individual concerns as they relate to and impact on the family. Practitioners should assess and observe the contributions each family member makes to the problem and how each family member could contribute to the solution.

After meeting with each family member, the practitioner can then decide which combinations of dyads or even triads are best to observe and assess together. When making this decision, it is important to consider the safety of each family member. Interviews, observation and reviewing available collateral evidence can provide important information about family history, their needs, function and structure.

Box 14.1 Psychologist: I once saw a family who was court ordered to see me for family therapy. The family consisted of a three-year-old boy and his parents who were separated. The boy was living with his mother and she was refusing to let the boy spend time with his father. The mother claimed the father was unfit to be a parent. I met with the parents separately first. There were no historical or present facts they could agree on. Their perceptions of their past relationship and how it ended were completely different. I could not say whose story was closest to the truth; however, the father told the most logically convincing story. The mother's story was unrealistic and contained many contradictory statements. I met with the boy in my rooms. He was pale in complexion and looked small and underweight for his age. He was still wearing nappies and he did not speak. His mother refused to leave the room and she encouraged him to stay close to her. He would not interact with me at all. I then saw the boy with his father. They had not seen each other for over a year. After an initial fuss separating from his mother (a fuss the mother encouraged), the boy eagerly engaged in a game of peek-a-boo initiated by his father. Within minutes, the boy happily engaged with his father, with me and with his surroundings. He was a completely different child in the presence of his father.

When meeting with the family members for the first time, it is important to establish the boundaries and limitations of confidentiality and consent. Practitioners must clarify their role and the limits to the intervention they may provide. Each member of the family should leave the first interview with a clear understanding of what is about to happen next, including children who are old enough to understand this information.

It is vital the practitioner remain non-judgemental. It can be easy for practitioners to blame the alienating parent for the family's problems. This will not help the family. Instead, the practitioner needs to listen to each family member and make every effort to understand each family member's frame of reference.

When approaching a family assessment, it is important for the practitioner to keep in mind prevailing theories of family functioning. This is because these theories can guide practitioners to observe and assess the dysfunction and complexities that exist within the alienated family. Let us give consideration to some of the important theories of family functioning.

Models of family functioning and attachment

When understanding the difficulties faced by the alienated family, the focus must shift from understanding the experience of the individual to the interactions and transactions that occur at a family systems level. Parental alienation does not occur in a vacuum. It occurs within the context of a family unable to adapt to stress in a productive way.

Minuchin and family stress

Minuchin (1) argued that family stress originates from four sources. These are:

1. When one family member comes under stress and their stress reactions infiltrate the entire family system.
2. When external pressures affect the entire family system.
3. When adapting to the life cycle, such as expected developmental changes in each family member.
4. When idiosyncratic problems arise that are unique to the family

Minuchin (1) maintained that all families are in a perpetual state of transition. How well a family functions depends on how the family members adapt to ongoing changes. For most families, the stress experienced during transitions is not pathological unless families, or one or more of the members, respond to stress by being rigid and resistant to exploring avenues for effective coping.

The interactional patterns seen in the alienated family can be considered pathological because the alienating parent and, subsequently, the alienated child avoids and resists opportunities to deal with family separation in an adaptive and functional manner. Their reactions infiltrate the entire family system including the wider extended family. The involvement of services designed to help the family, such as legal or mental health services, can act as an external source of stress for the alienated family.

When assessing the alienated family, it is useful to understand how each family member responded or reacted to stress before and after family separation. Also, it is useful to assess how stress reactions of one member affects other members. The practitioner should ask about the nature of stressors the family faced before separation as well as after in order to place the family's current difficulties in context. Moreover, it is important to determine if these stressors were expected life transitions or stressors unique to the family.

Minuchin (1) also described the concept of triangulation. Triangulation occurs when stress exists within a dyad and a family member tries to relieve this stress by involving a third family member. Hayley (2) referred to the perverse triangle when two family members of a different generational level form a coalition against a third family member. The perverse triangle has also been referred to as the rigid triangle (1). This form of triangulation typically involves a parent–child coalition against the other parent. This is central to parental alienation. The existence and nature of the perverse triangle within the alienated family should be examined as part of the family assessment.

McMaster model of family functioning

In addition to understanding family stress, it is useful to consider the organisational structure of the family and how family interactions maintain the problem. A useful model for practitioners to keep in mind during family assessment is the McMaster model (3), which is grounded in family systems theory. According to this theory:

1. All parts of the family are interrelated.
2. No one part of the family can be understood fully without understanding the rest of the family system.
3. Family functioning can only be understood when the whole family system is considered.
4. Family structure and organisation are important determinants of how family members behave.
5. The way family members interact with each other also determines how family members behave.

The McMaster model describes family functioning as a series of tasks family members need to complete to function effectively. Dysfunction in the family occurs when the tasks cannot be achieved. Table 14.1 provides a summary of the tasks or dimensions of family functioning.

Table 14.1 McMaster's six dimensions of family functioning.

Dimension	Description
Problem solving	A family's ability to satisfactorily resolve problems. Problems are broadly categorised as: *Instrumental*: day-to-day problems *Affective*: problems associated with emotional experience Family dysfunction occurs when families cannot find a solution to their problems
Communication	The way in which a family communicates or exchanges information with each other. Communication includes: *Problem solving*: communicating effectively with the aim of solving problems *Affective communication*: communicating about emotions and displaying empathy *Instrumental communication*: communicating about day-to-day activities and events Families experience dysfunction when they are unable to communicate with each other in a clear and empathic way
Roles	A family's ability to define, maintain and negotiate roles within the family. Roles can be considered recurring patterns of behaviour and tasks. These are divided into: *Instrumental roles*: these include division of labour within the household *Affective roles*: the emotionally supportive roles Families dysfunction if they are unable to negotiate these roles and when one family member becomes dissatisfied with the roles and the family cannot renegotiate them
Affective responsiveness	A family's ability to respond to each other emotionally This includes each family member's ability to respond to other family members' emotional reactions as well as the manner in which family members respond emotionally to situations and events Family dysfunction occurs if family members repeatedly cannot respond in an emotionally adaptive way to other family members and/or external situations and events
Affective involvement	The degree to which a family is interested in each other and values each other. Affective involvement considers the following: *Empathic involvement*: involvement because each family member is valued *Enmeshment*: over involvement whereby boundaries between members are blurred *Interest devoid of feelings*: involvement out of a sense of duty rather than genuine interest *Narcissistic involvement*: Involvement because of self-interest *Uninvolved*: No involvement or neglect
Behaviour control	A family's ability to develop strategies to manage behaviour in the following situations: Physically dangerous situations Meeting and expressing psychobiological needs Interpersonal socialising Family dysfunction occurs when a family is unable to develop and maintain acceptable standards of behaviour by setting appropriate family rules

Table 14.2 Six dimensions of family functioning related to the alienated family.

Dimension	Description
Problem solving	The alienated family adopts a pervasive pattern of poor problem solving that predates family separation. The alienating parent's inability to effectively problem solve ripples throughout the family. The targeted parent's capacity to solve problems created by the alienating parent becomes exhausted, which can trigger maladaptive reactions to the alienating parent's rigidity and refusal to make changes.
Communication	The alienating family describes a pervasive pattern of poor communication with each other. Communication can be devoid of empathy. Communication can be ambiguous, masked, camouflaged and open to misinterpretation.
Roles	Roles in the alienated family are rigid and the alienating parent's inability to renegotiate family roles as the family develops and changes reverberates throughout the family.
Affective responsiveness	The alienated family is unable to respond in an adaptive way to stress and consequently separation was inevitable. The family is then unable to respond in a functional way to family separation. The alienating parent is unable to respond appropriately to the needs of the child because they prioritise their own needs. The targeted parent's ability to respond to the child's needs is diminished as the alienation progresses and their ability to cope with family dysfunction is exhausted.
Affective involvement	The targeted parent's opportunity to be empathically involved in their child's life is diminished as a consequence of the alienation. The alienating parent and alienated child's relationship is enmeshed. The alienating parent's involvement in their child's life is typically narcissistic and, when their involvement is no longer of benefit to them, their child's needs are neglected. Observing this is distressing for the targeted parent. Their distress is compounded by their inability to find a solution for their child.
Behaviour control	The alienated family is unable to set and maintain consistent standards of behaviour. The alienating parent repeatedly changes these rules for each family member and sets a standard for others they do not set for themselves.

The alienated family may have difficulty in all of these dimensions. Table 14.2 provides a brief summary of the ways in which the alienated family is unable to achieve the tasks of family functioning.

Dysfunctional and circular patterns of behaviour within a family are associated with family impairment and this must be considered when assessing the alienated family. It is also useful to consider the level of cohesion and flexibility that occurred in the family prior to separation as well as the level of cohesion and flexibility within the dyadic relationships post separation. To understand the alienated family as a whole, it is useful to examine the flexibility, cohesion and communication between the various dyads within the family (i.e., alienating parent–alienated child dyad, alienated child–targeted parent dyad, alienating parent–targeted parent dyad).

Circumplex model of family cohesion

Olson's circumplex model (4) identifies flexibility, cohesion and communication skills as central to family interactions. Families function well when these components of family interactions are in balance. Families function better when they can flexibly respond to stress. The alienated family is unable to find this balance. There is no shared understanding of family rules and roles before and after family separation. This leads to chaos within the new family structure.

The circumplex model also considers the level of emotional bonding or cohesion between family members. When a family is cohesive, they can balance independence and togetherness while maintaining healthy relationships. The alienated family is unable to strike this balance. The alienating parent and targeted parent are unable to achieve a level of cohesion post separation to be able to effectively co-parent. The alienating parent remains focused on their individual concerns. Within the alienating parent–child relationship, emotional closeness is too high, leading to dependency and reactivity in this relationship. As a result of triangulation, the alienated child–targeted parent relationship is disengaged. The imbalance of cohesion is so severe that no family member can function effectively.

The circumplex model also refers to communication. Communication is essential for facilitating movement towards balance in flexibility and cohesion. The alienated family has poor communication within the family system and, as a result, stays in perpetual imbalance if there is no intervention.

The alienating parent–alienated child dyad is chaotically enmeshed. The loyalty the child has to this parent is too high and the level of closeness leads to blurred boundaries. There is lack of appropriate parental leadership as well as shifts in roles and erratic changes in expected standards of behaviour. The alienating parent–targeted parent relationship is chaotically disengaged. The alienating parent prioritises their own needs and dramatically changes the rules of co-parenting to suit themselves. As a result of these imbalances, the alienated child–targeted parent relationship can range from chaotically disengaged to rigidly disengaged depending on the severity of the alienation. The severely alienated child is rigidly disengaged from the targeted parent.

The circumplex model is useful when observing family interaction patterns when the alienated child is older. When the alienated child is below the age of five, attachment theory is a useful framework for consideration. Moreover, attachment theory can guide the practitioner's assessment of enduring attachment styles the alienating parent and targeted parent have with their family of origin. Understanding family of origin attachment styles can provide useful context to how the family became alienated, because parental alienation is intergenerational (5–7).

Attachment theory

Attachment is the state and quality of an individual's connection to a significant other (8). An attachment between parent and child must be warm, empathically involved and continuous in order to ensure the normal development of the child (9). Attachment behaviour is any behaviour that results in achieving or maintaining closeness to another person who is considered to be better able to cope with the world. Usually, it is triggered by separation or the perceived threat of separation from the attachment figure (10). When young children are separated from their caregivers, they will display attachment behaviours and experience separation distress.

Within the context of parental alienation, one of the child's attachment figures, the targeted parent, has been removed from their lives. The alienating parent positions themselves as the child's primary attachment figure. As a result of this, the child will display attachment behaviours when the child fears the loss of yet another attachment figure. Sometimes, practitioners can misinterpret attachment behaviour as fear of the targeted parent. Therefore, it is important to consider the attachment between the alienating parent and child as well as the attachment between the child and targeted parent.

However, it also is important to consider that for an attachment to be maintained, the parent–child relationship must be continuous as well as warm and empathically involved. When the targeted parent–child relationship has been disrupted, the child will inevitably be wary of the targeted parent unless the targeted parent is able to provide the child with a much-needed secure base and recommence regular contact.

When observing parent–child interactions as part of the family assessment, it is also useful to consider attachment styles. An infant who is securely attached to their caregiver will explore their environment comfortably in the presence of their parent. They will experience some distress in the absence of their parent but will settle quickly when comforted by either their returning parent or another attachment figure (11). The child with an anxious–ambivalent attachment to their parent will show extreme separation distress when their parent leaves them, and ambivalence or anger upon their return (12). The infant with an anxious–avoidant attachment to their parent will be distant and avoid their parent regardless of whether their parent is present (12).

Alienated children are typically insecurely attached to the alienating parent because the alienating parent prioritises their needs over having a continuous, warm and empathically involved relationship with their child. Attachment style at one developmental stage can impact attachment style at the next stage of development (13). It is useful for practitioners to consider the possible attachment style the alienating parent and targeted parent had with their parents. This is because attachment styles tend to be enduring.

Box 14.2 Psychologist: When assessing the alienated family, I keep in my mind the circular patterns of behaviour and interaction that occur within the family, even when the family is severely alienated. One action from one family member almost always reverberates throughout the whole family system. Although alienated, each family member is intrinsically linked and will always be linked and influence each other until each family member is no longer alive. When assessing family functioning, it is a bit like putting together a giant puzzle until the picture of the family makes sense. This is not an easy or quick task because alienated families are messy.

Assessment tools

When assessing dysfunctional patterns of family interactions, interviews with each parent, child interviews and parent–child observations are the most useful assessment strategies for the alienated family (14–16). Both assessment methods are an effective and readily available method of obtaining a clear picture of family functioning. Interviews and observational assessments encompass a wide range of skills the practitioner must juggle. These skills include active and empathic listening, managing multiple perspectives, navigating different motivations for and readiness to participate in the assessment and any subsequent intervention, working with different age groups and judging when to bring different subsystems of the family together.

Currently, there is no widely accepted valid and reliable assessment tool for the assessment of dysfunctional family interactions patterns in the alienated family. Assessment tools commonly used to assess family functioning have been developed for use with intact nuclear families and have not been validated for use with other family types. Having said this, there are some assessment tools described in the literature that can assist with assessing the alienated family.

Garber (17) described a "Hierarchical Decision Tree for Alienation". This decision tree prompts the practitioner to consider the following issues:

1. Is the child giving socially desirable responses?
2. Is the child unable to separate from the alienating parent?
3. Is the child resisting contact with the targeted parent?

4.   Are there differences and similarities in the way each parent sets and enforces household rules?
5.   Are both parents responsive to the child's needs?
6.   Do the parents support the child having a relationship with their other parent?
7.   Is the targeted parent able to provide the child with an environment that can counteract the impact of the alienating parent's behaviour?
8.   Is it necessary, practical and appropriate to remove the child from the care of the alienating parent?
9.   Is it necessary, practical, and appropriate to reduce interactions between the targeted and alienating parent?

Assessing dysfunctional family interaction patterns in the alienated family is challenging. This is because research in this area of assessment is limited. These limits are compounded by varying opinions about how parental alienation should be conceptualised (18–19). A variety of questionnaires have been described in the literature. A select few are mentioned here:

•   The Parental Acceptance–Rejection Questionnaire (PARQ)(20) is a 60-item questionnaire completed by children. The PARQ measures the extent to which children engage in splitting behaviour and lack ambivalence towards the targeted parent.
•   The Baker Parental Alienation Syndrome Questionnaire (BPASQ)(21) is a 28-item instrument that measures parent–child alignment in the context of family conflict and separation.
•   The Co-Parenting Behavior Questionnaire (22) measures parenting and co-parenting behaviour in a variety of domains such as inter-parental conflict, triangulation, cooperation, communication, discipline, parental monitoring, warmth, and parent–child communication.

Additionally, the practitioner should integrate information from any available collateral evidence into their understanding of the family. Collateral information can provide pieces of the puzzle that cannot be obtained from interviews and observations.

Best practice in family assessment

Family assessment for intervention is different to a forensic assessment for the Family Court. The purpose of a forensic assessment for the Family Court is to provide an evidence-based opinion to the court. The purpose of assessment for intervention is to gather sufficient information to develop an appropriate intervention pathway for the family. Regardless of the purpose of the family assessment, the following guidelines are suggested.

Standards of practice in parenting dispute evaluations vary across jurisdictions and countries. However, Martindale and colleagues (23) offered a model of best practice for parenting dispute evaluators that can also be applied to family assessment for the purpose of intervention planning. They maintained that an empirically driven approach should be applied to assessments. Each parent and all adults who live with the child and/or engage in caregiving responsibilities in relation to the child, as well as the child, should be included in the assessment. Each parent–child dyad should be directly observed unless doing so poses a known risk of harm to the child.

Assessments should be conducted in a non-judgmental manner that is fair to all family members and with accuracy. If using psychometric tools, practitioners should only use those that have acceptable psychometric properties and only with the populations the tests were designed to target. Practitioners should only use assessment tools they are qualified and trained to administer.

When conducting a family assessment, do no harm!

Concluding comments

Assessing dysfunctional family interaction patterns in the alienated family is messy and not for the faint-hearted. Each family member is part of a wider family system that is inherently entwined. In order to maintain an empirically driven approach to the assessment, consideration should be given to theories of family functioning and attachment. These theories can provide structure to the assessment approach. When conducting family assessment, be mindful to assess for the family's strengths as well as their difficulties. Ensure the assessment is free from bias and, importantly, do no harm.

References

1. Minuchin, S. (1974). *Families and family therapy*. Cambridge, MA: Harvard University Press.
2. Hayley, J. (1977). *Problem solving therapy*. California: Jossey-bass.
3. Epstein, N.B., Bishop D.S., & Levin, S. (1978). The McMaster Model of Family Functioning. *Journal of Marriage and Family Counseling, 4,* 19–31. doi:10.1111/j.1752-0606.1978.tb00537.x
4. Olson, D.H. (2000). Circumplex Model of Marital and Family Systems. *Journal of Family Therapy, 22,* 144–167. doi:10.1111/1467–6427.00144
5. Baker, A.J.L. (2005). The long-term effects of parental alienation on adult children: A qualitative research study. *The American Journal of Family Therapy, 33,* 289–302. doi:10.1080/01926180590962129
6. Baker, A.J.L. (2007). *Adult children of parental alienation syndrome: Breaking the ties that bind*. New York: W.W. Norton.
7. Baker A.J.L., Chambers J. (2011). Adult recall of childhood exposure to parental conflict: unpacking the black box of parental alienation. *Journal of Divorce Remarriage, 52,* 55–76. doi:10.1080/10502556.2011.534396
8. Holmes, J. (1993). *John Bowlby and attachment theory*. London: Routledge.
9. Bowlby, J. (1963). *Attachment and loss: Attachment* (Vol. 1). London: Hogarth.
10. Bowlby, J. (1988). *A secure base. Clinical applications of attachment theory*. London: Routledge.
11. Ainsworth, M.S., Blehar, M.C., Waters, E., & Wall, S. (1978). *Patterns of attachment: A psychological study of the Strange Situation*. Hillsdale, NJ: Lawrence Erlbaum Associates.
12. Feeney, J.A., Noller, P., & Roberts, N. (1999). Attachment and close relationships. In. I.C. Hendrick & S.S. Hendrick (Eds.). *Close relationships: A sourcebook* (pp.185–201). London: Sage Publications.
13. Kerns, K.A. (1994). A longitudinal examination of links between mother-child attachment and children's friendships in early childhood. *Journal of Social and Personal Relationships, 11,* 379–381. doi:10.1177/0265407594113004
14. Bow, J.N. (2006). Review of empirical research on child custody practice. *Journal of Child Custody: Research, Issues, and Practices, 3,* 23–50. doi:10.1300/J190v03n01_02
15. Gould, J. (2006). *Conducting scientifically crafted child custody evaluations* (2nd edn.). Sarasota, FL: Professional Resource Press.
16. Gould, J., & Martindale, D. (2007). *The art and science of child custody evaluations*. New York: The Guilford Press.
17. Garber, B. (2007). Conceptualizing visitation resistance and refusal in the context of parental conflict, separation, and divorce. *Family Court Review, 45,* 588–599. doi:10.1111/j.1744-1617.2007.00173.x
18. Baker, A.J.L. & Darnall, D. (2007). A construct study of the eight symptoms of severe parental alienation syndrome: A survey of parental experiences. *Journal of Divorce and Remarriage, 47,* 55–75. doi:10.1300/j087v47n01_04
19. Kelly, J.B., & Johnston, J.R. (2001). The alienated child: A reformulation of parental alienation syndrome. *Family Court Review, 39,* 249–266. doi:10.1111/j.174–1617.2001.tb00609.x

20. Bernet, W., Gregory, N., Reay, K.M., & Rohner, R. (2017). An objective measure of splitting in parental alienation: The parental acceptance-rejection questionnaire. *Journal of Forensic Sciences, 63,* 776–783. doi:10.1111/1556–4029.13625.

21. Baker, A.J.L. (2010). Adult recall of parental alienation in a community sample: Prevalence and associations with psychological maltreatment. *Journal of Divorce and Remarriage, 51,* 16–35. doi:10.1080/10502550903423206

22. Mullett, E., & Stolberg, A.L. (1999). The development of the Co-Parenting Behaviors Questionnaire: An instrument for children of divorce. *Journal of Divorce and Remarriage, 31,* 115–137.

23. Martindale, D., Martin, L., Austin, W., Drozd, L., Gould-Saltman, D., Kirkpatrick, H., ...Stahl, P. (2006). Model Standards of Practice for Child Custody Evaluation. *Family Court Review, 45,* 70–91. doi:10.1111/j.1744-1617.2007.129_3.x

Part Four

The alienated family

A legal perspective

Chapter Fifteen

Parental alienation in the courts

Introduction

An important aspect of parental alienation is that it often occurs in the context of legal proceedings. Failure of the targeted parent to obtain adequate time with their child motivates them to seek legal redress. The concept of parental alienation has been reported in many countries (1) and within many legal systems, even if the term 'parental alienation' is not always used (2).

An Internet survey of mental health professionals and lawyers who work in family law demonstrated that there is considerable awareness of parental alienation, including the debate about its validity. However, despite this level of understanding, it was found that most professionals were cautious in their approach to parental alienation (3). Of course, those who hold the view that the validity of parental alienation has not been determined also hold the view that courts should not base their decision-making on an unsubstantiated syndrome (4). Certainly, some have raised the issue of the failure of parental alienation syndrome to meet admissibility standards (3,5).

In general, the management of parental alienation within the legal system is challenging. Determining if a child not spending time with a parent is because of parental alienation or estrangement can be complex because the differentiation between those concepts largely relies on psychological factors. Therefore, the courts tend to rely on expert evidence. It is this evidence that is often given weight when deciding what outcome is in the best interests of the child.

The nature of parental alienation in the legal system

Parental alienation is one of a multitude of challenges faced in family law. It complicates decision-making by increasing the complexity of cases. It is necessary to consider how parental alienation affects parenting disputes in a legal setting.

The size of the problem in family law

Here we are not referring to the number of parenting order disputes in family law that involve parental alienation. Rather, we are referring to the extent to which the cases involving parental alienation make the application of the law and the management of cases more challenging.

The court processes for cases involving parental alienation are the same as other children's cases in terms of court processes and procedures. However, in Australia, cases where parental alienation is an issue are more likely to be heard in the Family Court of Australia rather than the Federal Circuit Court, particularly where there are allegations of sexual abuse. This is a reflection of the complexity of the cases and the difficulties faced in resolving parenting order disputes where parental alienation is a genuine issue.

Certainly, despite the court processes being the same irrespective of the presence or not of parental alienation, these cases do represent significant challenges for the court. Not least of these challenges is the need to have a cohesive response in a case involving numerous competing issues. These competing issues might include any number of the following factors that complicate cases before the court, including the views expressed by the child about with whom they wish to reside, and allegations of family violence and abuse.

Issues related to the views expressed by the child will be covered later in this chapter. In terms of family violence and abuse of the child, parental alienation cases often involve these types of allegations that are denied by the other party. The relatively high rate of false accusations of violence and abuse in the context of parenting disputes is well known (6–7), whether or not parental alienation is occurring. In cases involving parental alienation, alienating parents often make allegations of harmful behaviour by the targeted parent, with both the alienating parent and the alienated child being identified as the victims of this alleged violence and abuse. It also may be the case that the actions of the alienating parent are construed as abusive towards the child by the targeted parent. This can lead to an application for the child to live with the targeted parent because the alienating parent is placing the child at psychological risk.

These cases that involve allegations of violence and abuse by one party and denial of wrongdoing by the accused party are among the hardest of cases to achieve a satisfactory outcome. In these cases, and in cases involving parental alienation in general, without allegations of violence and abuse, it is difficult to discern the best outcome for the child or children involved. The child will often vehemently oppose knowing or communicating with the targeted parent and show great anxiety at the thought. Notwithstanding this in extreme cases, if a parent cannot promote the relationship between the child and the other parent it may be in the child's best interests to be removed from the alienating parent, which may itself cause the child distress. This creates an uneasy dilemma for the court. With the requirement that a child is not placed in a situation where there is risk of harm to that child, a pathway forward in a parenting dispute involving allegations of violence and abuse is not always clear.

Parental alienation cases tend to be complex and involve expert evidence from a variety of sources. In Australia, these cases almost always involve the appointment of an independent children's lawyer (ICL). An ICL is a lawyer appointed by the court to represent the interests of the children involved. The trials tend to be lengthy and use considerable resources. Often, there is a larger than normal amount of evidence presented at these trials. For example, this evidence can be provided by child protective services, centres that offer supervision of the time a child spends with a parent, and the police. As a result, these trials can be costly financially.

In addition, the cross-examination of witnesses providing evidence and the parents involved in the case can be exacting in nature and difficult for those involved. Often, the worst aspects of a parent's life will be considered and laid bare. The resultant difficulties of this process may move the focus away from the central issue, that is the child's best interests.

Lawyers' and the courts' approach to parental alienation cases

The difficult and complex nature of family law cases that involve parental alienation is recognised by lawyers in Australia. As a result, the parenting disputes that seem to involve parental alienation are handled with caution. Family lawyers dealing with these cases are required to use their experience and skill to advance the case as instructed while evaluating the evidence and reality checking their client's expectations. An alienating parent will often be forceful in their presentation and determined to keep the child from the other parent who, they say, poses a risk of harm. Challenging a client's position that is contrary to the emerging evidence is very difficult but important. Reluctance to challenge the alienating parent's viewpoint will give that parent more power in the context of a parenting dispute than is warranted or deserved. At a trial however, the alienating behaviour may be exposed with disastrous consequences.

Parental alienation is viewed seriously by the court. There is recognition of the impact of parental alienation on targeted parents and their relationships with their children. Section 60CC of the *Family Law Act, 1975* (8) sets out the factors that a court must consider when determining the parenting order to be made in the best interests of a child. A number of factors have relevance to cases where parental alienation is alleged. For example, the court must consider, among other things:

- The benefit of a child having a meaningful relationship with both of the child's parents.
- The need to protect the child from physical or psychological harm and the likely effect of any changes in the child's circumstances including the likely effect of the child being separated from either of his or her parents.
- The capacity of either of the child's parents to provide for the needs of the child including emotional and intellectual needs; and
- The attitude to the child and responsibilities of parenthood demonstrated by each of the parents.

For the lawyers representing the parents, the approach that they take to the court will depend very much upon the instructions they have received and the evidence before the court. For the lawyer representing the alleged 'alienating parent', the brief is likely to be that the 'targeted parent' is a risk to the child. Also, it often is the case that the child is expressing very clear and unequivocal views that that child does not want to see that parent. Further, the brief is likely to be that the child is exhibiting a high degree of anxiety at the prospect of spending time with that parent. There may be a lot of evidence supporting this position as the child will often have been seen by a number of experts, including psychologists, sometimes police officers, social workers and family consultants. These experts may have witnessed and provided evidence of the child exhibiting anxiety and provide evidence of the clear views stated by the child. The ICL also may have spoken with the children and have received some more information supporting these accounts.

The fact that a child is expressing a particular view is a matter that the court must take into account. However, it is one of a number of matters that a court must consider when determining the best interests of the child.

The evidence to support the veracity of the allegations made by parents is crucial as it gives context to the child's stated views and the anxiety around having a relationship with the other parent. Often such evidence can be hard to obtain and the only real forensic evidence available is that given by the 'alienating' parent and the child themselves. Experts are often called in to interview the child and provide some evaluation as to the weight to be applied to the stated views. A thorough expert will test what the child and/or the parents are saying against the other evidence, the history and the relevant background.

It is often difficult for the lawyer and advisors acting for that parent to determine whether or not such a parent is deliberately alienating the child or is motivated by a legitimate desire to protect the child. Malicious intent to deny the child a relationship with the other parent needs to be separated from a genuine desire to protect the child from harm. Often, the evidence is nuanced and complex and, for that reason, the evidence often needs to be tested in a court.

The lawyer acting for the alleged targeted parent has a difficult task, as it is often necessary to counter a large volume of unhelpful evidence, including vehemently held views of a child, allegations of abuse or observed anxiety of a child at the thought of having a relationship or spending time with the targeted parent. Again, it often is not until a trial, or at least a forensic examination by an expert, that there is any ability to challenge the allegations made and promote the prospect of the child either coming into that parent's care or spending time with the parent.

Lawyer and client relationship in alienation cases

All children's cases are challenging, with lawyers having to manage clients at their most vulnerable and emotional, with each parent instructing that their position best advances their child's best interests. Most experienced family lawyers are able to straddle the difficult balance of advancing their client's position while advising effectively and dispassionately as to the merit or otherwise of the same.

Alleged alienators will firmly instruct that their position keeps the child from harm. As stated, this often is corroborated with evidence, some of it from experts. The lawyer has to evaluate the strength or weakness of such evidence and manage the client's expectations. This is obviously a difficult task and requires a high level of training, experience and skill.

Targeted parents feel the need for justice in a situation they consider to be fundamentally unfair (9) and look to the legal system to give them this sense of justice. When the matter does not resolve in the way or as quickly as the targeted parent would like, they tend to feel let down. Despite lawyers working with their targeted parent clients to resolve the matter in their favour, targeted parents tend to view their lawyer in a negative way (10). This is likely to reflect the difficulties that exist in resolving cases involving parental alienation in a way that is satisfactory for all parties, and the challenges in resolving the cases in favour of the targeted parent, in particular.

One of the realities that the alleged targeted parent will find difficult to grasp is that their 'rights' are not the focus for the court. The child is the only participant who has 'rights'. Parents have responsibilities. The targeted parent often can feel that their right to see their child is ignored. Their lawyer has the very difficult task of fighting for their client's position while explaining that the court will focus on outcomes that meet the child's best interests, including ensuring the child is not subject to harm.

Further, a forensic examination of the allegations raised against a targeted parent can often only occur by way of an expert's involvement or a trial. Unfortunately, those processes take a long time to complete. In the meantime, the targeted parent is often left with restricted or no time with their child. If the child is young, this will affect the ability of the child to form an attachment with the parent. This can lead to great frustration and anger for the targeted parent.

Each case is different, and it is difficult for there to be well-developed guidelines to be used in the judicial system. Further, the difficulty in identifying true alienation, as against estrangement or legitimate cases of children at risk in a parent's care, can lead to targeted parents feeling disappointed with the outcome. Notwithstanding this, the judges deciding these matters usually are adept at weighing the complex evidence that typically arises from what are often lengthy trials. If the judge makes a fundamental error, the Full Court can be called upon to correct the same.

It has been recommended that a firmer and more consistent approach to legal decision-making when dealing with alienating parents be adopted (11). However, this is easier said than done. The focus is upon the child's best interests and judges have a wide discretion to fashion orders that meet that paramount consideration. Prescription and guidelines in relation to what a judge can take into account already exist in the *Family Law Act* (8). Nevertheless, legislators could amend section 60CC to refer explicitly to alienating behaviour of a parent. The definition of 'family violence' (section 4AB) could also be enhanced to incorporate explicitly alienating behaviour. That, of course, begs the question as to what exactly is meant by that term. Assuming a definition can be agreed and legislated, such amendments would ensure judges considered whether such behaviour existed in their particular case.

The lawyer for the targeted parent, among all mentioned challenges, will often be left to encourage their client to keep fighting notwithstanding the risk that, ultimately, they may lose. The client has to maintain a patient and measured approach, often over years. They have to behave well, avoid altercations, addictions and other poor behaviour in circumstances where they are under enormous pressure. The process sometimes can set them up to fail as a result.

Further, the client has to be able to meet ever-increasing costs. Given the complexity of these matters, the costs can become prohibiting. Costs not only include those of the lawyer but also the myriad of experts that often are involved. The court's administrative fees also can be significant. Even if legally aided, the client must continuously satisfy the relevant commission that their case has merit to be funded. Sometimes, the expert evidence received will put the funding at jeopardy, even though it is untested in a court. It is not uncommon for such a client to say that they will 'walk away' rather than fight. It is actually a reasonable response, at times, given the challenges. The lawyer has to be skilled to deal with such an emotional response.

The length and complexities of the process to a trial often advantage the alleged alienating parent. Courts are naturally cautious where allegations are raised against a parent that may place a child at risk. This usually results in the targeted parent having restricted or no contact with their child for the years it can take for a matter to go to trial. For the alleged alienator, this can be an advantage, particularly, when the child is young. The restricted or little time with the other parent impacts on the child's relationship with that parent.

A manipulative 'alienating' parent can stymie processes to ensure that they are drawn out and the trial process is delayed. Missing expert reporter interviews or having a sick child each time contact or an interview is to occur are familiar tactics.

Often the parties will agree to a process of 'family therapy' to try to repair the relationship between parent and child. Usually involving a psychologist, the parties and children will go through a process aimed at repairing the parent–child relationship. The process is usually reportable to the court and can take many months before the therapist is able to assess the prospects of success. However, that process can be used by a manipulating parent to delay the overall process. If that parent does not engage in the process and assist with the repair of the other parent–child relationship, months can be wasted. Ultimately, this may backfire on the recalcitrant party as the court may find such behaviour as indicative of a parent who will not promote the child's relationship with the other parent. Nevertheless, it can cause significant upheaval to the process along the way.

If a parent is not complying with a court-ordered process or is denying time with the child for the other parent contrary to an order, contravention proceedings can be filed. However, contravention proceedings are a process that has its own limitations. Apart from the usual issues of expense and delay, the process is one that requires the party alleging the contravention to prove their case. Given that the consequences of a proved contravention, in extreme cases, can be imprisonment, the process is a quasi-criminal one. The accused parent can rely on the defence of 'reasonable excuse' to avoid the contravention. Such an excuse includes action to protect the health and safety of the child. This defence feeds back into the original argument run by the alleged alienating parent that, in keeping the child from spending time with the other parent, they are acting to protect the child from harm. Therefore, it can be difficult to prove a contravention.

One of the other dangers is that the judge who deals with the contravention will be asked to make findings of credit. If that occurs, it may affect that judge's ability to hear the ultimate trial. This is particularly an issue in small registries where there may not be other judges readily available to take on the hearing. Therefore, delays often ensue or, more usually, the aggrieved party is advised to avoid the contravention process and leave it all to be considered at the trial.

That said, a finding that a parent has contravened an order is a significant event. A court can sanction that parent and compensate time for the aggrieved parent. It will reshape the focus of the proceedings on the parent who has contravened and place considerable pressure on them and their lawyer. It will raise the prospect of the child being removed from their care if they will not promote the relationship with the other parent. A proved contravention is also very helpful evidence for the other parent to take into a trial.

Ultimately, if a parent has behaved badly it will become a problem for them at the eventual trial. Also, it may create an impression for the ICL, who will be making recommendations to the court as to the outcome of the proceedings. The ICL will usually hold conferences with the parties throughout the proceedings and will use that opportunity to inform the parents of their thinking around the case and the recommendations they may make. Evidence of poor behaviour can have significant impact in those conferences and sometimes lead to the settlement of cases.

Involvement of the alienated child in proceedings

The views of the child and parental alienation

The views of the child in terms of their preferences for parenting arrangements can be presented to the court, including in cases involving parental alienation. Although consideration is given to the factors that might impact on a child's decision-making, the expressed views of the child in Family Court proceedings are still given weight in Australia as per section 60CC(3)(a) of the *Family Law Act, 1975* (8). Of course, it is the case that the more mature the child or the greater the chronological age of the child, the more weight is likely to be given to their expressed views. If a child's views have been clearly influenced by another, a judge may give little weight to those views, notwithstanding that child's age.

Contrary to popular belief, there is no set age where a child's views must be accepted. Therefore, it is not correct to assume that just because a child is older and expressing clear views that those views will be adopted by the court. That said, a 16-year-old expressing clear views, even if influenced by a parent, may be difficult to move even if time with the other parent is ordered. Usually, a targeted parent will not pursue time with an older child because of this practical limitation. The focus is usually on younger children.

In cases of suspected parental alienation, the court must evaluate the views being expressed by the child in an attempt to determine to what extent those views are influenced by an alienating parent. If it can be shown that such an influence existed, then less weight is given to the child's expressed views by the court than would otherwise be the case. In this way, it is recognised by the court that children can be encouraged to hold particular views that support one parent and reject the other without there being ample justification for the view being held.

To illustrate the issues that arise in relation to the consideration of views expressed by the child and parental alienation, a case will be presented here (available from AustLII). This case involved a parent who influenced the children to have a particular view. The High Court was called on to consider how such views should be assessed.

Case – Views of the child

This case involved an appeal to the High Court of Australia following the dismissal of an appeal to the Full Court of the Family Court of Australia. The case involved two boys aged 16 years and 14 years. The youngest child was a daughter aged 11 years. The appeal was against the decision by the primary judge to have the two eldest children return to Australia to complete a process initiated by the primary judge, that is the preparation of a family report by a family consultant. The father had taken the two oldest children overseas for a holiday and failed to return them. The mother sought to have the children returned to Australia.

The parents separated in 2010 and parenting consent orders were made in 2014 giving the parent's equal shared parental responsibility. It was ordered that the children live with both parents as decided by the parents or as elected by the children. Further, it was ordered that the children could go on holiday outside of Australia with one parent as long as the other parent was informed of the travel not less than 14 days prior to departure and that documentation relevant to the travel was provided. The Full Court agreed the orders did not allow for the children, independently of their parents, to make the decision about where they live.

An ICL was appointed after the 2014 parenting orders were made. By the end of 2015, further orders were made for family members to be involved in a child responsive programme that included a family consultant who was to produce a report for the court.

The father then opted to take the two oldest children overseas on a holiday in mid-January, 2016, without meeting the requirements of the existing orders regarding travel. From the overseas location, the father's lawyer informed the mother that the father had decided to move overseas and the boys had opted to reside with him. The mother used the legal options available to her to have the children returned to Australia, including the use of international agreements under the Hague Convention. The primary judge made interim orders that the boys be returned to Australia.

These orders were made despite the understanding that the boys were expressing the view that they wanted to remain living with their father overseas, that the father would not commit to returning with the boys or providing them with accommodation and supervision in Australia, and the boys may not choose to live with their mother on their return. The mother suggested the children reside with the families of their long-term friends. This was accepted by the court on an interim basis after due consideration.

When considering the statutory provisions, the court is able to make a parenting order it considers appropriate and the order can be made in favour of a parent or some other person the court considers acceptable. The issue of paramount importance in making parenting orders is the best interests of the child. In determining these best interests, the court must give consideration to the benefits to the child of having a meaningful relationship with both parents. Consideration must be given to the views expressed by the child although the weight given to these views may be influenced by other factors, such as the maturity of the child.

In making parenting orders, other considerations include the nature or character of the relationship the child has with each parent, the potential effects of changing the child's circumstances, and any practical difficulties that may make it difficult to maintain relationships. In addition, there are underlying principles that guide the making of parenting orders. These include that a child has a right to know both parents and to be cared for by them with this requiring that the child spend time with both parents on a regular basis. Further, the best interests of the child require that the parents fulfil certain obligations, such as fulfilling parenting duties, meeting the responsibilities associated with caring for the child, addressing welfare needs, and promoting the development of the child.

When making his decision as to whether the boys should return to Australia, the primary judge accepted what the father said about the boys expressing the view that they wished to remain living with him overseas. He had rejected the father's request for a 'wishes report' to be prepared overseas outlining the boys' expressed views, because he was already aware of the views being expressed. The judge also had other information that supported the notion that the father had been influential in the formation of the views expressed by the boys with regard to them remaining with their father. Some of this information was obtained from text messages between the middle child and the mother.

It was apparent that the father was offering the boys an opulent and indulgent lifestyle, and this was influencing the boys' rejection of their life in Australia and their relationships, including with their mother and sister. As a result, the primary judge reached two conclusions: (a) that the father had acted in a prejudicial way, and (b) this had influenced the boys' expressed views. The primary judge formed the view that the father's actions had negatively impacted and would be likely to continue to impact on the relationships between family members, especially the relationship between the mother and the younger son, and the relationship between the daughter and her father.

The decision of the primary judge to have the boys returned to Australia was appealed to the Full Court of the Family Court. The appeal was dismissed in a majority decision.

Parenting orders made by the primary judge can only be set aside on the basis of a limited number of factors. The father argued that greater weight to the views expressed by the children should be given. A judge can give these views considerable weight, but is not required to do so. There are a number of considerations the judge needs to take into account in the determination of what is in a child's best interests and the expressed views of the child is only one of these considerations. The primary judge did take into account significant issues that needed to be considered, including the effect on them in the future of their separation from both their mother and sister. In addition, the judge took into account the effect of any decision on the relationship between the father and daughter. The judge formed the view that the best option for managing these issues was through the process involving the family consultant that was initiated in the parenting orders of 2015 but was not completed because the father took the boys out of the country and did not return. Interim parenting orders were made to that effect.

In his appeal, the father contended that the primary judge had made errors in two ways. Namely, by failing to obtain a wishes report, the judge had failed to give the boys' views proper consideration. He also contended the judge's negative opinions about the father's behaviour meant that he did not give proper consideration to the boys' expressed views about where they wished to live.

The High Court determined that it was appropriate for the primary judge to have considered the father' behaviour. This is because it was in breach of the 2014 parenting orders. Further, the father's behaviour could have negatively impacted on the boys' relationships with family members. The orders made in 2015 were directly addressing the issue of problematic family relationships. It was concluded that the father's actions in disregarding the parenting orders may be inconsistent with the responsibilities of parenting and, therefore, it was appropriate to consider them. It was pointed out that the primary judge did not fail to take into account the boys' views; he just gave them less weight than desired by the father and he did so for appropriate reasons.

The father then contended that the primary judge should have both given more weight to the boys' expressed views and he should have sought the boys' opinions about any parenting orders. However, the Act is clear. The judge must take into account any view expressed by the boys, which he did, but it is not required that he seek their opinion. Interestingly, the most appropriate means of exploring the boys' views was through the process initiated in the 2015 parenting orders and that was avoided by the father when he took the boys overseas and failed to return.

Comment

The issue of how much weight is given to the expressed views of the child in parenting disputes is an important one, especially in cases of parental alienation. Most alienated children will be likely to express the view that they want to live with the alienating parent. Clearly, it is not only the age of the child or that child's perceived maturity that should determine the weight that is given to the child's views. In cases where the child is unduly influenced by a parent or any other person, the extent to which that view can be considered to be the child's own is limited. It may fall to the expert witness to explain to the court how such influence or the impact of parental alienation can determine a child's expressed view. However, proving alienation is easier said than done.

The need for a legal response to parental alienation

The need to resolve parental alienation

Appeals have been made for the courts to better manage parental alienation cases, primarily because of the short- and long-term impact of parental alienation on the wellbeing of the alienated child but also to assist targeted parents (12). However, in practice, it is difficult to see how courts could manage alienation cases much differently.

The court is increasingly being asked to determine cases where it is alleged a child is at risk in the other party's care. The court is aware of the need to move such cases as quickly as possible to a trial. However, a lack of funding and judicial resources is significantly impacting on the court to hear matters within a reasonable time. This is particularly the case in the bigger registries around Australia. Alleged alienation cases are no different to the many pressing risk cases before the courts.

There have been attempts to develop guidelines in relation to alienation and estrangement cases, including by some judges. However, none of these attempts have been successful or widely accepted. The lack of success may reflect shortcomings with the guidelines that were developed but may simply reflect the lack of understanding of, and agreement about, parental alienation in general. Also, it is the position of many that the existing legislative framework is sufficient to deal with these and any other children's cases. Many see danger in overly prescribing the matters a court must consider when ultimately the courts' aim is to make a parenting order that meets the child's best interests whatever the facts. Further, given the concept of parental alienation has no accepted definition or universal acceptance, it is unlikely that the courts will create law around the concept without clear legislative change.

As it stands, each case involving alleged parental alienation currently is considered on the basis of its own facts. If the legislative pathways offered by the relevant sections of a Family Law Act (8) are followed (in Australia, sections 60B, 60CA, 60CC, and 65DA of the *Family Law Act, 1975*), then the action taken by the court cannot be criticised.

Collaboration between law and psychology

The courts rely on information about psychological matters from the family consultants who work for the court and from expert witnesses. With regard to parental alienation, there is certain information that experts can provide that will assist the court in making decisions. These include the following:

1. The signs or indicators of parental alienation.
2. The differentiation between parental alienation and estrangement.
3. What psychology can offer in terms of resolving parental alienation.
4. The dangers and benefits of a child transferring to live with the other parent.
5. Ways to manage a child's resistance to spending time with the targeted parent.
6. Whether the transfer should be considered if the targeted parent has identified flaws.
7. The ways lawyers can deal with alienating parents.
8. An explanation of the difference between family therapy and reunification.

From expert witnesses, the court needs to be offered solutions so that decisions can be made that directly address parental alienation. If there is strong and accepted expert evidence, particularly where the expert has been cross-examined, it can lead to confidence among the lawyers arguing a position and courts accepting the same. Strong academic literature providing evidence-based conclusions also is very helpful to the lawyers and, ultimately, the court. Such literature can often assist with the preparation of cross-examination and help challenge existing thinking. Tested and accepted expert evidence is often crucial in parenting cases.

The nature of the legal response to parental alienation

Legal responses to parental alienation

One of the hardest aspects to overcome in these cases is the reality of a child vehemently not wanting a relationship with the other parent. Even if deliberate alienation is suggested, the court often still will be faced with a dilemma of how to move a child to the other parent where the child may be distraught at the suggestion and the other parent may not be able to take on that role full-time.

One factor that contributes to these decisions is that the alienating parent often is identified as the parent the child most prefers. The decision to leave the child in the care of the alienating parent may reflect a desire not to destabilise a child's current circumstances and cause the child distress by removing them from their preferred parent and placing them in the care of the rejected parent. In this way, the court is focusing on what is considered to be the best for the child in their current situation. However, there is often a failure to recognise that there are potentially negative longer-term consequences for alienated children to be left in the care of the alienating parent, especially if parental alienation is understood to be a form of abuse.

Under other circumstances of abuse or potential abuse, the court would consider the risk to the child to be too great for the child to be left in the care of an abusive parent and remove that child even if the child wants to remain. This happens in child protection jurisdictions all the time with children regularly placed in foster care. It begs a question as to whether a similar response would occur if parental alienation was also recognised as a form of family violence and/or abuse. Given the long-term consequences of deliberate alienation upon a child, there is argument for this different approach. However, as said, it may need to come from the legislators before the court would of itself make that finding.

A primary factor that must be considered under section 60CC of the *Family Law Act, 1974* (8) is the need to protect children from physical and/or psychological harm. Alienation can be considered in this context if the evidence shows that a parent's behaviour is causing harm to a child. Expert evidence confirming this is crucial.

The courts' position may be made easier if the definition of family violence specifically included deliberate alienating behaviour. However, that again will require legislative change.

Court support for psychological intervention

An option is available to the court to ensure that the transition from living with the alienating parent to living with the targeted parent is easier for the child, and to increase the chances that the longer-term benefits of such a move are realised. Psychological intervention can assist. However, it has to be the right type of intervention.

Family therapy tends to be recommended in cases of parental alienation before the final hearing. In this way, it is proposed as a possible means of obtaining a resolution and avoiding the matter going to trial.

However, the court and lawyers often do not fully understand the nature of family therapy and the goals of the therapeutic intervention. The steps involved and the expected efficacy are largely unknown. Some lawyers see family therapy as a 'magical fix' that will resolve all obstacles to good parenting in the future. Lawyers also have limited information about the appropriateness of family therapy for their individual cases. These represent genuine obstacles to the useful application of court-ordered therapeutic intervention. Better guidelines for courts, lawyers and therapists would assist.

Court orders for psychological intervention

Despite the fact that therapy for parental alienation is often seen by lawyers as a way of avoiding trial by resolving differences between the parties, the nature of parental alienation often makes this difficult. Alienating parents can sabotage therapeutic attempts. If there are court orders for the parties to comply with therapy and stipulated court sanctions for non-compliance, the chances of a good therapeutic outcome are enhanced. The importance of linking the authority of the court with the need to engage in therapeutic efforts has been recognised by others (13). It is worth noting that although a court can make an order, that order does not teach parents how to parent, how to collaboratively parent, or how to get along with each other.

Case comparison

In concluding this discussion of parental alienation in a legal context, two cases and their legal outcomes can be compared (available from AustLII). One case involves parental alienation and the other involves an allegation of parental alienation without supporting indicators of this occurring. The cases will be presented here, followed by an identification of the indicators of parental alienation that assisted the court in reaching decisions regarding parenting orders.

Case A: Parental alienation

Introduction and background

In this case, the applicant father sought to have his three children, a daughter aged 14 years, a son aged 12 years and a daughter aged eight years, reside with him and that he be given sole parental responsibility. He claimed that the mother had acted in a way that was causing his children to be alienated from him. The mother denied alienating the children, claiming that the children's rejection of their father was based solely on their own experience with him and was not influenced by her in any way.

The respondent mother sought to have the children continue to live with her and spend school holiday time with their father and some weekends. She said this time with the father should be determined by the views expressed by the children and they should not be forced to spend time with their father if they did not wish this time to occur.

The father's application to the Family Court was triggered by the mother making a unilateral decision to move herself and the children to a town a six-hour drive away from where the father was residing. This involved a change of schools for the children. At the time of making his application, the father did not know where the children were residing or what school they were attending.

The parents' relationship began in the late 1990s and ended in 2013. For 12 months prior to separation, the father worked in City B, returning to City A each weekend to spend time with his family. After the separation, the father continued to return to City A every second weekend and the children stayed with him in a hotel. The mother remained living in the family home until property settlement was decided. The children would spend half of their school holidays with their father in City B.

In 2014, the mother and the children moved to a rental property when the family home was sold. The father paid the substantial monthly rental on this property for the mother. In addition, he paid more than double the assessed amount in child support and paid for the children's schooling, clothing, electronic devices, health insurance, holiday trips and extra-curricular activities above the child support payment. He also paid various personal costs of the mother, such as car maintenance and registration, and he paid off a substantial personal loan she had taken.

In early 2015, parenting consent orders were made. The parenting agreement allowed for equal shared parental responsibility. The children were to live with their mother and spend four consecutive nights per fortnight and half the school holidays with their father. During the school term, the time spent with the father was in City A and school holiday time was spent in City B.

The financial strain on the father was considerable. An agreement with the mother that the father pay extra child support expired at the beginning of 2016, but he continued to pay this extra amount until late 2016. Even then, he continued to pay almost $2,000 more per month than the assessed amount until late 2017. The father gave the mother ample notice that the amount of child support would reduce to the legally assessed amount in keeping with the agreement they had made.

The mother later claimed that she had only signed the consent orders of 2015 because she felt pressured to do so. She claimed she could not afford legal advice and had only agreed to the consent orders because she could not afford to support herself and the children. She said she had been threatened with eviction from the rental property for non-payment and she was fearful she and the children would be homeless.

The father said that by late 2014 he was overwhelmed with debt because his expenditure exceeded his income. He said there was a short period when his payments to the mother were delayed but he had caught up with these payments several months prior to the signing of the consent orders. The amount he had paid far exceeded his legal obligation.

The mother coped poorly with the end of the marital relationship and she became angry and bitter with the passage of time. She blamed all of the problems she experienced on the father and was resentful that she had to find paid employment. She had no empathy for the father's dire financial position.

Within 60 days of the consent orders, the mother made a unilateral decision to move to another suburb and change the children's schools. Although disturbed by her actions, the father was accepting of the decision because, on investigation, he found the new schools acceptable. He did address with the mother her failure to engage in collaborative parental decision-making. The mother became angry and responded by demanding sole parental responsibility.

At the end of 2016, the mother obtained paid employment. She denied the father time with the children during the school holidays, claiming that she had taken time off work to care for them.

In fact, the maternal grandparents were caring for the children and the mother had instructed the grandparents and the children to lie to the father. The father's attempts to contact the children were rarely successful.

The father learned the mother was making denigrating and vilifying comments about him to the children. Among other things, the mother told the children they had been evicted from their rental property because the father had failed to pay child support then reduced the amount to a level that could not financially sustain them. Neither of these allegations were true. Further, the eldest daughter formed the view that the father had been charged with rape and the mother failed to correct this assumption. There were various text exchanges between the mother and the eldest daughter that made derogatory and offensive references to the father's partner. There was no evidence the father made denigrating comments about the mother to the children. Also, the mother broke or allowed the children to break the expensive electronic devices he had bought the children that he would then replace.

In late 2017, the father's lawyer wrote to the mother to resolve the problems that had been developing. The content of the letter was gentle and non-offensive. The mother had her legal representative respond, conveying her displeasure and accusing the father of offensive and controlling behaviour. She made allegations of wrongdoing by the father and claimed that his actions had caused her to be evicted from a rental property. She blamed the father for the unilateral decisions she made about the children's schooling.

Early in 2018, the father learned that the mother had moved to a town that was a six-hour drive away from City B and that the children would be attending new schools in this town. He did not know where his children were or whether they had already changed school. The mother, the children and the maternal grandparents lied to the father about this move, claiming no move had taken place. The father initiated proceedings in the Family Court.

In response to the application, the mother claimed she was forced to move because the father had made a unilateral decision to reduce child support payments and she had been evicted from the property she was renting. She labelled the father as controlling and intimidating, but was unable to provide examples of this type of behaviour. She reiterated that she would not force the children to spend time with their father if they chose not to do so.

A report was prepared by Mr P, a clinical psychologist. He supported the father as a parent who was responsive to the children's needs. In contrast, he described the mother as self-focused, tense and distressed, with a restricted emotional range. He said the mother could not differentiate her children's needs from her own.

Mr P said the mother perpetuated the erroneous view that the father was controlling and that he had caused her and the children to be evicted from their rental property. She claimed he controlled her by limiting the amount of child support he paid. She identified herself as the victim rather than the person interfering with the father–child relationships.

Mr P reported that all children expressed strongly positive views about their mother and strongly negative views about their father. They were protective of their mother's feelings. He identified that the eldest daughter was strongly aligned with her mother and blamed her father for her mother's anguish. She berated her father for failing to explain his actions in leaving the marriage, but made it clear she had no intention of forgiving him even if an explanation was forthcoming. She expressed no concern that her mother's actions were in breach of the consent orders.

The middle child presented as anxious and stressed, whereas the younger child was the most engaging during interview. However, both children's understanding of the situation was the same as the one presented by the mother. Mr P was concerned about the world view taken by all the children and their lack of ambivalence in their views about their parents. Although the children viewed their father as untrustworthy, a view supported by the mother, Mr P did accept that when away from their mother's influence the children tended to have a more positive relationship with their father than they claimed.

Legal considerations

The father's lawyer argued that the behaviour of the mother fell within the definition of family violence. It was argued that the coercive and controlling characteristics of the mother's behaviour were what made it a form of family violence. This was one factor the judge could consider, but it was one of a myriad presented to the court and to be considered pursuant to section 60CC of the Act. This included the views of the children. In this case, all of the children expressed the view that they wished to live with their mother in Town X.

The eldest child was approaching 15 years of age. Under most circumstances, considerable weight would be given to the views expressed by a young person of this age. However, in this case it was evident that the child's views were being strongly influenced by the mother's version of events. She was presenting herself as a child whose role was to protect her mother from the perceived harm done by the father. In listing the things she saw as her father's wrongdoings, the eldest daughter identified some terrible behaviours that were not supported by the evidence. Nevertheless, the mother supported the child's views and reinforced them. Certainly, the mother did nothing to correct the child's erroneous and vilifying comments about the father's behaviour.

Mr P identified that there was an unhealthy hierarchy in the mother's household, with the mother and the eldest daughter interacting as friends and confidants and not mother and daughter. The mother was failing to make the adult decisions and inform her daughter of the outcome. Instead, she was involving her daughter in the decision-making process. As a result, it was determined that the weight that should be given to the eldest daughter's expressed views was less than it would have been without the mother's adverse influence on her attitude towards her father and her perception of the dynamics in her family relationships.

The middle child, at the age of 12 years, should also have his views considered. However, it was determined that he was under many of the same influences as his older sister, although he acted as less of a confidant and more of a protector of his mother. It was established that this child suffered the most psychologically. In the case of the youngest child, although her views were given some weight, it was also determined that her views were greatly influenced by both her mother and her older sister.

The children's relationships with their parents and extended family members were considered. The children undoubtedly had a close relationship with their mother. Throughout their lives their mother had been their primary carer. The children felt most comfortable living in their mother's home.

However, there was strong evidence that the children's relationship with their mother was not healthy in every respect. The mother had failed to maintain appropriate boundaries that are typical of healthy parent–child relationships. She did not shelter the children from the bitterness she felt towards their father. She encouraged loyalty towards her and an alliance, so the mother and the children worked as a team to deceive the father. As a result of the mother's actions, the children developed problematic relationships with both parents that lacked healthy ambivalence.

It was recognised that the children had a close and loving relationship with their maternal grandparents. However, the grandparents' actions associated with following the mother's instruction to deceive the father were not seen to be in the children's best interests.

The court accepted that the children had a loving relationship with their father despite the efforts of the mother to undermine it. Despite the children acting to support their mother and, seemingly, reject their father when placed in situations that demanded they adopt this role, it was accepted that, when not observed, they would settle when in their father's presence and present as happy and relaxed. In addition, there was evidence that there were good foundations for a close and loving relationship to develop with the father's partner.

It was considered whether both parents had taken the opportunity to involve themselves in decision-making relating to the children's futures, to spend meaningful time with the children, and to communicate with them in a consistent way. It was recognised that the father's opportunities for involving himself in the children's lives in these ways had been limited by the actions of the mother. Nevertheless, the father had demonstrated considerable commitment to maintaining his relationships with his children by travelling from City B to City A to spend time with his children on a regular basis. The mother, of course, had demonstrated her involvement with the children.

The court considered the impact upon the children of moving to the full-time care of their father. The court recognised that the children would likely be distressed if such a decision was made as they strongly expressed the view that they wished to remain living with their mother. As the children had adopted a protective role with regard to their mother, it was likely they would be worried about her wellbeing if they went to live with their father. This increased the risk that the children would leave their father's residence and return to their mother's residence. However, it was recognised that the chances of this occurring would be reduced if the mother supported the move. During her evidence, she undertook to do this because she recognised the importance of supporting her children to reduce their distress.

The practical difficulties of a parenting arrangement were considered. It was evident that if the mother continued to live in Town X, there would be continued difficulties related to the children spending time with the other parent outside of school holiday times.

Consideration was given to whether the parents were capable of meeting all the children's needs. This included their emotional and intellectual needs. The court was satisfied that the father was well able to meet the children's needs in this regard. He had demonstrated the capacity to understand the needs of his children and to give them greater priority than his own needs. Also, he had demonstrated that he was willing and able to work with the mother in a civil manner so they could co-parent well.

In contrast, the level of confidence in the mother's ability to meet the children's needs was low. There had been a consistent pattern of her putting her own needs before those of her children. Although under cross-examination the mother claimed that she recognised the problematic nature of her behaviour and the impact that might have on the children, it was considered to reflect the mother's understanding that her favoured outcome might have been out of her reach because of her actions and she wished to offer the court an alternative view of her that would increase the chances that the children would remain living with her.

Parenting orders

The relevant parenting orders were:

- The father was given sole parental responsibility.
- The children were to live with the father in City B.

- The mother was ordered to support the children in the changes they faced and to return the children to the father if they ran away to her.
- The mother was not permitted to have face-to-face contact with the children for term three of the school year to allow the children to settle into their life with their father.
- If the mother moved closer to City B, the mother was to spend time with the children every second weekend. However, if she chose not to move closer to City B, the mother could spend time with the children for ten consecutive nights per school term in City B.
- During school holidays, the children were to spend half their time with the father and the other half with their mother.
- The mother was ordered to undertake personal counselling.
- The father was ordered to arrange counselling support for the children.

Case B: No parental alienation

Introduction and background

Involved in this case was one 12-year-old boy. In 2010, parenting orders were made allowing the father to have unsupervised overnight time with the child one night per fortnight with additional time during school holidays. This ceased when the father assaulted the child in 2015. The applicant father sought the parenting orders of 2010 be reinstated. Further, he sought that if the court determined that the mother was not capable of caring for the child and had alienated the child against him, that the mother have supervised time with the child for a period of two years with telephone communication on Wednesday evenings, followed by unsupervised overnight time every second weekend. The respondent mother proposed that she have sole parental responsibility and that the child live with her and spend independently supervised time with the father up to six times a year for three hours. She also sought to relocate to Town Y.

In 2015, the child reported that the father had hit him in the face. The father asserted the child had hit himself in the face while the father was trying to restrain the child. Consequently, criminal proceedings against the father were instigated. The day after the incident, the child stopped spending time with the father.

Later in 2015, the Federal Circuit Court of Australia put aside the previous parenting orders of 2010. Interim orders made at that time allowed the father to spend independently supervised time with the child for three hours every second weekend with weekly telephone contact. The father was found guilty of assaulting the child and causing actual bodily harm, with an appeal against the criminal conviction being unsuccessful.

Early in 2016, a family report was ordered. A final hearing was set down for May 2017.

Relevant evidence

The parents' relationship began in 1996 and ended late 2007. Parenting orders were made in late 2010 and were enacted when the child commenced school in 2011. From 2011 until February 2015, the father and child spent regular time together in accordance with the parenting orders of 2010. After the assault incident and the matter being brought back to court, the father spent independently supervised time with the child from late 2015 until April 2016, and again from late 2016 until early 2017.

In February 2015, the mother learned of the assault from school staff as the child had been dropped off at school with a black eye. The mother sought medical support for her son and, after talking to him about what had happened, she contacted the police. The child reported that his father had struck his face because he could not tie his shoelaces. He reported that his father gave him a bag of frozen vegetables to hold on his eye. He reported that the father's partner had asked the father why he had hit the child and had been critical of the father's actions. The child also said his father said if he did not tell his teacher that their dog had caused the injury, he would blacken the other eye. The mother sought an apprehended violence order (AVO) and an interim order was obtained in early March 2015. This order was for the protection of the child.

Starting on the day after the assault, the child repeatedly told his mother he did not wish to see his father because he had hurt him. The child then was reluctant to talk to his father on the telephone despite the mother's encouragement.

A child inclusive conference was held in late 2015. The child was anxious about seeing his father because he was scared his father would hurt him. Despite this, he said he missed his father.

By late April 2016, the child began telling the mother that he was worried that this father would turn up at his school. His nervousness at school events was noted by teaching staff. He told his psychologist that he only wanted to see his father if a police officer was present. He started to question whether his father cared about him.

The child had a congenital condition that affected some physical functioning and caused a degree of developmental delay. Early intervention had assisted the child in a number of ways, but he continued to have problems with his gait and with fine motor skills.

The mother and the child lived at a rental property with a friend, Mr F. The mother had completed some tertiary education qualifications and planned to continue to do so to increase her skills in her chosen area. The mother was the primary carer of her son and had support from Mr F and her father. She wished to relocate with Mr F to Town Y for a fresh start after the assault and because her mother and brother lived close by. She was concerned that the child's father knew where they lived. Relocation would not prevent her from delivering the child to the location of the supervised time he would spend with his father.

Under cross-examination, the mother acknowledged that the child was aware that the relationship between the mother and father was not good. However, she indicated that the child was not aware of the discomfort she felt about the child spending time with his father. She said her son continued to be afraid of his father.

The mother said she supported the notion of the child having a relationship with his father and was accepting of him having telephone contact with his father, although she felt too uncomfortable to directly communicate with him. She acknowledged that if she was given sole parental responsibility, it would be important that she provide the father with information about the decisions she makes about the child's life.

The mother acknowledged she had ceased including the father in decision-making about the child after 2015. She said she believed her obligation to keep the father informed ceased when the original parenting orders of 2010 were suspended.

The mother accepted that the child loved his father. However, she pointed out that the child had been experiencing anxiety since the assault. The mother denied that the child had a general tendency to make untruthful statements or that he would lie to support her in achieving her goals in relation to her proposed parenting orders.

When cross-examined, the father re-stated the view he had expressed to the family consultant that the conviction for the assault of the child was wrong. He refused to acknowledge that he had hit the child in the face. He reported that, despite his claims, the child was not aware of what occurred at the time of the incident.

The father acknowledged that between 2010 and 2015 the mother had not interfered with the time he spent with the child. He acknowledged that his relationship with his child currently was strained. He believed this could be rectified simply by being able to spend time with his child. Nevertheless, he said he would be open to the notion of undertaking a programme that would help facilitate the repair of his relationship with the child. Although he was seeking equal shared care of the child with the arrangement being on alternate weeks with the two parents, the father was aware that some intervention may be needed before this could be implemented.

The father reported being aware the child had told the family consultant that his father had not apologised for the assault. He said this was because the child had not asked him to do so. He said he would apologise to the child if it would make the child feel better.

The father undertook to use better communicate strategies with the child. When asked how he would achieve this, he reported that he would communicate with the mother and, perhaps, ask her for the advice. The father blamed the mother for poor communication between the parents.

The father's partner gave evidence. She supported the father's version of events in relation to the assault. Mr F gave evidence that he was willing and available to offer care assistance to the mother.

Exhibits

The independent supervisor of the time the father spent with the child provided recorded aspects of the father's behaviour towards the child. It was reported that, during supervised time, the father had spoken harshly to the child, had threatened to tell the child's psychologist if he did not oblige the father, and had repeatedly questioned the child about Mr F.

Further, the psychologist's clinical notes about sessions with the child often referred to the child's anxiety about spending time with his father. It also was recorded that the child did not wish to see the father without a police officer present. The child was concerned that his father would hit him again. Reference also was made to the child's unhappiness that his father had failed to apologise for hitting him.

Child inclusive conference

In November 2015, a child inclusive conference was conducted by the family consultant. At this conference, the parents confirmed they were unable to communicate about the child's needs. The mother identified the father's aggressive communication style as intimidating for her.

Both parents were able to identify the child's limitations in terms of his poor fine motor skills. The mother also identified some cognitive limitations and the family consultant noted that the child, aged almost 11 years at the time of the conference, presented as a child younger than his chronological age.

The child was insistent that he did not wish to spend time with his father because his father had hit him in the face. The child recalled being interviewed by the police and having to attend court. The child was certain that the father hitting him in the face had not occurred as part of the father disciplining him. He reported that there were other times when his father had hit him on other areas of his body. The child was insistent that he did not wish to spend time with his father, even if his father promised not to hit him again or if he was in the presence of an independent supervisor. When discussing what he thought about talking to his father on the telephone, the child said that sometimes his father was nice to him but, if the child did not want to speak to him, he would hang up the telephone.

Overall, the child expressed concerns about his personal safety when around his father. He did not express similar concerns about his mother or Mr F, who he spoke about in positive terms.

The family report

The family consultant conducted interviews and prepared a family report in August 2016. The mother reported that the child was afraid to spend time with his father. She said there were no noticeable differences in the child's behaviour before or after spending time with his father other than he seemed quieter. However, she said that after speaking with his father on the telephone, the child demonstrated regressive behaviour that had to be addressed by his psychologist. The mother went over her reasons for wishing to relocate. These reasons predominantly related to the mother wanting to protect the child from the father.

The father told the family consultant that his inability to spend time with his son was due to difficulties with the mother. He reiterated that he had been unfairly treated by the criminal justice system and the conviction was flawed.

When the child was interviewed, he relaxed only after he was reassured that his father was not in the immediate vicinity. The child was able to identify the difference between his father physically disciplining him by smacking him on the bottom or on the hand and being hit in face because his father was angry that he was struggling to tie his shoelaces. The account he gave the family consultant about the events on the day he was hit in the face was the same as those he had provided to others.

When discussing with the child the reasons why he did not want to see his father, the family consultant learned that the child was worried that his father would be angry with him for disclosing what happened. He believed that he would be hit again as soon as he spent time with his father. Also, he worried that his father did not care about him. He said this was because his father did not pay him very much attention and tended to spend his time looking at his phone when the child spent time with him. The child indicated that he had no confidence that his father would not hit him again even if an independent supervisor was present. The child said his mother did not say negative things about his father.

The family consultant observed the father with the child. The child was anxious prior to the session. He did relax at times and engaged in a game with his father that he seemed to enjoy. However, there were comments made by the father that caused the child to become tense. At these times, the child would ask his father if he could leave. When the father repeated the question of whether the child wished to engage in a particular activity at the father's home, the family consultant ended the session.

When formulating her opinion, the family consultant adopted the position that the father had assaulted the child. This view was adopted because of the father's conviction and because the father's appeal was dismissed. It was noted that the father maintained his innocence and blamed other parties for the conviction, including the mother, the police, the child's teacher and the court. This demonstrated a lack of insight into his actions and a failure on his part to accept any responsibility for his own behaviour.

The family consultant was concerned about the child's vulnerability, not only because of his age, but because of the disabilities associated with his congenital condition. His condition would make him physically and psychologically more vulnerable.

The family consultant raised the issue of the child's anxiety about spending time with the father and how this would be likely to affect his wellbeing. She also noted the difficulties the parents had in communicating with each other and identified that this may impact on the child's wellbeing.

The family consultant said that it could not be recommended that the child spend unsupervised time with his father. She said it would not be appropriate for the father's partner to supervise the child's time with the father as she had chosen to support her partner's account of the assault. As a result, she could not be relied upon to protect the child from his father's behaviour.

The family consultant could offer no solution to the situation. There was no intervention that would be effective in resolving the problems the family faced while the father refused to accept responsibility for his actions.

When the family consultant was cross-examined, the issue of parental alienation was raised by the father. The family consultant provided a description of parental alienation. The family consultant, when cross-examined, said her opinion did not change because of the issues that had been raised by the father. She continued to have concern about the risk to the child if he had unsupervised time with his father. She contended that independent supervision would allow the child to have positive experiences when he spent time with his father.

When questioned about the possibility of parental alienation, the family consultant identified the difference between realistic estrangement and parental alienation. She said that although realistic estrangement may seem to be similar to parental alienation, parental estrangement is based on an actual event or series of events or a poor relationship between the parent and the child that has been caused by identifiable factors. Further, the family consultant highlighted the potentially negative impact on the child if he was separated from his mother or their time was significantly reduced for a two-year period because of the father's claim of parental alienation.

Relevant issues

The court, when determining the matter, considered the benefit of the child having a meaningful relationship with both parents, as required by section 60CC(2a). It was determined that the child had an already established meaningful relationship with his mother and that there would be clear benefit to the child for this relationship to continue.

The child's relationship with his father had been more problematic since February 2015. The assault by the father of the child at that time caused an estrangement that was understandable.

The court rejected the father's claim that the mother had acted to alienate the child from his father. Of particular importance was the fact that the relationship between the father and the child and the time they spent together from when the original parenting orders were made in 2010 and the assault in 2015 was unimpeded by the mother.

It seems that the child became aware that the mother had negative views of the father. This occurred from the time of the assault. The reason for this change in attitude was the assault of the child, although not an excuse for the child to be exposed to this attitude.

The court accepted that the child may benefit from having a relationship with his father that was meaningful, as long as by allowing this the child did not experience psychological harm. The court determined that unsupervised time with the father would represent too great a risk of psychological harm for the child. If this psychological harm was to occur, it would increase the potential for the child's relationship with the father to be damaged in the longer term.

The court was of the view that the risk of psychological harm was substantially reduced if the time the child spent with the father was supervised. This is true even if the supervision placed limitations on the father–child relationship.

The court considered the need to protect the child from harm. The court determined the child was at significant risk of psychological harm from the time he spends with the father being unsupervised.

The child presented as tense and anxious when discussing the possibility of spending time with his father. He was worried that his father would assault him again and there was little that reassured him this would not occur. In addition, he was concerned that his father would be displeased that he had disclosed information about the assault. He feared retribution. The child's anxiety was observed to persist to an unacceptable degree when around his father.

The father demonstrated little insight into his actions and the impact they may have on the child. He did not apologise to the child for the assault despite being made aware that this was an important issue for the child. Further, the father had no clear idea of the potential impact on the child of being separated from his mother and placed with the father who evoked anxiety in the child. Concern was raised about the way in which the father questioned the child even when under supervision. It was apparent that the father prioritised his own need to find out information about the mother over his need to protect his child from feelings of anxiety and discomfort.

Although recognising that he would be expected to change his parenting style and that the child held the view he had been assaulted by his father, the court was not convinced that the father had enough insight to be able to meet the child's emotional needs. The court decided that the child was at risk of psychological harm if he spent unsupervised time with his father. The ICL and the family consultant shared the lack of confidence in the father's capacity to meet the child's emotional needs.

As a result of these arguments, the court determined that the time the child spent with the father needed to be supervised. It was decided that the supervisor would need to be an independent person as the proposal that the father's partner supervise the time was rejected by the court on the basis that she had supported the father's position about the assault. It was concluded that she would not act to protect the child from the father's behaviour.

The court accepted that if the child was to have a positive experience of the time spent with his father that time had to be supervised. The court accepted that therapeutic intervention had a limited chance of success given the father's attitude and may be a difficult process for the child to be involved in with only a low chance of positive outcome.

The court considered the risk to the child of physical harm from his father was low. The experiences of the father since the assault and the direct consequence of the assault would act as a catalyst for the father to change his behaviour. However, it was recognised by the court that the father continued to insist he was innocent with regard to the assault.

Despite the father raising the issue of the mother's parenting competence, the court did not accept that there was evidence for this proposition. She had a history of caring for the child on a daily basis, including meeting his health needs. She demonstrated protective actions when she learned of the assault of the child.

When considering the views expressed by the child, the court accepted that the child's anxiety about spending time with his father was a result of the assault. Even taking into account the child's developmental status, the court gave significant weight to the child's expressed views about spending time with his father.

The court accepted that the child would experience a negative impact on his emotional state if he went to live with his father and spent only limited time with the mother. The mother had the capacity to meet the child's needs. The father had limited ability to meet the child's emotional needs.

The father contended that the mother had deliberately withheld information from him about the child. However, the court accepted that it was the mother's belief that she was no longer legally obliged to do this as a result of the original parenting orders being suspended. Also, the father's contention that the mother had created problems for him so that she could obtain more child support payments from him was rejected.

With regard to the mother's proposal to relocate, the court acknowledged the concern of the mother about the child's anxiety about his father knowing where he lived. The court also accepted that the area to which the mother wished to relocate increased the support she could access, as her mother and brother would be living close by.

It was the father's contention that the mother wished to relocate with the child to further alienate the child from him by minimising the contact between the father and the child. The father also raised the issue of the difficulties he would face caused by the geographical distance. The court rejected the allegations of parental alienation and formed the view that the issue of geographical distance would not create a problem because of the mother's willingness to transport the child to spend time with the father.

The presumption of equal shared parental responsibility was rebutted in this case. This is because of the father's conviction for assault occasioning actual bodily harm upon the child. Further, the communication between the mother and the father was ineffective. To a large extent, this was a result of the mother being fearful of the father and her inability to deal with what she perceived as his aggressive and controlling behaviour towards her.

There was little reason to believe the parents could communicate effectively about matters relating to the child. The mother did not trust the father. As the child would remain living with the mother and the time the child spent with the father would be supervised, it was determined to be in the child's best interests for the mother to have sole parental responsibility, as long as the mother kept the father informed of her decisions and took into account any views he may have about the matter being considered.

Parenting orders

The relevant parenting orders were:

- The parenting orders of September 2010 were discharged.
- The mother was to have sole parental responsibility provided the mother:
    - Notified the father in writing of any proposed decision and the reason for the decision regarding the long-term care and welfare of the child;
    - Notified the father six weeks before the final decision is made, except in emergency situations;
    - Took into consideration the views of the father;
    - Advised the father in writing of the final decision made.
- The child would live with the mother.
- Unless otherwise agreed in writing, the father was able to spend supervised time with the child up to six occasions per calendar year for up to three hours under the following conditions:
    - The supervised time was to take place at a contact centre; or
    - The supervised time was to take place at a venue nominated by the father but supervised by an independent supervisor.
- Unless otherwise agreed in writing:
    - The father was to give notice in writing of no less than four weeks of the time and date of the supervised visit.
    - Any nominated times must take place on non-school days between 9am and 3pm.
    - The father was to pay all costs.
    - The mother was responsible for delivering and collecting the child from these visits.
    - The mother and the father should comply with all directions from the supervising service.
- Unless otherwise agreed in writing, the father could have telephone communication each Wednesday between 5.30pm and 6pm.

- If the father did not choose to contact the child, the father must notify the mother by text 12 hours beforehand.
- The parents should not denigrate each other around the child and should ensure no third party denigrated the other parent around the child.
- The mother was permitted to relocate upon the child completing primary school.

Comparison between cases

Contained below (Table 15.1) is a comparison of the cases in terms of the indicators of parental alienation. This comparison focuses on the tactics known to be used by alienating parents and the ways in which the indicators of parental alienation manifest in the child's behaviour.

It is evident from this comparison that the court is able to identify and take into account the indicators of parental alienation in the decision-making process. The absence of indicators in Case B supported the decision to reject the father's contention that the mother was trying to alienate the child from his father. In comparison, there was ample indication of a parental alienation process in Case A. These indicators were noted and contributed to the decision both to move the children to their father's care and to limit the influence of the mother's views on the children's world views.

Concluding comments

The challenges of dealing with parental alienation in a legal setting are manifold. These include issues related to the identification of parental alienation as a factor in a case, the management of the presentation of individual clients and the demands they make on legal processes, the complexity of cases involving parental alienation in terms of the increase in court time used when parental alienation is involved, and what the court can do to try to resolve these cases. In part, there needs to be collaboration between the courts and psychology to effectively address and manage parental alienation.

Ultimately, the court is able to manage these types of cases within the existing legislative framework. However, there is a case for legislative change, particularly by bringing alienation into the definition of family violence. The courts also clearly require greater judicial resources to deal with these cases in a timely manner. This, again, is a matter for government. It is not sustainable for a parent to be prevented from spending quality time with their child due to inordinate delays, particularly in the big city registries. Delay does nothing to enhance the court's ability to make orders that meet the best interests of children.

References

1. Bernet, W., von Boch-Galhau, W., Baker, A.J.L., & Morrison, S.L. (2010). Parental alienation, DSM-V, and ICD-11. *The American Journal of Family Therapy, 38,* 76–187. doi:10.1080/01926180903586583
2. Gith, E. (2013). The attitude of the Shari'a Courts to parental alienation syndrome: Understanding the dynamics of the syndrome in Arab society. *Journal of Divorce and Remarriage, 54,* 537–549. doi:10.1080/10502556.2013.828982
3. Bow, J.N., Gould, J.W., & Flens, J.R. (2009). Examining parental alienation in child custody cases: A survey of mental health and legal professionals. *The American Journal of Family Therapy, 37,* 127–145. doi:10.1080/01926180801960658

Table 15.1 A comparison between Cases A and B in relation to the presence of alienation indicators.

Case A	Case B
Tactics of alienating parents	
Denigration of the targeted parent	
Mother's claims of the father leaving her financially bereft	Some negative attitudes made known
Mother's claims that the father caused her to be evicted	to the child since the assault
Vilification of the targeted parent	
Father guilty of rape	No evidence
Father threatening and intimidating person	
Interference with time spent with the targeted parent	
Mother moving the children further away from father	Mother stopped the time spent with
Mother failing to tell father of new address	the father after the assault and
	following suspension of the orders
Eradication of the targeted parent from the child's life	
Mother making unilateral decisions and keeping them secret from the father	Child refusing phone contact
Father cannot contact the children by telephone	
Information gatekeeping	
Mother not providing information to the father about move, change of schools, dental appointments	Mother stopped providing father with information when orders suspended
Interrogation of the alienated child	
No information	Father interrogated the child
Damage to the loving connection with the targeted parent	
Mother makes negative reports about father to children	No evidence
Inappropriate disclosure about the targeted parent	
Mother exposes to children to legal documents	No evidence
Encouraging child defiance	
Mother told daughter she did not have to attend school interview	No evidence
Mother told children not to disclose information to father	
Forcing loyalty to the alienating parent	
Mother created opportunities for children to express loyalty (e.g., having the children agree to lie to their father to support their mother's actions)	No evidence
Encouraging an unhealthy alliance	
Oldest daughter acting as mother's confidant	No evidence
Mother plotting with children against father	
Emotional manipulation	
No evidence	No evidence
Utilising outside forces	
Mother instructed grandparents to lie to father to support her actions	No evidence
Alienating child's presentation	
Expression of negative views about the targeted parent	
Oldest daughter expressed view father was a rapist	No evidence
Children's belief father caused family financial difficulties	
Children's belief father failed to meet their emotional needs	
Extreme and opposite views about parents	
Children believed mother good, father bad	Child recognised father sometimes nice to him

Table 15.1 (Cont.)

Case A	Case B
Situationally determined changes in the child's behaviour	
Evidence that children settle when with father	Child continued to be worried about threat from father
Denial of positive regard for the targeted parent	
Tendency to loss of positive regard	Child worried about threat from father but worried his father does not care about him and says his father can be nice
Oldest daughter claimed she would not forgive father even if he could explain his actions	
Distorted views about the targeted parent	
Evidence of distortion (e.g., commitment to a marital relationship should not change)	No evidence
False memories or accounts of events not experienced	
Evidence of erroneous views held by oldest daughter	No evidence
Lack of concern about internal inconsistency of information provided	
Insufficient information	Child consistent in his account
Relating targeted parent's faults as a litany	
Oldest daughter tended to do this when interviewed	No evidence
Fear response	
No	Yes
Dependent or symbiotic relationship with alienating parent	
Children believes mother meets all their needs and their father does not	Dependent on mother as his primary carer
Compliant with adults other than targeted parent	
Yes, to a degree. Oldest daughter broke school rules	Well behaved in general
Believes alienating parent persecuted by targeted parent	
Children believe mother treated unfairly by father	No
Lack of empathy for plight of targeted parent	
Yes	No
Targeted parent holds no important position	
Increasingly so	Child worries his father does not care about him
Rigidity of belief system regarding targeted parent	
Oldest daughter said she would not change her views about father irrespective of his explanations	Justifiably believes father is threatening to him
Independent thinker phenomenon	
Children insistent their views are their own	Child expressed his own view about spending time with his father

4. Zirogiannis, L. (2001). Evidentiary issues with parental alienation syndrome. *Family Court Review, 39,* 334–343. doi:10.1111/j.174–1617.2001.tb00614.x
5. Williams, R.J. (2001). Should judges close the gate on PAS and PA? *Family Court Review, 39,* 267–281. doi:10.1111/j.174–1617.2001.tb00610.x
6. Lowenstein, L.F. (2012). Child contact disputes between parents and allegations of sex abuse: What does the research say? *Journal of Divorce and Remarriage, 53,* 194–203. doi:10.1080/10502556.2012.663267
7. Trocme, N., & Bala, N. (2005). False allegations of abuse and neglect when parents separate. *Child Abuse and Neglect, 29,* 1333–1345. doi:10.1016/j.chiabu.2004.06.016

8. *Family Law Act, 1975 (Cth)*. Retrieved from *www5.austlii.edu.au/au/legis/cth/consol_act/ fla1975114/*

9. Vassiliou, D., & Cartwright, G.F. (2001). The lost parents' perspective on parental alienation syndrome. *The American Journal of Family Therapy, 29,* 181–191. doi:10.1080/019261801750424307

10. Baker, A.J.L. (2010). Adult recall of parental alienation in a community sample: Prevalence and associations with psychological maltreatment. *Journal of Divorce and Remarriage, 51,* 16–35. doi:10.1080/10502550903423206

11. Lowenstein, L.F. (2011). What if the custodial parent refuses to cooperate with child contact decisions? *Journal of Divorce and Remarriage, 52,* 322–325. doi:10.1080/10502556.2011.585088

12. Lowenstein, L.F. (2015). How can the process of parental alienation and the alienator be effectively treated? *Journal of Divorce and Remarriage, 56,* 657–662. doi:10.1080/10502556.2015.1060821

13. Sullivan, M.J., & Kelly, J.B. (2001). Legal and psychological management of cases with an alienated child. *Family Court Review, 39,* 299–315. doi:10.1111/j.174–1617.2001.tb00612.x

Chapter Sixteen

Parental alienation and parenting dispute evaluations

Introduction

Parenting dispute evaluations are an important means of determining whether parental alienation is influencing the post-separation functioning of parent–child relationships and identifying the factors that need to be taken into account when deciding on the best options available for the parenting orders of any children involved (1). They require a combination of scientific analysis, clinical experience and psychological testing (2). These evaluations allow for a critical analysis of the factors that may distinguish parental alienation from parental rejection that is a function of some other process (3).

Extreme and opposing views about parental alienation have been reported to be held by parenting dispute evaluators (4) and psychologists, in general (5). Some authors report general consensus about the existence of parental alienation among professional parenting dispute evaluators (6). Others debate this. It has been asserted that parenting dispute evaluators too often mislead courts by disregarding allegations of family violence and the abuse of children in favour of erroneously asserting that estrangement is due to parental alienation and discounting the seriousness of the impact on abused children (7). In response, it has been argued that there is no evidence for these claims and parenting dispute evaluators do consider the role of family violence and are aware of the impact on the victims of that violence (8–9).

Whatever the point of view, it remains a fact that expert witnesses are called in family law matters to offer opinions that affect parenting decisions, including opinions about parental alienation. If this work is going to be undertaken, it is necessary to both be fully informed about the factors that should be taken into account and to do it well.

Do no harm

The actions of mental health professionals typically are guided by the principle of non-maleficence that requires that practitioners do no harm (10–11). The notion of non-maleficence provides mental health professionals with a solid basis for guiding their actions when making decisions about and interacting with the people in their care. The notion of non-maleficence takes into account the fact that your clients are considered to be vulnerable individuals whose rights should be protected.

Also, an approach of not doing any harm protects an individual from the power imbalance that is inherent in a relationship between a mental health professional and the vulnerable client. As an over-arching principle, non-maleficence guides the professional not to act in a manner that, in any way, would be detrimental to the client even if the professional could do otherwise or believes that the end result would be warranted despite distress or difficulties experienced in the process of achieving that end result.

Herein lies the problem. The decisions you make, the opinions you formulate and share and the actions you take in parenting dispute evaluations can have significantly negative effects on at least some individuals. If you think about it, the decisions you make can result in families being separated and parent–child relationships changing. Your decisions may be contrary to the views expressed by the children, who may strongly desire something you consider to be too great a risk for them. In effect, your decisions can contribute to events that change the course of people's lives both in a positive and a negative way.

The burden of this can weigh heavily on you. The weight will be greater in cases where the challenges on you to do the right thing in terms of your role are severe. Of course, this process should weigh heavily on you. You are then less likely to act rashly or impulsively, fail to give the matter the attention and consideration it warrants, or act without due consideration to the fact that you are making potentially life-changing decisions. Of course, it should be said that these factors that make the role so challenging also have the potential to make it so rewarding.

Although this all sounds quite overwhelming, the answer to the problem is quite simple. Your end goal should always be the same. That is, you should always act to protect children from further harm, to formulate a plan for them that is in their best interests in terms of their future wellbeing, and to be driven by the need to act in a way that will optimise the child's chances of a good and healthy future.

Approach to evaluation

Although expert witnesses clearly serve a function in the court system, many critical comments have been made about their role and their ability to influence the decision-making process about parenting issues (12). Rather than rejecting these criticisms, they should motivate parenting dispute evaluators to do their very best and to ensure their opinions are not flawed and biased. With this goal in mind, it is necessary to undertake parenting dispute evaluations in a way that will minimise potential biases. This begins with the approach you take from the outset of the evaluation.

Neutral position

It is absolutely essential when undertaking parenting dispute evaluations that a neutral position is adopted at the outset of the assessment process. Your position must be that you do not know what is happening until you undertake the assessment. There are a number of reasons for this. Firstly, no matter how much you know or no matter the nature of your past experience, you really do not know what is happening in this particular case. Secondly, you need to be able to defend your opinion as being unbiased and based on all the available information. So, you should approach the undertaking from a neutral position and then start to gather the information you need to ultimately formulate your opinion.

Serious errors can occur if assumptions are made about parental behaviours based on one's own views, generalities, past experience, the influence of the views of others, or a range of other factors. If you take a particular view about a matter, your interpretation of the information you gather is likely to be influenced by this view. For example, if you believe that 'once a wife beater, always a wife beater', then your interpretation of the information you have available to you may be biased in favour of labelling the father as a 'wife beater' in cases where family violence is alleged. Your value as an evaluator is then compromised. If you cannot adopt a neutral position when undertaking these types of assessments, do not accept the request to undertake the assessment.

Information gathering

When presented with the task of assessing the functioning of a particular family, you commence an undertaking of information gathering. The sources of information include interviews, opinions sought from others (e.g., doctors, teachers) and other documentation (e.g., police records, medical records) as well as the use of psychological tests.

The amount of information you must consider can seem quite daunting. This is particularly true when the information you gather tends to be contradictory in content. We will discuss how to manage this in an upcoming section. From this point, the information you gather is evaluated and hypotheses are developed.

Hypothesis building

Once you have gathered the information, you begin to build hypotheses about what might be happening for this family. Indeed, you may start to formulate hypotheses as you gather the information although it is better to delay the formulation of hypotheses for as long as possible or at least until a considerable proportion of the information you need to gather has been obtained.

The formulation of hypotheses is an important part of a scientific process. Before testing any idea of what might be occurring within a family setting, it is necessary to develop hypotheses that can be tested against the available information.

Box 16.1 Psychologist: During a supervision session with a psychology intern, she discussed with me her tendency to believe the person she was talking to at that time, even if she believed the account provided by the person she interviewed previously. Her budding hypotheses seemed to be based on who she interviewed last rather than on what all the information was telling her. If her tendency to do this had not been corrected, she would have offered opinions that were based on her bias towards believing the person she was interviewing in combination with a recency effect. Clearly, unchecked, this would have resulted in erroneous opinions and opened her up to considerable criticism with regard to the quality of her work.

Hypothesis testing

After your hypotheses have been formulated, they must then be tested. Rather than conducting a research project that tests your hypotheses, you test them against the information you have available to you. If you consider that a particular conclusion is warranted, you test the hypothesis by considering whether all the information you have available to you is accounted for by the hypothesis.

This undertaking protects you from the distortions or biases that can influence the interpretation of the information you have available to you. It does not rule out you giving greater weight to some information than other pieces of information. However, the relative weight you give the information that will form the basis of your opinion will need to be backed up with a rational account of why this greater weight was apportioned to some information over other information.

Opinion formulation

After completing these previous steps, an opinion should be formulated. An opinion should not just be the re-telling of the information you gathered, but reflect your professional interpretation of this material. That is, you are providing an opinion that offers the reader the meaning of the various pieces of information and how they come together.

The recipient of the opinion should be able to determine how you reached your conclusions. This is achieved by you making it clear on what you based your decisions. Your interpretations need to be evidence-based, drawing on the body of professional knowledge that is available to you, both to guide your decision-making and support your expressed opinion.

Approach to interviewing

An important part of the information-gathering process is the interviews you conduct with people related to the matter (13). The quality of your interviewing will influence the quality of the final formulated opinion.

Interviewing parents

The interviews conducted in this type of assessment are not the same as would take place in a typical therapeutic encounter (14). At the commencement of a therapeutic relationship you might explore the client's presenting problem by asking more questions than you would otherwise ask but you are still focused on developing therapeutic goals and allowing the client to present their views about their situation from his or her perspective.

Although it is still the aim to obtain from the client what their view is about a situation, parenting dispute evaluation interviews are much more directive than more therapy-focused interviews. Remember, your goal is to have the person you are interviewing answer the questions you pose rather than explore an issue as you would in a therapeutic setting. The directive nature of the interviewing style does not prevent the interviewee adding information along the way or particular issues being explored more fully.

Starting point

You need to be able to have an overview in your mind of what you are trying to achieve from the interview. This seems straightforward. However, you are actually faced with the challenge of obtaining as much information as possible within a limited period of time. In most cases, you may not have the luxury of repeated interviews or unlimited time. So, you have to get to know your client as well as possible in a short period of time.

It is worth remembering that most people who attend such interviews are anxious. In their minds, their relationship with their child or children can be affected by the outcome of the interview. In some cases, the people being interviewed are overly cautious, suspicious and determined to make you see they have done nothing wrong. This tends to make them give a less than genuine account of the situation. They will exaggerate the wrongdoing of others and minimise their contribution to the problem situation. It is your job to interview the person in a way that allows you to gather useful information that enables you to distinguish between truthful and embellished or fabricated information. The way you do this is important.

Interviewing style

The interviewing style you adopt will allow you to gather the information you need and manage the bias in what the person you are interviewing is reporting. It is not really your aim to develop a typical therapeutic relationship with your client. However, in effect, you may obtain more useful information if you use some counselling skills.

It is certainly the case that you will gain more information from the interview if you use a directive questioning style. In fact, it is necessary that you do so in most circumstances. In general, your primary goal is not to explore a client's perspective of a problem, but to gain factual information or to make enquiries about a person's already formed ideas about a situation. You may ask a person's views, such as asking what they would consider to be the best outcome, if the enquiry is still within the more directive framework of your questioning.

Box 16.2 Psychologist: I tend to take a chronological approach to interviewing for these purposes, at least in most cases. I know I need to find out about the problem situation, but I prefer to obtain that information in the context of a person's life. I also have limited time to gather all of this information, so I tend to start at the beginning. In this way, I can learn about the person's earlier life experiences that might have shaped their adult behaviour, the person's relationship history, the issues surrounding the development of the relevant relationship and what caused the breakdown of that relationship. In this way, I can address the arrival of the children and how this might have influenced the relationship as well as the parenting of the children. When I have gathered all the information, I will ask the person about their expectations for the future. Any missed information can be gathered at the end. I also ask the person if there is something they want to tell me that I had not asked them about, although I welcome any additional information provided along the way. It makes sense to me to do it this way as I can see early on how one event can influence other events.

Detection of deceptive responding

It is rarely the case that the people you interview will be objectively truthful in the account they provide. Even without witting attempts to deceive you, one's own perception of events can influence how a situation is understood. There are a number of ways that witting deception or unwitting mistakes can be identified.

Consistency of account provided

One way of determining whether the person you are interviewing is giving a genuine account of the events, from their perspective, is to look for consistency in the information provided. If a person is intentionally distorting the information they provide, inconsistencies may occur.

Although you may question why a person who is intent on deceiving you did not get their story straight before talking with you, the answer is quite simple. The person may have rehearsed what they are going to say but they have no way of knowing what you are going to ask or in what order you are going to ask the questions. This can be disconcerting for the person who is being interviewed if they have an intention to deceive you. Errors in fabricated accounts can occur because the complexity of the information being asked for does not lend itself to a straightforward and well-rehearsed account. It is easy for interviewees to make mistakes if their intention is to deceive.

There can be inconsistencies in the account being provided by the person being interviewed without there being a genuine effort to deceive, at least not in the usual sense. A person might say one thing but hold different views. For example, a person may say they are supportive of the other parent when, in fact, they are anything but supportive. They may say they do not care about the other parent, but present as overwhelmed by jealousy of a new partner in the other person's life. They may believe that the account they are providing is the genuine one because they have convinced themselves these views are accurate.

Below is part of an interview with a mother who has been reported to have a significant problem with alcohol use. The father had made an application to the Family Court to have the children live with him.

Box 16.3 Interviewer: There have been concerns raised about your use of alcohol.

Mother: Oh, I know what he's said, but that's not fair. I'm only a social drinker.

Interviewer: I noticed in the information given to me that there have been times when the children have reported that they have been unable to wake you after you've been drinking.

Mother: No, that's not true. I wasn't very well, and I got really tired. I was asleep on the couch. I don't know why the children over-reacted. I expect their father put them up to it.

Interviewer: We'll come back to that in a moment. Can you tell me how much you drink?

Mother: Hardly anything. I will have a couple of glasses of wine when I'm with my friends, you know, at a social event. Other than that, I don't drink. I don't drink every day and I don't even drink every week. And when I do drink, I don't get drunk.

Interviewer: You said you drink when you're with your friends. What about when you're alone?

Mother: No, I've never done that.

Interviewer: Some people like to use alcohol to feel better when they've had a stressful day. Do you tend to drink to cope with stressful times?

Mother: No, I only drink when I'm happy and with friends.

Later in the interview …

Interviewer: Well, thanks for coming in for the interview.

Mother: That's ok. It wasn't as bad as I thought it was going to be. But I feel quite exhausted. I think I'll go home and have a couple of glasses of wine to recover. Um … you know, just as a treat.

This is a fairly blatant (and true) example of the inconsistencies that can occur. This mother said she is a social drinker who does not drink alone or drink to cope. However, as soon as her guard was down, she said she was going home to drink as a means of coping with the pressure she was under for a couple of hours.

You can notice inconsistencies as you interview someone and challenge them as you go along. Alternatively, you may notice the inconsistencies when you review the information you gathered during the interview. It is worthy of note that inconsistencies do not only occur within an interview. Indeed, more often they occur between interviews or interviewees.

Discrepancies between accounts

It is always the case in parenting dispute evaluations that you will be confronted with discrepancies between the account provided by one person and that provided by another person. This is not particularly surprising given that most parenting dispute evaluations become necessary because of conflict or disagreement between the people involved.

The nature of the discrepancies between accounts will vary. Some will reflect differences of opinion or differences in how a particular event is perceived. These are the normal inconsistencies that occur between two people's reports or points of view. Other discrepancies between accounts will exist because one or both parties are trying to distort what occurred and to put themselves in a better light. Given the adversarial nature of many of the circumstances that lead to a parenting dispute evaluation being necessary, the tendency for the parties to do this is not surprising.

The challenge for you is to identify these discrepancies and determine how much weight you are going to give to each person's account of what has taken place. Here is an example of the types of discrepancies you might notice when undertaking parenting dispute evaluations. We will consider what the now separated husband and wife have to say about a particular matter.

Box 16.4 Ex-wife: The pregnancy wasn't planned. I was completely shocked. We hadn't been going out for very long when it happened, about six months. I didn't even know if I really wanted to be in a relationship with him and he certainly turned out to be horrible. And I was taking the contraceptive pill. So, the pregnancy was a complete surprise. I told him he didn't have to commit himself to me or the baby if he didn't want. I gave him the option of getting out of the situation.

Ex-husband: I was freaked when she told me she was pregnant. I had only known her for five weeks. I couldn't believe it was happening. She told me she was on the pill, but her sister told me that wasn't true. Look, I'm glad I have my child in my life now, but I do believe I was set up. And she was desperate to be married. She asked me to marry her and, while I was considering it, she had already started arranging the wedding. Her parents dived in as well. It was only her sister who made any sense. I just felt really rushed, like my head was spinning. I don't think I was very supportive during the early stages of the pregnancy, but that's because I couldn't believe it was happening. I felt like a stranger in my own life. We were married by the time she was four months' pregnant and I don't even recall ever saying I wanted to marry her.

Here we have two completely different accounts of events that cannot be a result of differences in how a situation is perceived. It is these types of discrepancies that have to be resolved when forming your opinion.

Inconsistencies with collateral information

There can be inconsistencies evident between what is told to you during interviews and what is available to you from collateral information. Collateral information is the type of information you receive from external sources, such as police records, medical records, and reports from teachers. Here is an example of the discrepancy between what a teacher and the parent have to say.

Box 16.5 Mother: Bella is terrified to go to school. I think it's because her father goes there and helps out. Bella told me she doesn't want to go to school because her father is always there. I just don't see why he won't leave her alone. I take Bella to school and she clings to me. Look, her father is allowed to have her overnight two nights a fortnight, so I don't see why he has to go and harass her at school.

Teacher: I'm Bella's grade 2 teacher. It's my experience that Bella's fine at school and she seems to enjoy having her father come and help around the place. She always seems proud that it's her dad doing the heavy lifting. I do agree that there are some tears when Bella is dropped off in the morning by her mother. I don't see that when she's dropped off by her grandmother or father. All I'm saying is that I don't think the problem is with her father. To be honest, I think Bella has a problem when she is dropped off by her mother because her Mum tends to create a bit of drama.

Here we have a difference of opinion about the cause of a problem rather than the problem itself. The mother is motivated to blame the father in a way that is not supported by the collateral information that is available.

What they do not say

The problem of the detection of deception may not just be a matter of evaluating what is said. It may be necessary to pay attention to what is not said or what the person being interviewed refuses to say. The interviewee may simply refuse to answer a question, may divert attention away from the question or may refuse to agree or disagree with a proposition about which there is already considerable evidence.

Box 16.6 Interviewer: On the day he hurt his foot, did you lock Harrison outside the front door when he was misbehaving?

Mother: You know, it's been really hard coping without any support from Harrison's father. You would think that he'd want to be there for his son, but he doesn't bother to make any effort with him.

Interviewer: On that day when Harrison hurt his foot, had you locked him outside the house?

Mother: We have always struggled to make ends meet because Harrison's father won't pay his child support payments on time. I have tried to make him see that withholding the money is hurting Harrison more than it hurts me. But he thinks he is causing me trouble, so he doesn't pay on time.

Interviewer: These are important things to talk about but first I need you to answer the question. On the day that Harrison hurt his foot, did you lock him outside the house because he was misbehaving?

Mother: Harrison's behaviour has been difficult for some time. I put this down to his father's influence. I think his father has told him to play up when he's with me. He wants to make it seem like I'm a terrible parent and can't handle Harrison's behaviour.

Interviewer: I draw your attention back to the question I asked. Did you lock Harrison outside the house that day?

Mother: I don't think you understand how difficult it's been for me.

You can see the problem here. The interviewee is trying to avoid directly answering a question, most likely because she wishes to cover up something she does not want you to know or does not wish to discuss.

So, deception attempts can take a variety of forms. When it is detected during interview, it may be necessary to challenge what is being said.

Challenge skills

It is imperative in these types of interviews that your counselling challenge skills are well developed. This includes you having the confidence to challenge the discrepancies you identify as well as knowing how to challenge. If you are uncertain that you have the counselling challenge skills to be able to take on this task, we recommend that you undertake some professional development. It will make your job easier.

The challenge skills used in these types of interviews are probably more direct than would be used in a typical therapeutic session. You will have limited time to try to determine the veracity of what is being said. Therefore, you will need to confront discrepancies, hidden agendas, or efforts to deceive earlier than you would do in a therapeutic process.

Let us see how challenging can be managed. This is an abridged version of what would be likely to take place.

Box 16.7 Interviewer: You have said you don't use drugs, even marijuana.

Mother: Yeah, that's right. Everyone says I do, but it's not true.

Interviewer: But you said you've used drugs in the past.

Mother: Yep. That was because of a guy I was with a while back. He turned me onto drugs, and I got into them a bit. But not anymore.

Interviewer: You say a bit?

Mother: Yeah, not as much as him, but I suppose I was using every day, but not very much.

Interviewer: You say that your partner at the time turned you onto drugs. But your mother said your drug use started earlier than that.

Mother: What would she know?

Interviewer: I noticed that you had been charged in relation to drug offences.

Mother: That's because of my association with that person. The police just picked on me because I was with him.

Interviewer: What about this charge from two months ago? That was a long time after your relationship with this person ended.

Mother: That was just because the police were after me because of my past association with that guy.

Interviewer: I also noticed from your medical records that you were admitted to the hospital following an accidental overdose of morphine.

Mother: Yes, but that wasn't my fault. My boyfriend back then gave me the drugs. I just took what he gave me. He shouldn't have given me so much. But that all makes it seem worse than it was.

Interviewer: And your oldest son ... I understand he went to live with your mother for 12 months because of your drug use. You weren't in a position to look after him.

Mother: That was more because he didn't like my boyfriend. He asked to go and stay with his grandmother. I don't know what I was thinking then. I think it was my boyfriend's influence. I was really into him and I wasn't thinking straight. But I spoke to my son every day. We are still close.

Interviewer: And now you say you're not using?

Mother: No, I'm not.

Interviewer: But there've been reports of you being under the influence of drugs as recently as last week.

Mother: No, that's not right.

Interviewer: Well, the reports have been made. There is a police report of a welfare check from two weeks ago that indicated that you were under the influence of something and they called an ambulance because they were concerned about you. Also, your mother told me she is very concerned about your current drug use.

Mother: My mother has got it in for me. She just doesn't want me to be happy. She wants to take my kids.

Interviewer: Why?

Mother: I don't know. I think she's just jealous. She's so uptight and can't relax and enjoy herself. She just wishes she was more like me.

Interviewer: I noticed that you have failed to undertake the drug tests the court ordered.

Mother: Well, I forgot to take my ID when I went there to take the test.

Interviewer: But there have been four occasions when you have failed to take the random drug tests.

Mother: They didn't let me know one of them and I had an appointment when another was scheduled.

Interviewer: So, let's see. You said you used to have a drug problem that wasn't too bad but resulted in drug charges and an admission to hospital with a morphine overdose. Also, your son went to live with your mother, she says because of your drug use. Now you say you're not using, but there are reports of current drug use, including from your mother and the police, a trip to hospital, recent drug-related charges and you have failed to undertake the drug tests ordered by the court. I am concerned that what you are telling me is not consistent with the information that has been given to me. Are you able to see why the court is questioning whether your drug use was more serious than you are saying and whether your drug use isn't in the past as you've claimed?

Here, the inconsistencies in the person's account have been outlined for her. Continued failure to adequately address these inconsistencies provides additional information about deception attempts. This failure would need to be taken into account, down the track, when allocating weight to the mother's comments. Challenge skills will be central to your interviewing of parents.

Interviewing children

An integral part of parenting dispute evaluations involves child interviews (15) although they are fraught with difficulty (16). Certainly, interviewing children is a more complicated task than interviewing adults. The way you interview a child will need to be adjusted depending on the developmental stage of the child. Also, children are much more vulnerable to suggestion than are adults, so you need to be careful about the nature of the questions you ask and the way they are asked. We suggest that you undertake specific training in interviewing children.

Here are some of the issues you need to take into account when interviewing children in the context of parenting dispute evaluations.

Starting point

Firstly, it is necessary to consider the developmental stage of the child being interviewed. In general, the younger the child, the more vulnerable the child is to influence by the interviewer. It is important to make every effort to avoid influencing what the child reports to you.

Remember that it is difficult for children to say negative things about their parents. Indeed, young children often do not think in those terms. Although they may understand better when someone is behaving negatively towards them, young children struggle to express genuine negative feelings towards a parent. Even maltreated children love their parents and can be strongly attached to them.

You also need to remember that children like to please. They will try to determine what it is they think you want from them and then give it to you. You need to be careful that you do not reinforce this expectation that the child should provide you with an answer that pleases you.

As a result of this effort to please, children may demonstrate a tendency to tell both parents what they think they want to hear. Parents will report to you that a child is expressing dissatisfaction with their treatment at the other parent's home while the other parent reports the same. This occurs because the child perceives that it pleases a parent to say negative things about their treatment in the care of the other parent.

This is not inconsistent with the report that children find it difficult to say negative things about their parents. It seems that children find it difficult to report genuine negative feelings but have less trouble in relaying information they know to be false when it pleases the parent to whom they are telling the story.

It is worth remembering that the children you interview should view the experience in a positive light, or at least as an emotionally neutral event. The way in which you conduct the interview will determine the nature of the experience for the child. We recommend that you tell the child from the outset that it is your job to help families and sometimes that means helping families to fix problems they might be experiencing. The way this information is conveyed will depend on the developmental stage of the child. Indeed, your chosen interview style also will be developmentally determined.

Interviewing style

As stated, your goal is to make the interview experience as easy as possible for the child. Tell the child you are going to be asking lots of questions. Set the child up as the expert on their family. That is, tell the child that they know lots of things about their own family that you do not know so you will be looking to them to help you get to know their family members.

There are guidelines for asking children questions in an effort to obtain information. Although considerably more complex than outlined here, which is why we suggest you undertake child interview training, here are some simple rules from an interview guide we have found useful (17).

Invite

Invite the child to provide you with information about a topic. Here, you are trying to establish a narrative or have the child provide an account of what occurred, in their own words. For example:

"What happened at Dad's house yesterday?"

Use open-ended questions like this one that will encourage the child to relate information to you. Closed-ended questions that invite a 'yes' or 'no' answer do not encourage the child to tell their story about what occurred. Closed-ended questions are associated with a greater tendency for the child to be influenced by what they think the interviewer wants to hear.

Elaborate

After the child has been invited to provide an account of their experience, you then ask the child to elaborate. For example:

"Tell me more about the fight at Dad's house."

Here, you are encouraging the child to provide more details about the important aspects of what they told you. It allows you to obtain more information about a matter of interest. It also allows you to ensure that all freely recalled information has been provided by the child.

3. Focus

The child is then asked to focus their attention on specific aspects of their account. You might ask the child to focus on a particular period of time, what they saw or heard, or some key facts. For example:

"What happened from the time the man arrived at Dad's house until the time he left?"

You can encourage the child along the way by using prompts, such as, "What happened next?". By focusing the attention of the child, you can obtain more information about specific events.

Clarify and elaborate

Then, after focusing in on specific aspects of the account provided by the child, you can then ask for clarification and further elaboration. For example:

Clarification: "Did Dad ask him to leave before or after that happened?"
Elaboration: "What did the man say when Dad asked him to leave?"

Here is this process in action.

> **Box 16.8 Interviewer:** Tell me what happened at the party.
> **Child:** It was Jack's birthday. He turned five. Mum had bought him a cake, and everything was ok. But Mum drank lots of wine and then she got angry. She usually gets angry when she drinks lots of wine. Then she fell over a bit and the birthday cake fell on the floor.
> **Interviewer:** Tell me about what happened when the cake fell on the floor.
> **Child:** Well, Mum was really angry and blamed Jack. She pushed him and he fell down on the floor and landed on the cake.
> **Interviewer:** What happened from the time Mum started to get angry up to when she pushed Jack and he fell on the floor?

> **Child:** I thought Mum was going to get mad. I was watching her, and she started to look angry. Her voice got louder and that usually means she's getting mad.
>
> **Interviewer:** What happened next?
>
> **Child:** Well, Peter, you know Mum's boyfriend Pete, well he told Mum to be quiet and that just made Mum madder. She shouted at Pete then but she sort of tripped and bumped into the table and the birthday cake fell on the floor.
>
> **Interviewer:** Then what happened?
>
> **Child:** Pete called Mum a not very nice name and Mum got madder. She started yelling at Jack then. She said it was Jack's fault the cake fell on the floor, but it really wasn't his fault. Jack looked really scared. Mum doesn't like it when Jack looks scared so she sort of pushed him and he fell over and landed on the cake.
>
> **Interviewer:** What was the reason why Jack was looking so scared?
>
> **Child:** Jack was scared because Mum and Pete were fighting. And then he got scared because Mum yelled at him.
>
> **Interviewer:** How hard did Mum push Jack?
>
> **Child:** She pushed him really, really hard. He just sort of flew backwards and landed on the cake.

You can see how the application of these simple interviewing guidelines can assist you in obtaining information from the child. Of course, the application of these guidelines does not guarantee that the information you obtain is truthful.

Detection of deceptive responding

The biggest problem of deception occurs when a child is coached by an adult to provide you with a particular version of events. The child is likely to have rehearsed what they should say. So, look for the child doing the following:

Using words outside the child's normal vocabulary

When interviewing children, pay attention to the wording they use. Children who have been coached will often use words that they would not normally use, or you would not expect a child of that age to use.

> **Box 16.9 Interviewer:** So, do you like living with Grandma?
>
> **Child:** She looks after us and she always respects me.
>
> **Interviewer:** Grandma respects you?
>
> **Child:** Yes, Grandma always respects me, but Mum never respects me.
>
> **Interviewer:** In what way does Grandma respect you?
>
> **Child:** Um … in every way.
>
> **Interviewer:** And what about Mum? In what ways doesn't she respect you?
>
> **Child:** She just doesn't respect me.
>
> **Interviewer:** Can you tell me what respect means?
>
> **Child:** Umm …

Picking up on the word 'respect', further questioning indicated that the child really did not know the meaning of the word.

Using language not typical of a child of that age

In addition to coached children using words that are unexpected for a child that age or when it seems apparent that the meaning of the word is not known, children will also use phrases or refer to matters using unexpected language. They will sound like adults or will use phrases that are likely to have little meaning for them.

Box 16.10 Interviewer: And how have things been since that big fight between Mum and Dad?
  Child: It wasn't Mum's fault. It was Dad's.
  Interviewer: Ok. We'll talk about what happened in a minute. But how have you been feeling since then?
  Child: I've been having intrusive thoughts and back flashes.
  Interviewer: Back flashes? You've been having back flashes?
  Child: Yes, that's because my father traumatised me.
  Interviewer: What's a back flash?
  Child: Umm … well … you should know. You're the doctor.
  Interviewer: Do you mean flashbacks?
  Child: Oh, yes, that's right. I've been having flashbacks.
  Interviewer: And who told you that you were having flashbacks?
  Child: No-one. I just know.
  Interviewer: So, tell me what happens when you have a flashback?
  Child: Well … um … I don't want to. I just know I have them.

This child is giving little indication that he is aware of the meaning of what he is saying.

Talking about events about which they have no first-hand knowledge

Children who have been coached will talk about events they have not experienced as if they have direct knowledge of these events. Children can describe confidently such events although, when questioned about these events, the answers tend to lack sufficient detail.

Box 16.11 Interviewer: So, you said Dad is scary when he's been drinking.
  Child: Yes, that's right. He is scary and he hurts people. That's why I don't want to go to stay at his house.
  Interviewer: Tell me about a time that you remember when Dad was drinking, and you were scared.
  Child: Well, Dad came home drunk and Mum was scared. Dad started shouting at Mum in the kitchen and then he pushed her against the fridge.
  Interviewer: Do you remember that happening or did someone tell you about it?
  Child: I remember.

> **Interviewer:** But everyone I spoke to told me that happened before you were born. They also told me Dad stopped drinking alcohol before you were born. Have you ever seen Dad drink?
>
> **Child:** No but Dad is scary when he's been drinking and he hurts people. That's why I don't want to go to stay at his house.

This also will occur when children have been repeatedly exposed to conversations about events they had not experienced. Listening to others talk about events can lead children to believe they have experienced them.

Challenge skills

In the context of a parenting dispute evaluation it may sometimes be necessary to challenge children. Challenging the inconsistencies in children's accounts of their experiences should be done gently and with caution. Rather than directly confronting the child with the inconsistencies in what they are saying, you could express confusion or ask for clarification.

> **Box 16.12 Interviewer:** Tell me about your Dad.
>
> **Child:** Well, he's mean.
>
> **Interviewer:** How is he mean?
>
> **Child:** He's just mean. He's always in a grumpy mood. And he gets mad at me. I don't like going to his house.
>
> **Interviewer:** Don't you do nice things with Dad?
>
> **Child:** No, never. He never does anything with me. He just watches TV or reads a book and never even talks to me.
>
> **Interviewer:** Oh, I'm a bit confused then. I saw some photos of you and Dad fishing and you and Dad at your Nan and Pop's barbecue.
>
> **Child:** Except for those times. He never does anything except for those things.
>
> **Interviewer:** Mmm. I thought Dad took you camping during your last school holidays.
>
> **Child:** Well, yeah.
>
> **Interviewer:** So, help me understand because it seems like you have done some fun things with Dad.
>
> **Child:** Maybe I just don't want to do them anymore. I'd rather do them with Mum.

So, by expressing confusion, you have learned that it may be the case that it is the child's relationship with the mother rather than the father's neglect of the child's needs that has created a problem.

We cannot underestimate the challenges for evaluators associated with interviewing children. The differences between the skills needed to interview a four-year-old child and a 12-year-old, for example, are considerable. We strongly suggest you prepare yourself to conduct a forensic interview with children prior to undertaking parenting dispute evaluations.

Interviewing others

It is reasonably commonly the case that you will be required to interview other people as part of a parenting dispute evaluation. For example, these people might include extended family members.

In general, your goal here is different. In effect, unless you are assessing the person as a potential kinship carer, you are using these interviews to gather collateral information that will assist you in formulating an opinion about the parents and the child or children involved in the parenting dispute.

Starting point

At the outset, you need to make your position clear when interviewing other individuals as part of a parenting dispute evaluation. You need to explain your role and identify what type of information you expect to be able to obtain from the person you are interviewing. You can do this by offering them the opportunity to contribute to the evaluation process.

However, it is the case that you need to determine the agenda of the person you are interviewing. It would be nice to think that people providing collateral information would be able to provide you with unbiased information that would add to the body of knowledge you have about the family being assessed. Unfortunately, it is rarely the case that the information you obtain can be accepted without consideration of the motivations of the information giver. In a sense, the biases of family members can be understood. Nevertheless, although wanting to support their family member who is the focus of the parenting dispute evaluation, most family members can be encouraged to provide a more balanced view of the situation if they are reminded that the wellbeing of the child is your main concern.

When interviewing other people, you have to be careful to distinguish between their first-hand knowledge of what has occurred and either what they believe has happened or what someone has told them has happened. People will talk confidently about matters they do not really have direct experience of or knowledge about. Consider this interview with a person who claimed to know about the family situation.

Box 16.13 Relative: They were at my place, pretending like everything was ok. The kids were there, and they were playing happy families. But then Steve and I had a disagreement and I told him to leave. He's hard to get along with and I got fed up with him. They put the kids in the car and took off. That night they took morphine while the kids were in their care.

Interviewer: How do you know?

Relative: Pardon?

Interviewer: How do you know they used morphine that night?

Relative: They did.

Interviewer: I just need to clarify how you know this happened.

Relative: Well, I bet they did.

Interviewer: So, you're not sure.

Relative: Oh, I'm sure.

Interviewer: Let me put it another way. You weren't there at their house that evening?

Relative: No, I wasn't. I was at home.

Interviewer: So, what you're saying, really, is that you believe they used morphine that evening but you don't have any first-hand knowledge that is what occurred.

Relative: Yeah, I suppose.

Interviewer: Thanks. I just needed to make that clear in my mind.

As stated, you need to make clear the motivation of the interviewee and evaluate the information you obtain for accuracy and usefulness. The way you interview these people will assist in this process.

Interviewing style

When interviewing people who are not central to the parenting dispute, you are undertaking an information-gathering exercise. You can be quite direct and focused in your questioning. Ask the questions you need answers to, then offer the person the opportunity to add extra information they might have that you have not yet considered.

It is a good idea to create an atmosphere of collaboration. This will encourage the person being interviewed to disclose information that they might not otherwise have planned to provide. Counselling skills can be used, such as empathic statements, prompts and probes. Appropriately used counselling skills will enhance the quality and the quantity of the information you obtain.

Box 16.14 Interviewer: Thanks for coming in to talk with me today about your grandchildren's situation.

Grandmother: That's ok. I don't know what I can say that will help.

Interviewer: Well, I really appreciate you working with me. I like to be able to get a really good picture of the family I am interviewing. And I guess you are one of the people who would know the family the best.

Grandmother: Um, yes. I've been there for the kids since they were babies. I try really hard to make sure they have everything they need. I look after them a lot.

Interviewer: The children told me how much they love you. I certainly believe you've been a really important person in their lives.

Grandmother: I love them, too.

Interviewer: I'm sure you do. I suppose there's been times when you have been quite worried about them.

Grandmother: I'm worried all the time. Right from when they were tiny. But I always made sure they had food to eat and they got to the doctor if they were sick.

Interviewer: So, you've helped out your daughter and the children quite a lot, then, even with things like groceries.

Grandmother: Yes, it would break my heart to think of the children going hungry because my daughter wasn't looking after them properly.

By creating an atmosphere of collaboration, this grandmother has begun to talk about her concerns about her daughter's family. She moved from saying she had little to offer in identifying problems the children face. Of course, you still have to evaluate the truthfulness of what is being related.

Detection of deceptive responding

When evaluating how much weight you are prepared to give to the information provided by the other people you interview, there are some factors you need to consider. Always keep in mind their agenda. If the agenda is to do the best for the children, then the agenda is a good one. However, they may present with a need to punish people they perceived as having wronged them, a need to maintain control over the other parties, a need to keep the children away from their parents because of their own needs, a need to be praised and rewarded, or a desire to help one of the parents.

Evaluate these people's capacity to accept information that might contradict their own views. Rigidity in their thinking may make it difficult for them to accept points of view that are contrary to their own beliefs about the situation. This inflexibility may be specific to the situation being investigated or may be a more generalised characteristic.

Pay attention to exaggerations or embellishments in the information they provide. Note intensifiers in the language they use, such as, "She was really very difficult to manage" rather than "She was difficult to manage". Take note of comments such as, "She was always a problem" or "She never did anything right".

Take note of what is not said. A failure to mention information about events of which you are already aware may indicate a desire to cover up and deceive. Notice how they respond to disclosure of your knowledge about events.

Box 16.15 Interviewer: I understand you have experienced some difficulties as a result of your daughter's problems managing her anger.

Grandmother: Oh no. We get along all right.

Interviewer: Has she ever harmed you?

Grandmother: No, she'd never do that. She's a lovely girl, really. Her father and I don't have many problems with her. That might be because she stays away from us when things are going badly for her.

Interviewer: I've been told she assaulted you in your driveway when you refused to give her money.

Grandmother: Oh, that was blown out of proportion. She didn't assault me. That's just what Tony says because he wants the kids to live with him. He just tries to make it seem worse than it is.

Interviewer: My difficulty here is that I've seen a copy of the police report about this incident and your daughter confirmed it happened when I questioned her about it.

Grandmother: Oh. Well ... I'd still say she didn't mean to hurt me.

You would have to reach the conclusion that the quality of the information being provided is problematic. It can be difficult for a mother to convey to strangers information that can negatively affect their child. Certainly, it would be necessary to challenge this person's intentions.

Challenge skills

You have to walk a fine line between offering an environment of collaboration and challenging inconsistencies or blatant attempts to deceive. We recommend that you try to offer a collaborative interaction but abandon that in favour of more direct confrontation or challenge if the need arises. It is more important that you have an understanding of events and, indeed, the extent to which the person you are interviewing will use deception to support a family member, than it is to have them on side. Remember, you are not engaging in a therapeutic process.

However, also remember that challenging an interviewee is not the same as inciting conflict with that person. You are not attacking them or interrogating them. You are trying to obtain information. Use counselling challenge skills.

So, we have considered interviewing family members to gather information on which you will base your opinion, at least in part. There are other sources of information.

Parent–child observations

You may wish to or you may be asked to observe parent–child interactions as part of the parenting dispute evaluation process. Although some argue these observations are an important component of the evaluation process (18–19), there are pros and cons in relation to doing this. Such observations may provide useful information, but they may not. Also, they are time consuming and, therefore, costly. If the option for a parent–child observation is made available, you need to consider whether there is benefit in doing this.

Organising observations

When organising parent–child observations, you must realise there is no such thing as unobtrusively observing a child in his or her natural environment. Your presence alters the dynamic so the people being observed will not act normally. So, you might as well observe the parent and child in your environment as long as there are not overriding reasons to conduct the observation elsewhere. Indeed, a survey of parenting dispute evaluators indicated that few conducted observations in the parents' homes (13).

Some psychologists have facilities to observe a parent–child interaction without the need for them to be present in the room. We are sorry to inform you that this does not mean that your presence does not influence the interaction. You cannot observe an adult without informing them of your intention. Even if a young child does not know they are being observed, the parent's behaviour is likely to be affected by the knowledge that the observation is taking place.

When organising observations, please keep in mind family violence orders or restraining orders. Bringing in the child on a single occasion, then observing the children with one parent followed by the other parent may not work if the parents cannot cope with being in the same place at the same time or there are legal implications of such an arrangement. Even if you can arrange it so that there is no face-to-face contact by placing people in separate rooms, victims of family violence often are not comfortable with the knowledge that the perpetrator is close by. Also, you have no control over what happens after these people leave the building. An undertaking by the perpetrator that he or she will leave the area before the victim leaves the building does not guarantee that this will occur. Allowing the victim to leave first does not guarantee that the perpetrator has not arranged for someone to follow the victim.

Also, it is not good practice to expose children to abusive parents unless you can guarantee their safety and wellbeing. All the reassurances in the world will not make an abused child feel better about being in the room with someone they fear. Sometimes, observations can be arranged under special circumstances, but you would have to make sure that the child is both well protected and emotionally ready to see the alleged abuser.

Keep in mind the child's needs. It may be convenient for you to arrange interviews and observations on the same day but a child who has to be there for hours will become tired. This will influence their behaviour and the information you obtain may be compromised.

Conducting observations

Although some parents will bring along an activity (and snacks) for their child, when conducting an observation you may wish to provide a focus for the interaction, such as toys. Of course, although older children might not need to have an activity provided, many younger children will wish to play.

If you are in the same room as the people you are observing, the decision has to be made whether or not you join in. Sometimes it is hard not to be part of the interaction and, certainly, it is hard for parents and children to ignore you if you are in the room. However, we recommend that you keep your interaction with the people you are observing to a minimum. Respond when needed but do not make the interaction about you.

Although your task is to observe and record, you may wish to delay taking notes about the session until after its completion. Older children and parents tend to become self-conscious if you are seen to be taking notes when certain events during the interaction occur. Younger children can become more interested in what you are writing than their reason for being there. I recall a three-year-old watching a psychologist writing observation notes before she turned to me asking, "What him doing?".

Despite the artificial nature of the observation, there are some things you should be looking for. These include:

- The way in which the parent responds to the child's presence.
- The way in which the child responds to the parent's presence.
- The way the parent engages the child and the way the child responds.
- The way the parent manages the child's behaviour and the way the child responds.
- Non-verbal signs of discomfort in the presence of the other person.
- Non-verbal signs of affection towards the other person.
- Problematic child behaviours that occur in the presence of the parent but not observed at other times.
- The way the parent copes with competing demands for attention when there is more than one child present.
- The way the child reacts to separation and the way the parent handles that reaction.

There may be other observations you can make that are relevant to the particular case on which you are working.

Usefulness of observations

The usefulness of these parent–child observations varies. Certainly, there are limitations in what can be learned about the way a parent and child interacts because of the artificial nature of the situation.

Nevertheless, observations can provide useful information. They can be used to identify discrepancies between what has been said (e.g., "I don't like my father") and the way the child acts around the parent (e.g., reaches out for physical contact). They can be used to identify differences in the way a child responds to one parent and the other parent by comparing the child's behaviour during observations with both parents separately. They can be used to gather additional information to support evolving ideas about the nature of the parent–child relationship (e.g., the strength of attachment).

So, it is possible to obtain useful information from observing parent–child interactions that can supplement information obtained from interviews. You also may obtain information from other sources.

Use of collateral information

Collateral information already has been mentioned. Collateral information refers to data gathered from sources other than the family being assessed that may be used to determine how much weight is given to certain information provided by family members, or to identify inconsistencies in the account provided by family members. It can offer a different perspective that would not be available otherwise.

The quality of the collateral information needs to be established. Some information you obtain is more objective in nature, such as medical records or police records. Other information is more subjective and reflects the views of the person who is the source of the information, such as, teachers.

Information provided in documents

You will be provided with some additional documents. These may include affidavits prepared by the people you are interviewing. However, the documents may also include affidavits from other people, reports from other professionals, or records, such as medical and police records.

Further, you may seek to have available to you other information. Ask for what you want, and you may be provided with it. However, be aware that some information would need to be subpoenaed and this may take some time. You need to make a judgment whether the information you are able to obtain merits delaying the production of your report.

Information from teachers

Information provided by teachers can be useful. You can learn about the general state of the child's adjustment and how the child functions away from the family. You can learn the following and more:

- Whether the child presents as clean and tidy at school.
- Whether they are fed, tired or happy.
- Whether they demonstrate problematic or inappropriate behaviour around other children and/or adults.
- Whether the child demonstrates good social skills.
- Whether the child's parents behave appropriately when they are at the school.
- Whether the parents are engaged in their child's education and responsive to their child's needs.

We consider it is better to talk with the teacher who spends the most time with the child. Sometimes it is the principal who elects to talk with you. Although this person may know something about the child in question, the teacher who spends the most time with the child will have considerably more information. The teacher often is the person who has the most interaction with the child's parents or has had an opportunity to make comparisons between the involvement of one parent and the other parent.

Information from health professionals

Information from health professionals can be useful collateral information. However, there are some issues to consider. Although a family doctor may know the family members well, he or she also may take a more positive or protective view of their patient than would be the case if the information being obtained was more objective in nature. Here we are not being critical of family doctors. We are saying that their role may make it difficult for them to give negative accounts of their patient's functioning. Hospital records relating to admissions and/or treatment tend to provide 'snap shots' of a person's life or adjustment but rarely give a complete view of a person's functioning over time.

Information from mental health professionals

Information from other mental health professionals may provide you with useful information. However, you must be cautious because of the potential for a biased account of a family member's functioning to be offered. That is, a parent's therapist may act to protect their client and fail to adequately disclose concerns.

As previously stated, mental health information obtained from hospital admissions may be useful but may only provide 'snap shots' of a person's life. This is because such records often do not provide an overview of how a person is functioning between admissions. Also, it is often the case that there is no consistency with regard to the person making diagnostic judgements as people often do not see the same doctor with repeat admissions. This can result in a confusing number of seemingly competing diagnoses.

Police records

Information obtained from police records can be very useful. This is particularly the case when this type of collateral information is used to determine the degree or fullness of disclosure by parents. For example, a parent may downplay their own aggressiveness, which may be inconsistent with police records of repeated physical assaults.

Police records also can provide you with useful information about family violence episodes that involved the police attending the home. Often these records are accompanied by a description of what took place at the time of the family violence incident. Police records can also provide support for concerns about substance use with drug-related charges or charges related to the effect on behaviour of substance use being recorded.

Police records must always be subpoenaed. This is done by the lawyers involved in the case. The request for police records may take some time to process.

Other information

Sometimes parties to these assessments will provide you with documents, articles, recordings and transcripts that they believe will support their case. If this information is not already being considered as part of the legal process, and you wish to use it in formulating your opinion, you must append a copy to the report you prepare. This is because the court must have available any information on which you based your opinion.

Role of the expert witness

By conducting a parenting dispute evaluation, you are being appointed as an expert witness who is being asked to provide objective opinion about matters being considered by the court. There are some things about being an expert witness that you need to know.

Expert witness

This is you. An expert witness is a professional who, by virtue of their qualifications and/or experience, is in a position to provide an opinion to the court to assist the court in making parenting orders.

Roles when offering opinions

There are a variety of roles you might fulfil when offering an opinion in the Family Court.

Court-appointed single expert

You may be appointed by the Family Court to fulfil the role of single expert. The single expert is the person who undertakes a parenting dispute evaluation for the Family Court and reports to the court their opinions related to the terms of reference that have been provided. The single expert is someone who is accepted by the court and, indeed, all parties involved, as having the appropriate qualifications, expertise and experience to offer the court sound opinions about psychological matters related to parenting disputes.

The single expert has the advantage of being able to interview all the relevant parties. They have access to collateral information in the form of documents provided by the court as well as through interviewing individuals peripherally involved in the case, such as teachers or therapists.

In general, the single expert works with the independent children's lawyer (ICL), who is a lawyer who has been appointed by the court to assist the court in making parenting orders that will be of benefit to the child. Ultimately, the decision about the parenting arrangements for the child will be determined by the court. People acting in the role of ICL typically are experienced, senior lawyers.

The ICL will assist the single expert by making documents available, arranging for the parties to be informed of scheduled appointments, and offer any other assistance that is needed. If additional information is needed by the single expert, the ICL may seek to make it available.

Box 16.16 Case example: A single expert was appointed to provide an opinion to the Family Court about the risk to the children. The mother claimed that the father had sexually abused the oldest of their four daughters. There were also claims that the father had acted in a sexually inappropriate manner with other children. The father was asserting that he did not have sexual interest in children and that his alcohol use had influenced his behaviour. He also claimed that his playful behaviour with these children had been misinterpreted as sexual in nature. The court wanted the expert to offer an opinion on the risk to the children of the father being allowed to spend time with his children and what aspects of the father's behaviour needed to be addressed before it would be safe for the children to spend time with their father, if it was considered that a risk to their safety existed.

Expert for one party

You may be asked by the lawyer for one of the parties to act as an expert, providing information to the court in relation to that person. In this role, you would have the opportunity only to interview one of the parents and, potentially, family members of that person.

Typically, an expert in this role is sought to counter the opinions formulated about the lawyer's client by the single expert or a family consultant who works for the Family Court. Alternatively, an expert in this role would be asked to provide additional information about the client that was not addressed by the single expert or family consultant.

Although employed by one side in the dispute, it is the expectation that psychologists in this role do not act as a 'hired gun'. There is an expectation that the opinion being expressed will be offered to assist the court. That is, the psychologist in this role should not act as an advocate for the client but as an expert for the court.

Box 16.17 Case example: A request was made for an assessment of the mother and her relationship with the children by the mother's lawyer. The court-appointed single expert had prepared a report outlining her opinion that the mother was deliberately alienating the children from their father. The expert suggested that despite some behaviour problems with the father, the children would be better off if they lived with their father and spent limited time with their mother. The mother's lawyer asked for an assessment of the mother's functioning and the relationship between the mother and the children. The aim of the lawyer was to challenge the single expert's opinion.

Critiquing the work of others

You may be asked to provide a critique of the work of others. This might involve the critiquing of the report of the single expert or the family consultant, who is a mental health professional who is employed by the Family Court to offer the court an opinion about the functioning of the family in relation to appropriate parenting orders.

This is interesting work. It allows you to draw on a broad range of knowledge about psychological matters. It demands that you apply a cogent strategy to evaluate the argument being presented by the other professional. It offers the opportunity for you to develop your own argument about the merits or limitations of the other person's work and the conclusions they reached.

When undertaking this type of work, it is essential that you stay focused on the goal. That is, it is essential that you critique the work of the other professional. You are not making a judgment about the person whose work you are critiquing.

Box 16.18 Case example: A report was being used in the Family Court to determine appropriate parenting orders in relation to two children, aged 12 and eight years. The report was prepared by a psychologist who had been working with the youngest child and the mother and was being offered as evidence by the mother's lawyer. The father's lawyer sought a critique of the report because of concerns that the opinions contained in the report seemed to be contrary to other evidence suggesting that the mother was falsely claiming family violence by the father and the absence of evidence supporting the father's alleged violent

---

behaviour. The report prepared by the therapist offered conclusions about the risk presented by the father that were made without the therapist ever having met the father. Also, strong indicators of parental alienation by the mother were potentially misinterpreted by the report writer as indicators of rejection of the father by the children because of the alleged family violence. The therapist gave no weight to the fact that the children were unable to provide any detailed information about family violence episodes and the fact that the mother's account was inconsistent with its repeated telling. The lawyer used the critique of the report to challenge the writer of the report during cross-examination.

Advisor

Another interesting role is that of advisor to lawyers. The lawyer of one of the parties may seek your advice about the meaning of the evidence provided by another psychologist. The lawyer also may seek your advice about how to cross-examine an expert witness.

> **Box 16.19 Case example:** A lawyer for a father sought advice about the indicators of parental alienation. It was his strategy in court to prove that the mother was deliberately turning the children against his client, their father. To develop a good cross-examination strategy, this lawyer needed to be educated about the indicators of parental alienation with regard to the mother and the child. This would allow him to target his cross-examination and challenge the interpretations being placed on the mother's behaviour and the children's behaviour by a number of witnesses. What was being sought was information about the indicators of parental alienation and not specific indications in the case.

Parenting dispute evaluation issues

If undertaking parenting dispute evaluations, it is necessary to understand the issues that both guide and impact on opinion formation. Even if the primary focus is on whether parental alienation is relevant in a particular case, the issues that are fundamental to parenting dispute evaluations need to be taken into account.

Complexity of cases

It is worth saying at the outset that the cases you will be presented with are likely to be complex. This complexity can make it more difficult to ascertain the appropriate course of action for a child in terms of the parenting orders that would meet a child's needs.

Firstly, it often is the case that both parents contribute or have contributed in a meaningful way to the quality of a child's life. Parents may make complaints about each other based on the animosity they feel towards each other rather than focusing on what is the best outcome for the child. In these cases, both parents have strengths and weaknesses and the child would be safe with either parent.

Secondly, there are cases where neither parent has the capacity to adequately care for a child although the court has to make a decision between the two parents as to which would offer the child the best life circumstance. Although child protective services may be notified if abuse has occurred, it is more likely the case that both parents have significant parenting weaknesses that make neither candidate problem free.

It is probably easier to formulate opinions about parents when there is one parent who offers considerable advantages for the child. In reality, the factors that you need to consider are not so straightforward.

Lives with/spends time with orders

For a long time, family law has been driven by the requirement to meet the child's needs by determining parenting orders that are in the best interests of the child. This notion of the best interests of the child has underpinned the 'lives with/spends time with' parenting order preferences that have existed until relatively recently. This type of parenting order means that a child will live most of their time with one parent and spend 'meaningful' time with the other parent. A 'lives with/spends time with' parenting order used to allow a child to spend time with the non-residential parent for two nights per fortnight although there has been considerable variation in this time allocation. However, there is a body of literature that strongly indicates that a lives with/spends time with approach is problematic in comparison with equal parental responsibility and shared care (20).

The value of a 'bests interests of the child' approach is that the needs of the child remain the strong focus of attention in determining parenting orders. It has been suggested that the standard allows for each case before the court to be considered on the basis of its own merits. This has been an important feature of family law.

However, the best interests of the child approach that results in a lives with/spends time with order is considered to be a parent-deficit approach (20). It focuses on the problems experienced by one parent relative to the other parent as a reason for a lives with/spends time with parenting order. Although it is still the case that lives with/spends time with parenting orders are necessary, as a starting point, such an approach makes the assumption that there typically will be one parent who is superior to the other in relation to their parenting capacity. Of course, this is not always the case.

It has been suggested that the seeming benefits of the best interests of the child approach should be considered with caution (21) if that translates to a lives with/spends time with order. It is considered to be vague and relies on judges making decisions about matters outside their training, such as child development (22). The standard also requires that predictions are made about future parenting without the benefit of clear guidelines about how to make those predictions. It has been suggested that these problems make it impossible to determine what is in a child's best interest with any degree of certainty.

It has been argued that the parenting orders that tend to be made are based on the way in which a case is presented in court (23) rather than on more objective means of determining what is truly in a child's best interest. There is reliance on experts to offer to the court information or opinions on which decisions can be made. However, it is evident that the empirical support for the parenting dispute evaluation process is limited (21), especially given the variability in the quality of the expertise and methods of evaluators. In fact, as a result of the lack of evidence base, it has been argued that it is not ethically sound for evaluators to make parenting dispute recommendations (24).

It has been suggested the best interests of the child standard can leave parenting orders open to challenge. Parents can dispute the findings of one parenting arrangement being more advantageous to a child than another parenting arrangement because of the lack of a research foundation to support the process. In any case, the standard seems to encourage a stronger adversarial approach to the resolution of parenting disputes than would otherwise be necessary if there were more objective means of determining parenting orders. A lives with/spends time with order leads to the belief that there is a 'winner' and a 'loser' in any parenting dispute determination.

Kruk (20) makes a good point. Parenting orders made that are based on a 'best interests of the child' standard resulting in a lives with/spends time with order do not, as is claimed, favour one parent in terms of living arrangements. In fact, the parenting orders take the time a parent spends with a child away from one parent where more time previously existed. It has been suggested that this results in the discrimination of the children of divorce by having a different standard applied than would be applied in intact families.

The notion of meaningful time

It must be understood that for a parent to contribute in a meaningful way to the responsibilities of child management and socialisation, it is necessary that day-to-day involvement in the child's life occurs (25). Without that type of involvement, the non-residential parent faces the risk of being forced to the periphery of the child's life and, as already covered, this has the potential to have detrimental consequences for the child. The parent forced to the periphery is most often the father, although not always so. In many cases and despite a commitment to remain involved with their children, many fathers are prevented from spending sufficient time with their children to allow them to maintain a close and psychologically meaningful relationship with their children (26). Limited time does not allow the non-residential parent to act in a parenting role. The parent ends up acting like a playmate rather than a parent.

It is structural factors (e.g., shared care) and early contact (greater percentage of time spent with the father post-divorce) that are the best predictors of nurturant fathering and active involvement in a child's life (27). For the general population of divorces, the issue is how to develop parenting plans that provide adequate opportunity for a positive relationship with both the mother and the father. It has been recognised that spending time with a parent every other weekend is not optimal for facilitating an active ongoing involvement in children's lives of the parent who gets to spend time with their children (28).

Willingness to facilitate contact with the other parent

In making decisions about the living arrangements of children, the Family Court needs to make orders that are likely to be effective. One factor that needs to be taken into account is whether or not one parent is willing to facilitate contact of the child with the other parent. Reluctance or refusal to do so by one parent has the capacity to make parenting orders ineffective, as is often the case with parental alienation.

It is necessary that the Family Court make orders that are likely to reduce the chances that the matter will be brought back to court. If one parent refuses to facilitate contact with the other parent, a common enough scenario, the result is a breach of orders and, potentially, more time spent in court.

It may be the case that one parent is more open to facilitating contact than the other parent. In cases such as this, it must be considered whether it is better for the child to live with the parent who will encourage the relationship with the other parent than with the parent who is reluctant or refuses to facilitate this contact. In the former arrangement, the child will get to spend time with both parents. The likelihood of this occurring is reduced in the latter arrangement. Clearly, this has implications in relation to the management of parental alienation cases.

Shared care

As stated, for a long time it was the case that a child would live predominantly with one parent and would get to spend time with the other parent, usually for one weekend a fortnight or one weekend a month. This arrangement resulted in one parent being pushed into a peripheral role in their child's life. It is not possible to function adequately in the role of parent with such limited time with the child.

Now, it is considered a better option for the child to have a shared care arrangement where a child can live with both parents in an equal or close to equal shared experience. The evidence to support the notion that children's needs are best met by having meaningful relationships with both their parents is growing (29). Complementing this is the evidence to suggest that sole-parent living arrangements do little to support the parent–child relationship with the other parent (20).

There is now strong evidence that shared care parenting is more effective than sole parent parenting. Interestingly, despite the claims to the contrary, this holds true for cases with high parental conflict. Also of interest is the fact that the outcomes are the same whether the shared care parenting is by consent or whether it is court mandated (30). It seems to be the case that shared parenting works well even in cases where the parenting arrangements are court mandated or in cases of high parental conflict because there is a decrease in parental conflict with the passage of time. There tends to be a decrease in parental cooperation with sole parenting arrangements (31). This supports the literature that indicates that most parents can find a way to engage in cooperative parenting after the end of litigation (29).

Equal shared parental responsibility

With a shift to the understanding of the benefits to children of shared care, changes in family law have meant that the principle of equal shared parental responsibility is applied as the starting point in parenting disputes. A presumption of equal parental responsibility means that, in contested cases, children will continue to reside with both parents and that both parents will have a say with regard to decision-making about the children's lives as long as other factors, such as family violence, do not indicate a different course of action (32). Although the legislation relates to shared parental responsibility, this, in effect, translates to shared care. In most cases, if there can be shared parental responsibility, there is likely to be no real impediment to shared care.

Views expressed by the child

There is another component to the parenting order decision-making process that is considered by those charged with being the decider, that is the judiciary. You may be asked to provide information about the expressed views of a child in relation to a family law matter. However, you will also be asked what weight you believe should be given to these views.

This issue can be a complicated one. It is true to say that children's views about what they want do not necessarily take into account the factors that could influence the outcome for the child if these wishes are granted. It is necessary to take into account the cognitive and emotional development of the child when determining whether the views expressed by the child should be given weight by the court. It is necessary that the child understands the consequences of the choices they make, and this requires that the child can identify various pathways that would lead on from the choices and evaluate them in terms of the likelihood of a good outcome.

If weight is to be given to a child's expressed views, then it would be necessary that it could be determined that the child had not been placed under undue pressure to express a view that was consistent with the one expressed by the person placing the pressure on the child. The influence on a child's expressed views can be direct or indirect. A child can be coached about what to say when asked with whom the child wishes to reside. Alternatively, a child may be promised desired things in an effort to encourage the child to want to live with one parent.

One last word. You must be careful not to promise a child that their expressed views will lead to an outcome in the desired direction. That is, do not tell the child that they will get what they want. It is not in your power to ensure that a child's expressed wishes will be considered in a way that allows the child to have what they desire.

Dispute issues relevant to parental alienation

When undertaking parenting dispute evaluations, there are certain factors that can influence cases characterised by parental alienation. These influences need to be understood and taken into account when conducting these evaluations.

The role of conflict

The majority of separated parents will be able to resolve parenting issues between themselves and without the support of the Family Court. Interestingly, though, is that the minority of cases that cannot be resolved and end up going to trial are the ones that define legal norms. In effect, they determine what happens with regard to the negotiation process for the majority of cases.

Those parents who are unable to resolve their differences with regard to determining a parenting dispute outcome often are labelled as 'high conflict', despite the fact that the majority of these cases will not involve any form of family violence or abuse (20). Nevertheless, because these parents have to resort to the court for decision-making assistance, it is assumed that the children's needs are better served by a lives with/spends time with order rather than a shared care order (33). This assumption seems to be made because, once the label of 'high conflict' is given, it also is assumed that the children will be negatively affected by the parental 'conflict'.

Certainly, it can be argued that parental conflict is undesirable in terms of a child's psychological functioning. There are particular characteristics of parental conflict that are associated with greater concern regarding a child's longer-term adjustment. For example, when parental conflict influences the amount of time one parent spends with their child, there is a greater risk of harm of the child. When considering the nature of the conflict, the most detrimental effects occur when the conflict is emotionally hostile rather than characterised by disagreements, when the conflict is associated with verbal or physical aggression, when the conflict is not resolved within a reasonable period of time, when the child is directly exposed to the expression of that conflict, and when the child is the subject of the conflict (25), as is the case with parental alienation, at least on the surface.

Despite the emphasis on parents in high conflict, it is the case that over half of divorcing parents are cooperative and another fifth of divorcing parents could be considered to fall in a mid-range between cooperation and conflict. With only the minority of parents experiencing conflict to any significant degree, there should be an expectation that parents will find a way to be supportive of one another post-divorce (25). Also, it is a mistake to focus solely on the level of conflict during the separation and divorce process as an indicator of the extent to which conflict is going to influence subsequent parenting roles. In most cases, parenting conflicts will not persist and resolution of legal proceedings most commonly triggers the commencement of resolution of open conflict.

Most parents will find co-parenting challenging but most will find a way to work cooperatively to parent their child even if a level of conflict exists at the time of separation and during the process of determining care arrangements. There are factors that increase the likelihood that conflict will persist. These include (a) the presence of a high level of hostile conflict prior to separation; (b) a lack of respect for each other and lack of confidence in the other's competence as a parent; and (c) a relationship history characterised by family violence. Even with these factors being present, cooperative parenting still can develop, especially if parents can learn to accept that cooperative parenting has considerable advantages for the child and they choose to focus on the needs of their child irrespective of their feelings about each other (25).

It seems, then, that cases of parental alienation that can easily be classed as high in conflict, fall into a special category. That is, the parents involved in these cases cannot and are unlikely to be able to find a way to parent collaboratively or, at worst, unobtrusively, even with the passage of time. Intervention then becomes necessary to effect a good outcome for alienated children.

Child abuse and family law

It is necessary to consider child abuse in the context of family law and with regard to parental alienation cases. Child abuse is considered as a special issue in family law. It is relevant to mention here because of the high rates of accusation of child abuse made by alienating parents about targeted parents (or extended family members of targeted parents).

In Australia, the Magellan Programme guides the actions of the court in relation to Family Court cases that involve allegations of sexual and physical abuse. The programme is based on a case-management model that allows for the fast-tracking of cases because sexually and physically abused children are considered to be vulnerable and their circumstances require rapid attention (34).

The Magellan Programme involves the following:

- Close judicial management of Magellan cases.
- The early allocation of resources including the early appointment of an ICL.
- Early accessing of information from child protective services.
- Close contact with a team comprising judges, registrars and family consultants and providers of information who are external to the family court.

The particular approach adopted by the Magellan Programme involves the following:

- A cooperative approach between all authorities involved with the family.
- A primary focus on the children involved in the case.
- The proceedings being guided by a judge who will act to maintain the short time frame, with the goal being to complete these cases within a six-month period.
- The ability of the court to make orders for evaluations or investigations by child protective services or Family Court family consultants.
- An ICL appointed for each child with that person's services being legally aided.

Events occur earlier with Magellan cases than with other cases. These events include the following:

- To protect the child before the case comes to trial, interim orders are made.
- A report is ordered from the child protection agency seeking the following information:
    - Whether there is an intention to intervene in this matter;
    - Whether there have been any earlier investigations in relation to this child or the parents;
    - Whether a conclusion has been reached following the investigation and the basis for the conclusion;
    - Recommendations or any other information that might be considered to be relevant.
- A subpoena is ordered to obtain relevant case material from the child protection agency.
- The appointment of an ICL is ordered.
- A family report is ordered from a family consultant with the aim of determining family dynamics and the child's needs.

Evaluation of the Magellan programme found that the cases were being managed more quickly, that there were fewer court appearances, cases were resolving early, and fewer cases were returning to the court as a result of problems with the orders (34).

Although effective in processing cases and acting on decisions in cases of the abuse of children, it is evident that these processes additionally complicate already complex and difficult cases involving parental alienation. It may fall to the parenting dispute evaluator to provide the court with information about the indicators of genuine versus fabricated allegations of abuse so that appropriate decisions can be made. Despite some authors alleging that parenting dispute evaluators fail to do anything other than misguide the court with biased opinion based on poorly conducted evaluations (7), others recognise that most parenting dispute evaluators do take allegations of abuse seriously and properly investigate these allegations from a psychological point of view (9).

Formulating your opinion

As a parenting dispute evaluator and expert witness, after gathering all the information you are able, and after considering the issues that should be taken into account when conducting parenting dispute evaluations, you must then form an opinion related to the terms of reference you have been provided. In some cases, this will be a straightforward matter. It will be clear to you how to address the terms of reference. However, in other cases, the issues may not be quite so clear cut. Nevertheless, you will be required to formulate a response to the terms of reference.

Formulating a response

In formulating your response, remember that your starting point is that you do not know what is going on in any case. You then gather information, start to form hypotheses and then test these hypotheses.

Biases can infiltrate your response if you abandon this procedure and jump to a conclusion too early in the process of evaluation. This is something that can easily happen when you start undertaking these evaluations and before you have sufficient experience.

Reconciling opposing accounts

You will have to reconcile opposing account provided by the people you interview. After all, if there were no differences in perceived facts or points of view, no parenting dispute would exist. There is no truly objective way of determining truthfulness without corroborating, objective evidence to support one view. In effect, you must rely on your clinical or professional judgment with regard to the weight you are going to give one point of view over another.

It is worth remembering that you are not required to determine fact. You are required to give an account of the opinion you formulated, the basis of that opinion, and why you used some information to form the basis of your opinion but rejected, or partially rejected, other information.

As stated, you will need to rely on your professional or clinical judgment because there is no formula you can apply that will assist in this process. As a guide, you should consider the following when determining the weight given to one piece of information on which you rely in the formulation of your opinion over another piece of information. In no particular order, consider the following:

- The internal consistency of the account.
- The extent to which the account is consistent with other, supporting information.
- The extent to which the account is consistent with what is generally known to be the case as indicated by the psychological literature.
- Whether there is an indication of consistency across time of the account provided.
- Whether the account contains obvious distortions or misinterpretations of the intentions of others.
- The timing of any allegations of wrongdoing by the other party in the account provided that would suggest strategic reinterpretation of events or false allegations of wrongdoing.
- The extent to which the interviewee gave focused, relevant responses to questions posed, even the difficult questions, without need to embellish or evade.

It is essential that these differences be reconciled in the formulation of your opinion. In addition, it is necessary that you give an account in the report you prepare for the court of your reasoning for giving one account more weight than another.

Evidence base for opinion

You have two sources of information that will form the basis of your opinion. These should be your clinical experience and the current empirical literature. Of course, if you give this matter any consideration, you should realise that your clinical experience and the current literature should not really diverge. As an aside, in the same way, your clinical view and the results of psychological testing should be consistent. The results of psychological testing should support your clinical opinions rather than produce surprising new information.

This issue is important. If your clinical opinion is not consistent with the literature base, then you must question on what you are basing your clinical opinion. Remember, just because you believe something to be true, this does not necessarily make it true. Your clinical opinion should be based on an understanding of what the research has offered. This is the foundation of the notion of evidenced-based practice.

Remember your audience

Remember that you are not writing your reports for an audience with a good understanding of psychological issues. Therefore, you must make sure that your reports are understandable given the targeted audience. You may need to explain aspects of your opinion so that the recipient of the report has a clear understanding of what you wish to convey.

Effect of your opinion

You must remember that the opinion you express can have life-changing effects for the families involved in these cases. Parents and children may be separated, and the course of children's lives may be changed. Although you will not carry the burden of the entire responsibility for these potential events, what you have to say contributes, sometimes to a significant degree.

Therefore, you need to be confident that the views that you express can be supported by the information about the family you have available to you and the current empirical literature in relation to the issues that are affecting the families.

Openness to additional information

The best you can do is formulate an opinion on the information you have available to you at the time of formulating that opinion. It is worthwhile making this statement at some point in your report. For example, you might say, "On the basis of the available information, it is my opinion that …".

You are more credible as an expert witness if you are open to the notion that there might be information that you do not yet have available to you that may alter your opinion. This does not mean that you should change your opinion without good cause. However, you need to recognise that your opinion is not a definitive statement of the truth. It is an opinion that is based on available information that may be modified if new information is presented to you.

Cross-examination of opinion

You should be prepared to go to court and be cross-examined about your opinion if you undertake this type of work. This will involve you having to defend the opinions you have formed and included in your report. You have to be sure that the opinions you express are defensible under cross-examination.

Concluding comments

Parenting dispute evaluations are complex assessments that contribute to the body of information presented to the decider of facts, that is the judge or a person who holds a similar position. When you are asked to evaluate cases involving parental alienation, the opinion you form about whether or not parental alienation is affecting a parent–child relationship should be evidence-based with robust information available to support the opinion.

There are many challenges that come with undertaking parenting dispute evaluations. When parental alienation is present, the complexity of the case increases as do the challenges the evaluation presents.

References

1. Saini, M.A. (2008). Evidence base of custody and access evaluations. *Brief Treatment and Crisis Intervention, 8,* 111–129. doi:10.1093/brief-treatment/mhm023
2. Gould, J.W., & Stahl, P.M. (2000). The art and science of child custody evaluations: Integrating clinical and forensic mental health models. *Family and Conciliation Courts Review, 38,* 392–414. doi:10.1111/j.174–1617.2000.tb00581.x

3. Lee, S.M., & Olesen, N.W. (2001). Assessing for alienation in child custody and access evaluations. *Family Court Review, 39,* 282–298. doi:10.1111/j.174–1617.2001.tb00611.x

4. Sanders, L., Geffner, R., Bucky, S., Ribner, N., & Patino, A.J. (2015). A qualitative study of child custody evaluators' beliefs and opinions. *Journal of Child Custody, 12,* 205–230. doi:10.1080/15379418.2015.1120476

5. Viljoen, M., & van Rensburg, E. (2014). Exploring the lived experiences of psychologists working with parental alienation syndrome. *Journal of Divorce and Remarriage, 55,* 253. doi:10.1080/10502556.2014.901833

6. Baker, A.J.L. (2007). Knowledge and attitudes about the parental alienation syndrome: A survey of custody evaluators. *The American Journal of Family Therapy, 35,* 1–19. doi:10.1080/01926180600698368

7. Kleinman, T.G., & Kaplan, P. (2016). Relaxation of rules for science detrimental to children. *Journal of Child Custody, 13,* 72–87. doi:10.1080/15379418.2016.1130596

8. Bow, J.N., Gould, J.W., & Flens, J.R. (2009). Examining parental alienation in child custody cases: A survey of mental health and legal professionals. *The American Journal of Family Therapy, 37,* 127–144. doi:10.1080/01926180801960658.

9. Erard, R.E. (2016). Maybe the sky isn't falling after all: Comment on Kleinman and Kaplan (2016). *Journal of Child Custody, 13,* 88–96. doi:10.1080/15379418.2016.1130597

10. Brennan, C. (2013). Ensuring ethical practice: Guidelines for mental health counselors in private practice. *Journal of Mental Health Counseling, 35,* 245–261. doi:10.17744/mehc.35.3.9706313j4t313397

11. Jennings, L., Sovereign, A., Bottorff, N., Pederson Mussell, M., & Vye, C. (2005). Nine ethical values of master therapists. *Journal of Mental Health Counseling, 27,* 32–47. doi:10.17744/mehc.27.1.lmm8vmdujgev2qhp

12. Blank, G.K., & Ney, T. (2006). The (de)construction of conflict in divorce litigation: A discursive critique of 'parental alienation syndrome' and 'the alienated child'. *Family Court Review, 44,* 135–148. doi:10.1111/j.1744-1617.2006.00072.x

13. Gourley, E.V. III, & Stolberg, A.L. (2000). An empirical investigation of psychologists' custody evaluation procedures. *Journal of Divorce and Remarriage, 33,* 1–29. doi:10.1300/j087v33n01_01

14. Patel, S.H., & Choate, L.H. (2014). Conducting child custody evaluations: Best practices for mental health counselors who are court-appointed. *Journal of Mental Health Counseling, 36,* 18–30. doi:10.17744/mehc.36.1.e00401wv7134w505

15. Hynan, D.J. (1998). Interviewing children in custody evaluations. *Family and Conciliation Courts Review, 36,* 466–478.

16. Warshak, R.A. (2003). Payoffs and pitfalls of listening to children. *Family Relations, 52,* 373–384. doi:10.1111/j.1741-3729.2003.00373.x

17. Sternberg, K.J., Lamb, M.E., Orbach, Y., Esplin, P.W., & Mitchell, S. (2001). Use of a structured investigative protocol enhances young children's responses to free recall prompts in the course of forensic interviews. *Journal of Applied Psychology, 86,* 997–1005. doi:10.1037//0021-9010.86.5.997

18. Hynan, D.J. (2006). Scientific considerations in observing how children interact with parents. *Forensic Examiner, 15,* 42–47.

19. Saini, M., & Polak, S. (2014). Observations: A review of empirical evidence related to custody evaluations. *Journal of Child Custody, 11,* 181–201. doi:10.1080/15379418.2014.953661

20. Kruk, E. (2011). A model equal parental responsibility presumption in contested child custody. *The American Journal of Family Therapy, 39,* 375. doi:10.1080/01926187.2011.575341

21. O'Connell, M.E. (2009). Mandated custody evaluations and the limits of judicial power. *Family Court Review, 47,* 304. doi:10.1111/j.1744-1617.2009.01256.x

22. Woodhouse, B.B. (1999). Child custody in the age of children's rights: The search for a just and workable standard. *Family Law Quarterly, 33,* 815–832.

23. Firestone, G., & Weinstein, J. (2004). In the best interests of children: A proposal to transform the adversarial system. *Family Court Review, 42,* 203–215. doi:10.1177/1531244504422003

24. Tippins, T.M., & Wittmann, J.P. (2005). Empirical and ethical problems with custody recommendations: A call for clinical humility and judicial vigilance. *Family Court Review, 43*, 193–222. doi:0.1111/j.1744-1617.2005.00019.x

25. Whiteside, M.F. (1998). Custody for children age 5 and younger. *Family and Conciliation Courts Review, 36,* 479–502. doi:10.1111/j.174–1617.1998.tb01092.x

26. Amato, P.R., & Sobolewski, J.M. (2004). The effects of divorce on fathers and children: Nonresidential fathers and stepfathers. In M.E. Lamb (Ed.), *The role of the father in child development* (4th ed.). pp.341–363. New York: Wiley.

27. Peters, B. & Ehrenberg, M.F. (2008). The influence of parental separation and divorce on father–child relationships. *Journal of Divorce and Remarriage, 49,* 78–109. doi:10.1080/10502550801973005

28. Sandler, I., Miles, J., Cookston, J., & Braver, S. (2008). Effects of father and mother parenting on children's mental health in high- and low-conflict divorces. *Family Court Review, 46,* 282–296. Doi:10.111/j.1744-1617.2008.00201.x

29. Nielsen, L. (2011). Shared parenting after divorce: A review of shared residential parenting research. *Journal of Divorce and Remarriage, 52,* 586–609. doi:10.1080/10502556.2011.619913

30. Bauserman, R. (2002). Child adjustment in joint-custody versus sole-custody arrangements: A meta-analytic review. *Journal of Family Psychology, 16,* 91–102. doi:10.1037//0893-3200.16.1.91

31. Gunnoe, M.L., & Braver, S.L. (2001). The effects of joint legal custody on mothers, fathers, and children controlling for factors that predispose a sole maternal versus joint legal. *Law and Human Behavior, 25,* 25–43. doi:10.1023/a:1005687825155

32. Kruk, E. (2005). Shared parental responsibility: A harm reduction-based approach to divorce law reform. *Journal of Divorce and Remarriage, 43,* 119–140. doi:10.1300/j087v43n03_07

33. Mcintosh, J., & Chisholm, R. (2008). Cautionary notes on the shared care of children in conflicted parental separation. *Journal of Family Studies, 14,* 37–52. doi:10.5172/jfs.327.14.1.37

34. Higgins, D.J. (2007). *Cooperation and coordination: An evaluation of the Family Court of Australia's Magellan case-management model.* Canberra: Family Court of Australia.

Part Five

Intervention with alienated families

Chapter Seventeen

The need for intervention

Introduction

Psychological intervention is a therapeutic approach underpinned by psychological theory and methods. The aim of psychological intervention is to improve psychological functioning or well-being in the recipients of the intervention. It should be evidence-based and provided within the structure of a therapeutic relationship between the practitioner and recipient of the intervention.

Psychological intervention can take different forms depending on the theory on which it is based. It can include elements of supportive counselling as well as providing psychoeducation about the intervention recipients' difficulties. Within the context of parental alienation, the goal of psychological intervention includes re-establishing the relationship between the child and targeted parent by addressing any psychological processes that hinder the reunification, establishing a co-parenting relationship where it is possible to do so and helping the intervention recipient manage and resolve any psychological distress experienced as a consequence of family dysfunction and separation. Psychological intervention can include any or all family members of the alienated family.

As discussed in Chapter Fifteen, it is most often the case that court decisions result in the alienated child being left in the primary care of the alienating parent. Sometimes this decision includes an order or recommendation for therapeutic intervention or no therapeutic intervention at all. The arguments for and against therapeutic intervention in cases of parental alienation have been debated in the literature. In this chapter, the utility of psychological intervention in parental alienation cases is discussed.

To intervene or not to intervene? What does the research say?

Within the literature there has been much commentary on how best to intervene in cases of parental alienation. Arguments against intervening in cases of parental alienation are based on the notion that intervening could cause further harm to the child or, at best, provide no benefit to the child and/or family. Some believe that if the child appears to be functioning well in other aspects of their life, such as in school and with peers, intervention is not required. Some also argue that intervention will be futile if the alienated child is an adolescent who exhibits resistance to change. Others believe that leaving the child in the care of the alienating parent is enough because of the belief that this will end the child's exposure to interparental conflict (1–3). Further, there is a concern that there is insufficient evidence supporting the benefit of existing intervention programmes resulting in a reluctance to recommend any existing programmes.

alienating parent and shared care is possible as long as there are strict visitation schedules and court sanctions that are applied for non-compliance. One of these sanctions needs to be change of primary parental responsibility to the targeted parent if the alienating parent cannot facilitate contact.

Psychological intervention in these cases may follow an integrative family therapy approach as described by Lebow and Rekart (8). This approach involves the therapist using systemic and individual therapeutic techniques to help the family adjust to the new post-divorce environment and establish a new family structure where the parents can maintain distance from each other and minimise conflict and triangulation. Therapy sessions may not follow the typical weekly sessions in the therapy room.

In severe cases of parental alienation, the alienating parent uses deliberate and targeted strategies to sever the targeted parent–child relationship. The child refuses all contact with the targeted parent and is vehement in their rejection of the targeted parent (9). In such cases, transfer of the child to living with the targeted parent is necessary to ameliorate the alienation (6–7). The targeted parent and child need to attend a specialised intervention programme to support the change in living arrangements. To ensure the alienating parent cannot sabotage this intervention, a no-contact period is necessary between the alienating parent and child. During this period, the alienating parent must make gains in their own therapy by demonstrating insight into their behaviour and willingness to support the child having a relationship with the targeted parent. After the no-contact period has ended and assuming therapeutic gains have been made, a visitation schedule with the alienating parent and child can be implemented.

All intervention programmes described in the literature are centred on providing each involved family member with psychoeducation. The aims of these programmes are to: (a) protect children from further harm caused by parental alienation; (b) improve the child's critical thinking skills and psychological wellbeing; (c) improve the targeted parent–child relationship; and (d) strengthen family communication and boundaries within the new family structure (6).

Specific intervention programmes have been described in the literature. In the next section, each of the intervention programmes will be described along with the evidence base for them. We acknowledge that there are other programmes being conducted around the world. However, the focus here is on programmes where there is published data pertaining to their efficacy.

The evidence for interventions

The most well-known programme for severe parental alienation is the Family Bridges Programme for Alienated Children and Families (FBAC). FBAC was first developed and delivered in the US and is now offered in Canada, South Africa and Australia. FBAC is an evidence-based programme that uses psychoeducation and experiential learning to repair the relationship between severely alienated children (including adolescents) and targeted parents. When a court determines that it is in the best interest of a child to have a relationship with the parent they have unreasonably rejected and the alienation is severe enough to warrant a change of living arrangements for the child, the court can order the family attend FBAC to support the transfer of residence.

FBAC includes a structured four-day workshop for the child and targeted parent. The workshops occur on four consecutive days and the content is based on scientifically validated psychological constructs. Following the workshops, the child and targeted parent are required to take a vacation together in order to consolidate the changes made and strengthen their relationship. FBAC aims to prepare children to live with the parent they have rejected and improve the quality of the targeted parent–child relationship.

FBAC also includes a mandatory period of time in which the alienating parent must have no contact with the child. During this time, the alienating parent is required to attend the Aftercare Programme (ACP). The ACP is delivered by different facilitators to the ones delivering the four-day FBAC workshop. The aim of the ACP is to protect the relationship between the targeted parent and child and educate the alienating parent about their behaviour and provide them with an opportunity to make changes that will enable the child to have a relationship with both parents.

Research has shown that FBAC produces significant improvement in targeted parent–child relationships (10–11). Further, the majority of children who have participated in the workshop rated the experience positively and reported that they were treated with kindness and respect throughout the workshop (11).

The Overcoming Barriers Family Camp (OBFC) is another residential programme involving a five-day, overnight family camp. OBFC includes all family members within the new family structure post-separation. This may include any step-parents and step-siblings. The programme consists of psychoeducation about the impact of high conflict family separation on children and the importance of children having both parents in their lives. Families also participate in therapeutic intervention tailored to the needs of the family. Therapeutic interventions may consist of individual sessions, sessions with different combinations of family members as well as whole of family sessions. Children are taught critical thinking skills and parents are taught effective co-parenting skills. The camp is experiential, and it is facilitated by a team of professionals. Participation in the camp requires a court mandate. Programme evaluation data indicate that participants are satisfied with the intervention. However, it may not reduce the incidence of alienating behaviours in all families (12). Further published data are needed to establish the efficacy of this programme.

The Family Reflections Reunification Programme (FRRP) is another residential programme that was initially based on FBAC and OBFC. The goals of this programme are the same as the others previously mentioned. The components of FRRP include the child and their siblings attending a retreat while having no contact with the alienating parent. During this retreat, the children are provided with psychoeducation to prepare them for reunification with the targeted parent. The targeted parent also attends the retreat and works with a psychologist to prepare them for reunification before the parent and child come together to engage in experiential activities. Following this the parent and child share large living quarters and share a celebration chosen by the child before leaving the retreat. While this occurs, the alienating parent is required to engage in counselling with a certified FRRP practitioner. When the child and targeted parent leave the retreat, both parents and the child are required to engage in an aftercare programme tailored to the needs of the family to support the maintenance of their relationship. FRRP requires a court order and an order for a non-contact period between the child and alienating parent for the duration of the retreat. Preliminary research has shown that the majority of children who complete the programme re-establish and maintain a relationship with the targeted parent (13). An important observation from this study is that separation from the alienating parent was not harmful to children.

Residential intervention programmes can provide a swift and effective solution to moderate and severe cases of parental alienation when other interventions have been unsuccessful. Residential programmes come at a high financial cost to parents at a time when their financial resources already may be depleted due to the expensive nature of ongoing litigation. The cost of residential programmes may be prohibitive to many parents.

One non-residential programme is Parallel Group Therapy. Parallel Group Therapy consists of 16 90-minute group sessions for children and their parents delivered over 16 weeks. Children and parents participate in separate groups that run in parallel with each other. The parent groups consist of equal numbers of alienating and targeted parents. Ex-couples do not participate in the same group. The groups involve psychoeducation, cognitive-behavioural interventions, interpersonal skills and coping strategies. The groups are structured but allow flexibility to address the specific needs of the group. At the conclusion of the programme, participants experience a reduction in anxiety, improved mood and greater cooperation between parents (14).

Another intervention delivered in the therapy room is the Multimodal Family Intervention (MMFI). MMFI involves mental health and legal practitioners working collaboratively with the alienated family. Therapy may be delivered by a single mental health practitioner who can enlist other practitioners as needed. It includes all involved family members and it can be conducted with and without a court mandate. This intervention incorporates case management, psychoeducation, individual therapy and family therapy. The programme aims to teach the family about the impact family separation has on children, provide coping skills and teach critical thinking skills. The ultimate goal of MMFI is to restore the relationship between the targeted parent and child and achieve an appropriate co-parenting relationship. With this approach, the practitioner needs to develop a therapeutic relationship with both parents and the children and work with them concurrently. It is a structured approach that allows sufficient flexibility to ensure the particular needs of the family are met. This programme can lead to a reduction in alienating behaviours and an increase in the time the child spends with the targeted parent (15).

Consequences of no intervention

The long-term outcomes for alienated children have been well documented in the literature involving adults' reports of their alienation experience as a child. As seen in Chapter Eight, adults who were alienated from a parent during childhood experience negative psychological consequences. Parental alienation can result in the child internalising a sense of worthlessness and conditional value that continues into adulthood. Loss of self-confidence, low self-esteem, anxiety, depression, substance abuse and difficulty trusting others as a consequence of parental alienation have been reported by adults who have been alienated from a parent (16–20). These are the consequences for children if there is no intervention.

Consequences of no intervention for targeted parents are similarly serious. Targeted parents grieve for the loss of their child and for the loss of their parenting role. Targeted parents experience helplessness, anxiety, depression and suicidal thoughts. An increased risk of suicide among targeted parents has been reported (21–23).

Box 17.1 Targeted parent: This is the most terrifying, painful, defeating, hopeless thing I have ever experienced. Nothing will ever replace the huge whole in my heart for my kids and the precious years I have missed. I fear that my children will never come back to me. I fear that it may be something they will never be able to overcome. It will likely be something that will haunt them for the rest of their lives.

When there is no intervention for parental alienation, the child and targeted parent are faced with the real likelihood that their relationship is lost forever. Without intervention spontaneous reunification is possible but it is a difficult process that rarely leads to a happy family reunion (24). Spontaneous reunification can be motivated by a crisis about which the child, who has typically reached adulthood, needs to approach the targeted parent (25). The reunification process is difficult because it can be hindered by a number of factors. These include the alienating parent sabotaging reunification efforts, the targeted parent not being psychologically ready to respond empathically and patiently to the child and the difficult reunification process, and the child's expectations of the targeted parent not being met (24–25). Below is the conundrum an adult child might face during the reunification process when there is no intervention to facilitate it.

Box 17.2 Adult alienated child: You're constantly evaluating: "Should I or shouldn't I?" "Can I or can't I?" "What does this mean?" "What's the ulterior motive here?" "Is this genuine? Is this not genuine?" Decades later I still have this conflict in my head – "Do I or don't I?"

Concluding comments

When faced with the seemingly intractable complexity of parental alienation it can be easy to assume that leaving the child with the parent they express as their preferred parent is the best outcome. Leaving the child with the alienating parent with or without some form of traditional therapy for the child does not lead to the best outcome psychologically for children. Leaving the child in the care of the alienating parent is tantamount to leaving the child with an abusive parent. This is unacceptable when there are evidence-based intervention programmes that are effective when coupled with court mandates and sanctions for non-compliance. In the next chapter, best practice guidelines for working with alienated families will be described.

References

1. Bala, N., Hunt, S., & McCarney, C. (2010). Parental alienation: Canadian court cases 1989 2008. *Family Court Review, 48,* 164–179. doi:10.1111/j.1744-1617.2009.01296.x
2. Jaffe, P.G., Ashbourne, D., & Mamo, A.A. (2010). Early identification and prevention of parent–child alienation: A framework for balancing risks and benefits of intervention. *Family Court Review, 48,* 136–152. doi:10.1111/j.1744-1617.2009.01294.x
3. Warshak, R.A. (2015). Poisoning parent–child relationships through the manipulation of names. *The American Journal of Family Therapy, 43,* 4.
4. Dunne, J., & Hedrick, M. (1994). The parental alienation syndrome: An analysis of sixteen selected cases. *Journal of Divorce and Remarriage, 21,* 21–38. doi: 10.1300/J087v21n03_02
5. Rand, D., Rand, R., & Kopetski, L. (2005). The spectrum of parental alienation syndrome part III: The Kopestski follow-up study. *American Journal of Forensic Psychology, 23,* 15–43.
6. Templer, K., Matthewson, M., Haines, J., & Cox, G. (2017). Recommendations for best practice in response to parental alienation: findings from a systematic review. *Journal of Family Therapy, 39,* 103–122. doi:10.1111/1467–6427.12137
7. Gardner, R.A. (2001). Should courts order PAS children to visit/reside with the alienated parent? A follow up study. *American Journal of Forensic Psychology, 19,* 61–106.
8. Lebow, J., & Rekart, K.N. (2007). Integrative family therapy for high-conflict divorce with disputes over child custody and visitation. *Family process, 46,* 79–91. doi:10.1111/j.1545-5300.2006.00193.x
9. Gardner, R.A. (1998). Recommendations for dealing with parents who induce a parental alienation syndrome in their children. *Journal of Divorce and Remarriage, 28,* 1–23. doi:10.1300/J087v28n03_01
10. Warshak, R.A. (2010). Family bridges: Using insights from social science to reconnect parents and alienated children. *Family Court Review, 48,* 48–80. doi:10.1111/j.1744-1617.2009.01288.x
11. Warshak, A.A. (2018). Reclaiming parent–child relationships: Outcomes of family bridges with alienated children. *Journal of Divorce and Remarriage, online first.* doi:10.1080/10502556.2018.1529505

12. Sullivan, M.J., Ward, P.A. & Deutsch, R.M. (2010). Overcoming Barriers Family Camp: A program for high-conflict divorced families where a child is resisting contact with a parent. *Family Court Review, 48,* 116–135. doi:10.1111/j.1744-1617.2009.01293.x

13. Reay, K.M. (2015). Family reflections: A promising therapeutic programmes designed to treat severely alienated children and their family system. *The American Journal of Family Therapy, 43,* 197–207. doi:10.1080/01926187.2015.1007769

14. Toren, P., Bregman, B.L., Zohar-Reich, E., Ben-Amitay, G., Wolmer, L. et al. (2013). Sixteen-session group treatment for children and adolescents with parental alienation and their parents. *The American Journal of Family Therapy, 41,* 187. doi:10.1080/01926187.2012.677651

15. Friedlander, S., & Walters, M.G. (2010). When a child rejects a parent: Tailoring the intervention to fit the problem. *Family Court Review, 48,* 98–111. doi:10.1111/j.1744-1617.2009.01291.x

16. Baker, A.J.L. (2005a). The long-term effects of parental alienation on adult children: A qualitative research study. *The American Journal of Family Therapy, 33,* 289–302. doi:10.1080/01926180590962129

17. Baker, A.J.L. (2005b). Parental alienation strategies: A qualitative study of adults who experienced parental alienation as a child. *American Journal of Forensic Psychology, 23,* 1–23.

18. Baker, A.J.L. (2006). Patterns of parental alienation syndrome: A qualitative study of adults who were alienated from a parent as a child. *The American Journal of Family Therapy, 34,* 63–78. doi:10.1080/01926180500301444

19. Baker, A.J.L., & Verrocchio, M.C. (2016). Exposure to parental alienation and subsequent anxiety and depression in Italian adults. *The American Journal of Family Therapy, 44,* 255–271. doi:10.1080/01926187.2016.1230480

20. Godbout, E., & Parent, C. (2012). The life paths and lived experiences of adults who have experienced parental alienation: A retrospective study. *Journal of Divorce and Remarriage, 53,* 34. doi:10.1080/10502556.2012.635967

21. Balmer, S., Matthewson, M., & Haines, J. (2017). Parental alienation: Targeted parent perspective. *Australian Journal of Psychology,* 1–8. doi:10.1111/ajpy.12159

22. Poustie, C., Matthewson, M., & Balmer, S. (2018). The forgotten parent: The targeted parent perspective of parental alienation. *Journal of Family Issues, 39,* 3298–3323. doi:10.1177/0192513x18777867

23. Baker, A.J.L., & Fine, P.R. (2014). *Surviving parental alienation: A journey of hope and healing.* Lanham, Maryland: Rowman & Littlefield.

24. Ward, S. (2016). *Reunification of alienated parents and their adult children: A qualitative investigation.* (Master's thesis, University of Tasmania, Hobart, Australia).

25. Darnall, D., & Steinberg, B.F. (2008). Motivational models for spontaneous reunification with the alienated child: Part I. *American Journal of Family Therapy, 36,* 107–115. doi:10.1080/01926180701643131

Chapter Eighteen

Family therapy and beyond

Introduction

Many practitioners can feel daunted by the task of helping the alienated family. Some practitioners feel so overwhelmed and helpless by these families that they choose not to intervene. Instead, they claim it is best for the child to be left with the alienating parent without any further therapy because the child has had enough therapy already. It is important to remember the helplessness felt by a practitioner daunted by the challenge of intervening in an alienation case is nothing like the helplessness felt by an alienated child. It is this understanding of the experience of the child that drives some practitioners to do what they ethically can to end the alienation campaign.

It is unsurprising that many practitioners recommend no further actions for alienated families when there is an absence of clear published guidelines for working with parental alienation cases. However, despite the intractable nature of parental alienation, intervention is comparatively straightforward once the practitioner knows how to go about it.

As we saw in Chapter Seventeen, a number of intervention programmes have been described in the literature, all of which have carefully designed protocols that are based on the available research findings about parental alienation and behaviour change principles. Although there are some differences in these intervention programmes, they all share the same goal and essential ingredients to achieve this goal. In this chapter, the essential components needed in intervention programmes for parental alienation and how practitioners can intervene in mild–severe cases of parental alienation are explored. It is beyond the scope of this chapter to provide a step-by-step intervention guide. However, examples of how to go about particular aspects of intervention are provided.

The essential ingredients

> **Box 18.1 A common story:** Elizabeth's parents separated when she was eight years old. After that she lived with her mother most of the time and she saw her father for five days every fortnight. As her parents continued to dispute Elizabeth's living arrangements and the division of their assets in the Family Court, Elizabeth increasingly had difficulty separating from her mother at handovers. By the time she was nine years old she refused to spend time with her father without a clear reason for this decision. By the time she was 11 years old Elizabeth had seen three different psychologists in an attempt to address her contact refusal. The last psychologist attempted family therapy, which resulted in Elizabeth spending no time with her father. Eventually, the family saw a family consultant for an assessment. The

family consultant determined that parental alienation was occurring. Because Elizabeth expressed that it was her preference to live with her mother and not see her father, the family consultant recommended Elizabeth live with her mother and see her father when she chooses. Because Elizabeth had already seen three psychologists and she was adamant she would not see another, no further psychological intervention was recommended. The matter went to trial and the magistrate made orders that were consistent with the family consultant's recommendations. Elizabeth continued to live with her mother and did not see her father.

This scenario is all too common. This outcome may appear to be in the child's best interest because it is consistent with her apparent views and, on the surface, offers no further disruption to the child's life. As we have seen in previous chapters, this outcome could result in the worst long-term consequences for Elizabeth. With the right intervention, Elizabeth could maintain a relationship with her mother and father and have better long-term outcomes.

Consideration should be given to how Elizabeth's situation could have been managed. Traditional forms of therapy are ineffective in resolving parental alienation and repeated experiences with traditional therapy will only compound parental alienation. Interventions for parental alienation are specialised programmes and, despite the variety of programmes available, they all include specific strategies.

Psychoeducation

The central component of interventions for parental alienation is psychoeducation for all members of the alienated family. Family members need to learn about the nature of the intervention and what is required of them in terms of engagement. It is important the boundaries and expectations of any intervention are set early. Asking family members to enter into a contract that clearly outlines the nature of these expectations and intervention goals is particularly useful. Such contracts should be written in clear language and in age-appropriate language for children and teenagers. Family members can decline to enter into these contacts. However, they need to be informed of the possible consequences of declining. These consequences are discussed later in the chapter.

All family members should receive psychoeducation about parental alienation, as well as the impact of parental alienation and inter-parental conflict on children. Psychoeducation needs to be delivered in a respectful and face-saving manner so that no family member feels judged or shamed.

Children can benefit from learning more about the impact inter-parental conflict and parental alienation has on children's wellbeing. This acts to normalise their emotional experiences in response to the exceptional circumstances with which they are faced. Learning about the processes used when a parent attempts to control a child and how false memories can develop is also useful. It is vital that this information is provided in a face-saving and non-confrontational way. Children can respond well to psychoeducation being presented through the use of audio-visual media and/or casual conversation in a manner that is not personalised but highly relevant to their experience. This will allow children to digest the information in a face-saving way while making the connections between the information and their experience themselves, thus minimising resistance.

Box 18.2 Alienated child: I really don't understand what's happened. It's really confusing.

Psychologist: Would it help if I told you what I think has been happening to you and your family?

Alienated child: Yes. I'd like to know. My mum always told me not to trust you. She says such awful things about you, but none of them are true. You're the only one who helped us, so I'd like to know what you think.

Psychologist: I'll tell you what I've observed, and you tell me if you think it fits with your experience.

Alienated child: Ok.

Psychologist: When your parents separated, everyone in your family struggled to cope with that. When families breakup it's understandably hard for everyone. Your Mum especially had trouble adjusting afterwards. Up until that point your Mum was a wife and mother. When being a wife changed, she did everything she could to hang on to her role as your mother. So, your Mum did all kinds of thing to try and push your Dad out of her life and your life because she thought that would make it easier. When your Dad made it clear he was going to remain in your life, your Mum felt threatened by this. As your parents continued to fight over where you should live, your Mum did more and more things to push your Dad away.

Alienated child: Yeah. She said Dad was violent. She kept saying it over and over. She told us we had to say he was violent. At the time I knew he wasn't but I kind of came to believe it at the same time. It's hard to explain how you can know one thing and believe something else.

Psychologist: It's been really difficult for you being in the middle of Mum and Dad fighting. Understandably, it's been very confusing for you. Despite all of the information to the contrary, your Mum came to believe your Dad was dangerous and she thought he might hurt you. When someone you love and trust believes this, it's easy for them to convince you of the same. In fact, there's even been research showing how easy it is to convince people events happened in their lives that never happened. This research was with adults and they came to believe made-up stories about their lives from the researchers. So, if researchers can do this with adults, parents can do this with their children. Your Mum believed your Dad was dangerous and you came to share this belief with her.

Alienated child: Wow. That's amazing. And a bit scary.

Psychologist: The good thing is you were able to separate a belief about your Dad from the reality of your Dad. Now you're able to have your Mum and Dad in your life.

Alienated child: Yes. It isn't always easy because Mum still believes Dad is the most dangerous person on the planet.

Psychologist: You've been able to spend a lot of time with your Dad to be able to form your own view of him. Because your Mum and Dad had a different relationship, a husband and wife relationship, it's different for your Mum. She may continue to feel hurt for years to come by the losses she felt when your family separated. She's unlikely to spend time with your Dad now and consider information that contradicts her view of him.

Alienated child: Yeah, but now I know this I don't have to keep feeling like I have to convince her that dad's ok.

Psychologist: That's right. That isn't your job. Your job is to enjoy having Mum and Dad in your life and stay away from any lingering conflict they might have with each other. When you're a child or teenager, it's hard work being in the middle of two parents who can't agree on anything. You've done your time with that hard work.

> **Alienated child:** Now I just have to figure out how I handle my 18th birthday party. I know I can't have Mum and Dad there at the same time.
>
> **Psychologist:** Well, let's see what solution we can figure out for this dilemma.

The teenager in this scenario had been alienated from her father for most of her childhood until she was reunified with her father following a court order for this to happen. Her mother exhibited borderline and narcissistic personality traits and experienced narcissistic injury and an abnormal grief reaction when family separation occurred. She came to believe her ex-husband posed a risk of harm to her children and made allegations against her ex-husband to that effect. By the time reunification was ordered, the teenager in this scenario was moderately alienated from her father. Reunification was swift. This conversation occurred shortly after reunification. The practitioner was careful to speak about the alienating parent in a respectful way and information provided was based on a thorough assessment of the family and knowledge gained from scientific research. The practitioner made it clear to the teenager that this was an opinion and invited her to decide for herself if this opinion was consistent with her experience.

Targeted parents can benefit from understanding more about the alienation process their child has been experiencing. This can help them to separate their child from their child's rejecting behaviours. Targeted parents also can benefit from learning effective coping skills and assertive communication skills. These skills will help them to better respond to any future alienating behaviours they may encounter without engaging in further triangulation with their child. Targeted parents can learn better ways to respond to any provocative or contemptuous behaviour the alienating parent or the child may continue to demonstrate. Effective co-parenting skills are essential including how to co-parent on a 'needs-to' basis with an uncooperative parent.

> **Box 18.3 Targeted parent:** She's just so rude to me. I don't understand how the little girl I raised and was so close to can be such a nasty piece of work. She yells at me, deliberately defies me and, if I hear her tell me she hates me one more time, I'm done. She can go back to her mother's. I can't do this anymore. I don't understand it. She's starting to sound just like her mother when we used to argue.
>
> **Psychologist:** Seeing your daughter so angry is distressing and it's confusing when she directs her anger at you. It's really important to separate your daughter from her behaviour and understand where her behaviour is coming from. She's still the girl you raised. Just like you, she's hurt, confused and afraid.
>
> **Targeted parent:** Yes. Of course she is. She must feel at least ten times worse than me because she's just a child. But I don't understand why she's turned on me. She was always Daddy's little girl. I never hurt her. I wasn't even the one who left. It was my ex-wife who walked out. She walked out on our daughter, too, but my daughter hates me. It doesn't make sense.
>
> **Psychologist:** When parents separate, and that separation is as difficult as yours, children really struggle with that. Your daughter's life as she knew it was tipped upside down. That's hard for a child to adjust to. She has seen her parents unable to agree on anything and that upheaval takes its toll on children. They feel caught in the middle of the two people they love the most in the world and there's nothing they can do to stop the conflict. So, they develop a loyalty conflict. They want Mum to be happy, so they tell her things they think Mum wants to hear. And they want Dad to be happy, so they tell Dad things they think he

wants to hear. Then, when one parent, in this case your daughter's mum, starts to form an unhealthy alliance with their child, their loyalty conflict reaches crisis point and they feel forced to choose. Eventually, the pressure to choose builds up and children will reduce the stress by siding with one parent. This parent is usually the one where the consequences of rejecting them are higher than the consequences of rejecting the other.

Targeted parent: Oh, and my ex-wife makes our daughter choose. It isn't immediately obvious, but it's clear in what she says and doesn't say that our daughter has to pick her as the only one who cares for her. I just don't understand how my daughter can believe all the horrible things she's been told about me. Surely she knows I'm not the way her mother says.

Psychologist: If you think that adults can easily come to believe the distorted view of cult leaders, then it's easy for children to come to believe what isn't true from their parent. Research has shown just how easy it is to plant false memories into perfectly healthy, well-adjusted adults, so it's just as easy to do this with children.

In this conversation, a targeted parent struggles to understand the behaviour of their child. The psychologist empathises with them and then reminds the targeted parent to separate their loved child from their behaviour. Reminding the targeted parent about the difficult position their child is in is distressing for the targeted parent, but necessary. It helps the targeted parent to look beyond their child's rejection of them to fully appreciate the predicament their child is facing. The conversation is handled with respect for the targeted parent, child and alienating parent and the information provided is evidence-based. The conversation can continue to explore the reasons why alienating parents are motivated to behave in this way. This insight can help targeted parents to change the way they respond to their child's behaviour and the alienating parent's behaviour.

In mild to moderate cases of parental alienation, alienating parents may benefit from learning about children's psychosocial developmental processes and how alienating behaviours and interparental conflict can negatively impact this development. It is important for alienating parents to learn about different parenting styles after separation and their impact on children's development. This can lead to useful discussions about the benefits of parallel parenting or co-parenting, whichever parenting style is more realistic for the family. If an alienating parent has a diagnosed mental health condition, including a personality disorder, this also needs to be considered and addressed in individual therapy separate from family-related work.

Box 18.4 Psychologist: There are four broad styles of parenting after family separation. The first one is cooperative parenting. These parents have low levels of conflict between them and they can get along for the benefit of their children despite their differences. This type of post-separation parenting has the best outcomes for children and it's the type of parenting children say they want after their parents separate.

Alienating parent: That's just not possible with her. Cooperative parenting is a pipedream, I'm afraid.

Psychologist: The next style is parallel parenting. These parents find a way to have parallel homes for their children to go back and forth between. Both parents have limited contact with each other and as a result have low or no conflict with each other. The parents and children accept there are different rules in the two homes and the children are free from having to deal with their parents' disagreements.

Alienating parent: The children wouldn't cope with this situation. I just can't trust her to parent properly. The children won't know where they are. It'll be far too confusing for them …

Psychologist: Psychologists have been researching this very topic for a long time now and have found that children can cope very well going between two homes and they can cope with different rules in each home. It's exposure to conflict between parents and inconsistency in rules within one home children struggle with. Let's look at the next two parenting styles before we talk more about this. There's the mixed style. This group of parents have little to do with each other but, when they do, they argue and they don't care if they do this in front of the children.

Alienating parent: I can't help it if she picks a fight in front of the children.

Psychologist: Regardless of who starts the fight and who ends it, this type of parenting is not good for children because children exposed to their parents fighting develop problems such as anxiety, anger, depression. The fourth style is called the parental alienation group. This group of parents can't stand each other.

Alienating parent: I'm not vindictive. I've never suggested I can't stand her. I just don't trust her.

Psychologist: This group of parents can't agree on anything and they wish the other parent would go away because they think this would end the agony. Their desire for the other parent to go away can become so strong that they start doing things to try and push the other parent out of their lives. This type of parenting is associated with very poor outcomes for children because not only are children exposed to their parents fighting, they suffer the loss of a parent. From all of the information I have about your family, I can see this is the parenting style happening here and the court has made an order for you to see me to change this. If you want the best outcomes for your children's psychological health, and I'm sure you do, this is your chance to make changes. Cooperatively co-parenting is the ideal situation, but you've shown already that this might be unrealistic at this stage. While I'd like to see your family reach this goal, the parallel parenting style is a more realistic option. Parallel parenting involves low levels of engagement with the children's mother and low levels of conflict. Your children don't need to see or hear the conflict anymore.

In this conversation with an alienating parent, the psychologist provides information about different parenting styles and the emotional outcomes for children of each one. The information provided to the alienating parent is based on science with reference to this fact being made. When the alienating parent tries to derail the conversation or shows signs of resistance, the psychologist remains on track by bringing the conversation back to the topic of parenting styles. When the alienating parent tries to argue against the most realistic parenting style for their family, the psychologist challenges their argument with information while remaining focused on the goal of the conversation, not with further argument. In this conversation, the therapist uses the term parental alienation. However, some therapists prefer not to use this term because they are concerned the term is divisive.

If the alienation is severe, the nature of the work with the alienating parent is directive and educative, and, in essence, it is crisis management because their behaviour is abusive in nature. It is vital that alienating parents are clear on the expectations for their behaviour and the goals they need to meet and the consequences for not meeting these. Without such a contract and without set consequences for not meeting expectations and goals, alienating parents in severe cases will derail the intervention. To this end, the example, the conversation between the alienating parent and psychologist seen in this chapter would need to be far more directive and supported by court orders that stipulate clear consequences for non-compliance and no behaviour change towards the preferred parenting style outlined.

Critical thinking

All members of the alienated family can benefit from learning critical thinking skills, but this is particularly important for alienated children. It is essential the alienated child be exposed to information that counteracts their irrational beliefs about the targeted parent. This is best achieved experientially. In intervention programmes delivered via camps or retreats, the child spends an extended amount of time with the targeted parent where they can see them as not 'all bad'.

In workshops or interventions delivered from the practitioner's office, the alienated child can spend time with the targeted parent engaged in shared activities. Initially, these shared activities should be engineered and facilitated by the practitioner and then continued without the practitioner being present. As the contact between the child and targeted parent continues, the practitioner can use cognitive restructuring and solution-focused strategies with the child to address any cognitive distortions associated with parental alienation. This approach can be considered an adaptation of cognitive behavioural therapy applied to cognitive distortions seen in parental alienation. Children can benefit from learning about different unhelpful thinking styles, such as black and white thinking commonly associated with parental alienation. How unhelpful thinking styles can drive emotions and behaviour should be discussed and strategies for identifying and challenging these should be taught. Children should also be taught assertive communication skills.

Box 18.5 Alienated child: It's really good with my Mum. It's relaxed and easy. At John's house it's stressful and there was this one time John only fed me instant noodles. I always eat properly at Mum's. She never feeds me instant noodles.

Psychologist: I notice you call your dad John. Tell me about that?

Alienated child: Well … John hasn't been much of a father to me. I see my stepdad as more of a father. He's kind and generous. I know John doesn't really care about me. He says he does but it's a lie.

Psychologist: Do you believe your Dad doesn't care about you?

Alienated child: Yes. I know he doesn't.

Psychologist: How do you know this?

Alienated child: He stresses us out because he's always there.

Psychologist: Who's us?

Alienated child: Us is me and Mum.

Psychologist: When you say your Dad is always there, what do you mean by that?

Alienated child: Well … there was this one time when he turned up at my school unannounced.

Psychologist: Your Dad turned up at school. How come?

Alienated child: It was my birthday. He brought me some presents and sat with me. It was stressful because we didn't know he was coming.

Psychologist: Who's we?

Alienated child: Me and mum.

Psychologist: Was your mum there, too?

> **Alienated child:** No. She saw the presents when I took them home.
>
> **Psychologist:** Your Dad came to see you on your birthday and gave you birthday presents. I'm confused, because some people would say that's a nice thing to do, but are you saying your Dad giving you birthday presents is a sign he doesn't care about you?
>
> **Alienated child:** Um. I don't know. Maybe when you put it like that. I don't know.
>
> **Psychologist:** It's really confusing when your Dad tries to do something nice for you and your Mum thinks differently.
>
> **Alienated child:** Yeah. It is. (The child starts to cry).
>
> **Psychologist:** What would you say if I told you that your Dad started to cry when he told me how much he misses you?
>
> **Alienated child:** Mum would get upset.
>
> **Psychologist:** Why would Mum get upset about that?
>
> **Alienated child:** Mum gets upset about everything to do with Dad.
>
> **Psychologist:** That's got to be tough on you. Would it be easier for you if Mum didn't get upset about Dad?
>
> **Alienated child:** Yeah. It would.
>
> **Psychologist:** Would you like me to help with that so you could see your Dad?
>
> **Alienated child:** Yes.

During the course of this conversation, the alienated child demonstrated black and white thinking (Mum is the good and competent parent, Dad is the bad, incompetent parent). The child demonstrates his alliance with his mother by using the words "us" and "we" when the questions refer to his individual experience. He also denounces John as his father by referring to him by his first name. With careful questioning in the style of empathic curiosity, the practitioner was able to challenge the child's distorted thinking. Despite the child calling his father "John", the practitioner reinforced throughout the conversation that he is his father. The child's thinking started to turn around before he started to cry. At this point, further empathic inquiry revealed the behaviour of the child's mother as well as the child's desire to see his father who he is no longer calling John.

Of course, these conversations are not always this easy. When a child is severely alienated from a parent, a conversation will unlikely facilitate a cognitive shift. Let us consider the conversation with this child's older sister.

> **Box 18.6 Alienated child:** I'm really anxious about being here today.
>
> **Psychologist:** Thank you coming despite feeling anxious. What is it about today that's making you feel anxious?
>
> **Alienated child:** Every time I have to think about John I get really anxious. It's really good at Mum's. It's relaxed and easy. I can forget about John. And then I have to come to these kinds of appointments, and I have to think about him again.
>
> **Psychologist:** What is it about your Dad that makes you feel anxious?
>
> **Alienated child:** I don't know. He just makes me feel anxious.
>
> **Psychologist:** I can see you're feeling quite anxious now. Your hands are shaking and you're a little breathless. There must be a reason why thoughts of your Dad are causing these feelings?
>
> **Alienated child:** Well … John's really selfish. When I had to go to his house, he fed me instant noodles. Sometimes he didn't feed me at all. I had to get my own food. I don't remember John ever cooking.

Psychologist: I notice you call your dad John. Tell me about that?

Alienated child: Well … John hasn't been a father to me. My stepdad is more of a father to me. John doesn't care about me. If he did, he would have fed me better.

Psychologist: Do you believe your Dad doesn't care about you?

Alienated child: Yes. I know he doesn't.

Psychologist: How do you know this?

Alienated child: John's done nothing for me. All he ever does is cause trouble.

Psychologist: When you say your Dad causes trouble, what do you mean?

Alienated child: John keeps taking us to court when he knows we don't want to see him.

Psychologist: Who's us and we?

Alienated child: Me, Mum, my brother and stepdad.

Psychologist: I'm curious to know why you think your Dad is going to court … not what anyone else thinks, what do you think?

Alienated child: I think he has a cheek costing us so much money and stress. I know he's making us come here.

Psychologist: I noticed you said us again.

Alienated child: Well … that's what I think.

Psychologist: That your Dad is costing you money and stress by going to court?

Alienated child: He's costing Mum money and John's made us do stuff like this I don't want to do.

Psychologist: I can see how upset this is making you. It's hard to be a kid in the middle of separated parents and having court stuff intruding on your life.

Alienated child: Yeah. I'm over it.

Psychologist: I'm curious about your thoughts on why your Mum and Dad are going to court?

Alienated child: John just needs to respect that we don't want him in our lives anymore. He's causing us too much stress.

This conversation continued until the practitioner had tried various ways to challenge the alienated child's cognitive distortions. At every angle, the alienated child in this scenario persisted that her father was the cause of her distress. She continued to demonstrate her allegiance to her mother and stepfather and refused to refer to her father as anything other than "John". The practitioner ended this conversation when it was clear that, on this day, the wall of resistance was impenetrable. It is important to remember that resistance is a state, not a trait. It fluctuates over time (1). Therefore, the practitioner set about providing the child with a secure base from which to continue teaching this alienated child critical thinking skills. However, time with her Dad was the most powerful means of challenging her view of him.

Targeted parents also can benefit from learning critical thinking skills using cognitive restructuring and solution-focused strategies. Coupled with assertive communication skills training, targeted parents should learn to separate their child from their alienated behaviours. These skills also can help the targeted parent manage any ongoing interactions with the alienating parent.

The task of teaching some alienating parents critical thinking skills can be challenging, but not impossible. Outcomes with alienating parents depend on their motivation for alienating their children from the targeted parent, the severity and intensity of their behaviour and the presence of problematic personality traits. Outcomes also depend on the practitioner's capacity to work with the alienating parent. When working with the alienating parent, practitioners must take a directive approach and be proactive in implementing and maintaining appropriate boundaries. Some alienating parents are master manipulators and can act to coopt the practitioner into an alliance with them or even act aggressively to derail the process to maintain control. Practitioners must be assertive when working with the alienating parent.

Improving the targeted parent–child relationship

This is best achieved with the child and targeted parent spending quality time with each other. Some practitioners recommend children's time with the targeted parents start with short amounts of time and gradually increase that time consistent with graded exposure seen in the treatment of specific phobia. This approach is inappropriate for parental alienation. All this approach achieves is appeasing the irrational fears of the alienating parent and buys them time to perpetuate the alienation. To counteract the brainwashing, the child needs to spend substantial periods of time with the targeted parent so they can have sufficient exposure to information and experiences that dispels the distorted picture of the targeted parent. To begin with, the practitioner can facilitate a session with the alienated child and targeted parent. It is best to engage the dyad in a shared activity where the focus is on the parent and child cooperatively working on an activity. In mild to moderate cases of parental alienation, this can be achieved with strict adherence to visitation schedules supported by the interventions described in this chapter with consequences for non-adherence.

Box 18.7 Psychologist: I recall the first reunification session I facilitated between an alienated mother and her teenage daughter. Before the session, I met with the mother to discuss the best ways to communicate with her daughter and how best to respond if her daughter wanted to confront her about certain topics. I also met with the daughter to explain to her what was going to happen in the session with her mother. I then brought mother and daughter into the room together and sat them down expecting to facilitate the perfect mediation session. How wrong I was! Within seconds, it all fell apart. The daughter accused Mum of all sorts of things and Mum forgot everything we'd talked about and launched into defending herself. The conversation became a horrible, angry game of verbal tennis. Every time I tried to stop them, they talked over me, like I wasn't there until the two were shouting at each other. I found myself jumping to my feet as I sternly commanded them to stop it now! We were all shocked at my inner school principal being unleashed. I was completely naïve to the beast that is parental alienation and had no control over the session. I don't know if it was skill or pure luck, but I somehow managed to salvage the session and both agreed to return for round two. The second time around was very different. I immediately put mother and daughter to work playing a board game – a game they hadn't played before, so they had to teach each other the rules. At the end of the game, the daughter reminded her mother of a funny moment they once shared. Mum reciprocated by recounting more positive memories. Then they hugged. I felt so privileged to have witnessed this moment. I've since witnessed many of these moments and the significance of these moments is never lost on me. I now know mediation is completely inappropriate and an experience I will not put another child or parent through again.

In severe cases of parental alienation, it is vital there is no contact between the child and alienating parent for a period of time so the child and targeted parent can reconnect without the ongoing interference from the alienating parent. While the targeted parent and child reconnect, the alienating parent must engage in interventions that teach them to support the relationship between the child and targeted parent. Research shows that despite initial resistance to spending time with the targeted parent, once they reconnect with that parent and they are no longer exposed to alienating behaviours, children and teenagers settle very quickly. Any behavioural or emotional problems seen before reunification are no longer evident (2-3).

Preparing the alienating parent for an improvement in the targeted parent–child relationship

It is essential alienating parents are part of the solution. In mild to moderate cases of parental alienation, alienating parents can respond well to psychoeducation. Some alienating parents are motivated to change their behaviour when they see their child coping well with time spent with the targeted parent. Unfortunately, some alienating parents are unable to make changes necessary to support the targeted parent–child relationship. Their need to control or seek revenge outweighs a desire to act in the best interest of the child. In these cases, as it is in other cases of family violence, it is in the best interest of the child and their safety to have limited, if not no contact with the alienating parent until they are old enough to make their own decisions about whether or not it is safe for them to have this parent in their lives.

Establish healthy boundaries and communication within the family

Psychoeducation, coping skills and assertive skills training will help targeted parents to feel confident to parent their child again. These same skills can help children realise that love and care from their parents is not conditional on them meeting the needs of their parents.

When alienating parents demonstrate a capacity for co-parenting with the targeted parent, it is possible for co-parenting skills to be taught to alienating and targeted parents. Indeed, it is possible for joint sessions to occur with these parents in mild to moderate cases of parental alienation when targeted parent–child reunification has occurred and individual intervention goals have been achieved.

In severe cases of parental alienation, it would be unethical and atherapeutic for alienating parents and targeted parents to have joint sessions. Numerous studies have suggested that joint sessions are contraindicated when family violence has occurred, unless the perpetrator of the family violence has sufficiently changed their behaviour and no longer pose a risk of harm to others and their partner/ex-partner feels safe to be in the same room as the perpetrator (4). This approach should be followed in severe cases of parental alienation.

Strict visitation schedules

In all cases of parental alienation, courts need to implement strict visitation schedules. Parenting orders need to be written in clear and concrete terms that cannot be open to interpretation. In mild to moderate cases of parental alienation, equal shared care arrangements are achievable with intervention. However, in severe cases and cases where the alienating parent has demonstrated an inability to change their behaviour, changes in where the child lives to the targeted parent or changes in child and targeted parent visitation arrangements are required to resolve the alienation (5-6).

Collaborating for effective outcomes

Interventions for parental alienation should include both a legal and therapeutic response. In essence, the court can make the orders needed to make family members accountable for their behaviour while therapists teach family members the skills needed to make the required behaviour change. In parental alienation matters, orders are necessary external motivators for alienating parents to participate in interventions where the outcomes are counter to their wishes. When alienating parents resist the intervention or refuse to attend to therapeutic tasks needed to achieve the goal of improving family functioning, therapists and the judiciary need to work together to ensure there are consequences for non-adherence. These consequences may include reducing the time the child spends with the alienating parent, implementing or extending a no contact order or giving the targeted parent primary parental responsibility.

Interventions should be delivered by court-appointed psychologists, social workers or counsellors. Complex matters may require a coordinator who can act as a conduit between therapists and the court. The role of the coordinator is to monitor compliance with court orders.

It is preferable that this work is not conducted alone. At the very least, two practitioners should work as a team. It can be useful for a different practitioner to work with the alienating parent while a second practitioner works with the child and targeted parent. This separation can prevent the practitioner from encountering numerous ethical pitfalls.

Ethical dilemmas and pitfalls

There are many ethical dilemmas and pitfalls practitioners can encounter when working with the alienated family. Let me count the ways ....

Boundaries

This work is not for the faint-hearted or inexperienced practitioner. It goes without saying practitioners need to have a thorough understanding of parental alienation, how it manifests and the processes underlying it in order to do this work. Additionally, a good understanding of behaviour modification processes, developmental theories, attachment theory, systemic family theories and family violence, at the very least, is required. Practitioners should be knowledgeable in the laws and ethical guidelines that govern their practice as well as ethical decision-making processes. A thorough understanding of risk assessment and response procedures is also necessary.

Practitioners working with the alienated family can easily fall into the trap of wanting to advocate for the child or the targeted parent. Advocacy falls outside of the role of practitioners working in this area. Once a therapist acts outside of their role, their work ceases to be therapeutic in nature. Having a contract where the roles of the practitioners are stated clearly and regularly engaging in mentoring and reflective practice can prevent this from occurring.

Practitioners also need to be cognisant of their own beliefs, values and biases and how these can impact on their work in subtle and at times not so subtle ways. Counter-transference can lead a practitioner to over-identify with one member of the family and critically judge another. This is atherapuetic and unethical. Acting to understand each family member's frame of reference and motivations for behaving the way they do can assist. Working in a team where constructive feedback is provided between team members can also be useful in monitoring how biases can manifest in intervention delivery.

Informed consent and signed contractual agreements

Even when family members have been ordered by a court to attend therapy, they still have the right to autonomy, which means any individual family member can choose not to participate in therapy. In order for the family members to make an informed decision, practitioners should provide each family member with an orientation regarding the intervention, what it involves and the mutual expectations of family members and practitioners.

Family members need to know that, unlike traditional forms of therapy, their confidentiality is limited because a report to the court will be made about intervention progress. Each family member needs to know who their information will be released to and under which circumstances information can be released. If family members agree, they should sign a contract to that effect. All adults and teenagers capable of giving informed consent should be asked to sign a contract. Family members need to know the possible consequences to them if they choose not to participate. The consequences should be predetermined by the court.

Confidentiality in the face of reportable work

The alienated family engaging in an intervention programme has very limited confidentiality. Family members need to know this so they can make an informed decision about how much information they disclose about themselves during the course of the intervention. It is difficult for a practitioner to build a trusting rapport with family members when every communication they have with the family is reportable, but this is not impossible provided that practitioners are transparent about their role, the limits of their role and the fact that reports to the court will need to be made.

Working with multiple clients

Working with multiple clients poses many ethical issues. It is very difficult for one practitioner to manage the demands of each family member while remaining neutral with regard to their presenting concerns in alienation matters (7). For this reason, it is best practice to work in a team. Preferably, a different practitioner should work with the alienating parent to avoid the conflict of interest. Indeed, as previously mentioned, it is best practice in family violence cases for the perpetrator of the family violence to work with a practitioner who is different to the one working with the survivors of their violent behaviour.

Record keeping

Keeping an accurate record of the intervention delivered, responses to the intervention and all communications with the family members and about the family members is an ethical and legal requirement. This includes records of telephone calls, electronic communication and non-attendance. When working with a family, it is best practice to keep a separate file for each family member. When keeping records, it is important to write in a clear, objective and non-judgmental manner. Keep in mind the potential audiences of the records, which includes the family members, the court and regulatory bodies.

When the subpoena comes

It is inevitable in this work that the practitioners delivering the intervention will be subpoenaed to produce documents and/or attend the court in person for examination and cross-examination. When the subpoena comes you are legally obliged to respond to it.

Firstly, check the date you must respond to the subpoena and what the subpoena is requiring. If the subpoena is requiring documents, check if original documents or copies are being requested. Where possible, inform the clients of the subpoena and your legal requirement to comply with it (8).

You can object to a subpoena on certain grounds. These grounds include:

1. The documents being requested are irrelevant to the matter before the court.
2. Releasing the documents would pose a serious threat to the life and safety of an involved family member or member of the public.
3. Release of the information being subpoenaed would undermine the therapeutic relationship and consequently cause irreparable harm to the psychological wellbeing of the family member(s).
4. Privacy of other individuals not involved in the court matter would be breached.
5. The documents being requested are written in specialised language requiring interpretation. Without explanation the information will not be useful.
6. The request for the documents is frivolous or vexatious.
7. The documents being requested are not in your possession or control.
8. The documents are protected test material or data (8).

If a practitioner is uncertain about the subpoena, they should contact the lawyer who issued the subpoena for further information and/or seek legal advice from another lawyer.

Complaints

Due to the complexity of family law matters, it is unsurprising that complaints against practitioners to regulating bodies are common. When a practitioner is notified that a complaint has been made about them, it is important to remain calm and seek as much information as possible about the nature of the complaint from the regulatory body. Find out about the complaints process, timelines and requirement for responding to the complaint. It is important the professional indemnity insurer is informed. Also, it can be useful to obtain legal advice and mentoring support throughout the complaints process.

Being on the receiving end of a complaint is stressful. It shakes a practitioner's confidence and forces them to evaluate their practice. No matter how stressful and distressing the complaints process, it is important to remember to act with integrity, honesty and within accepted professional and ethical standards of behaviour. Importantly, self-care during this process will help to reduce the personal impact.

Self-care

Working with alienated families is rewarding but extremely stressful. It is vital all practitioners working with these families engage in good self-care practises. Practitioner wellbeing is important because practitioners who are feeling unwell or burnt-out will be ineffective. Burn-out is disabling. Knowing the warning signs can help to prevent it from having a negative impact on practice. Watch out for the following signs:

*   Feeling emotionally exhausted.
*   Experiencing a desire to withdraw from work and others.
*   Feeling overworked and overloaded.

- Feeling like you have no control over your workload.
- Experiencing non-specific physical symptoms, such as headache, stomach ache, muscle aches and pains, increased susceptibility to viruses.
- Developing a negative attitude towards your clients and finding it difficult to suspend critical judgment.
- Developing a negative attitude towards colleagues.
- Feeling disillusioned by the work you are doing.
- Feeling like a failure.

If a practitioner notices any of these signs, there are strategies that can be implemented to prevent burn-out from having a profound effect:

- Have realistic expectations of yourself, clients and colleagues.
- Obtain regular mentoring or peer supervision.
- Engage in regular self-reflective practice.
- Engage in regular training and professional development programmes.
- Know when to take a break from work.
- Know when to reduce your hours at work even if this is a temporary measure.
- Spend time with the people in your life who support and care for you.
- Schedule positive activities that make you smile and laugh.
- Engage in regular exercise, healthy eating and good time management.
- Practice healthy sleep hygiene.
- Practise what you preach!

Concluding comments

Despite the seemingly intractable nature of parental alienation, intervention is possible. There is ample research evidence showing that reunifying the targeted parent and child can be a quick and relatively straightforward process. However, working with alienating parents can be challenging. For this reason, it is important that interventions comprise a coordinated approach between court-appointed therapists and the judiciary. Further, this work should not be conducted by a sole practitioner in order to avoid serious ethical dilemmas and therapist burn-out.

References

1. Miller, W.R., & Rollnick, S. (2013). *Applications of motivational interviewing. Motivational interviewing: Helping people change* (3rd edn.). New York: Guilford Press.
2. Reay, K.M. (2015). Family reflections: A promising therapeutic program designed to treat severely alienated children and their family system. *The American Journal of Family Therapy, 43,* 197–207. doi:10.1080/01926187.2015.1007769
3. Warshak, A.A. (2018). Reclaiming parent–child relationships: Outcomes of family bridges with alienated children. *Journal of Divorce & Remarriage, online first.* doi:10.1080/10502556.2018.1529505
4. Karakurt, G., Whiting, K., van Esch, C., Bolen, S.D., & Calabrese, J.R. (2016). Couples therapy for intimate partner violence: A systematic review and meta-analysis. *Journal of Marital and Family Therapy, 42,* 567–583.
5. Darnall, D. (2011). The psychosocial treatment of parental alienation. *Child and Adolescent Psychiatric Clinics of North America, 20,* 479–494. doi:10.1016/j.chc.2011.03.006

6. Templer, K., Matthewson, M., Haines, J., & Cox, G. (2017). Recommendations for best practice in response to parental alienation: findings from a systematic review. *Journal of Family Therapy, 39,* 103–122. doi:10.1111/1467-6427.12137
7. Fidler, B., & Bala, N. (2010). Children resisting postseparation contact with a parent: Concepts, controversies, and conundrums. *Family Court Review, 48,* 10–47. doi:10.1111/j.1744-1617.2009.01287.x
8. Australian Psychological Society. (2016). *Managing legal requests for client files, subpoenas, and third-party requests for psychological reports.* Melbourne: Author.

Chapter Nineteen

Individual therapy with each family member

Introduction

Often therapists can find themselves working with individual family members affected by parental alienation rather than the alienated family system. A targeted parent can seek help from a therapist when they do not know where to turn, an alienating parent can seek an ally in a therapist, and alienated children can be mandated by a court or alienating parent to see a therapist. Sometimes, adults who were alienated from a parent during childhood can seek support from a therapist. When faced with the task of working with an individual family member, therapists can be overwhelmed by their perceived limited capacity to intervene when they cannot influence the family system.

When working with individual family members, therapists need to focus on their role as a practitioner providing therapy to an individual. Therapists need to remember that their role is not to resolve the alienation, but to support the individual to cope more effectively. The most important role the therapist can assume when working with an individual affected by parental alienation is to function as a secure base.

The concept of a secure base originates from attachment theory. Bowlby (1) detailed how the first task of therapy is for the therapist to provide their client with a secure base from which they can explore the painful aspects of their life. A secure base is a safe and reliable haven. Each time the client returns to the therapist they can be safe in the knowledge that, no matter how chaotic their life is and how distressed they are, they will always receive the same non-judgmental care and support from the therapist (1). This is vital for an individual experiencing the storm of parental alienation, even if that individual is the one engaging in alienating behaviours.

In this chapter, an overview of how to provide individual therapy with the aim of reducing psychological distress in the client will be provided. Therapeutic boundaries and avoiding manipulation will be discussed.

Working with targeted parents

> **Box 19.1 Targeted parent:** Please help! I haven't seen my child in two years. I'm not a bad person. I haven't done anything wrong but my child refuses to see me and my ex has done things you wouldn't believe to stop me from seeing my child. I've been to court and jumped through every hoop. I've spent thousands of dollars for things to get worse. I don't know what to do next. What can I do? Can you help me get my child back?

Knowledge is a double-edged sword

Targeted parents can seek therapy at different stages of parental alienation. Sometimes they seek support and advice as soon as their ex-partner has become uncooperative or after years of battling to maintain a relationship with their child. Regardless of when targeted parents seek help, providing them with information about parental alienation can be helpful.

As any valid and reliable assessment of parental alienation requires meeting with each involved family member, the therapist must be careful not to draw a definitive conclusion that the client is a targeted parent. Instead, it is more productive to provide information to the parent about alienating behaviours and allow the parent to determine for themselves if they are a targeted parent. This revelation can be beneficial for a parent because it helps them to understand their confusing experience and it helps to give their experience legitimacy. It is then the task of the therapist to balance working within the parent's frame of reference as their therapist as opposed to acting as a single expert for the court.

When targeted parents have been on the receiving end of false allegations while feeling unable to defend themselves, it can be therapeutic for them simply to be heard. To this end, targeted parents need to feel heard in a non-judgmental and validating manner. Therapists can do this through good use of the core counselling skills of active and empathic listening. Simply hearing back from another that they have been heard and understood is an experience targeted parents rarely encounter in the context of a parental alienation campaign (2).

Many targeted parents want to understand the reasons why their ex-partners have chosen to alienate them from their children (3). For this reason, it can be useful to explore what the targeted parent believes are their ex-partner's motivations. Also, it can be useful to provide generic information about the behaviour of alienating parents as described in research. This insight can help targeted parents to change the way they react to the alienating parent's provocative behaviour. Targeted parents can find it helpful to understand why their child is rejecting them. This knowledge can help targeted parents separate the child's behaviour from their much-loved child. This, in turn, can help targeted parents to feel differently about the rejection and change their reactions to their child's behaviour. Of course, the therapist must disseminate information about alienating parents and alienated children in a sensitive, empathic and non-judgemental manner. The aim of providing this information is not to perpetuate anger and resentment towards others, but to promote awareness and insight that can be the catalyst for adaptive coping.

However, knowledge is a double-edged sword. Although it can be therapeutic to discover that your experience is a legitimate one, it also can be overwhelming. Targeted parents can find it confronting to learn about the plight of their child while they remain exposed to alienating behaviours. Also, targeted parents can feel helpless when faced with the knowledge that their avenues to resolve the alienation are limited depending on the jurisdiction in which they live. Most intervention programmes described in the scientific literature are based in the US, UK and Canada. There are limited options for intervention in the southern hemisphere. Despite this, it is important targeted parents are aware of the reality of their situation so they can make informed decisions about what to do next.

The hard road or the hard road?

Targeted parents often question whether they should continue to pursue a legal pathway to maintaining a relationship with their child or whether they should give up the legal fight (3). Targeted parents need to know they have done everything they possibly could do to resolve the alienation. The criteria for "I've done everything I can do" differs for every targeted parent. It is the therapist's role to help the parent explore this. Using decisional balance (4) to explore the pros and cons of various courses of action can be useful. It is not the role of the therapist to tell the targeted parent what to do. Continuing the 'fight' and walking away are equally difficult and painful roads to walk. Only the targeted parent can make the decision about which road to take. Both journeys will demand impeccable self-care.

Time to grieve

Targeted parents need to give themselves sufficient time to grieve. The grief experienced by targeted parents is complex (2-3). Targeted parents must grieve for the loss of a child who is still alive, the loss of a loving relationship with their child and the loss of their identity as a parent. Also, it is important to recognise that targeted parents grieve for the lost relationship with the alienating parent because, before the hurt and anger of separating, the targeted parent once cared for the alienating parent.

In many respects, targeted parents experience disenfranchised grief because parental alienation is a poorly understood phenomenon in society. Disenfranchised grief is defined as grief experienced when the loss cannot be openly acknowledged or openly mourned (5). Targeted parents find it difficult to openly grieve for their child who is still alive (3). Further, when targeted parents have been subjected to false allegations of wrongdoing, their expressions of grief can be misconstrued or, at the very least, they may fear their grief response will be misconstrued.

The tasks of grief are:

1. To accept the reality of the loss.
2. To work through the pain of grief in order to accept the reality of the loss.
3. To adjust to life without the lost loved one.
4. To move on with life while maintaining a connection with the lost loved one, even when that person is no longer physically present.

These tasks of grief have been described by Worden (6) and adjusted here to apply to the experience of targeted parents. The task of the therapist is to provide targeted parents with a secure base from which to grieve. The therapists should make good use of core counselling skills and true therapeutic dialogue (7). Encouraging targeted parents to talk about their child is important. Targeted parents also need time to explore their identity as a parent. The role of the therapist here is to reinforce that they are still a parent even if they are unable to fulfil parenting responsibilities.

> **Box 19.2 Targeted parent:** When people ask me if I have children, I don't know what to say. When I tell them I have a son but I don't see him, I just can't deal with the funny looks or the questions I get from people. So, I often say I don't have children. It's easier to say this and it stops the conversation.
>
> **Therapist:** When you say to people "I don't have children", you're also saying I'm not a parent, when you are. It might be easier in the short term to say you don't have children, but how does it impact you later?
>
> **Targeted parent:** I hate it. I hate myself for saying it. I feel so guilty when I say this.
>
> **Therapist:** If your son passed away, you would still say you are his mother. If your closest friend was alienated from her child, you would still say she is their mother …

> **Targeted parent:** I know. You're right. But how do I handle it when people ask me if I have children?
>
> **Therapist:** You could say, "I have a son. He's called Ben. He's 14 years old and he lives with his dad right now. How about you, do you have children?" It's all true and then you shift the focus of the conversation on to the other person.

Suicide ideation is common among targeted parents (3). Therapists must continually monitor risk of self-harm in targeted parents by conducting regular risk assessments and implementing safety plans when needed.

When the targeted parent met cognitive behavioural therapy

Although therapists cannot resolve parental alienation when working with targeted parents alone, they can help them to improve the quality of their life despite the alienation. Cognitive behavioural therapy (CBT) is one therapeutic approach that can be used to achieve this goal. CBT is based on the premise that thinking patterns and beliefs influence emotions and behaviour. By identifying unhelpful thinking patterns and irrational beliefs and learning to think in more realistic and adaptive ways, individuals can experience an improvement in the way they feel and how they behave. CBT also incorporates behaviour change strategies to assist in improving mood and adaptive patterns of behaviour (8). Identifying unhelpful thinking patterns that compound distress and learning ways to think differently can help to reduce distress for targeted parents.

When targeted parents have an emotional experience, such as sadness, mindfulness of emotions can be helpful. Becoming mindful or aware of emotions, identifying and accepting the emotions and learning self-compassion also can help to reduce distress (9). Therapists can teach targeted parents mindfulness of emotions exercises to use when emotional distress is not due to cognitive distortions.

Additionally, behaviour change can help targeted parents manage their distress. When targeted parents experience mood instability they also can experience reduced motivation and energy levels. In time, targeted parents can shrink their world by having a singular focus on their experience of parental alienation. This perpetuates depressed mood. Over time, targeted parents can feel overwhelmed by simple daily tasks, such as cooking a meal for themselves. Scheduling simple tasks as well as pleasurable activities can help to improve mood, and increase energy and motivation (10), and it can help targeted parents to invest in their new reality. Positive activity scheduling may also include activities that involve connecting with a support network. This might include becoming involved in a support group or simply connecting with important people in their support network. Maintaining social connections is an important part of surviving parental alienation (2-3).

Also, targeted parents can benefit from assertiveness skills training. Assertiveness skills can be useful when targeted parents need to remain in contact with the alienating parent to co-parent their child, when interacting with their child and when communicating with legal and/or mental health professionals who may not understand parental alienation. Assertiveness skills training can help targeted parents to assert their needs, defuse conflict, protect themselves from abusive behaviour and help them to put structure into the chaos created by alienating behaviours.

Therapists should teach targeted parents strategies to avoid the vortex of emotions alienating parents create. Teaching targeted parents how to implement and enforce boundaries and how to be brief, to the point and factual in communications with others can help to reduce stress and anxiety. Knowing how to avoid confrontation and knowing when to walk away from aggressive behaviour can be empowering for targeted parents. Many targeted parents continue to assume that alienating parents may suddenly become rational in their thinking and reasonable in their behaviour when this is unlikely. Once targeted parents understand that alienating parents may not change in this way, they can focus on using assertive communication strategies that work with individuals with dysfunctional cognitions and chaotic behaviour.

Preparing for reunification

Targeted parents should never lose hope that one day they will reunite with their child. There are changes targeted parents can make now to prepare for reunification that increase the chances of it being successful. The reunification process is not easy and targeted parents need to be realistic about this. It is common for alienated children who are curious about their rejected parent to reach out and then withdraw again. This approach and withdraw pattern of behaviour can cycle for some time. During this time targeted parents need to be patient and learn to manage the anxiety, frustration and the rollercoaster of anticipation and disappointment. Targeted parents can support themselves through this time by engaging in the strategies already discussed. Targeted parents can support their children through this time by moving at their child's pace, avoiding emotionally laden conversations and refraining from blaming others. Also, assertive communication skills will be important during this time. Implementing boundaries and modelling how to have healthy, unconditional relationships with others are important.

Box 19.3 Targeted parent: My daughter contacted me yesterday. It's the first time in three years. I couldn't believe it when I realised it was her on the other end of the phone. My heart just burst with so many emotions. She said she needed to talk to me. She needed to talk to me! She said she needs me to buy her a car. She's found one she likes. I can't afford to buy her a car but I'm afraid she'll reject me again if I don't figure out a way to buy it for her.

Therapist: You must be elated to hear from your daughter after all of this time. I'm sure you were experiencing a number of emotions during your call. And now she's made this connection with you, you want to hang on to it. I'm curious though … do you want your daughter to form the view that having a relationship with you is conditional on you buying her things? Is that a healthy relationship for both of you?

Targeted Parent: No. I don't want her to think that. I don't want to lose her again, but I don't want her to only come to me when she wants something. Obviously, I'll help her out when I can, but I can't buy her a car.

Alienated children can approach the parent they rejected for a variety of reasons (11) and wanting the targeted parent to buy them something can be one of them. This is quite the dilemma for the targeted parent and only they can decide if their child's request is reasonable. It is the therapist's job to teach targeted parents about boundaries and how to implement them with their child who may resemble nothing of the child they once knew.

A word of caution

It is unsurprising that when hearing descriptions of targeted parents' experiences, therapists can feel overwhelmed and helpless (12). Targeted parents experience and express intense emotions, such as anger, frustration, fear, sadness and pain. They experience and express intense emotions associated with the perception of being let down by legal and mental health services with limited understanding of parental alienation (3). Therapists can feel powerless to do or say anything that they believe will make a difference. Although there is little the individual therapist can do to directly resolve the alienation and 'fix' the problems faced by targeted parents, there are still ways a therapist can assist.

In response to the targeted parent, therapists can feel motivated to advocate for them. Therapy and advocacy are different approaches and no therapist can juggle these two roles at once without facing ethical dilemmas. The most common ethical violation therapists make when they blur the boundaries between therapist and advocate is to write reports and letters of support for the targeted parent including content that falls outside of their role. This includes the therapist concluding in reports that the parent is the victim of parental alienation. As previously mentioned, only the practitioner who has assessed each family member and the family dynamics is in a position to conclude this. Therapists should only write reports detailing how the targeted parent presents in therapy, the nature of the therapy being conducted and the targeted parent's response to it. Therapists can avoid the ethical pitfalls of blurring the boundaries between therapist and advocate by being clear themselves on the boundaries of their role and communicating this clearly to their clients.

> **Box 19.4 Targeted parent:** I'm worried my child will see me doing well in life and accuse me of moving on without them.
>
> **Therapist:** Living well isn't a rejection of your child. If your child accuses you of this you can tell them "I wasn't moving on without you, I was getting ready to have you back in my life."

Working with alienating parents

> **Box 19.5 Alienating parent:** My ex abandoned us three years ago. My ex is a complete idiot and can't parent to save themselves. Unsurprisingly, my child isn't coping with shared care. Going to my ex's house is stressing my child out and isn't the same child when back in my care. I'm sure things aren't right at my ex's house. I'm sure my ex is abusing my child in some way. My lawyer suggested I see a psychologist. I'm at my wit's end. Can you do anything to support me in stopping the visits?

There are alliances and then there are alliances

We have already discussed the nature of intervention when working with alienating parents as part of family intervention in Chapters Seventeen and Eighteen. In this section, we will discuss the nature of therapy with alienating parents when they voluntarily present to a therapist for help. Alienating parents typically present voluntarily for individual therapy for three reasons: (a) to co-opt a therapist into an alliance with them against the targeted parent; (b) because is it strategic for them to do so in relation to the legal demands they face; and (c) because they are genuinely distressed about the situation they are in, but have limited or no insight in to their contribution to the problems.

Indeed, it is not always easy to identify an alienating parent when they attend therapy on their own. Of course, if a parent reports to a therapist that they are the victim of family violence, the therapist would be negligent to automatically assume these allegations are false and, therefore, alienating tactics. Similarly, it would be negligent of a therapist to assume that every allegation of family violence had occurred. Therapists should always start their assessment for therapy objectively. They should always seek to understand their client's frame of reference without being seduced by their story. When therapists can balance these tasks, they will be able to appropriately attend to issues of reported risk while being alert to indicators of possible alienating behaviours (as discussed in previous chapters).

Alienating parents can be quite skilled in garnering sympathy from healthcare professionals and manipulating them into behaving in ways that are violations of codes of conduct and even breaking the law. Just as it is unprofessional and unethical for a therapist to categorically conclude that their client is a targeted parent, it is unprofessional and unethical for a therapist to categorically conclude that when a parent says they "think" their child is being abused by the ex-partner that the ex-partner, whom the therapist has never met or assessed, is the perpetrator of violence and abuse.

Box 19.6 Psychologist: Alienating parents can be interpersonally warm, friendly and very convincing in the way they present their stories. I remember meeting one mother who described being emotionally and physically abused by her ex-husband. Her descriptions were detailed, horrific and plausible. She told me she had been to the emergency department for her injuries on many occasions and there were multiple police reports about her ex-husband's violence. Her distress seemed genuine and, upon meeting her alone, it would have been easy for me to conclude that she had been the survivor of family violence. I then met her ex-husband, their children and the maternal grandmother, and read over a thousand pages of collateral evidence. I discovered there had only been one police report where the mother called the police to attend a handover with the children in case her ex-husband became aggressive. The police report made note of the mother being agitated and verbally aggressive towards the father in front of the children while the father was cooperative. The mother had attended the emergency department on many occasions for attempting suicide. There were no medical reports about injuries that could be attributed to physical assaults. Then, as the parenting dispute continued, the mother alleged the father was sexually abusing the children. She had not reported concerns about this previously but managed to convince another psychologist that this was true. Without meeting the father, this psychologist concluded in a report that the father was a paedophile and the risk of harm he posed to his children was so severe that he should not have any contact with his children. Psychologists are obliged to draw conclusions that are evidence-based. They should not diagnose any person with a mental health disorder (e.g., paedophilic disorder) without conducting a diagnostic assessment with that person. The psychologist who formed the potentially career-ending alliance with the mother was experienced and highly skilled, but experience and skill were no match for this mother's alienating behaviours.

When a therapist has formed the view that their client may be an alienating parent, it is important that they develop a workable therapeutic alliance with the parent while implementing strong boundaries. Many alienating parents who see a therapist voluntarily are unlikely to continue to attend appointments if the therapist does not offer them what they seek. Therapists should not necessarily be disappointed by this outcome because, by refusing to join the alienating parent's alliance, the therapist has helped by not becoming an outside force perpetuating or exacerbating the alienation.

If therapists can implement clear boundaries in relation to what they can and cannot do to help the alienating parents, while balancing the task of understanding their frame of reference without being seduced by their story, the therapist can forge a therapeutic alliance with the alienating parent. If an alienating parent continues to attend sessions with a therapist, the therapist needs to act as a secure base. As we saw in Chapter Six, alienating parents tend to have poor relationship histories and problematic families of origin. Therefore, it is possible that alienating parents have never had a secure base. The role of the therapist is not to resolve the alienation, but to provide the alienating parent with information and skills that may help to reduce their distress.

Education

Some alienating parents may benefit from hearing information about the impact of family separation on parents and children. Also, they may find it useful to learn about the influence parents can have on their children's psychological wellbeing, particularly during parenting disputes. Discussions about the long-term consequences of feeling pressured to choose between parents on children's social-emotional development can be enlightening for some parents, particularly alienating parents who unwittingly use mild to moderate alienating behaviours. This information must be delivered empathically through the use of techniques such as circular questions, socratic questioning, empathic and advanced empathic highlights, and the skill of immediacy.

Shifting locus of control

Some alienating parents may respond well to learning skills that teach them to take greater personal responsibility and enhance their internal locus of control. This can be achieved by using solution-focused (13) and motivational interviewing strategies (4).

> **Box 19.7 Psychologist:** If you're waiting for another person to change, you might be waiting forever because you can't control how other people behave; you can only change the way you behave and respond to others.

When the alienating parent met dialectical behaviour therapeutic strategies

As many alienating parents exhibit narcissistic and borderline personality traits, they can benefit from Dialectical Behaviour Therapy (DBT) or some components of DBT for alienating parents presenting with sub-clinical personality traits. DBT is a variant of CBT that was developed for individuals with borderline personality disorder, but it can be used with individuals with other mental health concerns. Some people, such as alienating parents, are prone to having intense emotional reactions to certain situations such as those involving family relationships (14). DBT can help alienating parents manage their extreme mood swings, cognitive distortions and tendency to jump from crisis to crisis. It can be useful to teach alienating parents some or all of the components of DBT (14-15):

- Mindfulness to learn how to identify emotions.
- Interpersonal effectiveness to learn how to better interact with others in an assertive and respectful manner.
- Distress tolerance to learn how to tolerate and better cope with crises through distraction, self-soothing, acceptance and problem solving.
- Emotion regulation to learn adaptive ways for managing emotions.

Therapists may need to be creative in how they encourage the alienating parent to become motivated to participate in these therapeutic tasks, particularly if the alienating parent continues to externalise the cause of their difficulties.

Risk assessment and a word of caution

When working with alienating parents, therapists need to be aware of issues of risk. Alienating parents can detail reports of harm they believe have been perpetrated against them and/or their children. Therapists must conduct evidence-based risk assessments and remember to draw evidence-based conclusions while being mindful of not being seduced by the story. Therapists should be well-versed in how best to respond to issues of risk in order to avoid getting caught in the alienating parent's catastrophising and, subsequently, overreacting.

Even the most experienced therapist can be seduced by the alienating parent's story. However, this is no excuse for unethical and unprofessional conduct. So, when a parent asks the question, "Can you support me in stopping my child from seeing their other parent?" the answer should be, "No. My role as a therapist is to help people to cope better with difficult situations and distressing emotions by providing them with information and teaching them skills. Stopping visitation or making recommendations to that effect are outside of my role."

Working with children

> **Box 19.8 Alienated child:** I hate idiot! I never want to see idiot again! You can't make me. No one can make me.

Beware of an alliance with falsehood

Alienated children typically make their way to individual therapy in two ways:

1. They can be court ordered to attend individual therapy or counselling under the well-intentioned but ill-informed notion that individual therapy will resolve the alienated child's rejection of the targeted parent and associated behavioural problems.
2. They can be taken to a therapist by the alienating parent. In this instance, the alienating parent does this in order to manipulate their child's therapist to join their alliance against the targeted parent.

Unfortunately, while the alienated child continues to be influenced by the alienating parent and has limited contact with the targeted parent, the therapist's ability to address parental alienation is very limited. However, while the child continues to attend appointments, the therapist can be the child's secure base they do not have elsewhere during this time. The therapist's task is to develop a trusting and dependable therapeutic relationship with the child. The therapist must remember that they are the child's therapist, not the family therapist or advocate for either parent.

The way in which therapists engage alienated children will depend on the age of the child. Therapists may need to be creative in how they engage children. Also, they should be interpersonally warm (16), respectful, open-minded and willing to share their time with the child (17). Importantly, when working with the alienated child, therapists need to understand the child's frame of reference without being seduced by the story and becoming an ally in their seemingly delusional belief system. Therapists should be empathic without reinforcing the child's distorted beliefs. Instead, they should adopt a stance of empathic curiosity, which serves to model critical thinking skills.

Armour of coping skills

If the alienating child is being exposed to alienating behaviours, they will need to be armed up with coping skills. Alienated children can benefit from CBT and even some DBT skills if they are externalising their emotions. For very young children, play therapy can be an effective means of helping children to explore their self-concept, develop social skills and skills for social-emotional adjustment (18). Alienated children need to be taught critical thinking skills and reality testing skills. Reality testing is an important part of working with the alienated child because it will help the child to distinguish between what is and is not real, how to judge situations more rationally and how to respond more adaptively to situations. Therapists should not get into a battle of wills with the child. This is atherapeutic. Therapists should build rapport, teach coping and cognitive restructuring skills and allow the child to apply these skills.

Box 19.9 Psychologist: I remember being ordered by the court to provide therapy for a 13-year-old boy who had refused contact with his mother. The court was concerned that the boy's father was unsupportive of the boy having a relationship with the mother and the boy was caught in the middle of his parent's difficult separation. By the time I saw the boy he had not seen his mother for two years and had already seen three psychologists. The boy made it clear to me at the first session that he "hated" every psychologist he saw because "they were all making me see my mother". He believed I would do the same. I assured him that I was not powerful enough to make people do anything. I empathised with him that it is hard work being a kid stuck in the middle of two parents who do not like each other and cannot agree on anything. To which he replied "Gee. You're telling me! You have no idea!" He then went on to list just how much hard work it had been for him. I then told him it was my job to help him and only him to see if we could work together to ease the load. My primary goal with this boy was to build rapport and to earn his trust. Sessions included chatting about topics such as cars, girls, his preferred fast food, and how to stop your hair from flopping to one side by lunchtime. These seemingly unnecessary conversations were incredibly important. These were the conversations he could not have with anyone else and they served to build a solid secure base for him. When I had the opportunity to do so, I would carefully weave in 'words of wisdom'. These were essentially tiny digestible pieces of CBT. Then one day he said, "I'm really confused. I just can't work out fact from fiction, fact from fantasy and fact from people's opinion." I replied with "That sounds like quite a dilemma. Tell me more and we'll see what we can untangle." It seemed all the digestible pieces of CBT had now added up and the boy had started to question the distorted reality his father had created. By the end of the session the boy asked if I could arrange for him to see his mother. It was arranged.

Words of wisdom

Therapists working with alienated children must be clear that their role is to provide therapy for the child. Their role is not to provide family therapy or to provide therapy or advocacy to the child's parents. To be effective, therapists need to avoid entering, reinforcing and participating in the shared beliefs that exist between the child and the alienating parent. Therapists need to be well versed in ethical and professional guidelines for working with minors. Specifically, therapists need to be aware that, with limitations, children have a right to confidentiality. Therapists must not violate the child's trust by reporting back details of therapy sessions to either parent. The boundaries of confidentiality must be clearly stated for the child and for both parents.

If therapy is court ordered, the alienated child and their parents (the alienating and targeted parent) need to be told this. Reportable therapy poses a fundamental ethical dilemma for therapists. The foundation of any therapeutic relationship is confidentiality. This is the foundation on which trust is built. Reportable therapy negates this. To manage these competing professional, ethical and legal demands, the therapist must make the limits of confidentiality known to the child and parents. When the request to report comes, the therapist must be careful to report sufficient information to satisfy the court's need to make informed decisions that are in the child's best interests while preserving the therapeutic relationship. This is not an easy tightrope to walk. If any therapist cannot walk on that wire, they should not do the work.

When working with minors, therapists must be well versed in risk assessment and response protocols. They should be aware of legal and ethical mandates to report suspected cases of child abuse and make such reports when the therapist has reasonable belief the child is in danger. Again, if therapists must make reports to child safety agencies, they should be transparent about the need to report by informing the alienated child and their parents (the alienating parent and targeted parent), and report sufficient information to keep the child safe while acting to preserve the therapeutic relationship.

If one parent presents a child for individual therapy during the course of a parenting dispute, the therapist must check important facts before proceeding. Firstly, the therapist must check who has primary parental responsibility for the child. Therapists should see copies of any court orders verifying this. If there are no court orders, then assume the parents have shared parental responsibility for the child and proceed accordingly. When parents have shared parental responsibility, therapists should not engage a child in therapy without the knowledge and consent of both parents. Therapists also should be mindful of the blurry line on which an adolescent becomes a mature minor. This is determined by age and level of cognitive functioning when an adolescent can give their own consent to participate in healthcare. Therapists must judge what is in the mature minor's best interest depending on their individual circumstances. If in doubt, the therapist should seek advice from colleagues.

Working with adults alienated during childhood

> **Box 19.10 Adult alienated child:** My childhood was chaotic and confusing. I don't understand a lot of it. I was raised by my mother and I hardly saw my father. My parents split up when I was little. I don't remember much about it other than there was a lot of yelling. Mum left with us kids and she wasn't quite right after that. Growing up with Mum was like being raised by a toddler. Everything was about her and she would throw tantrums at any given time. It was like walking on eggshells with Mum. She despised my father and she never

really got over the fact that their relationship ended. The weird thing is she always blamed
him for leaving us, but she was the one who left. I met my Dad once. He said he did everything he could to try and see me again but, if that were true, why did I see him again when
I was in my 30s and not before? I don't know what to believe. What was that chaos some
people call childhood?

An adult alienated child is an adult who was alienated from a parent during their childhood. Any
therapist can find themselves working with an adult alienated child who may come to therapy with
varying levels of insight into their experience of parental alienation. Some adults alienated during
childhood may seek therapy because they are of the view that they were alienated from a parent
as a child. They may want to understand their experience better and learn ways to cope with the
aftermath. Some may not know about parental alienation and disclose to the therapist their confusing childhood experience as described in the example above.

Understanding the confusion

Adults alienated during childhood can benefit greatly from learning about parental alienation.
It is not the role of the therapist to tell the client that they were alienated as a child, but to provide enough information about parental alienation for the client to draw their own conclusions.
Therapists should provide accurate up-to-date, evidence-based information in a non-judgmental
manner. It is not the role of the therapist to speak disparagingly about the behaviour of the client's
family members, but to aid understanding and insight.

Dealing with trauma

Numerous researchers have detailed the abuse and neglect experienced by alienated children (19-
26). Undoubtedly, the experience of being alienated from a parent and being raised by an alienating parent has a profound effect on the person's life (see Chapter Eight for a detailed summary
of the experience of the alienated child). When parental alienation is considered as a form of
family violence and child maltreatment, it is unsurprising that adults alienated during childhood
present with the same traumatic responses as adults who have survived other forms of childhood
abuse. To this end, the therapist must provide a secure base and work sensitively with their client
to ensure that therapy does not exacerbate their distress because adult alienated children may be
hypervigilant to the way the therapist responds to them. Therefore, the therapist should be alert to
issues of transference where the client interacts with the therapist in a similar way to the way they
interacted with their alienating parent. Adult targeted children may benefit from CBT and DBT
strategies already described.

Supporting through reunification

The decision to reunify with the targeted parent is one only the client can make. Therapists will
need to be mindful of remaining impartial to the outcome of this decision. They can help their
clients to make the decision by using decisional balance and providing up-to-date information
about the reunification process. The reunification process is not easy. Adults who were alienated
during childhood may struggle with the contrast between the reality of their once rejected parent
and the distorted view of them they may hold as well as the difference between the reality and any

fantasies they have created about their rejected parent and how reunification might look. They may benefit from being supported through this process and being taught targeted coping skills such as assertive communication skills.

Concluding comments

Working with individual family members involved in parental alienation can be challenging and rewarding. Therapists need to be clear that when working with individual family members, it is not their role to resolve the alienation. The therapist's focus is to therapeutically support the individual family member and help them to cope more effectively through the chaos – even if the client is the one creating the chaos. As we have seen in Chapter Nine, parental alienation affects the wider family system. To this end, other family members, such as grandparents, siblings or step-parents, may approach therapists for help. Therapists need to determine whether the family member is being alienated from the child or if they are a contributor to the alienation process. Then therapists should act accordingly to teach their client effective coping skills tailored to the needs of the client.

References

1. Bowlby, J. (1988). *A secure base. Clinical applications of attachment theory.* London: Routledge.
2. Baker, A.J.L., & Fine, P.R. (2014). *Surviving parental alienation: A journey of hope and healing.* Lanham, Maryland: Rowman & Littlefield.
3. Poustie, C., Matthewson, M., & Balmer, S. (2018). The forgotten parent: The targeted parent perspective of parental alienation. *Journal of Family Issues, 39,* 3298–3323. doi:10.1177/0192513x18777867
4. Miller, W.R., & Rollnick, S. (2013). *Applications of motivational interviewing. Motivational interviewing: Helping people change* (3rd edn.). New York: Guilford Press.
5. Doka, K.J. (Ed.). (1989). *Disenfranchised grief: Recognizing hidden sorrow.* Lexington, MA, England: Lexington Books/D.C. Heath and Com.
6. Worden, J.W. (2009). *Grief counseling and grief therapy: A handbook for the mental health practitioner* (4th edn.). New York: Springer.
7. Egan, G., & Resse, R.J. (2018). *A Problem-Management and Opportunity-Development Approach to Helping* (11th edn.). Belmont, CA, US: Cengage Learning.
8. Beck, J.S. (2011). *Cognitive behavior therapy: Basics and beyond* (2nd edn.). New York: Guilford Press.
9. McKay, M., Fanning, P., & Ona, P.E.Z. (2011). *Mind and emotions: A universal treatment for emotional disorders.* Oakland, CA: New Harbinger Publications.
10. Rees, N.P., Lim, L., & Correia, H. (2003). *Back from the bluez.* Perth, Western Australia: Centre for Clinical Interventions.
11. Darnall, D., & Steinberg, B.F. (2008). Motivational models for spontaneous reunification with the alienated child: Part I. *American Journal of Family Therapy, 36,* 107–115. doi:10.1080/01926180701643131
12. Baker, A.J.L. (2013). Introduction. In A.J.L. Baker & S.R. Sauber (Eds.), *Working with alienated children and families: A clinical guidebook* (pp. 1–9). New York: Routledge/Taylor & Francis Group.
13. De Jong, P., & Kim Berg, I. (2012). *Interviewing for solutions* (4th edn.). Belmont, CA: Brooks/Cole.
14. Neacsiu, A.D., Bohus, M., & Linehan, M.M. (2014). Dialectical behavior therapy: An intervention for emotion dysregulation. In J.J. Gross (Ed.), *Handbook of emotion regulation* (pp. 491–507). New York: Guilford Press.

15. McKay, M., Wood, J.C. & Brantley, J. (2007) *The dialectical behavior therapy skills workbook*. New Harbinger, Oakland.

16. Shirk, S.R., & Karver, M. (2003). Prediction of treatment outcome from relationship variables in child and adolescent therapy: A meta-analytic review. *Journal of Consulting and Clinical Psychology, 71*, 452–464. doi:10.1037/0022-006X.71.3.452

17. Martin, J., Romas, M., Medford, M., Leffert, N., & Hatcher, S. (2006). Adult helping qualities preferred by adolescents. *Adolescence, 41*, 127–40.

18. Bratton, S., & Ray, D. (2000). What the research shows about play therapy. *International Journal of Play Therapy, 9*, 47–88. doi:10.1037/h0089440

19. Baker, A.J.L. (2005). The long-term effects of parental alienation on adult children: A qualitative research study. *The American Journal of Family Therapy, 33*, 289–302. doi:10.1080/01926180590962129

20. Baker, A.J.L. (2005). Parental alienation strategies: A qualitative study of adults who experienced parental alienation as a child. *American Journal of Forensic Psychology, 23*, 1–23.

21. Baker, A.J.L., & Ben-Ami, N. (2011). To turn a child against a parent is to turn a child against himself: The direct and indirect effects of exposure to parental alienation strategies on self-esteem and wellbeing. *Journal of Divorce and Remarriage, 52*, 472–489. doi:10.1080/10502556.2011.609424

22. Baker, A.J.L., & Ben Ami, N. (2011). Adult recall of childhood psychological maltreatment in adult children of divorce: Prevalence and associations with outcomes. *Journal of Divorce and Remarriage, 52*, 203–219. doi:10.1080/10502556.2011.556973

23. Baker, A.J.L., & Chambers, J. (2011). Adult recall of childhood exposure to parental conflict: Unpacking the black box of parental alienation. *Journal of Divorce and Remarriage, 52*, 55–76. doi:10.1080/10502556.2011.534396

24. Baker, A.J.L., & Verrocchio, M.C. (2013). Italian college student-reported childhood exposure to parental alienation: Correlates with well-being. *Journal of Divorce and Remarriage, 54*, 609–628. doi:10.1080/10502556.2013.837714

25. Clawar, S.S., & Rivlin, B. (2013). *Children held hostage: Identifying brainwashed children, presenting a case, and crafting solutions*. (2nd edn.). Chicago, IL: American Bar Association.

26. Godbout, E., & Parent, C. (2012). The life paths and lived experiences of adults who have experienced parental alienation: A retrospective study. *Journal of Divorce and Remarriage, 53*, 34–54. doi:10.1080/10502556.2012.635967

Part Six

Identifying parental alienation

Chapter Twenty

A decision-making process

Introduction

For those at the beginning of the process of understanding parental alienation, there can be a confusing array of factors that need to be considered when determining whether a child's relationship with a parent has been negatively influenced by the actions of the other parent. Making sense of these factors and understanding how they interact can be a challenge.

Further, when confronted with a single indicator of parental alienation, such as an insistent rejection of a parent by a child, it can be easy to ignore all of the factors that should be considered when making a decision about whether or not parental alienation is occurring. Focus on a single indicator that is strongly evident can lead to confirmation bias. That is, an opinion is formulated on the basis of that single indicator and that view remains steadfast because too little attention is given to factors that may influence that opinion and all other aspects of a child's behaviour are interpreted in light of that one accepted indicator. In determining whether parental alienation is occurring, it is necessary to consider all ways it may present, even though not all aspects of parental alienation may be evident in all cases.

In any assessment process that relies of clinical judgment, more weight can be given to one component as long as the rationale for doing so is sound. In this way, one element may be strongly evident. However, it is necessary to consider all the ways parental alienation may present to determine the strength of any decision that parental alienation has affected a parent–child relationship.

Below are ways in which the various indicators of parental alienation may present. This is not a definitive list but provides examples of what you should be looking for when formulating an opinion about whether an alienation process has occurred. As part of this decision-making process, it is necessary to consider all the ways the features of parental alienation present so that the best judgments can be made.

Characteristics of alienating parents

Problematic personality traits

- This parent presents him or herself as superior to other people even though there is no real reason for this.
- This parent is more hostile than the demands of the situation would warrant.
- This parent is struggling to cope with the humiliation caused by the breakdown of the relationship.

- This parent feels abandoned or rejected, whether or not that is the case, and seems unable to get over it.
- This parent expects to deal only with 'upper management'.
- This person expects you to appreciate their importance.

Abnormal grief reaction

- This parent seems unduly focused on the loss of the marital relationship.
- There has been a focus on the loss of the relationship that has endured for an unreasonable amount of time.
- This parent sometimes talks about reconciliation with the former partner, even when the situation does not support this.
- This parent seems bitter and hurt about the breakdown of the relationship beyond what you would consider to be reasonable.
- This parent reacts like the breakdown of the relationship has just occurred even though time has passed.
- This parent is so angry about the breakdown of the relationship that it colours their thoughts and actions.

Externalisation of responsibility

- This person solely holds other people responsible for the problems they face.
- This parent struggles to understand their own contribution to the problems they experience.
- This parent avoids taking responsibility for the resolution of the problems they face.
- This parent believes other people cause their negative emotions.
- Even when they are challenged about their views, this parent refuses to accept that they have contributed or are contributing to the current conflict.
- This person avoids answering questions about their own behaviour, preferring to focus on the other parent's wrongdoing.

Family of origin

- This parent struggles to act independently from his or her extended family.
- The relationships this parent has with extended family members seem problematic.
- This parent is being unreasonably influenced by the negative views about the targeted parent held by extended family members.
- This parent gives an overly idealised account of their own childhood or their parents.
- This parent was raised by a single parent.
- This parent did not have contact or had only limited contact with their non-custodial parent (if their parents were separated/divorced).

Deflection of attention from own problems

- This parent refuses to acknowledge their own problems that are separate from the targeted parent's behaviour.
- This parent experiences conflict with people other than the targeted parent.
- This parent seems to fail to cope with normal life demands and challenges.
- This parent makes a point of saying the other parent's problems are greater than their own.

- This parent holds the other parent responsible for the breakdown of the relationship even though this parent's actions contributed to the relationship failure.
- There is collateral information that suggests this parent has problems they are not reporting.

Poor relationship history

- This parent has a history of problematic romantic relationships.
- This parent has a child or children from a past relationship other than the one that is the focus of the current case.
- This child (or the children) from a previous relationship does not have contact with their other parent or has only limited contact.
- This parent has no history of romantic relationships other than the one that is the focus of the current case.
- A pregnancy occurred within the first 12 months of the relationship that is the focus of the current case.
- There is an indication that this parent pushed for the relationship while the other parent was drawn into the relationship.

Desire for control

- This parent tries to control events or dominate others.
- This parent talks as if their decisions are superior to the decisions made by others because they know best.
- This parent has a history of contravening court orders when these orders conflict with their own wishes.
- This parent contravenes court orders despite recently consenting to those orders.
- This parent struggles to understand why others do not agree with their way of doing things.
- This parent blames their lawyer or others for forcing them into agreeing with case direction despite them freely agreeing prior to their change of mind.

Desire for vengeance

- This parent wants the targeted parent to pay for or be held responsible for their unhappiness.
- This parent prevents or attempts to prevent the targeted parent from seeing their children because of a need for revenge.
- This parent sees the targeted parent as their only source of unhappiness despite facing other or normal life stressors.
- This parent fails to see that by targeting the other parent they are hurting the child(ren).
- This parent fails to see that by adopting a more moderate view of the other parent the quality of their own life would improve.
- Mediation or negotiation processes are compromised or complicated by the anger this parent feels towards the other parent.

Alienating tactics by alienating parents

Denigration associated with the targeted parent

- This parent makes denigrating comments about the other parent.

- This person is grudging in their acceptance of positive statements made by others about the other parent.
- This parent refuses to use the name of the other parent.
- This parent refers to the other parent using an unflattering name (e.g., Idiot).
- This parent struggles to admit that the other parent is capable of caring for the child(ren).
- The denigration of the targeted parent is implied rather than stated (e.g., "I suppose he does the best he can, given his background").

Vilification of the targeted parent

- This parent makes allegations about the dangerousness of the other parent without adequate supporting evidence.
- This parent makes claims about the abuse of the child by the other parent without substantiation.
- This parent makes reference to the possibility of abuse of the child by the targeted parent without actually making the allegation.
- The timing of any claim of abuse of the child by the targeted parent is linked to legal events or parenting changes (e.g., upcoming court appearance, progression of more time for the targeted parent with the child).
- This parent makes sinister interpretations of normal events (e.g., the child sitting on the father's lap, the child getting into bed with the father in the morning).
- The child's reluctance to see the targeted parent is used as 'evidence' of wrongdoing by the other parent.

Interference with time spent with the targeted parent

- This parent puts obstacles in the way of the child spending time with the other parent.
- This parent offers the child alternative, favoured activities that compete with time they are supposed to spend with the other parent.
- This parent insists on repeatedly contacting the child while the child is with the other parent.
- This parent fails to produce the child so the child can spend time with the other parent.
- This parent keeps the child out of school or collects them early from school so that the other parent cannot collect the child to spend time with them (if the other parent is to collect the child from school).
- This parent schedules medical, dental, counsellor or other appointments for the child during time they are scheduled to spend with the other parent.

Eradication of the targeted parent from the child's life

- This parent fails to pass on gifts, cards or letters to the child from the other parent.
- This parent makes it difficult or impossible for the other parent to maintain contact with the child by telephone or other electronic means.
- This parent refuses to mention the other parent when talking with the child or around the child.
- This parent insists that the child call his or her new partner 'Dad' or 'Mum' even when the relationship is very new.

- This parent encourages the child to call the other parent by their given name rather than 'Dad' or 'Mum' (or some other title, such as Papa, that indicates the parent's role in the child's life).
- This parent acts to prevent the child from spending time with the extended family of the other parent.

Information gatekeeping

- This parent fails to inform the other parent about important events for the child that the other parent could attend (e.g., school plays, sports carnivals).
- This parent fails to inform the other parent about the child's medical appointments or about matters relating to the child's health.
- This parent fails to inform the other parent about the child's counsellor or psychologist appointments.
- This parent limits the information that is provided to professionals working with the child (e.g., counsellors, psychologists).
- This parent fails to provide the other parent with information about the child's school performance.
- This parent withholds information from the other parent about the child reaching developmental milestones.

Interrogation of the alienated child

- When the child returns from spending time with the other parent, this parent wants to know what occurred in detail from the child.
- This parent questions the child about the other parent's potential wrongdoing after the child spends time with the targeted parent.
- This parent questions the child about the time they spend with the other parent despite being told not to do this.
- It is your view that the child is feeling pressured to provide information to the questioning parent.
- The child tends to change their story about their other parent to a more negative one if this parent questions them enough about the targeted parent.
- This child avoids or would avoid spending time with the targeted parents to avoid having to be questioned by this parent.

Damage to the loving connection with the targeted parent

- This parent tells the child negative things about the other parent.
- This parent tells the child the other parent has a new family and does not want the child.
- This parent tells the child the other parent never wanted them.
- This parent tells the child the other parent is too busy for them.
- This parent tells the child the other parent does not care about them because they have not paid child support.
- This parent tells the child the other parent was unhappy about the pregnancy/wanted to terminate the pregnancy/was unsupportive during the pregnancy.

Inappropriate disclosure about the targeted parent

- This parent informs the child about negative events that occurred in the relationship that had nothing to do with the child or occurred before the child was born.
- This parent shows the child court documents or tells them about the content of court documents to reinforce the negative view being expressed about the other parent.
- This parent does not balance up negative comments about the targeted parent with positive comments.
- This parent does not filter what they say about the targeted parent when they are around the child.
- This parent discloses information about the targeted parent to the child as a means of strengthening the alliance between this parent and the child.

Encouraging child defiance

- This parent tells the child they do not have to obey the other parent.
- This parent tells the child they do not have to obey the other parent's new partner.
- The child is compliant with other people but not the targeted parent.
- There are complaints that the child has to comply with the parental demands of the targeted parent despite these demands being normal enough requests a parent makes of a child (e.g., doing homework, picking up their clothes, tidying the kitchen, not snacking before dinner).
- This parent makes the targeted parent's rules for the child seem unreasonable to the child.
- This parent rewards the child for non-compliance with the targeted parent's rules (e.g., letting the child know they are pleased, affection in the form of hugs, reinforcement of the alliance between this parent and the child).

Forcing loyalty to the alienating parent

- This parent pressures the child to take their side in the conflict between the parents.
- This parent insists the child tell others that they support this parent.
- This parent makes it clear to the child that positive feelings about both parents will not be tolerated.
- This parent makes it clear there will be negative consequences for failing to be loyal to the alienating parent (e.g., "You can go and live with your father").
- This parent creates opportunities for the child to express their loyalty towards this parent.
- This parent has an expectation that the child will be loyal to them.

Encouraging an unhealthy alliance

- This parent talks about the child as if they are friends rather than having a parent–child relationship.
- This parent actively encourages the child to be dependent on them.
- This parent encourages the child to believe they cannot function without them.
- This parent plots with the child against the other parent.
- This parent encourages the child to lie to support their point of view.
- This parent talks about only needing the child to make them happy.

Emotional manipulation

- This parent withdraws or threatens to withdraw love and affection if the child disagrees with their view about the other parent.
- This parent withdraws or threatens to withdraw love and affection if the child acts in a way they consider to be disloyal.
- This parent withdraws or threatens to withdraw love and affection if the child asks to see the other parent.
- This parent sulks if the child talks about the other parent.
- This parent expresses displeasure or becomes angry if the child mentions the other parent.
- This parent threatens abandonment if the child expresses a wish to see the other parent.

Utilising outside forces

- This parent makes notifications to child protective services about the other parent.
- This parent seeks restraining orders or family violence orders claiming the other parent represents a significant threat despite no evidence to support this threat existing.
- This parent uses the legal system to punish the other parent.
- This parent seeks out counselling for the child to support their view that the child should not spend time with the other parent.
- This parent informs the child's school of the threat the other parent represents to the child despite no evidence to support this threat existing.
- This parent seeks out sexual assault support or family violence support for the child despite no evidence that the other parent sexually abused the child or perpetrated family violence.

Presentation of the alienated child

Expression of negative views about the targeted parent

- The child expresses negative views about the targeted parent.
- The child believes the targeted parent is persecuting them or their other parent.
- The child gives accounts of how the targeted parent deliberately acted in ways to upset them or interfered with their happiness, even though these behaviours seem not to indicate malicious intent on the part of the targeted parent.
- This child states that the goal of the targeted parent is to make them unhappy.
- The child gives accounts of negative experiences when with the targeted parent, even though there is no evidence that they occurred.
- The child attributes negative traits to the targeted parent.

Extreme and opposite views about parents

- The child makes strongly positive statements about the alienating parent and strongly negative statements about the targeted parent, even in the absence of objective evidence of wrongdoing on the part of the targeted parent.
- The child views the alienating parent as entirely good and trustworthy and the targeted parent as entirely bad and untrustworthy.
- The child states that the alienating parent always cares for them well and the targeted parent always cares for them poorly.

- The child states they only want to spend time with the alienating parent and never wants to see the targeted parent.
- The child states that the targeted parent is entirely responsible for the martial relationship breakdown and the alienating parent is entirely not to blame.
- The child expresses negative views about the targeted parent's extended family and positive views about the alienating parent's extended family.

Situationally determined changes in the child's behaviour

- In the absence of a person the child does not wish to disappoint, the child's behaviour towards the targeted parent seems inconsistent with what the child says about the targeted parent (e.g., the child says they do not like their parent but then seeks physical contact with the targeted parent when they are together).
- The child's behaviour when they spend time with the targeted parent seems inconsistent with their stated reluctance to spend time with the targeted parent.
- The child will say that they do not care if the targeted parent is critical of them but is hurt if criticism is made.
- If time with the targeted parent occurs, the fear or distress claimed by the child is not evident.
- The child claims their negative views about the targeted parent are certain but then behaves as if they are unsure or have positive feelings for the targeted parent.
- Even when a child refuses to talk with the targeted parent they have not seen for an extended period, they respond in a yearning way when in the targeted parent's presence.

Denial of positive regard for the targeted parent

- The child refuses to acknowledge any positive aspect of the targeted parent's behaviour, even when evidence of positive actions exists.
- The child interprets positive or neutral events when with the targeted parent as negative in nature.
- The child denies that they love the targeted parent.
- The child denies that the targeted parent has any redeeming characteristic.
- The child denies they ever loved the targeted parent despite evidence to suggest otherwise.
- The child says that they only pretended to like the targeted parent in the past.

Distorted views about the targeted parent

- The child reports negative stories about the targeted parent that could not possibly be true.
- The child relates negative stories about the targeted parent that might be true but there is no evidence to support the claims.
- The child attributes ill intention to actions of the targeted parent that others would see as positive.
- The child misinterprets normal parenting activities on the part of the targeted parent as intending to aggravate or cause harm.
- The child refers to the targeted parent in extreme and negative terms (e.g., the targeted parent 'always' behaves poorly towards the child, the targeted parent 'never' talks to the child).
- The child gives accounts of previously pleasurable times with the targeted parent as if they were negative experiences.

False memories or accounts of events not experienced

- The child gives accounts of events they could not have witnessed or been involved in.
- The child claims they have first-hand knowledge of events that occurred before they were born or when they were too young to remember.
- The child states a belief in the account of wrongdoing of the targeted parent despite it being pointed out that the child could not know what they claim to know.
- The child provides little detail about the specifics of an event (e.g., when it occurred or where it occurred) when providing details about the wrongdoing of the targeted parent that they could not know.
- There is a likelihood that the child has been exposed to information about the targeted parent that they had not experienced.
- There have been complaints that the child has not been shielded from negative views about the targeted parent.

Lack of concern about internal inconsistency of information provided

- The accounts provided by the child about the targeted parent's behaviour are not consistent (e.g., "Dad never takes me anywhere" and "Dad took me to the park").
- The child fails to respond or reacts with indifference when inconsistencies in their account are pointed out.
- When challenged about the lack of consistency in what the child is saying, the child either ignores the fact that the challenge was made or becomes angry.
- The child adjusts what is said to answer new questions put to them despite the fact that new answers may contradict previous answers.
- This child can make several changes of the account they are providing during the course of a single interview or discussion.
- The child demonstrates little evidence of discomfort despite having to repeatedly adjust what they are saying to match collateral information.

A litany of complaints about the targeted parent

- The child's account of the targeted parent's shortcomings seems rehearsed or practised.
- The child makes statements such as, "Mum/Dad told me to remember ..." when asked to express views about the targeted parent.
- The child has a list of complaints about the targeted parent that they state and re-state.
- The child tends not to provide much detail about their complaints about the targeted parent.
- When questioned about the complaints, the child tends to revert to listing the complaints.
- When talking about the targeted parent, the child tends to use language not commonly used by a child of that age.

Fear response

- The child seems unreasonably frightened or upset about the idea of seeing the targeted parent.
- The alienating parent reports that the child is distressed or frightened when faced with seeing the targeted parent.
- The child's fear is out of proportion to the threat the child actually faces.

- The child refuses time with the targeted parent, claiming they are frightened by that parent.
- The child hides from the targeted parent when the targeted parent arrives to spend time with the child.
- The child refuses to go to school in case the targeted parent comes to collect them.

Dependent or symbiotic relationship with alienating parent

- The child copes poorly when separated from the alienating parent.
- The child sees him or herself as aligned with the alienating parent.
- The child has an expectation that the alienating parent will meet their needs, no matter how unrealistic the demand.
- The child cannot spend time with the targeted parent without contacting the alienating parent.
- The child holds the view that it is only the alienating parent who can meet their needs.
- The child will not respond to the targeted parent's attempts to negotiate without referring to the alienating parent.

Compliant with adults other than targeted parent

- The child seems polite and obedient despite reports of poor behaviour when with the targeted parent.
- The child is only disrespectful to the targeted parent and not to other adults.
- The child is reported to be defiant and difficult when with the targeted parent despite this not being the case in other circumstances.
- The child believes there is no real need to obey the targeted parent's requests.
- The child's behaviour with the targeted parent is problematic despite good school reports of appropriate behaviour.
- The child's non-compliant behaviour extends to the targeted parent's partner or extended family members.

Believes alienating parent persecuted by targeted parent

- The child believes the alienating parent is the victim of the targeted parent's abuse.
- The child's view of the alienating parent as the victim and the targeted parent as the perpetrator is difficult to sway.
- The child chooses to believe accounts of wrongdoing by the targeted parent despite the targeted parent not acting in these ways towards the child.
- The child talks about the harm the targeted parent has done to the alienating parent.
- The child talks about the threat the targeted parent represents to the alienating parent.
- The child's views about the targeted parent are reinforced by selective exposure to court documents.

Lack of empathy for plight of targeted parent

- The child seems not to care that the targeted parent is distressed because he or she does not spend time with the child.

- The child seems not to care that the targeted parent is perceived as someone who should be exploited for financial gain.
- The child fails to contact the targeted parent on important dates (e.g., parent's birthday or Father's/Mother's Day).
- The child does not feel guilty about the harsh attitude they adopt towards the targeted parent.
- Attempts to elicit an empathic response from the child about the targeted parent are unsuccessful.
- The child demonstrates empathic responses to others but not the targeted parent.

Targeted parent holds no important position in child's life

- The child is dismissive of the significance of the targeted parent in their life.
- The child refuses to refer to the targeted parent as 'Dad' or 'Mum'.
- The child treats the targeted parent with the same connection or warmth as they would treat an acquaintance or stranger.
- The child does not express an interest in sharing important news with the targeted parent.
- The child does not wish to share important occasions (e.g., birthday celebrations) with the targeted parent.
- The child is disinterested in the targeted parent's life.

Rigidity of belief system regarding targeted parent

- The child's negative views about the targeted parent remain rigidly in place despite more moderate explanations for the targeted parent's actions being offered.
- The child simply dismisses evidence that does not support their views about the targeted parent.
- When their views about the targeted parent are challenged, the child presents an argument in favour of their own point of view, no matter how illogical their argument seems.
- The child will stick to their point of view about the targeted parent even when it is clearly demonstrated to be based on wrong information.
- The child will reject the notion that it is possible they may be wrong in their views about the targeted parent.
- The child may accept benevolent intention in others who behave similarly to the targeted person while rejecting that the targeted parent's intention is benevolent.

Independent thinker phenomenon

- The child believes that they are the one who should decide whether they spend time with the targeted parent.
- The child states that their decision about not seeing the targeted parent is theirs alone and is not influenced by the alienating parent despite there being evidence to the contrary.
- The child states that the negative views they hold about the targeted parent are a result of their own experiences with the targeted parent.
- The child denies that the alienating parent's negative views about the targeted parent influence their own views.
- The child is protective of the alienating parent when questions are raised about their influence on the child's attitude to the targeted parent.

- The child states that they will refuse to do as the court orders if there are orders made for the child to spend time with the targeted parent.

Characteristics of targeted parents

History of passivity, emotional constriction and over-accommodation

- This parent was the less dominant partner in the relationship with the alienating parent.
- This parent tended to give in to the alienating parent during their relationship as a means of avoiding conflict.
- This parent tended to fail to meet the alienating parent's emotional needs during their relationship.
- This parent has demonstrated a tendency to overly accommodate to the demands made by the alienating parent during their relationship.
- There was a power imbalance in the parental relationship in favour of the alienating parent.
- At the end of the relationship, this parent gave up trying to meet the demands of the alienating parent.

Tendency to avoid self-assertion

- This parent sometimes struggles to stand up to the alienating parent.
- This parent is cautious about taking action that will upset the alienating parent.
- This parent feels helpless in the face of the alienating parent's behaviour.
- This parent sometimes seemed paralysed into inaction by the alienating parent's behaviour.
- This parent avoids doing anything that will further alienate their child.
- This parent tries to control the alienating parent's behaviour by not doing anything to upset him or her.

Potential for distress in response to alienating tactics

- This parent is showing obvious signs of stress and distress.
- This parent is exceedingly distressed in reaction to the alienating parent's vilification of them.
- This parent's ability to function is being compromised by the distress they feel because of the alienation process.
- This parent is consumed by the alienation from their children and they struggle to focus on other things.
- This parent sometimes lashes out and does unreasonable things because of the stress they feel about the alienation from their child.
- This parent sometimes talks about taking dire actions to rectify the situation caused by the alienating parent's behaviour (e.g., taking the child without permission).

Possible willingness to justify alienating parent's strategies

- This parent sometimes tries to justify or explain the alienating parent's behaviour.
- This parent sometimes believes the alienating parent will see reason and allow them to spend time with their child.
- This parent tries to make sense of the alienating parent's behaviour.

- This parent tries to reconcile the fact that the alienating parent loves their child but acts in a way that is damaging to them.
- This parent tries to explain the alienating parent's behaviour in terms of mental health issues.
- This parent tries to find a logical explanation for fundamentally unreasonable actions on the part of the alienating parent.

Withdrawal from high conflict

- This parent talks about withdrawing from the fight over spending time with their child.
- This parent talks about feeling too overwhelmed by the process to continue to fight for their child.
- This parent has reached their financial limits to fund the legal fight to spend time with their child and talks about withdrawing as a consequence.
- This parent talks about having no more avenues available to them to fight for time with their child.
- This parent has opted not to compromise any further with the alienating parent's demands in an effort to spend time with their child.
- This parent has refused to communicate with their child.

Rejection of the child in response to the child's rejection

- This parent presents as hurt by their child's rejection of them.
- This parent presents as angry with their child because of the child's rejection of them.
- This parent rejects their child in retaliation for the child's rejection of them.
- This parent is critical of their child in relation to the child's rejection of them.
- This parent believes their child should act more respectfully towards them.
- This parent expects an apology from their child for their child's rejection of them.

Inflexible parenting style

- This parent strongly enforces rules they set for their child.
- This parent sets high standard for their child's behaviour.
- This parent is insistent about what should take place when their child is with them despite this not being what the child wishes.
- This parent is insistent that the parenting orders are adhered to no matter the child's circumstances.
- This parent struggles to be flexible when dealing with their child despite the child's changed attitude towards them.
- This parent has failed to adjust his/her parenting approach despite the change in the child's attitude towards them.

Consequences of alienation campaign for targeted parents

Loss of parenting role

- This parent feels like their role as a parent is undermined.
- This parent feels they have little say about their child's life.

- This parent feels controlled in relation to when they can spend time with this child and how that time is spent.
- This parent is too afraid to discipline their child for fear of alienating them further.
- This parent is too afraid to refuse their child's unreasonable demands for fear of alienating them further.
- This parent resents the fact that a replacement parent (e.g., step-parent) gets to parent the child when they do not have that opportunity.

Feelings of injustice

- This parent feels let down by the legal system.
- This parent believes the alienating parent is not being held accountable for breaches of orders.
- This parent feels frustrated by the lack of knowledge about parental alienation or their experiences that reflect parental alienation.
- This parent feels that psychological interventions do not adequately address the parental alienation.
- This parent feels the alienating parent is deliberately sabotaging legal and psychological intervention efforts.
- This parent feels the legal system targets people in his/her position.

Personal costs

- This parent is grieving for the child s/he does not see.
- This parent is angry at the failure to resolve the conflict.
- This parent is distressed and volatile at times.
- This parent seems traumatised by the loss of his/her child.
- This parent is struggling to cope with the legal process and the loss of his/her child.
- This parent is facing financial difficulties because of the prolonged legal fight for their child.

Degradation of the parent–child relationship

Escalation of parental alienation

- The alienating parent has made increasingly serious allegations over time about the targeted parent.
- The alienating parent has made increasingly serious allegations about the targeted parent that coincide with legal events or changes in the time the child is expected to spend with the targeted parent.
- The targeted parent's behaviour has become increasingly desperate or demanding over time.
- The targeted parent's psychological adjustment seems to have deteriorated over time.
- The alienated child has become more rejecting of the targeted parent over time.
- The alienated child's behaviour over time seems more fearful of the targeted parent or their views have become more rigid and irrational over time about the targeted parent.

Gradual decrease in time spent with alienated child

- Over time, the consistency of the occurrence of time spent with the child changes in a negative way.

- Over time, more excuses are made by the alienating parent for the child not attending time spent with the targeted parent.
- Over time, the child demonstrates greater resistance to spending time with the targeted parent to the point where it interferes with visits.
- Over time, the pattern of visits changes (e.g., the child refusing overnight time with the targeted parent).
- Over time, there can be an increasing pattern of the child asking to cut short the time they are spending with the targeted parent.
- Over time, the frequency of visits decreases to the point where time the child spends with the targeted parent is occasional or rare.

Dysfunctional family interaction patterns

Family stress

- The family has a history of pathological patterns of interacting with each other in response to stress.
- The alienating parent uses the alienated child to communicate with the targeted parent instead of communicating directly with them (referred to as perverse triangulation).

Inability to achieve family tasks

- There has been a pervasive pattern of poor problem-solving before and after family separation.
- This alienating parent's inability to problem solve and refusal to make adaptive behaviour change has serious consequences for the whole family system.
- This family has a history of poor communication that is ambiguous, masked, camouflaged and open to misinterpretation.
- This alienating parent's inability to renegotiate family roles has a serious negative impact on the whole family system.
- This alienating parent is unable to respond appropriately to the needs of the child because they prioritise their own needs.
- This targeted parent's ability to respond to the child's needs has diminished as the alienation progresses and their ability to cope with family dysfunction is now exhausted.
- This targeted parent's opportunity to be empathically involved in their child's life has diminished as a consequence of the alienation.
- This alienating parent and alienated child's relationship is enmeshed.
- This alienating parent's involvement in their child's life is narcissistic.
- This alienated family is unable to set and maintain consistent standards of behaviour.
- This alienating parent repeatedly changes the rules for each family member and sets a standard for others they do not set for themselves.

Lack of cohesion and flexibility

- This alienating parent–alienated child dyad is chaotically enmeshed.
- This alienated parent–targeted parent dyad is chaotically disengaged.
- This severely alienated child is rigidly disengaged from the targeted parent.

Insecure attachment styles

- This alienated child has lost a significant attachment figure (targeted parent) and fears losing another (alienating parent).
- This alienated child displays attachment behaviour when faced with the prospect of being separated from the alienating parent.
- This alienated child is insecurely attached to the alienating parent.
- There is an indication that parental alienation has occurred in past generations in this family.

Concluding comments

When formulating an opinion that is based on clinical judgment, it is worthwhile to have a guide so that all factors that need to be considered are given adequate attention. By using such a guide as the one just presented, the overall presentation of the alienated parent, the targeted parent and the alienated child can be considered. This can protect you from confirmation bias, whether the original supposition was that parental alienation was occurring or was not occurring. It helps you avoid giving undue weight to a single aspect of a person's presentation. It is worth remembering that the tactics used by a parent to alter the relationship between the child and the other parent really can be understood only in the context of parental alienation if there is a corresponding effect on the child that leads to a change in the targeted parent–child relationship. Therefore, it is not enough to say that a parent's desire to form an unhealthy alliance with their child is evidence of parental alienation. In effect, for parental alienation to be occurring, the unhealthy alliance must be the result of the strategy used by the parent.

Chapter Twenty-One

Where to from here?

Introduction

Despite the relatively recent increase in interest in parental alienation, it is likely that the phenomenon has existed for as long as there have been parenting disputes. It has been reported that the earliest case of parental alienation was in 1804 when Leonard Thomas De Manneville took his baby daughter and refused to return her to her mother, Margaret Crompton. De Manneville used the legal system that was available to him at the time to successfully alienate their daughter from the mother (1). Modern day research on parental alienation dates back to the 1970s when it was described as 'pathological alignment', in recognition of both its effect on the parent–child relationship, and its unhealthy nature.

Despite this early information, our knowledge about parental alienation still is limited in many areas. This may be due, at least in part, to the stumbling blocks associated with definition and description that have hampered the progress of research and the focus of that research. Below are some suggestions about gaps in our knowledge about parental alienation although, undoubtedly, there are many others.

Future directions

The nature of parental alienation

Much of what is known about parental alienation relates to 'snapshots' in time. That is, at the time of assessment, or at the time of dealing with the immediate family problems in therapy, this was how the various family members were functioning and this was the influence of the parental alienation process. Less is known about the evolution of parental alienation, especially from the onset of the problems through to the resolution of the alienation and beyond. The knowledge base relating to parental alienation would benefit from longitudinal studies that follow members of an alienated family. This would allow for the determination of whether there are key factors that might trigger the onset, maintain or help resolve parental alienation.

Following from this idea of the way in which parental alienation evolves, it is important to identify the factors that trigger the onset of parental alienation. Although some information is available about the presentation of alienating parents, it is not yet known which of these characteristics strongly trigger the alienation process. Also, it is not known if the trigger of parental alienation may be a more complicated interaction between the characteristics of the alienating parent and, for example, the response they receive from the targeted parent or the alienated child. For example, if a particular child is more amenable to the message being received from the alienating parent, this may influence the development of the alienation process. Certainly, this type of information could help with the early identification of families vulnerable to the alienation process or assist in earlier recognition of these processes occurring. In turn, this information would inform when intervention should occur.

Also, it is necessary to determine if all cases of parental alienation have the same onset, maintenance and resolution factors. It has been suggested that there are what has been termed 'hybrid' cases of parental alienation (2). If these exist, it is necessary to be able to differentiate cases by type. From a clinical point of view, there seems to be cases where the presentation of the alienating parent differs, potentially resulting in differences in the way these cases should be managed and, possibly, the likelihood of successful outcomes. It was mentioned in Chapter Four that there may be differences in the belief systems of alienating parents, with some deliberately and knowingly setting out to damage the targeted parent–child relationship and other presenting as holding beliefs that are so distorted that they are fundamentally delusional in character. If these differences reflect type differences, they need to be established and their impact investigated.

More attention needs to be given to whether or not parental alienation can be understood in a family violence framework. The characteristics of parental alienation that are consistent with family violence need to be clearly identified. If it is demonstrated robustly that parental alienation is a form of family violence, it is likely that this would influence how cases are managed and the type of support that could be obtained in a legal context. There are ways to manage cases involving family violence in family law that have not yet been applied to cases of parental alienation.

There is some basic information about parental alienation that is not yet known. For example, there is limited information available about prevalence rates or what influences there might be on these rates. It would be interesting to determine if there are differences in prevalence rates between countries that might be influenced by general acceptance of parental alienation, available psychological support, or differences between family law jurisdictions.

Alienated family members

We need to know more about alienating parents. More knowledge needs to be gained about their characteristics and which of these characteristics most strongly triggers or maintains the alienation process. It would be interesting to learn whether successful legal outcomes or therapeutic intervention outcomes correspond with real changes in the alienating parent's attitudes and beliefs or whether alienating parents learn to alter their behaviour to allow them to have a continuing relationship with their children that may be threatened by a legal process that does not respond to their alienating behaviour sympathetically.

It is recognised that there are difficulties in obtaining information about alienating parents, especially during the period of time when they are actively alienating a child from the targeted parent. Most alienating parents do not identify themselves as such and inviting them to participant in research that labels them as the offending party in a parenting dispute is unlikely to be successful. A more sympathetic approach, allowing those identified by the court as an alienating parent to offer their side of the story, may result in important information being obtained that will help identify their characteristics and motives. The knowledge gained in this way could be used to better assist alienating parents who, undoubtedly, experience considerable distress.

Very little information is available about alienated children while they are children and experiencing the effects of the alienation process. Much of what is known has been obtained from adults who were alienated as children. It is important to be able to access information about alienated children that is not confounded by the passage of time, later life experiences, and the outcome of the alienation process, whether that is resolution of relationship problems or seemingly irreparable damage to the targeted parent–child relationship. It would be interesting to learn how alienated children experience the alienation at the time it occurs and as a reflection of developmental stage. Also, it would be important to learn more about how children cope with the restoration of the targeted parent–child relationship and how they experience any forced change in residence.

Assessment

There needs to be consensus about the identification of cases of parental alienation. This is the foundation of good quality research that allows for comparison of individual study results. For this to occur, our assessment techniques need to be improved. Practitioners need to be able to identify parental alienation and confidently differentiate between estrangement and alienation. Further, they need to be able to identify the differences between genuine cases of parental alienation and alleged cases where a parent tries to use parental alienation as a means of forcing the outcome of a parenting dispute in their favour without adequate justification. It would be worthwhile assessing the differential impact of attempted alienation and successful alienation of a child from the targeted parent.

To achieve these goals, it is necessary to have good assessment instruments with sound psychometric properties. The assessment methods should allow for a more definitive way of determining whether or not parental alienation is occurring. For example, it may be that a parent engages in one or two alienation tactics without that being considered to be parental alienation. During the separation and parenting dispute resolution period, not all parents behave impeccably because they are distressed and hurt and feel threatened. In most cases, it would not be appropriate to label these people as alienating parents despite them sometimes or for a short period of time acting in ways that mimic aspects of parental alienation. It is necessary to distinguish these cases from genuine cases of parental alienation.

Ideally, good quality assessment instruments or techniques should be developed on the basis of a better understanding of the relationships between alienation tactics used by alienating parents and the corresponding effects on alienated children. A tactic used by a parent is only an alienating tactic if it has the effect of causing alienation between the child and the targeted parent. Without this effect, it may be a troubling behaviour, but it cannot be said to be an alienating behaviour. For example, many unhappy, newly separated parents make denigrating comments about their former partner. However, without the effect on the child being a change in the relationship between the child and a parent, the denigration is an inappropriate response to hurt feelings but not an alienation tactic.

Further, the relationships between the alienating tactic and the effect on the child might be a direct one or reflect a more complex chain of cause and effect. For example, an alienating parent may make denigrating comments about the targeted parent. This may directly cause the alienated child to express strongly negative views about the targeted parent. The expression of negative views about the targeted parent may then lead to the child developing distorted beliefs about the targeted parent that may then result in them having little positive regard for that parent. In a complicated chain of cause and effect, all demonstrations of alienation in the child should be linked to one or more tactics used by the alienating parent.

Unfortunately, we do not yet know the nature and strength of these relationships between tactic and effect on the child. It would seem that it is necessary for this information to be available for good quality assessment instruments or techniques to be developed. To gain this information, it is necessary for large sample size statistical analyses to be conducted. One way to achieve this is to have collaboration among researchers. It would be necessary for researchers to be working with consensus to gather the same information in a reliable manner. The benefits of undertaking such a large-scale project are many, including increasing the confidence in parental alienation as an entity and the valid and reliable identification of individual cases of parental alienation.

Intervention

Research also needs to focus on intervention, building an evidence base for efficacious therapeutic approaches to the management and resolution of parental alienation. Although some information exists, the robustness of the evidence base will rely on good quality evaluation studies. Importantly, it will be necessary to follow up families after the completion of therapeutic intervention to determine whether the therapeutic outcomes are maintained over time. It may be necessary to develop what amounts to relapse prevention strategies for use in the longer term if situational problem arise. This can be achieved through better understanding of the factors that might impact on long-term maintenance of therapeutic gain and good relationship functioning.

Collaboration of psychology and the legal system

Finally, the future of the management of parental alienation would benefit from better collaboration between psychology and law. Therapeutic outcomes have been demonstrated to be enhanced by support from the legal system (3), with sanctions being used to ensure engagement in therapeutic intervention that has the best interests of the child as its guiding principle.

Further, it would add to the body of knowledge about parental alienation to be able to follow families through the family court system to identify outcomes, particularly in relation to specific (or potentially specific) categories of family and parenting dispute type. In addition, it would be interesting to learn the differences between those alienated families who do and do not choose to seek a legal resolution. It is unknown whether the severity of alienation distinguishes these groups or whether therapeutic resolution is more achievable within or outside a supportive legal system.

Importantly, attention needs to be given to campaigning for legislative change that allows parental alienation to be considered a form of family violence in the context of family law. In all likelihood, this would involve only the expansion of accepted indicators of family violence to include the generation in a child of an unjustified fear response or feelings of hatred towards one parent by the other parent.

Concluding comments

There are many exciting avenues that can lead to a better understanding of parental alienation and the people involved. Although it is easy to see the alienating parent as the perpetrator and the child and the targeted parents as the victims, in reality the breakdown of relationships and the development of parental alienation is distressing for all those who experience it. The more we understand this process, the better we can assist in its resolution. Indeed, greater understanding of parental alienation could well lead to prevention strategies that could be offered to any family entering into a parenting dispute.

References

1. Lorandos, D., & Bone, J.M. (2016). Child custody evaluations: In cases where parental alienation is alleged. In M.L. Goldstein (Ed.). *Handbook of child custody* (pp. 179–232). Cham, Switzerland: Springer International Publishing.

2. Friedlander, S., & Walters, M.G. (2010). When a child rejects a parent: Tailoring the intervention to fit the problem. *Family Court Review, 48*, 98–111. doi:10.1111/j.1744-1617.2009.01291.x
3. Templer, K., Matthewson, M., Haines, J., & Cox, G. (2017). Recommendations for best practice in response to parental alienation: findings from a systematic review. *Journal of Family Therapy, 39*, 103–122. doi:10.1111/1467–6427.12137

Index

abnormal grief reaction 58–60
abusive relationships: characteristic features 172, 173
adolescents *see* alienated child
adultification of the alienated child 26–27
adults alienated during childhood 326–328; adult consequences of parental alienation 287–298; alcohol use 113; CBT 327; DBT 327; dealing with trauma 327; divorce rates 114; individual therapy 326–328; influence on partner selection 114; learning about parental alienation 327; reasons for seeking therapy 326–327; self-sufficiency difficulty as adults 115; subsequent alienation from own children 114; supporting through reunification 327–328; understanding the confusion 327
Aftercare Programme (ACP) 296
alcohol abuse/dependence: suicide risk factor 166
alcohol use: adults who were alienated children 113
alienated child 110–115; absence of guilty feelings about the way the targeted parent is treated 12; adolescents 18, 110; adoption of experiences of the alienating parent 13; adultification 26–27; alcohol and drug use as adults 113; anxiety 112; assertive communication skills training 306; beware of an alliance with falsehood 324–325; brainwashing by the alienating parent 22–23; CBT 325; children at risk of alienation 110–111; clarity about the role of the therapist 326; consequences of no intervention 297–298; control and manipulation of their behaviour 23–24; DBT 325; denigration of the targeted parent's extended family 13; depression as children and adults 112; detrimental effects throughout life 8; developing coping skills 325; disenfranchised grief 112; effects on wellbeing 3–4; emotional abuse inflicted upon 24–25; feelings of guilt and shame 112–113; functioning well outside the family 18–19; hatred and denigration of the targeted parent 11–12; identity issues 115; imposition of a single and extraordinary authority 25–26; independent-thinker phenomenon 12; individual therapy 324–326; indoctrination into an absolute belief system 25; infantilisation 28–30; insecure attachment style 348; isolation 23; lack of trust 113–114; learning about unhelpful thinking styles 306;

learning critical thinking skills 306–309, 325; learning reality testing skills 325; long-term effects 17–18; parentification 27–28; play therapy 325; poor self-esteem 111–112; psychological consequences 111–113; reasons to attend therapy 324; reasons for rejection of a parent 4–6; relationship breakdowns 114; relationship consequences 113–114; relationship with the alienating parent 110–111; response to parents' separation 17–18; school-related difficulties 115, 127–128; separating from an alienating parent 19; sibling relationships 122; Stockholm Syndrome and 47; strains on the daughter–father relationship 110–111; task of the therapist 324–325; unquestioning support for the alienating parent 12; unreasonable rejection of their mother 16–17; unreasonableness of rejection of a parent 16–17; use of phrases used by the alienating parent about the targeted parent 13; weight given to views expressed by adolescents 18; *see also* adults alienated during childhood
alienated child assessment 176–216; accounts of events not experienced 191–194; approach to assessment 215–216; believes the alienating parent is persecuted by the targeted parent 205–207; calling the targeted parent by their given name 209; compliant with adults other than the targeted parent 203–205; defiance towards the targeted parent 203–205; denial of positive regard for the targeted parent 186–188; dependent relationship with the alienating parent 201–203; distorted views about the targeted parent 188–191; exposure to court documents 207; expression of negative views about the targeted parent 176–180; extreme and opposite views about parents 180–183; false memories 191–194; fear response to the targeted parent 199–201; identifying alienated children 176–216; independent thinker phenomenon 213–215; indicators of parental alienation 176–216; lack of concern about internal inconsistency of information provided 194–197; lack of empathy for the plight of the targeted parent 207–209; possible indications of coaching 197–199; relating the targeted parent's faults as a litany 197–199; rigidity of belief system regarding the targeted

Printed in Great Britain
by Amazon